Communications
in Computer and Information Science   414

More information about this series at http://www.springer.com/series/7899

Faisal Karim Shaikh · Bhawani Shankar Chowdhry
Sherali Zeadally · Dil Muhammad Akbar Hussain
Aftab Ahmed Memon · Muhammad Aslam Uqaili
(Eds.)

Communication Technologies, Information Security and Sustainable Development

Third International Multi-topic Conference
IMTIC 2013
Jamshoro, Pakistan, December 18–20, 2013
Revised Selected Papers

 Springer

Editors

Faisal Karim Shaikh
Mehran University of Engineering
   and Technology
Jamshoro
Pakistan

and

University of Umm Al-Qura
Makkah
Saudi Arabia

Bhawani Shankar Chowdhry
Faculty of Electrical, Electronics
   and Computer Engineering
Mehran University of Engineering
   and Technology
Jamshoro
Pakistan

Sherali Zeadally
College of Communication and Information
University of Kentucky
Lexington, KY
USA

Dil Muhammad Akbar Hussain
Department of Energy Technology
Aalborg University
Esbjerg
Denmark

Aftab Ahmed Memon
Department of Telecommunication
   Engineering
Mehran University of Engineering
   and Technology
Jamshoro
Pakistan

Muhammad Aslam Uqaili
Department of Electrical Engineering
Mehran University of Engineering
   and Technology
Jamshoro
Pakistan

ISSN 1865-0929   ISSN 1865-0937   (electronic)
ISBN 978-3-319-10986-2   ISBN 978-3-319-10987-9   (eBook)
DOI 10.1007/978-3-319-10987-9

Library of Congress Control Number: 2014948787

Springer Cham Heidelberg New York Dordrecht London

Printed on acid-free paper

Springer is part of Springer Science+Business Media (www.springer.com)

Preface

This book constitutes the refereed proceedings of the Third International Multi-topic Conference, IMTIC 2013. The conference theme was "Communication Technologies, Information Security and Sustainable Development." IMTIC 2013 provided an opportunity for national and international researchers and practitioners to present state-of-the-art results and future challenges in the fields of information communication technologies along with security-related issues and their contributions toward sustainable development.

IMTIC 2013 received more than 140 submissions. All submitted papers went through a rigorous review process with each paper receiving at least three reviews. The review process included several stages including TPC member reviews, an online discussion among the reviewers, TPC lead summary recommendations, and additional reviews (as needed). Based on the TPC recommendations, we accepted a total of 27 papers for publication and presentation at IMTIC 2013. This represents an acceptance rate of 21.42 %.

With so many papers to choose from, providing a conference program with a high level of technical excellence became a task that was challenging and time-consuming, but ultimately a very rewarding one with the efforts of the Technical Program Committee (TPC). The TPC focused on two aspects while selecting the technical papers: first, to provide a forum for researchers from all over the world and, specifically, Pakistan to present and discuss their research results in the relevant areas covered by the conference; second, to maintain the highest technical standard for accepted papers. The conference program was structured with two parallel-track sessions for the presentation of papers, a PhD symposium and a poster session. The topics presented had a reasonable balance between theory and practice in multidisciplinary topics including wireless sensor networks, could computing, wireless communication, antenna design, signal processing, software engineering, image processing, bioinformatics and telemedicine, neural networks, automation and control, and green renewable energy. The program also included eight keynote speeches by renowned experts in the field and five parallel thematic tutorials.

This event would not have been possible without the enthusiasm and hard work of numerous colleagues. We express our gratitude to the General Chairs, for their assistance throughout the process, and the Steering Committee members for their supportive guidance. We also thank all the other members of the organizing committees for the fruitful cooperation. A special vote of thanks goes to the TPC members, and all the referees, for their invaluable help in reviewing the papers. We acknowledge all the authors for their overwhelming support in submitting their papers for consideration to IMTIC 2013. Last but not least, we thank all the participants for attending the conference. We sincerely hope that you enjoyed IMTIC 2013.

December 2013

Faisal Karim Shaikh
Bhawani Shankar Chowdhry
Sherali Zeadally
Dil Muhammad Akbar Hussain
Aftab Ahmed Memon
Muhammad Aslam Uqaili

Organization

Conference Chairs

Azizur Rahman	City University London, UK
Muhammad Aslam Uqaili	MUET, Pakistan
Abdul Qadeer Rajput	MUET, Pakistan

Steering Committee

Neeraj Suri	TU Darmstadt, Germany
Niel M. White	University of Southampton, UK
Ryszard Struzak	ICTP, Italy
Gul Agha	UIUC, USA
Tariq Munir	Edinburgh Napier University, Scotland
Mubark Shah	UCF, USA
Muhammad Yaqoob Siyal	NTU, Singapore
Franz Wotawa	Graz University of Technology, Austria
Javier Poncela Gonzales	University of Malága, Spain
Joseph Ronsin	Institut National des Sciences Appliquées de Rennes, France
Rezwan Khan	United International University, Bangladesh
Elfed Lewis	University of Limerick, Ireland
Mohd. Adam Suhaimi	International Islamic University, Malaysia

Technical Program Committee Chair

Faisal Karim Shaikh	MUET, Pakistan
Bhawani Shankar Chowdhry	MUET, Pakistan
Sherali Zeadally	University of Kentucky, USA
Dil Muhammad Akbar Hussain	Aalborg University, Denmark
Muhammad Aslam Uqaili	MUET, Pakistan
Aftab Ahmed Memon	MUET, Pakistan

Local Chairs

Mukhtiar A. Unar	MUET, Pakistan
Aftab Ahmed Memon	MUET, Pakistan
Ahsan Ahmad Ursani	MUET, Pakistan
Wajiha Shah	MUET, Pakistan

Abdul Sattar Larik	MUET, Pakistan
Tahseen Hafiz	MUET, Pakistan
Muhammad Zahid Shaikh	MUET, Pakistan

Poster Session Committee

Fahim A. Umrani	MUET, Pakistan
Imtaiz Kalwar	MUET, Pakistan
Muhammad Arif	MUET, Pakistan
Zafi Z. Shah	MUET, Pakistan
Yasmeen Panhwar	MUET, Pakistan

PhD Symposium Chairs

Tariq Jameel	MUET, Pakistan
Sheeraz Memon	MUET, Pakistan

Submission and Proceedings Committee

Sana Jokhio	MUET, Pakistan
Sania Bhatti	MUET, Pakistan
Umair Mujtaba Qureshi	MUET, Pakistan

Registration and Management Committee

Nafeesa Zaki	MUET, Pakistan
Fareeda Memon	MUET, Pakistan
Irfan Halepota	MUET, Pakistan
Narindar P. Chowdhry	MUET, Pakistan
Mansoor Soomro	MUET, Pakistan
Salman Afridi	MUET, Pakistan
Saba Baloch	MUET, Pakistan
Sanam Narejo	MUET, Pakistan
Mokhi Maan Chang	MUET, Pakistan
Shanzah Shaikh	MUET, Pakistan
Umair Mujtaba Qureshi	MUET, Pakistan
Madiha Majeed	MUET, Pakistan
Sanober Farheen	MUET, Pakistan
Jibran Memon	MUET, Pakistan
Attia Baqai	MUET, Pakistan
Shakeel Laghari	MUET, Pakistan

Zunera Aziz   MUET, Pakistan
Zartasha Baloch   MUET, Pakistan

Web and Publicity Committee

Ashfaque Issani   MUET, Pakistan
Saleem Memon   MUET, Pakistan
M. Murtaza Chang   MUET, Pakistan
Mustafa Baloch   MUET, Pakistan
Imran Qureshi   MUET, Pakistan

Finance Committee

Munir A. Shaikh   MUET, Pakistan
Zeeshan Memon   MUET, Pakistan
Lachman Das   MUET, Pakistan
Aftab Ansari   MUET, Pakistan
Muneer A. Memon   MUET, Pakistan

Program Committee

Arshad Ali   NUST, Pakistan
Yasir Arafat   Sindh University, Pakistan
Adnan Ashraf   MUET, Pakistan
Arabella Bhutto   MUET, Pakistan
Salim Bitam   University of Biskra, Algeria
Safdar Hussain Bouk   COMSATS, Pakistan
Bhawani Shankar Chowdhry   MUET, Pakistan
Flavia Delicato   Federal University of Rio de Janeiro, Brazil
Neil Grabham   University of Southampton, UK
Ian Grout   University of Limerick, Ireland
Manzoor Hashmani   IQRA University, Pakistan
Dil Muhammad Akbar Hussain   Aalborg University, Denmark
Imran Jokhio   MUET, Pakistan
Imtiaz Kalwar   MUET, Pakistan
Hameedullah Kazi   ISRA University, Pakistan
Abdelmajid Khelil   Huawei Technologies, Germany
Pardeep Kumar   QUEST, Pakistan
Winod Kumar   MUET, Pakistan
Athar Mahboob   DHA Suffa University, Pakistan
Naeem Mahoto   MUET, Pakistan
Qurban Memon   United Arab Emirates University, UAE
Sheeraz Memon   MUET, Pakistan

Tayab Memon	MUET, Pakistan
Zubair Memon	MUET, Pakistan
Syed Misbahuddin	SSUET, Pakistan
Shahzad Nizamani	MUET, Jamshoro, Pakistan
Christian Poellabauer	University of Notre Dame, USA
Javier Poncela Gonzales	University of Málaga, Spain
Abdul Qadir	PTCL, Pakistan
Nadia Qadri	COMSATS, Pakistan
Khairan Rajab	Najran University, Saudi Arabia
A. Qadeer Rajput	MUET, Pakistan
Shahid Raza	Swedish Institute of Computer Science, Sweden
Tahir Riaz	Aalborg University, Denmark
Akram Shaikh	PASTIC, Pakistan
Asadullah Shaikh	Najran University, Saudi Arabia
Faisal Karim Shaikh	MUET, Pakistan
Roshan Shaikh	Aisoft Inc., USA
Mohammad Shakeel	United Arab Emirates University, UAE
Jawwad Shamsi	FAST-NU, Pakistan
Waqas Sharif	Darmstadt University of Technology, Germany
Farhan Siddiqui	Walden University, USA
Safeeullah Soomro	SMIU, Pakistan
Jesus Tellez	Universidad de Carabobo, Venezuela
Suleyman Uludag	University of Michigan-Flint, USA
Fahim A. Umrani	MUET, Pakistan
Muhammad Aslam Uqaili	MUET, Pakistan
Ahsan Ahmad Ursani	MUET, Pakistan
Ziauddin Ursani	Oxford Brookes University, UK
Asim Imdad Wagan	UCET IUB, Pakistan
Ansar Yasar	Universiteit Hasselt – IMOB, Belgium
Nafeesa Zaki	MUET, Pakistan
Sherali Zeadally	University of Kentucky, USA
Zia Zeeshan	Swiss Federal Institute of Technology, Switzerland

Additional Reviewers

Abbasi, Abdul Rehman
Ali Khan, Sadiq
Ali, Ayesha Maryam
Amir, Samreen
Aziz, Zuneera
Bhutto, Arifa
Harijan, Khanji

Khan, Ghazanfarullah
Khoja, Shakeel
Lighari, Sheeraz
Noor, Fazal
Qureshi, Umair Mujtaba
Rao, Muzaffar
Shoro, Ghulam

Sponsors

 **Higher Education Commission PAKISTAN**

Organized by

 **MEHRAN UNIVERSITY OF ENGINEERING & TECHNOLOGY JAMSHORO, PAKISTAN**

Contents

Framework for Impact Analysis of Green Smart Grid Deployment in Energy Deficit Countries

Muhammad Aamir[1,2(✉)], Muhammad Aslam Uqaili[2],
Bhawani Shankar Chowdhry[2], Raiyah Rub[1], Andaleeb Ali[1],
and Mehwish Siddiqui[1]

[1] Sir Syed University of Engineering and Technology, Karachi, Pakistan
{raiyah90,mehwishsiddiqui2009}@hotmail.com,
{muaamir5,andleebali89}@yahoo.com
[2] Mehran University of Engineering and Technology, Jamshoro, Pakistan
aslamuqaili@yahoo.co.uk, c.bhawani@ieee.org

Abstract. Conventional grids are unable to deliver the escalating demand for electricity in this era of ever-increasing demand. Considering the increased requirements motivates the evolution of green smart grid technology. The smart grid technology introduces the new information and control technologies (ICT) enable the optimized approach to plan advanced, automated and centralized controlled system for power distribution and transmission. This paper provides a comprehensive study on comparative assessment of green smart grid versus conventional grids through highlighting the various factors such as reduction of CO_2 emission, self-healing and environment friendly, reliable operation, security provision, efficiency, cost management, energy empowerment, advance communication techniques, smart devices, smart controlling and monitoring, reduction in line losses and smart measurements. These factors will be used to propose an optimized solution based on green smart grid. The outcome of this research may be utilized to incorporate green technology in implementation of ICT infrastructure.

Keywords: Green ICT · Smart grid · Green energy · Conventional grid · Smart devices · Smart monitoring · Self-healing

1 Introduction

Increased demand of consumers [1], inadequate energy resources and the expensive procedure of exploiting new resources have put the reliability of the conventional grid in danger. In our conventional grid system we encounter losses when transmitting high voltages through transmission lines. In the developing countries like Pakistan pollution is a main environmental problem and unfortunately the major part of electricity generation is responsible for this dilemma. The fossil fuels used (coal, natural gas and oil) emits excess amount of CO_2. The most effective way to overcome this problem is to utilizing Green information and technology. Green Smart Grid incorporates Green communication protocols for smart grids, energy-efficient monitoring systems,

© Springer International Publishing Switzerland 2014
F.K. Shaikh et al. (Eds.): IMTIC 2013, CCIS 414, pp. 1–12, 2014.
DOI: 10.1007/978-3-319-10987-9_1

integration of green and renewable (wind, solar, geothermal, etc.) energy sources, Green sensor and actuator networks for smart grid and automation networks. By implementing green smart grid we can attain reductions in CO_2 emissions through energy efficiency and greater utilization of renewable resources. Energy-efficient technologies and practices reduce greenhouse gas emissions not only through energy savings but also through the deferral of new generation [12].

Thus, *Green Smart Grid* is a system that uses both hardware and software to enable the generators to efficiently route the power, and use digital technologies and smart devices and smart metering which uses sensors to provide a two–way real time information and flow of electricity between customer and demand side management through smart management and substations and provides a proper communication network to monitor the physical condition of grid devices, temperature, line losses, consumption of energy by customers, detect fluctuations and take immediate action to solve the existing problem and reduces the excess usage of electricity. It also provides an efficient delivery of energy by often generated the energy on the distribution side by using renewable energy resources like solar panels, wind turbines, small hydroelectric and hydro thermal technologies which reduces the emission of greenhouse gases and provides a healthy environment. The declaration of open communications standards through a Smart Grid will allow utilities to monitor and modulate the operating factors of what today are operationally incompatible components in the T&D infrastructure.

This automated controlled centralized monitoring system is self-healing with flawless interfaces between all parts of grids providing improved transmission and distribution networks and power generation, also enhance the quality, efficiency and makes the system secure, reliable and environment friendly. Figure 1 shows the burning of fossil fuel for generating electricity is the main reason for the emission of electricity.

The rest of the paper is organized as follows. Section 2 presents detailed infrastructure of smart grid followed by different available deployment options for communication network. Development of the framework is discussed in Sect. 3 by describing various subsystems for green smart grid. Advantages and disadvantages of the proposed framework are discussed in Sect. 4. Section 5 concludes the paper.

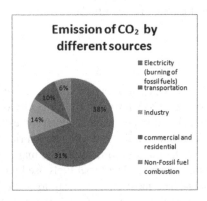

Fig. 1. Emission of CO_2 by different sources [12]

2   Smart Grid Infrastructure

The infrastructure of Green Smart Grid is subdivided into energy, information and communication system [2]. Smart Grid supports two-way real time information and flow of electricity; i.e. users can also generate electricity by using renewable energy sources and can also be put it back into grids. This reverse flow is extremely important in micro grid where islanded mode occurs due to power failures (Fig. 2).

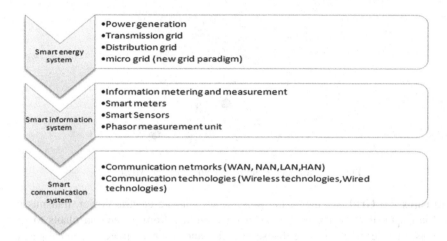

Fig. 2. Smart grid infrastructure

2.1   Smart Energy Subsystem

In conventional power grid, central power plants are only responsible for generating electricity where as in smart grid the power generation and the flow and distribution of electricity is more convenient [14]. By using renewable energy resources, the distribution grid may also be able of generate electricity. In this section, we further divide the green energy system into three subsystems power generation subsystem, transmission and distribution grid.

Power Generation subsystem. There are so many resources that are responsible to generate electric power. Particularly renewable energy resources take s significant part in power generation. Smart Grid enables the distribution grid to generate the electricity through renewable energy resources. Large-scale deployment of distributed generation grids changes the traditional power grid design methodology. Distributed generation grid permits the development of new grid paradigm called Microgrid.

MICROGRID. It is one of the cornerstones of the outlook Smart Grid, in which small areas are grouped for electricity generators and load distribution. By implementation of microgrid, electricity can produce using distributed generation grids using renewable energy resources [3]. This will result in an islanded microgrid, in an islanding mode the power is not coming from any outside source to consumers. In this system the user have option that whether they should connect to the macrogrid and get power from the electric utility or get power from microgrid and have the status of the load on each grid on basis of which they can take decision to connect with either of these grids. Thus, by using microgrids we can improve the power supply, reliability, high penetration of renewable sources, self-healing, and control active load (Fig. 3).

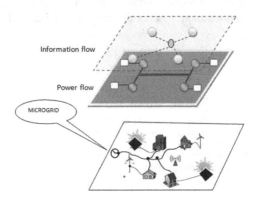

Fig. 3. Information and power flow through Microgrid

Transmission Grid. By increasing pressure to generate electric power, transmission grid is responsible for the bulk transfer of electricity from generation plants to sub-stations. In order to congregate this surging demand; we need more piecemeal patches to enable a smart transmission grid [2]. According to functionality smart green transmission grid consists of: smart control centers, smart transmission system and smart substations.

Distribution Grid. Distribution grid delivers power to the end users. For power generation distributed generators increases the system flexibility besides that, using distributed generators the control of the power flow becomes much more complicated. Two different switching systems in distribution domain can be used for delivering power, namely: AC power switching, and DC power switching system through energy packets [2]. The routers are placed to receive power packets. They will sort out the packets according to the information they contained and send them to the subsequent load. Power can be simply synchronized by controlling the number of energy packets. Therefore, power distribution systems become smarter to manage energy flow with the help of these systems.

2.2   Smart Information System

The growth of smart grid based in the enhancement of power technology as well as the complicated parameters such as computer monitoring, optimization and analysis [4]. In distributed system, atomization can be achieved from an information technology, such as interoperability of information exchanges and incorporation with existing and future devices. In this section, our center of attention is on the smart in-formation subsystem by examined the intelligent metering and measurement, which generates information for e.g. smart meters, sensors, and Phasor Measurement Units in a Smart Grid [4].

2.3 Smart Communication System

Some communication network and their properties are discussed below and according to these properties appropriate networks can be selected for the desired outcomes. We are discussing here some communication networks Wide Area Network (WAN), Local Area Network (LAN), Neighborhood Area Network (NAN), and Home Area Network (HAN) and how they can be implemented in green smart grid.

Wide Area Network. It covers the wide area and can connect other networks. It can connect long distant geographical sites and can be implemented using fiber or wirelessly. It also can connect utility centers with multiple substations and local control rooms. WAN technologies provide two-way communication in smart grid [6]. It includes several technologies like [7] WIMAX, cellular communication, satellite services etc. WAN can be used for communication path between concentrator and grid operator and capable of connecting information collectors to control room from utility centers.

Local Area Network. In contrast with WAN, LAN covers small geographical area so it can be used as field area network and can connects utility networks with central part or core network. LAN technologies can interconnect different smart devices and can be classified into wireless IEEE standards 802.x, wired Ethernet & PLC's etc. Wireless IEEE standards include Wi-Fi (IEEE 802.11), ZigBee (IEEE 802.15.4), WiMAX (IEEE 802.16) and Bluetooth (IEEE 802.15.1) [7].

Neighborhood Area Network. It is also known as WNAN and cover larger area than LAN. It helps to speed up the network with low cost. It can be used to manage smart meters data and convey it to WAN [8]. It provides control on end user devices for utility companies and sends real-time information to control the grid devices. It can be used to provide a communication path between WAN and HAN for monitoring and controlling.

Home Area Network. It covers less area than LAN and NAN and it can be used to facilitate communication between end user, all appliances inside the home and smart meters. It can be wired or wireless.

2.4 Communication Technologies

Communication networks can be used with different communication technologies. These communication technologies are subdivided into wireless and wired technologies. Wireless technologies are beneficial in many aspects than wired technologies like low cost, rapid deployment etc. However wired technologies can also be used and beneficial for the short distances like G3PlC can be used and as it can reduces infrastructure cost and transmit on medium voltage lines and can communicate across transformers, it also allow two way communication and provide power grid management in-home energy management, remote meter management and electric vehicle, in wireless communication network we have wireless mesh network, cellular technologies (GSM/GPRS/CDMA/LTE), WiMAX, microwave communication, wireless communication bases 802.15.4, satellite communication (Fig. 4).

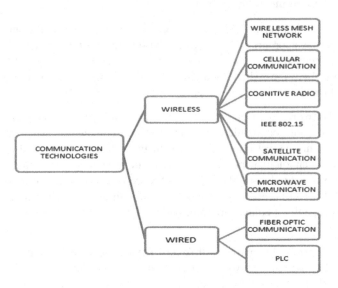

Fig. 4. Communication technologies

2.5   ICT Deployment Options

Different communication technologies are recommended for green smart grid, with the help of Table 1 we can analyze the pros and cons of the technologies and can select appropriate technology for our system as per our requirements. To select the communication system we have to keep in view that the system must be secure, reliable, cost effective, low power consuming, efficient, self-organizing or self-healing with high data rate and enough bandwidth [5] (Fig. 5).

2.6   Comparative Analysis of ICT Deployment Options

Table 1 compares the different ICT technologies that can be deployed for smart grid.

3   Proposed Framework

Considering the factors discussed above, the proposed energy efficient and Green ICT framework of smart grid is prepared below should be helpful to achieve a green, reliable, and proficient electricity usage in energy deficit countries like Pakistan. The steps involved in the proposed framework are shown in Fig. 6.

Table 1. Comparison between different ICT technologies for smart grid

FACTORS	IEEE 802.11/ 802.16	WIMAX	3G	ZIGBEE	SATTELITE	MICRO WAVE	FIBRE OPTIC	PLC (G3PLC)
coverage	wide	wide	wide	low	wide	low	wide	wide
cost	moderate	moderate	moderate	low	high initial cost	moderate	high	high
data rate	high	high	high	low	high	high	very high	high in short range, low in long range
power consumption	low	low	low	low	low	high	low	low
Losses	over long distances	no	depends upon weather condition	no	yes	no	no	no
self-organizing	yes	yes	yes	yes	yes	no	yes	yes
efficiency	yes	yes	yes	yes	yes	yes	yes	yes
reliability	yes	yes	less	yes	low	yes	yes	yes
security and privacy	yes	yes	security concerns	not more secure than 802.11	additional security required	yes	yes	yes
monitoring	good	good	good	good	good	good	good	good
speed	increase delay by multiple hops	faster	fast	moderate	high delay	fast	fast	fast
deployment in smart grid	• remote monitoring • demand response • AMI backhaul • residence • distribution automation	• AMI backhaul • demand response • SCADA backhaul	• Communication on network • AMI backhaul	• HAN • smart meters • smart devices	• remote monitoring and control • generation deployments • remote substation	• AMI • SCADA • demand response • distribution automation	• ICT backbone	• Remote monitoring • Load controlling • distribution grid • smart metering

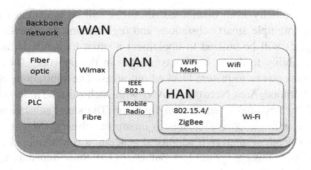

Fig. 5. Communication networks and technologies for ICT deployment

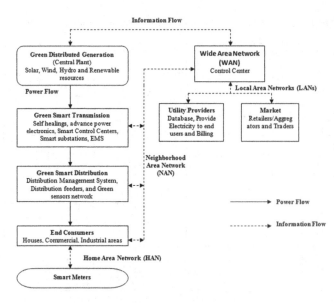

Fig. 6. Representation of Green Smart Grid framework

3.1   Integration of Distributed Generation: Utilizing Green Resources

Considering the growing demand for cleaner power and to reduce CO_2 emissions from atmosphere, distributed generation using green resources (solar, wind, hydro and renewable resources) are necessary to be accommodated in the [9] existing national grids of the energy deficit countries. Decentralized generation supplies power to the central generation unit. Green ICT (WAN-Based Network) is also involved to monitor the safe connection of distributed generation to the central grid. In this way we can achieve bi-directional exchange of information, optimized-generation, storage and delivery of green power. The scenario is presented by Fig. 7.

3.2   Allow Better Power Outage Management and Increased Grid Reliability: Smart Transmission

The generated electricity from distributed resources will be transmitted to the distribution grids via multiple smart substations and high tension transmission lines [10]. Self healings grids will be utilized to implement a smart transmission network. Self-healing has the ability to detect blackouts/outages in the network. These grids automatically re-routes power to restore blacked out areas. The substations are connected through Neighborhood Area Network (NAN) with each other. These substations are also monitored by Regional Transmission Operator. The smart substations share real-time information with the control centers to incorporate Energy Management System and smartly shed load, or analyze if additional generation is available elsewhere in the network and re-route this energy to black out areas [10]. Smart transmission uses Wide Area Networks for bidirectional communication between substations and control center

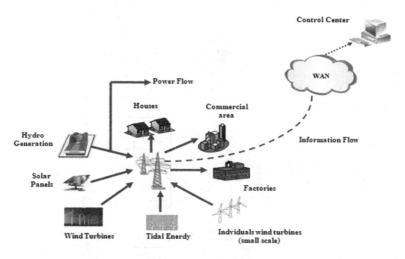

Fig. 7. Scenario of Green Distributed Generation [13]

to perform activities like fault management, monitoring and maintenance as well. The design and construction of power substation can be upgraded using green networks like fiber optic cables, advance power electronics and digitized equipment.

3.3 Assuring Security of Supply and Demand and Minimizing Downtime: Green Smart Distribution

In distribution domain delivery of electricity to end-consumers will be implemented by incorporating electrical and ICT infrastructure. It includes substations that contain feeders and step-down transformers. The substations are connected with the control center through Wide Area Network (WAN). The distribution domain is also connected with transmission domain via (NAN) to achieve bidirectional communication. Green sensor based networks are mounted on distribution feeders and transformers which enables remote monitoring of substations to encounter fault detection and send it to DMS, for e.g., [10] power lines or poles have been knocked down by storms, terror attacks and other accidents. Using real-time monitoring, distribution domain can detect and shut off the power lines before emergency. This domain will also provide Distribution Management System (DMS) which enables real-time load monitoring, automated demand response, asset monitoring and consumer load control [11]. This maintains continual supply to customers and ensures that the quality and level of power delivered meets customers' needs. The overall operation of distribution domain is shown in Fig. 8.

3.4 Network Management Protocol Can Be Used for Green Smart Grid Deployment

Simple Network Management Protocol (SNMP) is best suited for network management tool. SNMP manage information to exchange between agents that manage the system

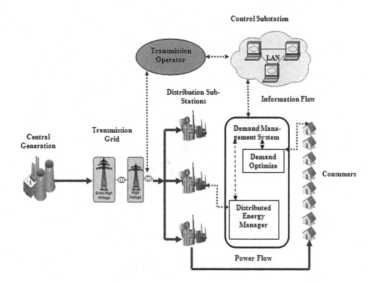

Fig. 8. Distribution domain operation

and network management applications. SNMP includes a network management application in a network management system. SNMP is a protocol for exchange of information throughout the system by using User Datagram Protocol (UDP) to send and retrieve information for the system management through a device which manages by the manager. Hence SNMP collect information, monitors and manages the system. For green smart grid we can use this protocol with communication technologies for the system management.

4 Advantages and Disadvantages of the Proposed Framework

4.1 Advantages

The proposed green smart energy framework exhibits the following advantages.

a. Environmental friendly because it reduces carbon emissions by integrating different renewables and improves consumption and delivery of generation.
b. Provide control over our energy usage.
c. Enables two way communications between power consumer and electricity provider.
d. Enhance security by reducing the probability of manmade attacks and natural calamities.
e. Self-healing grids reduce the cost of blackouts hence improve reliability.
f. Saves cost by keeping downward prices on electricity prices, reducing the amount paid by consumers.
g. Opens up new opportunities meaning, creating more jobs.

4.2 Disadvantages

Alongside advantages there are some disadvantages of the framework as well as discussed below.

a. Secure information storage and transportation are extremely important for power utilities, especially for billing purposes and grid control because automated meters can be hacked.
b. Various technology components are required for e.g. software, power generators, advanced sensors and system integrators.
c. Need for a two-way communication mechanism is crucial and investment-intensive.

5 Conclusion

In this paper, we represented a framework of green smart grid which will assure significant progress in the development of energy efficient and carbon reduced infrastructure and it shall be based on green communication technologies. This framework includes different deployment options regarding the implementation of smart communication network which monitors the exchange of information between different domains of the smart grid and ensure the management of balanced demand - supply of power. The proposed framework has taken the green energy resources into consideration for attaining a clean environment and to improve the energy production rate. Further green and smart devices networks are discussed for the up-gradation of transmission and distribution grids and to reduce substations power consumption. Smart metering structures are also proposed to facilitate the end-users. Such framework is cost-effective, intelligent, environmental friendly and can be a key enabler to help bring power savings in energy deficit areas.

References

1. Aamir, M., Poncela, J., Chowdhry, B.S., Uqaili, M.A.: Impact analysis of renewable energy in national grids for energy deficit countries. In: Chowdhry, B.S., Shaikh, F.K., Hussain, D. M.A., Uqaili, M.A. (eds.) IMTIC 2012. CCIS, vol. 281, pp. 1–9. Springer, Heidelberg (2012)
2. Fang, X., Misra, S., Xue, G., Yang, D.: Smart grid—the new and improved power grid: a survey. IEEE Commun. Surv. Tutor. 14(4), 944–980 (2012)
3. Lasseter, R., et al.: Integration of Distributed Energy Resources. The CERTS Microgrid Concept (2002)
4. Yan, Y., Qian, Y., Sharif, H., Tipper, D.: A survey on smart grid communication infrastructures: motivations, requirements and challenges. IEEE Commun. Surv. Tutor. 15 (1), 5–20 (2013)
5. Weber, V.: Smart sensor networks: technologies and applications for green growth. The Organization for Economic Cooperation and Development (2009)
6. Wang, W., Yi, X., Mohit, K.: A survey on the communication architectures in smart grid. Comput. Netw. 55(15), 3604–3629 (2011)

7. Gao, J., Wang, J.K., Wang, B.: Research on communication network architecture of smart grid. In: Proceedings of International Conference on Future Electrical Power and Energy Systems, vol. 6, Hong Kong Education Society, Hong Kong (2012)
8. Beigi, M.N.: An intrusion detection system for smart grid neighborhood area network. Dissertation, Ryerson University Toronto, Canada (2013)
9. Samad, A.: SMART GRID framework for Pakistan- perception to practicality. In: International Conference on Renewable Energies and Power Quality, Spain (2012)
10. General Electric: Real smart solution: distribution with digitizing equipment. http://www.gedigitalenergy.com/smartgrid_transmission.htm. Accessed 25 Dec 2013
11. Alstom Grid Smart Distribution: Solution for Smart Utilities. http://www.alstom.com. Accessed 20 Dec 2013
12. Inventory of U.S. Greenhouse gas emissions and sinks (1990–2011), Report No. EPA 430-R-13-001 (2013)
13. EPA: CO2 emissions. http://www.epa.gov/climatechange/ghgemissions/gases/co2.html. Accessed 18 Dec 2013
14. IEEE: The expertise to make a smart grid a reality. http://smartgrid.ieee.org/ieee-smart-grid/smart-grid-conceptual-model Accessed 19 Dec 2013

Impact of Wind Integration on National Transmission Network

Faheem Akhter[1,2(✉)], D. Ewen Macpherson[1], and Naeem Shahzad[3]

[1] Institute for Energy Systems, University of Edinburgh, Edinburgh, UK
{f.akhter,e.macpherson}@ed.ac.uk
[2] Department of Electrical Engineering, Sukkur Institute
of Business Administration, Sukkur, Pakistan
[3] Department of Electronic Engineering, International Islamic University,
Islamabad, Pakistan
naeem.chachar@gmail.com

Abstract. Due to the scarcity of fossil fuels and their increasing prices, adoption of renewable resources has become inevitable. Wind energy is being recognized as a potential renewable source of bulk power generation in Pakistan, just as across the world. The wind corridor located from Hyderabad to Keti Bandar has an immense potential for power generation, with two windfarms already in operation and many more planned. A stability analysis of installed and potential Wind Turbines Generators (WTG) type needs to be performed, to analyse the impact of power injection from wind turbines on the voltage level and grid stability of the power network. This analysis can further help to identify appropriate integration location and suitable wind turbine generator for AC network support. This paper presents the analysis of network strength at the point of wind the turbine generator's connection and a comparison of wind turbine generators to support the AC network, which will be useful for identification of suitable type of WTG for reliable operation of integrated system.

Keywords: Wind power integration · Network strength · Wind turbine generators · Stability analysis

1 Introduction

The generation deficit in Pakistan has peaked to 6000 MW in recent years, mainly due to over relaying on conventional resources of energy generation. The installed capacity of the country at the end of 2010 was 21,455 MW of which 31 % was hydro, 67 % thermal (gas & oil), 2 % nuclear and 0.1 % coal. However, due to seasonal variation of water flow it further decreases to 15,254 MW in winter [1]. Presently, this seasonal variation put a large burden on thermal generation due to the absence of renewable generation. This gap can be well filled by harnessing the vast wind resources located across different parts of the country.

According to the wind resource studies carried out by National Renewable Energy Laboratories (NREL) [2], Pakistan has a potential of more than 131,800 MW of wind energy across the country. The Alternative Energy Development Board (AEDB) has so

F.K. Shaikh et al. (Eds.): IMTIC 2013, CCIS 414, pp. 13–23, 2014.
DOI: 10.1007/978-3-319-10987-9_2

Table 1. Least cost generation plan [1]

	2010–11		2029–30	
	(MW)	(%)	(MW)	(%)
Hydro	6,555	31	41,546	37
Thermal-gas	6,571	31	12,015	11
Thermal-oil	7,838	37	6,855	6
Thermal-coal	30	0.1	37,774	34
Bagasse & Bio Waste Plant	0	0	100	0.1
Nuclear	461	2	6,947	6
Wind	0	0	5,400	5
Import	0	0	2,000	2
Total	21,455	100	112,639	100

far allocated land to more than eighteen (18) Independent Power Producers (IPPS) for wind power generation projects of 50 MW each. Twelve 50 MW wind power projects have completed feasibility studies. The plans are to achieve up to 1,800 MW from wind energy by the end of 2020 and a total of 5,400 MW from wind energy sources by 2030, shown in Table 1.

2   Related Work

Comprehensive studies have been performed for the integration of wind power into existing transmission network throughout the world, namely National Renewable Energy Laboratory in United States, Hydro-Quebec in Canada and Risø DTU National Laboratory for Sustainable Energy, in Denmark, Europe, considering both the technological and regional implementation aspects of the topic. Very few studies have been performed in the context of Pakistan. A regional study has been performed in [3], showing the need of regional interconnection for renewable energy integration and future energy security in SAARC countries. [4] presents the statistics of energy mix of sustainable energy option available for Pakistan. The evaluation of wind energy potentials at Keti Bander in particular is presented in [5]. The energy management from the renewable resources in energy deficit network is discussed in [6]. A co-ordination study of wind power and hydro power generation is performed in [7], mainly considering the loading capacity of transmission lines. However, no study has been performed to analyze the dynamic stability analysis of wind power integration into the power system network.

This study presents the stability analysis of the installed and potential Wind Turbine Generator (WTG) types, to analyze the impact of the power injection from wind turbines regarding the voltage level and grid stability of the power network. The existing transmission system has been designed for conventional power generation which is composed of synchronous generators, which can support the stability of the transmission system by providing inertia responses, oscillation damping, synchronizing power, short-circuit capability and voltage backup during faults. In contrast, wind turbine generators (WTGs) are characterized mainly as fixed speed and variable speed induction generators, doubly fed induction generators and full scale synchronous generators, which are very different from those of conventional generators. This paper presents a comparison of the grid support provided by different WTGs types to identify the most suitable type WTG at each location. A stability analysis of the 50 MW planned wind power project (WPP) is performed on the high wind potential site Jhampir, using PSCAD/EMTDC simulation software [8]. Different WTG concepts are simulated with given grid strength and wind speed at the location to determine the impact of wind turbine generators on the integrated grid. Dynamic analysis is performed to evaluate performance in accordance with the grid code description. Geospatial Toolkit map from NREL [9] shown in Fig. 1 is used to analyze the predicted average monthly wind speed in m/s at the location and the HOMER utility is used to obtain the frequency distribution at the locations.

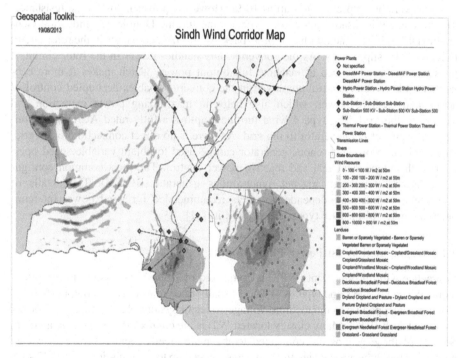

Fig. 1. Sindh wind corridor map (NREL) [9]

3 System Modelling

3.1 Wind Turbine Generator (WTG) Technologies

A wind turbine generator system is typically comprised of the turbine blades and rotor hub assembly to capture power from the wind, a drive-train to step-up the speed from low spinning turbine shaft to the high speed generator, and a generator as an electromechanical energy converter. WTGs are classified mainly into four types [10], according to their speed control characteristics, i.e., Type 1: Fixed speed wind turbines (SCIG), Type 2: Variable slip wind turbines (OSIG), Type 3: Double feed induction generator (DFIG) wind turbines, and Type 4: Full converter wind turbines (PMSG).

The fixed speed wind turbine is the most basic type turbine employed in wind energy market. It consists of a squirrel-cage induction machine (SCIG) directly connected to the grid and operates with very little variability in turbine rotor speed. It is very robust and reliable in operation but inefficient power capture capability and high reactive power consumption are its main disadvantages. Some of them do not even have pitch control capability. The remaining three types come under the broad category of variable speed turbines, as they are designed to operate over a wide range of rotor speed. Most of them also have the pitching controllability. Pitch and speed controllability enables them to capture more energy over a wide range of wind speed than fixed speed wind turbines. Type 2 wind turbines, the Opti-slip Induction Generator, employs dynamic rotor resistance to control the rotor resistance of the machine and provides variable slip operation up to 10 %. However, power is lost in the resistance. To overcome this disadvantage, the Type 3 wind turbine Double-Fed Induction Generator (DFIG) is designed with a back-to-back AC/DC/AC converter in the rotor circuit to recover the slip energy. As the converter only handles power in the rotor circuit, it does not have to be rated at machine full output power, which makes it more economical. Flux vector control employed in the converter enables decoupled control of active and reactive power, which also helps in maximizing power extraction and support to the grid. The type 4 wind turbine employs a fully rated AC/DC/AC converter to connect the generator to the grid. As there is no direct connection to the grid, so an induction or synchronous generator can be used to obtain variable speed operation with independent real and reactive power control. The most common configuration is the permanent magnet synchronous generator (PMSG). The details of universal manufacture-independent models recommended for wind power interconnection studies of all four types is described in [11].

3.2   Aggregated Wind Power Plant Model

In practice wind power plant (WPP) is comprised of a number of wind turbine generators (WTGs) of the same type. A WTG is usually rated at low voltage output (690 V). Voltage is stepped up to the medium voltage collector system (22 kV) by a transformer located at each WTG. Many closely located WTGs are connected in parallel in a group. Several of these groups are connected to the mains feeder, and several feeders are connected to a substation where the voltage is stepped up to transmission level (132 kV).

In many cases, it is desire able to model the WPP close to the actual implementation, but it may not be practical to model in detail each WTG and collector system for the WPP's power system integration studies. However, when the response to grid disturbances is required, dynamic models of the generator and related controls need to be implemented to know the turbine response. In this study an aggregated single turbine representation is taken to represent a 50 MW WPP comprising 33 units of 1.5 MW WTGs and low voltage pad-mounted transformers in a simplified manner, shown in Fig. 2.

Fig. 2. Single turbine representation of WPP

3.3 Power System Representation

For WPP integration studies, detailed representation of the whole network may not be practical and would involve excessive computational cost and time. So the actual system of the NTDC 132 kV grid shown in Fig. 3 is represented as an infinite bus connected to the PCC through equivalent impedance (Z_{grid}) of the system as shown in Fig. 2. This can be the most important parameter the network strength of the system. An important characteristic of determining the strength of the network is the short circuit ratio (SCR), connected with WPP of rated power $S_{N\,WT}$, can be defined as [10, 12]:

$$SCR = \frac{SCC}{S_{NWT}} = \frac{V_G^2}{Z_{grid} \cdot S_{NWT}} \qquad (1)$$

The SSC is the short circuit capacity which depends on voltage levels (V_G) and total power capability at the PCC. The SSC of the power grid is given in the National Power System Expansion Plan (NPSEP) [1]. Hence, the equivalent impedance of the grid (Z_{grid}) can be determined at the PCC as:

$$Z_{grid} = \frac{V_G^2}{SCC} \qquad (2)$$

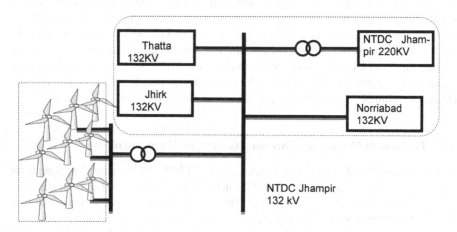

Fig. 3. Single line diagram of 132 kV Jhampir grid

4 Dynamic Simulation Results

4.1 Fixed Speed Wind Turbines

Figure 4 shows the dynamic behavior of the 50 MW WPP comprising fixed speed wind turbine (SCIG) following a rigid three phase fault for 200 ms at the PCC (132 kV) bus. The average wind speed is taken as 10 m/s at the location. The terminal and phase voltage of the wind turbine falls to zero during the fault and resumes to normal after the fault clearance Fig. 4(c) and (e). The electrical power and torque reduces to zero for the duration of the fault Fig. 4(b) and (g), while generator speed increases Fig. 4(d). When the fault is cleared at t = 10.20 s huge reactive power is drawn for excitation of the SCIG, along with the inrush current shown in Fig. 4(e) and (i). The wind turbine recovers to its normal condition 200 ms after fault clearance.

4.2 Variable-Slip Wind Turbines

Figure 5 shows the dynamic performance of the 50 MW WPP comprising variable slip wind turbines (OSIG) during rigid three phase fault at the PCC (132 kV) for 200 ms at average wind speed of 10 m/s. The dynamic behavior of the OSIG wind turbine appears to be the same as for the fixed speed turbine, except that power can be regulated to rated values in the event of higher wind speeds. The wind turbine system draws high reactive power for excitation of the induction generator, Fig. 5(f), after fault clearance and starts to supply active power, Fig. 5(a). The terminal voltage builds up, Fig. 5(c) and speed reduces down to the pre-fault value, Fig. 5(e).

4.3 Double-Feed Induction Generator Wind Turbines

Figure 6 shows the dynamic performance of the 50 MW WPP comprising double-fed induction generators (DFIG) during three phase rigid fault at the PCC (132 kV) bus. The average speed of 10 m/s is assumed with a fault of 200 ms. The wind turbine supplies active power to the grid from both stator and rotor sides. A low voltage protection is applied to avoid the very high rotor current during the fault, which blocks the rotor side converter. This compares the rms line voltage with a pre-set value of voltage dip and blocks the rotor side converter. The DFIG behaves as a squirrel cage induction generator and starts to draw huge reactive power, Fig. 6(g). After the fault clearance terminal voltage builds up and the rotor side converter is unblocked.

4.4 Permanent Magnet Synchronous Generator Wind Turbines

Figure 7 shows the dynamic performance of the 50 MW WPP comprising permanent magnet synchronous generators (PMSG) during a three phase rigid fault at the PCC (132 kV) bus. The fault is simulated for 100 ms and average wind speed is taken as 10 m/s. As observed previously in the dynamic behaviour of Type 1, 2 and 3 systems in Figs. 4, 5 and 6 respectively, the grid voltage drops significantly because of high

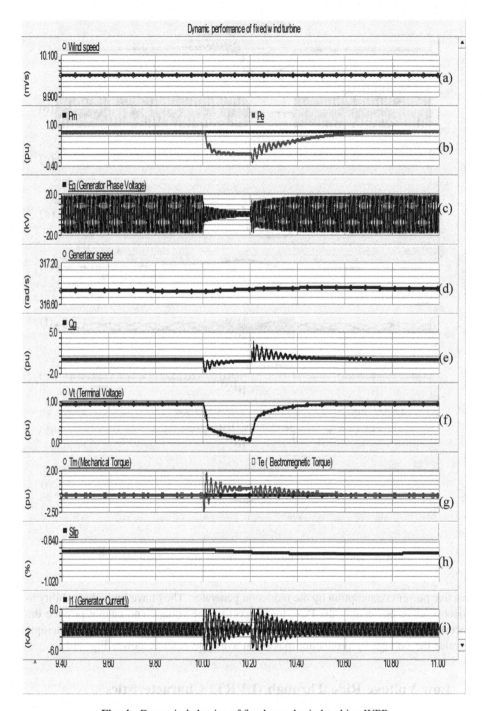

Fig. 4. Dynamic behavior of fixed speed wind turbine WPP

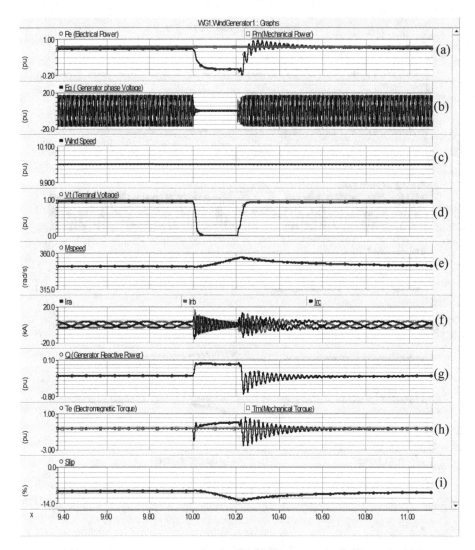

Fig. 5. Dynamic performance of variable slip wind turbine WPP

reactive power consumption by the induction generator. They have limited capability to inject reactive power into the PCC for supporting the voltage and cannot provide the necessary reactive power to raise voltage, whereas the PMSG control system attempts to raise the voltage by producing maximum available reactive power Fig. 7(d).

5   Low Voltage Ride Through (LVRT) Characteristics

One of the most important aspects of grid code compliance of WPP is Low Voltage Ride Through (LVRT) capability characterises. The Fig. 8 shows the LVRT requirement in

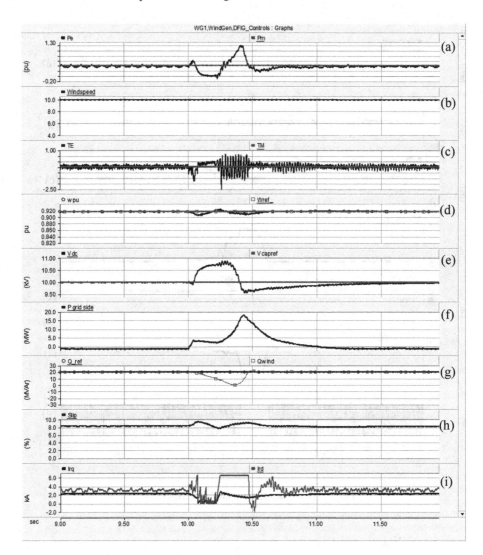

Fig. 6. Dynamic performance of DFIG WPP

German grid code. With the performance of further dynamic response analysis by varying voltage dip level at the PCC and fault duration, LVRT characteristics of each WPP type can be obtained, which can further confirm the grid code compliance of each type.

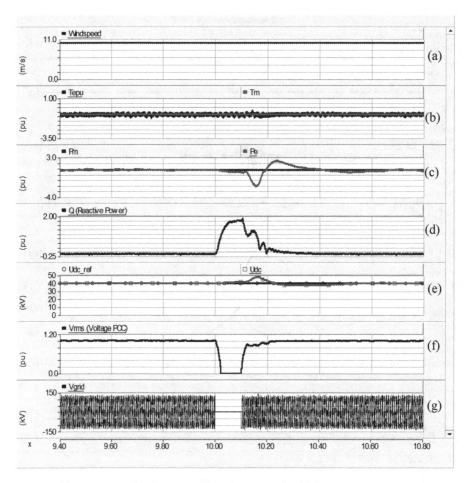

Fig. 7. Dynamic performance of PMSG WP

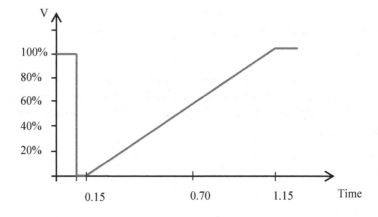

Fig. 8. VRT requirement in German grid code [13]

6 Conclusion

This paper presents the comparison of grid supportability of different WTGs types at the actual strength of the grid to identify the suitable type of WTG for the proposed location of Hyderabad-Keti Bander wind corridor. The active and reactive power controllability analysis of different WTGs types is performed to obtain the comparison of voltage and frequency maintaining capability within the prescribed range of rated values at the point of common coupling (PCC) in normal operation. The simulation result obtained shows that, Type 1, 2 and 3 systems, the grid voltage drops significantly because of high reactive power consumption by the induction generator. They have limited capability to inject reactive power into the PCC for supporting the voltage and cannot provide the necessary reactive power to raise voltage without addition protection and control. Whereas Type 4 (PMSG) wind turbines attempt to raise the voltage by producing maximum available reactive power. To further confirm with grid code compliance LVRT characteristic analysis is suggested to be performed.

Acknowledgement. The author would like to acknowledge the affiliation and funding resources for this research from Sukkur Institute of Business Administration, Sukkur.

References

1. Inc, S.-L.I.: National power system expansion plan. National Transmission and Despatch Company Limited. Final report 32 (2011)
2. Elliott, D.: Wind resource assessment and mapping for Afghanistan and Pakistan. National Renewable Energy Laboratory. Golden, Color, USA (2011)
3. Rashid, T.H.M.S., Islam, R.: Prospects of renewable energy resources and regional grid integration for future energy security & development in SAARC countries. IJRET 2(1), 43–51 (2013)
4. Asif, M.: Sustainable energy options for Pakistan. Renew. Sustain. Energy Rev. **13**, 903–909 (2009)
5. Ullah, I., Chaudhry, Q.-Z., Chipperfield, A.J.: An evaluation of wind energy potential at Kati Bandar. Pakistan. Renew. Sustain. Energy Rev. **14**, 856–861 (2010)
6. Aamir, M., Poncela, J.: Impact analysis of renewable energy in national grids for energy deficit countries. Commun. Comput. Inf. Sci. Second IMT, **218**, 1–9 (2012)
7. Awan, S.: Hydro and wind power integration: a case study of Dargai station in Pakistan. Energy Power Eng. **4**, 203–209 (2012)
8. User's guide (PSCAD) Power System Computer Aided Design (2010)
9. User manual Geospatial Toolkit (2010). www.nrel.gov/international/geospatial_toolkits
10. Ackermann, T.: Wind Power in Power Systems. Wiley, Chichester (2005)
11. Singh, M., Surya, S.: Dynamic models for wind turbines and wind power plants. National Renewable Energy Laboratory (2011)
12. Grunau, S., Fuchs, F.: Effect of wind-energy power injection into weak grids. In: Proceedings of EWEA Conference (2012)
13. Altın, M., Goksu, O.: Overview of recent grid codes for wind power integration. In: 12th International Conference Optimization of Electrical and Electronic Equipment, OPTIM, pp. 1152–1160 (2010)

Linear Discriminant Analysis Based Approach for Automatic Speech Recognition of Urdu Isolated Words

Hazrat Ali[1,5]([✉]), Nasir Ahmad[2], Xianwei Zhou[1], Muhammad Ali[3],
and Ali Asghar Manjotho[4]

[1] Department of Communication Engineering, School of Computer and
Communication Engineering, University of Science and Technology Beijing,
Beijing 10083, China
engr.hazratali@yahoo.com, xwzhouli@sina.com
[2] Department of Computer Systems Engineering, University of Engineering and
Technology Peshawar, Peshawar 25120, Pakistan
n.ahmad@nwfpuet.edu.pk
[3] Department of Electrical and Computer Engineering,
North Dakota State University, Fargo, ND 58108-6050, USA
muhammadali.sahibzad@my.ndsu.edu
[4] Department of Computer Systems Engineering,
Mehran University of Engineering and Technology, Jamshoro, Pakistan
ali.manjotho@faculty.muet.edu.pk
[5] Machine Learning Group, School of Informatics,
City University London, London EC1V 0HB, UK

Abstract. Urdu is amongst the five largest languages of the world and
enjoys extreme importance by sharing its vocabulary with several other
languages of the Indo-Pak. However, there has not been any significant
research in the area of Automatic Speech Recognition of Urdu. This
paper presents the statistical based classification technique to achieve
the task of Automatic Speech Recognition of isolated words in Urdu.
For each isolated word, 52 Mel Frequency Cepstral Coefficients have
been extracted and based upon these coefficients; the classification has
been achieved using Linear Discriminant Analysis. As a prototype, the
system has been trained with audio samples of seven speakers including
male/female, native/non-native and speakers with different ages while
the testing has been done using audio samples of three speakers. It was
determined that majority of words exhibit a percentage error of less than
33 %. Words with 100 % error were declared to be bad words. The work
reported in this paper may serve as a strong baseline for future research
work on Urdu ASR, especially for continuous speech recognition of Urdu.

Keywords: Urdu automatic speech recognition · Mel frequency cepstral
coefficients · Linear Discriminant Analysis · Isolated words recognition

© Springer International Publishing Switzerland 2014
F.K. Shaikh et al. (Eds.): IMTIC 2013, CCIS 414, pp. 24–34, 2014.
DOI: 10.1007/978-3-319-10987-9_3

1   Introduction

User friendly and natural interaction between man and machine has always been a complementary part of technological development. Speech is the most effective medium of communication between human and same is envisaged to be applicable for human-machine interaction. Therefore, Automatic Speech Recognition (ASR) has significantly grabbed the attention of researchers for the last five decades and has attained considerable success in noise-free environments. Successful ASR enables the computers to exhibit human-like behavior by understanding the voice input to them. Such hearing systems having been developed in various languages such as English, French, Japanese, Chinese and Arabic [1–5], and have wide-spread application ranging from data entry to security and surveillance. The research on ASR has enabled the communities with lower level of literacy to interact with machines, and similarly facilitated the interaction of blind and disabled people with the computers [6]. Despite the development of ASR systems in these languages, there has been no significant contribution to ASR of Urdu language, which is one of the largest languages of the world. Wiqas [7] has summarized the research work conducted on the ASR of the languages of the Indo-Pak, including the research work on Urdu ASR. A continuous speech ASR system for Urdu language has been presented in [8], however, no information on the use of a standard corpus of Urdu has been provided. The recognition rate is limited to 55 % accuracy for continuous speech. Furthermore, it lacks the information about the use of number of words/sentences and the training/test data. Azam [9] has proposed an Artificial Neural Networks (ANN) based Urdu speech recognition system however; this work is limited to digits recognition only. Moreover, the application of the system is limited to single speaker only. Ahad et al. [10] has used a different class of ANN called multilayer perceptrons (MLP) however; they have achieved recognition of Urdu digits from 0 to 9 for mono-speaker database only. Hasnain et al. [11] has made yet another effort to achieve the task of digits recognition for 0 to 9, based on the use of feed-forward neural network models developed in Matlab. A more recent contribution to isolated words recognition has been made by [12], developing a Hidden Markov Model (HMM) [13] based speaker-independent speech recognition system for Urdu. In this work the open source framework Sphinx-4 has been used for the classification. A wordlist grammar language model was adopted where each word was represented as a single phoneme instead of dividing into sub-units. An apparent limitation of this approach is that this may be applicable to shorter words but for longer words, the performance may degrade drastically. Huda [14] has used a relatively larger data set for the training purpose, however, the system developed is for continuous speech recognition task and the recognition results are yet modest. Research on ASR can be targeted at small, medium or large vocabulary applications; it may be for digits only, isolated words only or continuous speech applications. The applications of isolated words recognition are well known including the automated banking applications, automatic data and PIN codes entry applications, e-health monitoring and voice dialing phone applications etc. In this paper the ASR task for medium vocabulary isolated words has been undertaken containing 100 isolated words of Urdu. The three important components of an ASR system are the corpus i.e. the database of speech data, the features extraction and the classification. In Sect. 2 of this paper, the corpus used for this work has been discussed briefly. The features extraction approach and the major steps involved in the extraction of these features have been presented in Sect. 3. The classification of the different words based upon the features obtained for each word, has been discussed in Sect. 4. Finally, the results have been summarized in Sect. 5.

2   Corpus Selection

One of the most important components of an ASR system is the use of a standard corpus covering a range of acoustic variations and different aspects of a language. In this work, the corpus developed in [15], has been used. The corpus contains 250 isolated words selected from the list of most frequently used words, developed by the Center for Language Engineering [16]. Audio files for one hundred isolated words have been selected from the corpus and used in the training and testing of the system. The one hundred words used contain the digits from 0 to 9, names of seasons, days of the week and the names of months. Besides this, for few of the words, their antonyms have also been included. The words are available in separate audio files with an average length of 500 milliseconds and stored in mono format with .wav extension. Based upon the attributes such as age, gender and origin, this corpus provides a balanced distribution. The files include the words uttered by both male and female speakers of different ages. Similarly, a variety of accents has been covered by including the audio recordings by both native and non-native speakers originating from different areas. For example, Pashto speakers from different regions of Pakistan differ in the pronunciation of Urdu words, thus, data from these speakers provide a variety of samples for training and testing purpose. A sample representation of the attributes of the speakers has been shown in Table 1.

Table 1. Sample of representation of the speech data (as in [15])

S. No	Speaker name	Age group	Gender	Native non-native
1	AAMNG1	G1	Male	Non-native
2	ABMNG1	G1	Male	Non-native
3	ACMNG2	G2	Male	Non-native
4	AEFYG1	G1	Female	Native
5	AFFYG1	G1	Female	Native
6	AGMNG1	G1	Male	Non-native
7	AHMNG1	G1	Male	Non-native

3   Feature Selection

Feature Extraction is one of the most important modules of an Automatic Speech Recognition System. For continuous speech recognition, the feature extraction is typically aimed to capture the distinguishing characteristics of the phonemes i.e. the smallest unit of sound. However, for isolated words recognition, each word is usually split into equal number of segments and features are extracted from each of the segments. In this work, each word is split into four segments and the Mel Frequency Cepstral Coefficients (MFCC) based features have been obtained for each segment.

3.1   Mel Frequency Cepstral Coefficients

The MFCC features are the most commonly used features for Automatic Speech Recognition as MFCCs most closely resembles the human hearing mechanism. The Mel scale is based on the fact that the frequency response of the humans ear to the audio signal is not a linear function of frequency. This response can be best modeled on a Mel scale where the spacing between frequencies above 1000 Hz is logarithmic [17]. The relation between the Mel scale frequencies and the Hertz frequencies can be represented by Eq. 1;

$$f_{mel} = 2595 \times \log\left(1 + \frac{f}{700\,Hz}\right) \tag{1}$$

The Mel Frequency Cepstrum is the power spectrum of a speech signal for short term and is based upon a linear cosine transform of a log power spectrum on the Mel scale. The Mel Frequency Cepstrum comprises of the MFC coefficients. Several methods for MFCC extraction have been proposed by [17–19]. The major steps in the extraction of MFCC are shown in Algorithm 1.

In the pre-processing step, the segmentation of the words and noise removal have been achieved by using Adobe Audition Software. The sampling rate was set to 16000 Hz and the audio samples were saved as .wav files in mono format before being input to the algorithm. The Adobe Audition software has also been utilized for amplification or attenuation of the audio signal, as necessary, to obtain a uniform db level for all the samples. Besides, as the recording was performed in a controlled environment, this helps out in assuring minimum effect of noise. A snapshot of the Adobe Audition environment has been shown in Fig. 1.

The pre-processing stage also includes the Pre-emphasis of the signal to increase the energy of the higher frequency contents. The pre-emphasis is achieved using filter of the form, as in Eq. 2.

$$H(z) = 1 - 0.97z^{-1} \tag{2}$$

The pre-processing is followed by the windowing of the speech signal. A rectangular window as defined by equation for $w(n)$ in Eq. 3 has been used. For speech processing applications, hamming window is more commonly used to avoid information loss, however for isolated words processing, rectangular window is equally beneficial.

input : An isolated word - audio file
output: 52 Mel Frequency Cepstral Coefficients
initialization;
Preprocessing
for $i \leftarrow 1$ **to** 4 **do**
| Segmentation;
| Noise Removal;
| Pre-Emphasis $(1 - 0.97z^{-1})$
end
Windowing

if *isolated words* **then**
| Rectangular Window **else**
| | Hamming Window
| **end**
end
Discrete Fourier Transform

FFT Size = 552

Transformation to Mel Scale

linear scale $\rightarrow$ logarithmic scale

$f_{mel} = 2595 \times \log 1 + \frac{f}{700\,Hz}$

Discrete Cosine Transform

for $j \leftarrow 1$ **to** *4* **do**
| processing ;
end
Dimensionality Reduction

A single word $\implies$ 52 MFCCs

Algorithm 1: Extraction Algorithm for Mel Frequency Cepstral Coefficients

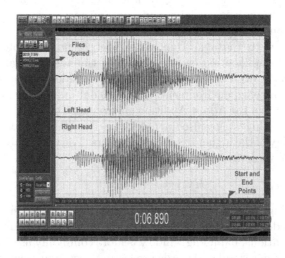

Fig. 1. Segmentation in adobe audition environment

$$w(n) = \begin{cases} 1 & 0 \leq x \leq M - 1 \\ 0 & \text{otherwise} \end{cases} \tag{3}$$

where $M = 128$. Fast Fourier Transform [20,21] is applied to the windowed frame of the signal. The size of FFT is $N = 512$. The spectrum, thus obtained, is transformed to the Mel scale, as defined by the equation for fmel. To imitate the logarithmic response of human ear, the output of the mel scale filters bank is subjected to base 10 Log. Finally, the application of Discrete Cosine Transform (DCT) [22] generates the MFCCs, i.e. 52 MFCCs for each isolated word.

4   Classification

The recognition on the basis of MFCCs requires a supervised classification technique for which Linear Discriminant Analysis is a strong candidate [23,24]. The classification includes; *training of the system* and *testing of the system*. 70 % percent of the data has been used for training the ASR system and the remaining 30 % data has been used for testing of the system.

4.1   Linear Discriminant Analysis

Linear Discriminant Analysis (LDA) is a classification as well as dimensionality reduction technique. LDA can be class-dependent or class-independent, based upon maximization of the ratio of between class variance to within class variance or maximization of the ratio of overall variance to within class variance, respectively.

4.2   Training and Testing Data

To evaluate the performance of the ASR system, the MFCCs of a total of hundred words have been used for training and testing of the system. As a simple case, the training and testing has been done with the speech data of first ten speakers. The training set contains data from both native and non-native speakers of Urdu. Similarly, it also contains male as well as female speakers.

4.3   Confusion Matrix

The number of correct matches from the testing data with the training data has been summarized in a Confusion Matrix. The confusion matrix is of size $N \times N$ for N number of words. It can be represented as shown by Mc.

$$M_c = \begin{matrix} m_{11} & m_{12} & m_{13}... & m_{1N} \\ m_{21} & m_{22} & m_{23}... & m_{2N} \\ m_{31} & m_{32} & m_{33}... & m_{3N} \\ . & . & .... & . \\ . & . & .... & . \\ m_{N1} & m_{N2} & m_{N3}... & m_{NN} \end{matrix} \tag{4}$$

The number of correct matches for a word i has been shown by the diagonal entries of the confusion matrix, i.e. m_{ij} for $i = j$. Number of confusions of word i with word j has been shown by non-diagonal entries, i.e. m_{ij} for $i \neq j$.

5   Results

The error in the recognition of any isolated word is calculated from the confusion matrix. For an isolated word i, the diagonal entry m_{ii}, divided by the sum of all the entries in row i, gives the fraction of test data correctly matched. The sum of all the entries in a row is always equal to the number of test signals. This ratio can be defined mathematically as;

$$Correct\ Match, C \equiv \frac{m_{ij}}{m_{i1} + m_{i2} + ...m_{iN}}, \text{for } i = j,\ j = 1, 2, 3...N. \quad (5)$$

Thus, the error is measured by using the following equation;

$$\%error = (1 - C) \times 100 \quad (6)$$

5.1   Results for First Ten Words

Figure 2 shows the confusion matrix graph for the first ten words. The x-axis and y-axis represent the indexes for the words i.e. 001 to 010. The number of successful or incorrect matches is represented by the height of the bars. As already mentioned, the maximum possible height is 3 as the number of test signals used here is 3. The percentage error and number of fraction of test signals correctly recognized has been summarized for the first ten words in Table 2. As shown in this table, the first word gives 66 % correct match, also depicted by the confusion matrix graph, by the first bar having a height of 2. The test signals for word 004 has undergone a 0 % error and the bar for this word has a height of 3. Similarly, the results for other words are obvious from the confusion matrix graph in Fig. 2 and the corresponding Table 2.

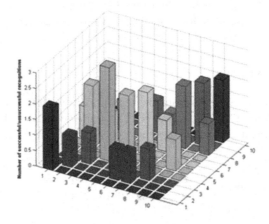

Fig. 2. Confusion matrix graph for first ten words

Table 2. Percentage error for words 001 to 010

S. No	Word number	Value of C	% error
1	001	0.667	33.33 %
2	002	0.333	66.67 %
3	003	0.333	66.67 %
4	004	1	0 %
5	005	0.667	33.33 %
6	006	0.667	33.33 %
7	007	0.333	66.67 %
8	008	0.667	33.33 %
9	009	0.667	33.33 %
10	010	0.667	33.33 %

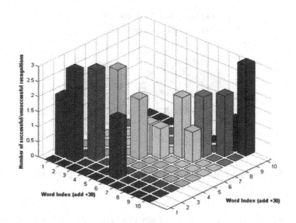

Fig. 3. Confusion matrix graph for words 031 to 040

5.2 Results for Words 031 to 040

As a second sample of the result, confusion matrix graph for word 031 to 040 has been shown in Fig. 3. The corresponding fractional values for correct matches and percentage error have been summarized in Table 3. The results shown in Fig. 3 are very important and needs to be discussed. As shown in Table 3, it is obvious that there is a zero percent error for words 032 through word 034. On the other hand, a complete mismatch exists for word 031, resulting in a 100 % error.

5.3 Overall Percentage Error

Figure 4 shows the proportion of the words with 100 %, 66.67 %, 33.33 % and 0 % error, respectively. The analysis shows that the percentage error is either zero

Table 3. Percentage error for words 031 to 040

S. No	Word number	Value of C	% error
1	031	0	100 %
2	032	1	0 %
3	033	1	0 %
4	034	1	0 %
5	035	0.667	33.33 %
6	036	0.333	66.67 %
7	037	0.667	33.33 %
8	038	0.667	33.33 %
9	039	0.667	33.33 %
10	040	1	0 %

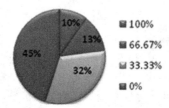

Fig. 4. Percentage of test data having different percentage error

or 33.33 % for majority of the words. However, for few of the words, the value is larger approaching the maximum possible value i.e. 100 %. The overall error, E, can be measured as;

$$E = \frac{100\% \; of(10 \times 3) + 66.67\% \; of(13 \times 3) + 33.33\% \; of(32 \times 3) + 0\% \; of(45 \times 3)}{(100 \times 3)}$$

(7)

From this calculation, $E = 29.33\%$. This is comparable with so many existing ASR systems as developed for other languages with audio-only based features. This value, however, can be reduced further by increasing the amount of training data.

5.4   Bad Words

The words having a 100 % error rate are referred to be the Bad Words. The primary reason for such a poor performance of the ASR system for these words, is the poor quality of recording which was determined through manual analysis of the audio files. Besides this, as each word has been divided into four segment, there is a possibility that more than one segment are matching exactly with segments of other words and the ASR framework is confused.

6 Future Work

This ASR system has been developed for speech recognition of isolated words only. This is a medium vocabulary application limited to a hundred words and can be extended to several thousand words. However, in that case, an even larger data for the training of the system will be required. Thus, there is need to increase the corpus size. This paper has provided a baseline for future research on ASR of Urdu language and can be extended to Continuous Speech Recognition of Urdu. This is an audio-only based feature extraction for ASR. The system can be evaluated by using audio-visual features which should result in the enhancement of the performance.

Acknowledgment. The authors are thankful to the supporting staff of the Department of Electrical Engineering, University of Engineering and Technology, Peshawar, Pakistan. It is due to their efforts which they put into keeping the Computer Lab open for extra hours and providing the authors with opportunity to use it. The authors also extend their gratitude to Engr. Salman Ilahi, Department of Electrical Engineering and Engr. Irfan Ahmad, Department of Industrial Engineering, UET Peshawar, for their valuable input and suggestions throughout this work.

References

1. Sakoe, H., Chiba, S.: Dynamic programming algorithm optimization for spoken word recognition. IEEE Trans. Acoust. Speech Signal Process. **26**(1), 43–49 (1978)
2. Gagnon, L., Foucher, S., Laliberte, F., Boulianne, G.: A simplified audiovisual fusion model with application to large-vocabulary recognition of French Canadian speech. Can. J. Electr. Comput. Eng. (Spring) **33**(2), 109–119 (2008)
3. Morii, S., Niyada, K., Fujii, S., Hoshimi, M.: Large vocabulary speaker-independent Japanese speech recognition system. In: IEEE International Conference on Acoustics, Speech and Signal Processing, pp. 866–869 (1985)
4. Shimizu, T., Ashikari, Y., Sumita, E., Zhang, J.: NICT/ATR Chinese-Japanese-English speech-to-speech translation system. Tshingua Sci. Technol. **13**(4), 540–544 (2008)
5. Mao, J., Chen, Q., Gao, F., Guo, R., Lu, R.: SHTQS: a telephone-based Chinese spoken dialogue system. J. Syst. Eng. Electron. **16**(4), 881–885 (2005)
6. Khadivi, S., Ney, S.: Integration of speech recognition and machine translation in computer-assisted translation. IEEE Trans. Audio Speech Lang. Process. **16**(8), 1551–1564 (2008)
7. Ghai, W., Singh, N.: Analysis of automatic speech recognition systems for Indo-Aryan languages: Punjabi a case study. Int. J. Soft Comput. Eng. (IJSCE) **2**(1), 379–385 (2012)
8. Akram, M.U., Arif, M.: Design of an Urdu speech recognizer based upon acoustic phonetic modeling. In: 8th International Multitopic Conference, pp. 91–96 (2004)

9. Azam, S.M., Mansoor, Z.A., Mughal, M.S., Mohsin, S.: Urdu spoken digits recognition using classified MFCC and backpropgation neural network. In: Computer Graphics, Imaging and Visualization, CGIV'07, pp. 414–418 (2007)
10. Ahad, A., Fayyaz, A., Mehmood, T.: Speech recognition using multilayer perceptron. In: Proceedings of IEEE Students Conference, ISCON'02, pp. 103–109 (2002)
11. Hasnain, S.K., Awan, M.S.: Recognizing spoken Urdu numbers using fourier descriptor and neural networks with Matlab. In: Second International Conference on Electrical Engineering (ICEE 2008), pp. 1–6 (2008)
12. Ashraf, J., Iqbal, N., Khattak, N.S., Zaidi, A.M.: Speaker independent Urdu speech recognition using HMM. In: The 7th International Conference on Informatics and Systems (INFOS 2010), pp. 1–5, March (2010)
13. Rabiner, L.R.: A tutorial on hidden markov models and selected applications in speech recognition. Proc. IEEE **77**(2), 257–286 (1989)
14. Sarfraz, H., et al.: Large vocabulary continuous speech recognition for Urdu. In: 8th International Conference on Frontiers of Information Technology (FIT'10) (2010)
15. Ali, H., Ahmad, N., Yahya, K.M., Farooq, O.: A medium vocabulary Urdu isolated words balanced corpus for automatic speech recognition. In: 2012 International Conference on Electronics Computer Technology (ICECT 2012), pp. 473–476 (2012)
16. Center for Language Engineering, May 2012. http://www.cle.org.pk/
17. Molau, S., Ptiz, M., Schluter, R., Ney, H.: Computing mel-frequency cepstral coefficients on the power spectrum. In: IEEE International Conference on Acoustics, Speech, and Signal Processing (ICASSP '01), pp. 73–76 (2001)
18. Han, W., Chan, C.-F., Choy, C.-S., Pun, K.-P.: An efficient MFCC extraction method in speech recognition. In: IEEE International Symposium on Circuits and Systems (ISCAS 2006) (2006)
19. Kotnik, B., Vlaj, D., Horvat, B.: Efficient noise robust feature extraction algorithms for distributed speech recognition (DSR) systems. Int. J. Speech Technol. **6**(3), 205–219 (2003)
20. Proakis, J.G., Manolakis, D.G.: Digital Signal Processing; Principles, Algorithms & Applications, 4th edn. Pearson Education Inc., Prentice Hall (2007)
21. Ingle, V.K., Proakis, J.G.: Digital Signal Processing Using Matlab, 3rd edn. Cengage Learning, Standford (2010)
22. Salomon, D.: Data Compression: The Complete Reference, 4th edn. Springer, London (2007)
23. Balakrishnama, S., Ganapathiraju, A., Picone, J.: Linear discriminant analysis for signal processing problems. In: Proceedings of the IEEE Southeastcon, pp. 36–39 March (1999)
24. Balakrishnama, S., Ganapathiraju, A.: Linear discriminant analysis; a brief tutorial. http://www.music.mcgill.ca/~ich. Accessed March 2012

Software Based Acoustic Modem

Samreen Amir[1](✉), Bilal Saeed[1], Mansoor Uz Zafar Dawood[2],
Danish Soonka[1], and Nimrah Ahmed[1]

[1] Sir Syed University of Engineering and Technology, Karachi, Pakistan
{samreen.amir4,dssoonka,nimra.ahmed99}@gmail.com,
smartstudent_732@hotmail.com
[2] King Abdul Aziz University, Jeddah, Saudi Arabia
mzdawood@kau.edu.sa

Abstract. In this paper, an acoustic band based software modem is
designed and implemented for wireless communication between two personal computers. Its based on an investigation of the theoretical techniques required to develop a modem capable of digital data transmission
in an indoor airborne acoustic environment, and the subsequent software development. Text files are used as information to demonstrate
the operation and are being built under MATLAB code, modem uses
4-QAM modulation scheme. To realize modem in real-time, the software
is developed that converts text in to voice, which is then modulated and
transmitted over wired or wireless medium and received on the microphone of the receiver side. This received voice is then again converted to
the text and displayed on the computer screen. The design encompasses
a significant proportion of the signal synthesis and recovery process is
performed digitally in software so that the burden on analogue RF hardware is minimized.

Keywords: Underwater acoustic system · AWGN · 4QAM · Gray code ·
Match filter

1 Introduction

Now a days most of the digital communication system is hardware based, so
modeling and designing have been increased in recent days [1]. There are several
approaches that have been published to design and simulate behavioral modeling
of communication system [2].

Latest advances in compactness and circuit integration have yield smaller
processors that are capable of running acoustic modulation and demodulation
software efficiently [3]. With these speedy processors, the idea of implementing software based acoustic modem became viable. Lope has explored aerial
acoustic communications by means of software modems for in ubiquitous computing application [4].

To understand the true digital communication system a software based platform is required to show the actual working of system. This makes clear in
understanding the complete flow of the system, design of the block diagram,

© Springer International Publishing Switzerland 2014
F.K. Shaikh et al. (Eds.): IMTIC 2013, CCIS 414, pp. 35–45, 2014.
DOI: 10.1007/978-3-319-10987-9_4

software and hardware implementation and performance evaluation. This software modem is very cost effective as it do not requires any expensive hardware as Many accessible wireless audio communications System rely on specialized hardware [5] all it requires is just a built in sound cards of the computer, speakers and microphone which are commonly available. By reduction of specialized hardware for acoustic communication trim down the price of network. To be more specific this modem has many merits. As it is Cheap and easily available equipments and has only two PCs, speaker and a microphone is required with MATLAB. This software modem has a flexible system that its parameters can be change in transmitter and receiver program in run time. It will motivate the readers and allow them to make new algorithms and learn the impact of updated techniques. Different topologies have been implemented such broadcasting, multi point and point to point can be implemented. It can also be used to implement the underwater wireless modem for data as Acoustic underwater communication is an established field and there are several commercial underwater acoustic modems are available [6] or for research work [7,8]. Utility Acoustic Modem (UAM) has been developed by the researchers at the Woods Hole Oceanographic Institution which is a self contained and independent acoustic modem which is able to communicate moderately with small power utilization [9]. It uses a specialized DSP board. For environmental research applications researchers at UC, are also so developing a DSP based acoustic underwater telemetry modem [10]. Whereas both aims at making cheaper acoustic underwater communications modem even more easy to get through the progress of software acoustic modems that can function on broad hardware platforms. Acoustical communication has wide effectiveness for consumer use, device-to-device communication, since it uses the standard tools; loudspeaker and microphone [11].

For our system, the hardware used consists of a speaker with Frequency range (90 Hz–20 kHz), a microphone with Frequency range (100 Hz–16,000 Hz), and same sound cards of sigmatel STAC 975XAC97 on both laptops. Matlab functions wav-play and wavrecord respectively are used to transmit and receive. Sampling frequencies of 8000, 11025 and 22050 Hz are used (sound card standard). This modem is a 4QAM based modem. It is the combination of amplitude modulation and phase shift keying. More technically, QAM is a system of modulation in which data is transferred by modulating the amplitude of two separate carrier waves, mostly sinusoidal, which are out of phase by 90° (sine and cosine). In practical application, higher order QAM greater receiver signal levels [12], delivers more data, but with less reliably (that is, with a higher bit error rate) than the lower order QAM [13]. But different modulation schemes such as 8QAM, 16QAM, QPSK,8PSK, 16PSK can also be implemented. For synchronization we use a chirp signal which indicates the preamble and post amble of the signal.

2   System Overview

Although it is based on the software implementation, but there are some aspects of hardware that requires consideration. It includes microphone, soundcard and speaker which can be seen in system setup in Fig. 1.

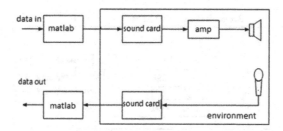

Fig. 1. The setup of software based acoustic modem

2.1 Microphone

A microphone (colloquially called a mic) is an acoustic-to-electric transducer or sensor that converts sound into an electrical signal. The sensitive transducer element of a microphone is called its element or capsule. A complete microphone also includes a housing, some means of bringing the signal from the element to other equipment, and often an electronic circuit to adapt the output of the capsule to the equipment being driven. Microphone also introduces internal noise and its precision depends up on the filters used in amplifier circuit. The specification of microphone used here is as following: Frequency range of 100 Hz–16,000 Hz and Sensitivity: -67 dB/Bar -47 dBV/Pa ± 4 dB.

2.2 Speaker

A speaker is an electro-acoustic transducer that produces sound in response to an electrical audio signal input. In our system, the quality of speakers is also a major consideration. Generally, the speakers also produce noise along with the applied signal and for accurate production of sound usually multiple speakers are used and for high sampling rates, higher output power is required. For this reason we have chosen speakers with following specification: Input sensitivity is 82 dB at 1 W, 1 m. Frequency range is 90 Hz–20 KHz, Amplifier distortion at rated power is maximum 1THD (Total Harmonic Distortion). Transducer of 2–3-inch full-range driver magnetically shielded. Maximum noise is -60 dB with no signal in and Maximum acoustic output is greater than 92 dB at 1 KHz, 1 m both speakers driven.

2.3 Sound Card

Sound card is the most important hardware consideration in our system since it requires same sound cards in both transmitter and receiver because of the difference of audio processors, A/D and D/A converters as well as the tuning frequency and frequency of oscillators, the block diagram of a sound card is shown in Fig. 2. Generally, the sound card is connected to a PC using Peripheral Component Interconnect (PCI) BUS interface, however it could also be also a Universal Serial Bus (USB).

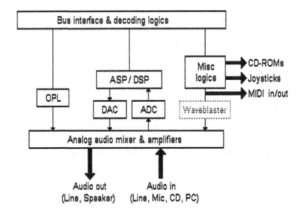

Fig. 2. Block diagram of a sound card

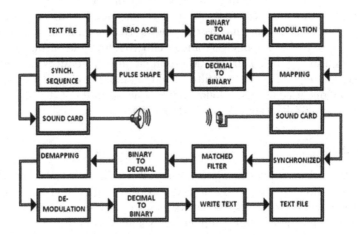

Fig. 3. Block diagram of software based acoustic modem

3   Design of the Software Based Acoustic System

The design consists of following building blocks and their functions are explained as under.

3.1   Block Diagram Representation of System

Figure 3 shows the block diagram of the system. It also helps in understanding the working of matched filter in real environment and different schemes can also be implemented.

3.2   Specification of Software Based Transmitter Design

The section below explains the working of the Modem.

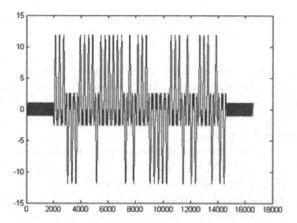

Fig. 4. Packet structure of data along pre and post-ambles

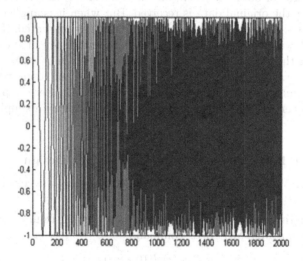

Fig. 5. Chirp sequence used for synchronization

System Parameters. The first step to begin with is to choose appropriate modulation schemes. Then the pulse shaping is done to decrease the impact of ISI. Following specifications are defined for operation as Modulation is 4QAM, Pulse shaping is Sinc pulse, sampling frequency is 8000 Hz, Bandwidth of pass band is 4000 Hz and Bit rate is maximum 100 bps.

Packet Structure Design. Packet structure design is shown in Fig. 4. The packet consists of a preamble followed by data and then a post amble signal. The preamble and post ambles are the chirp sequences shown in Fig. 5. These signals identifies the receiver the start and the stop of the data sequence. At receive these signals are correlated with a known sequence to indicate the start and the stop of the data sequence. For pulse shaping we use Sinc shape so that the issue of (ISI) could be covered.

Channel Emulation and System Performance. At the beginning, the transmitter converts the alphabets to their respective binary forms, after this gray coding and is performed. Then 4QAM modulation is performed. The modulated symbols were converted to real symbols and converted to bits again on which pulse shaping is performed.

To fully test the modem we emulate the channel with AWGN effects. Additive white Gaussian noise (AWGN) is a channel model in which the only impairment to communication is a linear addition of wideband or white noise with a constant spectral density and a Gaussian distribution of amplitude. The modem was first test over the wired channel with on ordinary auxiliary cable used for stereo systems. The result was satisfactory but at first time the receiver receives the complement value of data. At reception the receiver has to retransmit the data to itself so that the original data is received. But when it is applied on wireless system (with speaker and microphone) the data was corrupted. To cater this issue the SNR was increased. This increased the efficiency of the system. On wired network the system was tested at 10 dB SNR. On wireless channel the signal strength was increased. The noise variance of silent room was calculated up to 0.08 and measured through MATLAB it was 0.04. After the pulse shaping the data is converted in to sound and played by speaker by a simple MATLAB command.

3.3   Software Based Acoustic Modem Receiver Design

Following description shall provide better understanding of receiver operation.

Signal Recording. At reception first the data coming from outside world is recorded using a simple MATLAB command

$$rxcv = wavrecord(10 * 8000, 8000);$$

Here we have a limitation that the recorded length should be greater than the length of signal because the synchronization preamble and post amble should be recorded as they indicate the start and stop of the data signal.

Synchronization and Data Extraction. Since the so there is no clue about the start and end of the actual data. Synchronization is achieved through the correlation between two sequences in which one is known and another is unknown. The issue of latency is also covered with the same synchronization sequence as if the delay is present between transmitter and receiver, the synchronization takes only that part if data which is useful to receiver. Since both the signals are identical so the operator used is auto correlation in Eq. 1.

$$Rxx = \int \int_{-\infty}^{\infty} x_1 x_2 f(x_1) f(x_2)(x_1, x_2) dx_1 dx_2 \qquad (1)$$

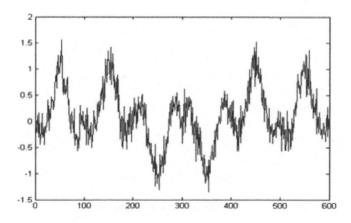

Fig. 6. Received waveform

Once the data is recorded, it is correlated with the known synchronization sequence using the following set of instructions.

$$data\_seq\_start = conv(rxcv, flipud(chirp));$$
$$[vals, pos\_start] = max(abs(data\_seq\_start));$$
$$data\_seq\_end = conv(rxcv, flipud(chirp\_rev));$$
$$[vale, pos\_end] = max(abs(data\_seq\_end));$$
$$data = [rxcv(pos\_start : (pos\_end - 2000))]$$

After the synchronization is performed the data signal is extracted.

Reconstruction of Signal and Evaluation of Binary Data. The basic problem that often arises in the study of communication systems is to detect the pulse transmitted over a channel as it gets corrupted by channels noise and external interferences which can be seen in Fig. 6. After the data signal is extracted this data is passed through the matched filter and reconstructs the data sequence using pulse shaping as seen in Fig. 7. If the x(t) is the received signal then Eq. 2 explains it as;

$$x(t) = g(t) + w(t) \tag{2}$$

where g(t) is the actual transmitted data symbol and w(t) is the noise of the channel.

The impulse response of the matched filter is then shown in Eq. 3.

$$H_opt(t) = kg(T - t) \tag{3}$$

where, k is a scaling factor and $g(T - t)$ is flipped and time delayed version of input sequence.

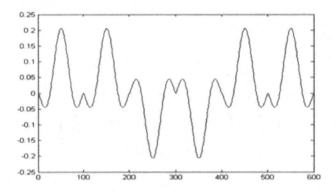

Fig. 7. Match filters matched output waveform

After the sequence is passed through the matched filter its form is reconstructed. Now this data signal is passed through the threshold detector which converts that data signal in to binary sequence. In threshold detector it simply convolutes the input sequence with a known sequence and map zero or one at their respective positions.

Reconstruction of Text. As binary sequences are obtained these binary digits are then converted in to decimal (example. 0, 1, 2, 3). These decimal numbers are then mapped to respective complex symbols so that 4QAM demodulation is performed. The demodulated output is passed through gray decoder to decode there values for error reduction. After decoding these decimal symbols are converted back into binary digits. And these digits are converted into the ASCII characters and written in a text file.

4   Results and Discussion

In our model, we have characterized the acoustic channel in three ways in order to get a better understanding of what happens to the transmitted signal as it passes through the channel, and is recorded by the receiver.

We analyzed background noise levels with respect to power over frequency and explored that background noise was corrupting our received signal. Along this we analyzed that our system is also hurt by Inter symbol interference. Although we use Sinc wave pulse shaping but still it did not eliminate ISI completely. Increasing sample per symbol of Sinc wave increases the efficiency but it decreases the data rate. To limit the outside noise we used a band pass filter with respect to AM and FM modulation we used butter worth filter with order between 2 to 4. By comparing the efficiency of the modem by using two analog modulation schemes AM Vs FM. We observed that up to 4–5 ft, we achieved 80 %–90 % efficiency but using FM gives better results. For synchronization, our system gives satisfactory result and gives 100 % synchronization of the receiver with transmitter. We used Chirp Sequences to synchronize the receiver with the data of the transmitter. The team used time domain synchronization for the data. Our designed modem is simplex but by using microphones and speakers at both computers, it can be used as a half-duplex system.

We try our modem first on simulation basis, the simulation results were 100 % but as we move on to wired channel we realized that soundcards behavior have disturbed our signal. The trouble shooting of second scenario; wired channel took time but it was covered, the issues of timing recovery and synchronization took time to get right, but the major problems turned out to be with how the transmitted signal is changed by the acoustic channel. We used butter worth band pass filter to cancel the noise of the channel and test several time to observed the best frequency response of the system. Before applying, any analog modulation scheme team analyzed that low frequencies are absorbed in the channel so the max range observed was 1 foot but after applying analog modulation the range of the system increases up 4 to 6 ft. We also analyzed that the distortion in the receiver was due to ISI of the received sequences and noticed that for correct reception sound cards at both end must be identical so that the sampling frequencies of both sound cards could be matched and proper reception could be achieved. The data rate of this modem is very low (up to 73 bps), but by using some good data compression techniques its data rate can be increased. On third scenario, we use speaker and microphones to transmit and received respectively. In wireless channel at first, the data received was totally corrupted but at increasing the signal strength its efficiency increased. Not all the alphabets were perfectly received but almost 70 % of them were received correctly.

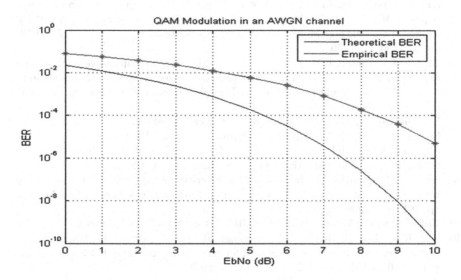

Fig. 8. QAM modulation SNR vs BER curve with AWGN channel

The Fig. 8 shows the BER of the implemented model versus the ideal. Our observations also showed that under noise free conditions reliable communication is achieved at the distance of approximately 6 ft. We also observed that high sampling frequency gave a higher data rate. The frequency spectrum showed that our output bandwidth is 4 KHz.

5   Conclusion

In this paper, we have proposed software based acoustic modem, which is very cost effective. The development of communication systems could be shifted away from traditional analog hardware designs towards systems implemented in software and reconfigurable digital hardware. The implementation is easy as well as easy to troubleshoot. Low cost of hardware allows easy research and development opportunities. It may be very useful for the development of the marine text messaging service with appropriate changes in the proposed scheme.

References

1. Aref, I., Algaid, K.: System level modeling of a digital communication channel based on systemC. Int. J. Future Comput. Commun. **2**, 210–214 (2013)
2. Bjornsen, J., Ytterdal, T.: Behavioral modeling and simulation of high-speed analog to digital converters using systemC. In: IEEE International Symposium on Circuits and Systems, pp. 906–909. IEEE press, Thailand (2003)
3. Jurdak, R., Aguiar, P.M.Q., Baldi, P., Lopes, C.V.: Software modems for underwater sensor networks. In: IEEE EurOCEAN, pp. 1–7. IEEE press, Scotland (2007)
4. Lopes, C.V., Aguiar, P.: Acoustic modems for ubiquitous computing. In: IEEE Pervasive Computing, Mobile and Ubiquitous Systems, vol. 2, pp. 62–71. IEEE press, Edinbugh (2003)
5. Jurdak, R., Aguiar, P.M.Q., Lopes, C.V., Baldi, P.: A comparative analysis and experimental study on wireless aerial and underwater acoustic communications. In: IEEE International Conference on Digital Telecommunications, pp. 397–420. IEEE press, France (2006)
6. Linkquest Inc., November 2013. http://www.link-quest.com
7. Freitag, L., Grund, M., Singh, S., Partan, J., Koski, P., Ball, K.: An acoustic communications and navigation system for multiple platforms. In: IEEE/MTS OCEANS, pp. 1086–1092. IEEE press, Washington, DC (2005)
8. Szer, E., Stojanovic, M.: Reconfigurable acoustic modem for underwater sensor networks. In: 1st International Workshop on Underwater Networks, Los Angeles, pp. 101–104 (2006)
9. Utility Acoustic Modem, November 2013. http://www.auvlab.mit.edu/
10. Iltis, R.A., Lee, H., Kastner, R., Doonan, D., Fu, T., Moore, R., Chin, M.: An underwater acoustic telemetry modem for eco-sensing. In: MTS/IEEE Oceans, pp. 1844–1850. IEEE press, Washington, DC (2005)
11. Shinmen, N., Ebihara, T., Mizutani, K.: Software-based modem for near field acoustic communication. In: 1st IEEE Global Conference on Consumer Electronics, pp. 152–155. IEEE press, Japan (2012)

12. Durso, C.M., McCulley, E.: The evolution of wireless video transmission technology for surveillance missions. In: SPIE, Tactical and Wireless Dissemination, Bellingham, vol. 8386 (2012)
13. Bhaumik, S., Chandrabose, S.P., Jataprolu, M.K., Kaumar, G., Muralidhar, A., Polakos, P., Srinivasan, V., Woo, T.: A framework for processing base stations in a data center. In: 18th International Conference on Mobile Computing and Networking, Turkey, pp. 125–136 (2012)

Design and Implementation of a Pressure Sensor on Proteus

Samreen Amir[1](✉), Ali Akbar Siddiqui[1], Nimrah Ahmed[1],
Bhawani Shankar Chowdhry[2], and Ian Grout[3]

[1] Sir Syed University of Engineering and Technology, Karachi, Pakistan
{samreen.amir4,nimra.ahmed99}@gmail.com, ali124k@hotmail.com
[2] Mehran University of Engineering and Technology, Jamshoro, Pakistan
c.bhawani@ieee.org
[3] University of Limerick, Limerick, Ireland
Ian.Grout@ul.ie

Abstract. This paper provides an overview of designing a Pressure sensor with its implementation on Proteus. We have worked on the concept of Autonomous Nodes with Control Unit (CU) and Master Unit (MU). When the pressure of gas increases in the pipe, the sensor senses it and the control unit will receive transmission from the active node, either to open or close the valve and actively communicates the result to master unit, whenever the status of signal changes. All the autonomous nodes are connected to MU. This system is designed to cope up with the excessive pressure of gas as to reduce the risk of accident.

Keywords: PIC16F627A · Spring based inductive pressure sensor · Multisim · Proteus

1 Introduction

Pressure sensor is the devices that measures pressure, usually of liquid or gas and is stated as force per unit area. It can be absolute, vacuum pressure static, gage, and dynamic pressure. Pressure can be measured by several derived methods like, hydrostatic pressure, elastic deformation, behavior of gases, dynamic pressure. Pressure compresses with increase in external pressure and expands as the pressure drops. It can be categorized in terms of their pressure range, design, cost, performance, operative temperature range and the kind of pressure they determine.

Piezoelectric sensors cannot sense static pressure and are used to measure fast varying pressure resulting from explosions, blasts or other cause of vibration, and are sensitive to temperature change. It can be used from about 3 psi to about 14,000 pounds per square inch (psi). Absolute pressure sensor measures the pressure relative to perfect vacuum and can achieve accuracy at high temperatures. Differential pressure sensor measures the difference between two pressures, and measures flow rate or fluid levels. The potentiometric pressure

© Springer International Publishing Switzerland 2014
F.K. Shaikh et al. (Eds.): IMTIC 2013, CCIS 414, pp. 46–55, 2014.
DOI: 10.1007/978-3-319-10987-9_5

sensor offers a method for obtaining an electronic output from a mechanical pressure gauge. Its pressure range is 5 and 10,000 psi.

They are used in many different applications like monitoring, calibration, Level and depth sensing, weather instrumentation, aircraft, industrial process control, etc. Sensor features depends on the construction, material and dimension of structure [1]. There are several pressure sensors, their selection can be made according to our demand, but few factors should be kept in mind such as indoor and outdoor usage, vibration, electrical and mechanical interference, shock, toughness, power consumption, accuracy, safety, temperature range, and hazardous areas like gas and oil applications. Electrical interface allows the user to attach the output of sensor to the system by means of cables or connectors. It can be chosen upon the environmental situation depending on the output signal. Mechanical interface describe the process link [2].

In this paper we have designed a sensor on Proteus which was founded in 1988. It enables our pressure sensor to tackle the pressure of gas pipeline. Gas is transported by means of gas pipelines in a compressed state; therefore in the incident of gas leakage this can be hazardous as there is stored energy [3]. The purpose of the gas pipeline application is to check critical notification about the gas and are not only limited to transmission, gathering and distribution systems. Gas can be stored for the time being in the pipeline, through line packing which can provide gas at the time of requirement. Under some situation when the pressure and temperature increases to some extent it is possible to cause spur-of-the-moment combustion of flammable gas [4]. Monitoring gas pipelines is a significant job for safety and economical operation, loss avoidance and environmental safeguard [5].

Whenever pressure of gas increases in our pipeline, expands and contracts with the decrease of the pressure this expansion and contraction is monitored and controlled by our proposed system. Sensor node gathers information and can also communicate with each other if necessary. RF (Radio Frequency) communication is used for transmission and reception of information between sensor nodes and main CPU. In most wireless systems, a designer has two limitations: it must function over a definite distance and within a time frame transfers some amount of information. Two parameters must be considered when determining range i.e. transmitting power and receiver sensitivity. Receiver sensitivity refers to the minimum level signal the radio can demodulate. For better receiver sensitivity; lower data rates are required so it will give more range. Thus 19200 baud module has less sensitivity than 9600 baud rate and the data transferred will miss out some of the data [6]. Higher data rates require more transmission power in minimum time. Here we are working with 9600 baud rate.

In our proposed system we have designed a spring based inductive pressure sensor. This sensor will be placed inside the pipeline for measuring the pressure, when the force is applied on the spring, it contracts and it changes its area, which causes its Induction to change as well.

2   Related Work

For designing Pressure sensor tools are rare, some companies are trying to develop Computer Aided Design tools for MEMS (Micro Electro Mechanical System), still they are not meeting their goal [7]. Some has designed sensor to monitor oil pressure in particular range of temperature by using FEA (Finite Element analysis) software ANSYS (Analysis System) tool [8]. The other paper focuses on the design and simulation of micro fluid sensor which can be attached to any pipe and they have been designed and simulated on MEMS tool Comsol multi physics [9]. Micro pressure sensors are used to monitor and measure pressure in various environments by using data mining software tool machine language- WEKA (Waikato Environment for Knowledge Analysis) [10]. In our proposed system we have designed a spring based inductive pressure sensor on Proteus.

3   System Description

In our proposed system, we have introduced PIC16F627A for operating the relays connected to valve as well as to transmit the condition of the valve that either they are ON or OFF. PIC16F627A is a flash based 8-bit microcontroller capable of executing a single instruction in approximately 200 ns. It features an internal 4 MHz oscillator, and 128 bytes of EEPROM data memory, it also has a USART (Universal Synchronous Asynchronous Receive Transmitter) that is used to communicate with other devices serially either by wired or wireless communication [11]. The purpose of PIC16F627A microcontroller is to monitor the pressure in the Gas line and adjust the valve according to the condition required, the calibration is done in accordance that if the pressure in the line rises up to 20 psi (Pounds per square inch) our PIC16F627A microcontroller will turn OFF the valve and then update this knowledge to the main CPU.

This main CPU will display the status of the values, which are wirelessly interfaced with the nodes via RF Transceivers. In our proposed system we have designed four identical nodes, and each node is wirelessly apart from each other are interfaced with the main CPU. We have designed a spring based inductive intelligent pressure sensor capable of measuring the pressure in psi; Eq. 1 demonstrates the formula for the conversion in psi.

$$P(psi) = (1.45 * 10^{-4}) * \frac{F}{A} \tag{1}$$

When force is applied on the pressure sensor it contracts. When this contraction occurs, the area of that spring changes, and will affect the inductance of the inductor. When a force in applied on the spring the area of that spring will change accordingly, this can be seen in Eq. 2.

$$L = \frac{\mu A N^{-4}}{\rho} \tag{2}$$

where, L is Inductance, N is the number of turn of winding, is the relative permittivity, A is the Area, ρ is the length.

$$Z_L = R + \jmath X_L \tag{3}$$

In Eq. 3, Z_L is the impedance, X_L is the reactance. Often it is required to measure the pressure in unsteady environmental conditions, the measurement of the time varying pressure sensor it of utmost important. Mathematical model of the Inductive sensor resembles to that of a simple RL circuit, with the Inductive change that occurs when the area contracts,

$$\frac{d}{dt}i(t) = -\frac{R}{\Delta L}i(t) + \frac{1}{\Delta L}V(t) \tag{4}$$

Equation 4 is the first order Time Domain representation, and by applying Laplace Transform we can convert it into frequency domain which is represented by Eq. 5.

$$G(s) = \frac{L(s)}{L(s) + R} \tag{5}$$

In our system area and length are the two factors affecting our Inductive Transducer. Figure 1 shows the step response of an uncompensated result of the inductive sensors transfer function. Due to this change in the induction there will be a certain change in the Inductor Voltage (VL); this is basically the Voltage that has to be fed to the PIC16F627A microcontroller for the purpose of controlling the valve, and to update the status of the value to the main CPU via RF Transceiver. Table 1 shows the changes occurs due to the certain change in inductance (L) when affected by the force. Table 1 represents the changes occurring till the value where it will turn off. It also shows the approximate change

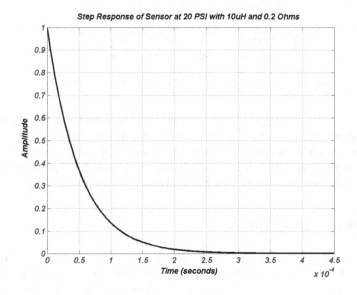

Fig. 1. Step response of uncompensated sensor at 20 psi

Table 1. The changes occurring in different parameters

Area (mm^2)	Change in inductance (uH)	VL (mV)	Pressure (psi)
2	10	3.77	20
4	9	3.39	19
6	8	3.02	18
8	7	2.64	17
10	6	2.26	16
12	5	1.88	15
14	4	1.51	14
16	3	1.13	13
18	2	0.753	12
20	1	0.337	11

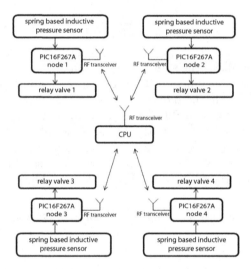

Fig. 2. Step response of uncompensated sensor at 20 psi

in the value of VL. This means the change in 1 uH inductance will change the VL by 0.38 mV approximately. Figure 2 demonstrates a complete block diagram of our proposed system, which shows four nodes with transceivers, interfaced wirelessly with main CPU. Each valve is also interfaced with our PIC16F627A microcontroller which is controlled by the relay separately.

4   Software Description

In our proposed system, we have used Micro C pro for programming or PIC16F6-27A. Micro C pro consists of all the libraries and tools to design our desired software. The simulated design of hardware is built on Proteus. The ISIS Schematic Capture of Proteus is used for the designing purpose. Multisim is used to design

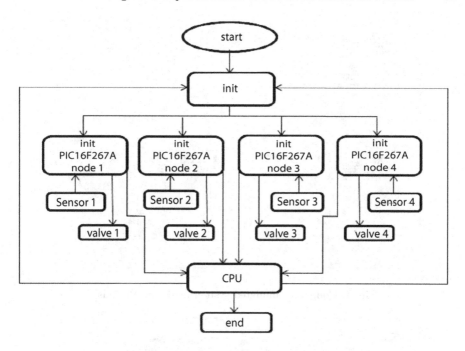

Fig. 3. Block diagram of the software system

an inductive Transducer. Mat lab is also used to simulate the result of the designed sensor to observe the parameters more closely. The flow chart of complete software Model is depicted in Fig. 3. After system initialization PIC16F627A microcontroller of every node continuously monitors the sensor interfaced to each of them, and turns the value OFF only if the Pressure reaches to 20 psi, and simultaneously also updates the main CPU via RF Transceiver about the status of the Valve that either it is in ON condition or OFF.

5   Results

The simulated system model on Proteus environment is shown in Fig. 4 and outcomes of our system are tested on it.

The status of the valves that were updated by the PIC16F627A microcontroller wirelessly, whether the valves are in ON or OFF condition is shown in Fig. 5.

Figure 6 represents an individual node with serial communication, which is used to interface the RF transceiver that communicates the main CPU and each node. The Inductive Transducer is tested using variable Inductor, and implemented on Multisim environment, thus the following results are obtained.

Figure 7 result demonstrates an output at 10 uH, at this point the Area of the spring is of 2 mm². This means that the spring is contract at the point representing the reading has reached to its maximum value that is 20 psi; we can clearly see the voltage output is 3.77 mV as shown in Table 1. This is the voltage

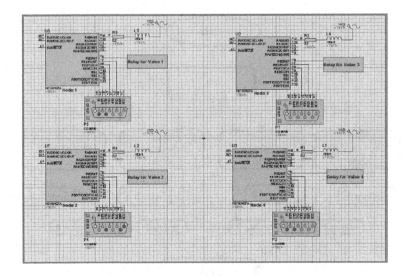

Fig. 4. Complete simulated system model on Proteus

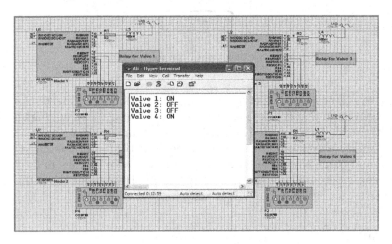

Fig. 5. Complete system with valve status

that is fed to our PIC16F627A microcontroller for processing after converting it in Digital format using ADC.

Figure 8 result demonstrates an output at 9 uH, at this point the area of the spring is of 4 mm^2. This represents that the spring has contracted and the pressure has reached to 18 psi, which represents the voltage output is 3.39 mV as demonstrated in the Table 1.

Figure 9 demonstrates an output at 1 uH, at this point the area of spring is 20 mm^2. This represents that the spring has not contracted enough and the pressure is at low level, that is 11 psi, and there is no danger to a gas line which

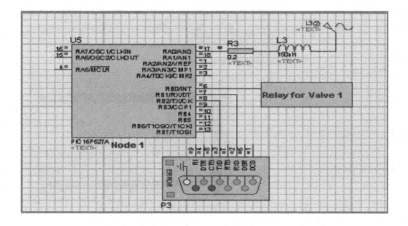

Fig. 6. Single node of a complete system

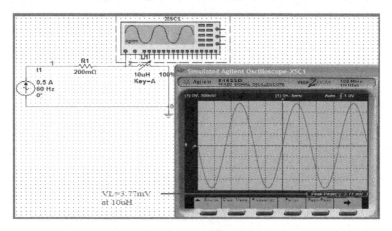

Fig. 7. The output at 10 uH

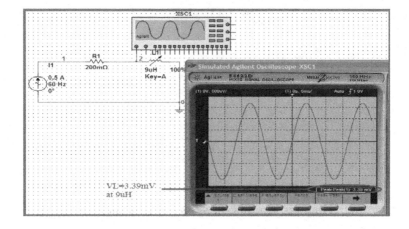

Fig. 8. The output at 9 uH

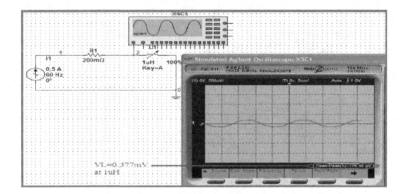

Fig. 9. The output at 1 uH

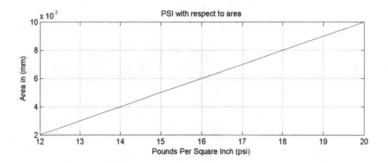

Fig. 10. Pressure with respect to area

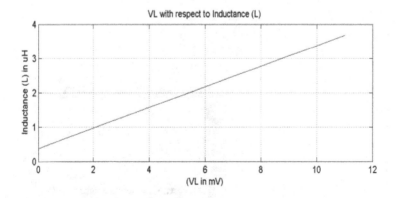

Fig. 11. Voltage with respect to inductance

represents the voltage output is 0.377 mV as shown in Table 1. These results are taken in accordance to the system operation.

Figures 10 and 11 represents the graphical output of parameters such as psi with respect to area, and voltage with respect to inductance.

6   Conclusion

In our proposed system, we have introduced an idea of cheaper way to measure pressure in environment such as pipelines. The entire system is simulated, and compiled in Proteus environment. The design of the pressure sensor using variable inductor is implemented in Multisim environment. Apart from our work, many different software tools are used to construct these sensors, which are either costly or unavailable for the commercially or for a small industry. Our proposed system performed according to our desired parameter, and can easily be implemented in industry for the monitoring purpose of gas, fluids etc.

References

1. Ionescu, C., Svasta, P., Marghescu, C., Zarnik, M.S., Belavi, D.: Study on optimization of capacitive pressure sensor using coupled mechanical-electric analysis. In: 32nd International Spring Seminar on Electronics Technology, Cehia, pp. 13–17 (2009)
2. Design essentials: how to select a pressure sensor for a specific application. Business Development American Sensor Technology. http://www.astsensors.com. Accessed Nov 2013
3. Rao, Y.C., Rani, S., Lavanya, P.: Monitoring and protection of oil and gas condition in industrial using wireless sensor networks. Int. J. Electron. Commun. Comput. Technol. **2**(5), 213–218 (2012)
4. Yong, W., Jiang, M., Tang, Y.: Study on liquid pipeline water hammer and protective device with gas concentration. In: Advanced Materials Research, pp. 616–618 (2012)
5. Fukushima, K., Maeshima, R., Kinoshita, A., Shiraishi, H., Koshijima, I.: Gas pipeline leak detection system using the online simulation method. Comput. Chem. Eng. **24**, 453–456 (2000)
6. Alam, S.S.: Electronics assembly and printed circuit board layout. Doctoral dissertation, California State University (2013)
7. Shing, T.K.: Robust design of silicon piezoresistive pressure sensor. In: International Conference on Modeling and Simulation of Microsystems, pp. 597–601 (1998)
8. Ye, F., Wang, Z.M.: Design of pressure sensor in common rail system by ANSYS tool. In: Computer-Aided Design, Manufacturing, Modelling and Simulation, Applied Mechanics and Materials, pp. 545–548 (2011)
9. Acharaya, P.N., Naduvinamsan, S.: Design and simulation of MEMS based micro pressure sensor. In: COMSOL Conference, Bangalore (2012)
10. Madhavi, K.Y., Sumithradevi, K.A., Krishna, M., Dharani, A.: Diaphragm design for MEMS pressure sensor using a data mining tool. In: World Congress on Engineering, London, pp. 1353–1356 (2011)
11. Electrosome. http://www.electrosome.com/category/tutorials/pic-microcontroller/mikroc/. Accessed Nov 2013

Filtration of Airwave in Seabed Logging Using Principal Component Analysis

Adeel Ansari[1](✉), Afza Bt Shafie[2], Seema Ansari[3],
Abas B. Md Said[1], and Elisha Tadiwa Nyamasvisva[1]

[1] Department of Computer Information Science, Universiti Teknologi Petronas,
Bandar Seri Iskandar, 31750 Tronoh, Perak, Malaysia
adeel.ansari@hotmail.com, abass@petronas.com.my,
tadiwa_g02172@utp.edu.my
[2] Department of Fundamental and Applied Science,
Universiti Teknologi Petronas, Bandar Seri Iskandar,
31750 Tronoh, Perak, Malaysia
afza@petronas.com.my
[3] Department of Electrical Engineering, Institute of Business Management,
Korangi Campus, Karachi, Pakistan
seema.ansari@iobm.edu.pk

Abstract. In this research, Independent component analysis using Principal Component Analysis (ICA-PCA) technique has been applied in the field of seabed logging application for the filtration of airwaves. Independent component analysis (ICA) is a statistical approach for transforming data of multivariate nature into its constituent components (sources) which are considered to be statistically independent of each other. ICA-PCA is applied in the domain of marine controlled source electromagnetic (CSEM), called seabed logging (SBL) sensing method used for the detection of hydrocarbons based reservoirs in SBL application. ICA-PCA has not been applied before in SBL application, and therefore may reduce exploration costs in deep sea areas. The task is to identify the air waves and to filter them out, hence, the ICA-PCA algorithm is carried out for airwave filtration, at varying seawater depth from 100 m to 3000 m. It is observed that the results are favorable upto 2500 m depth. Upon increasing seawater depth, the component representing the presence of hydrocarbon becomes more dispersed, vague and indistinguishable.

Keywords: Principal Component Analysis · Seabed logging · Independent component analysis · ICA · PCA · Data mining

1 Introduction

Independent component analysis (ICA) is method that is commonly applied into the blind source separation (BSS) problem. In BSS, no prior information is present to ascertain the constituent components within the mixed data set (useful information with noise). By blind we mean to say, we have no information about the sources of the signals. ICA implies a linear coordinate system (the unmixing system) such that the resulting signals are as statistically independent from each other as possible.

© Springer International Publishing Switzerland 2014
F.K. Shaikh et al. (Eds.): IMTIC 2013, CCIS 414, pp. 56–64, 2014.
DOI: 10.1007/978-3-319-10987-9_6

By independence, we mean that the resultant constituent signals have no correlation with each other.

A popular approach to statistical independence technique is the Principal Component Analysis (PCA) which has been applied and considered very useful in fields such as signal processing, image processing, and is a common technique for finding patterns in data of high dimension, data mining and data retrievals [14].

In this research the PCA algorithm is applied in the field of seabed logging. The dataset will be the resultant mixed response of electromagnetic (EM) waves at the receiver-end, in the form of electric field strength in Volts per meter unit. In seabed logging (SBL), hydrocarbon layers are detected by exploiting the highly resistivity contrast property of the hydrocarbon layers, that tends to reflect and/or refract the EM signals upwards (see Fig. 1).

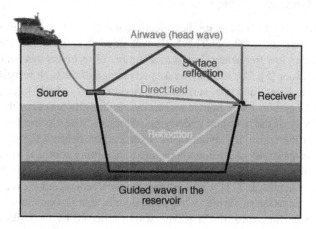

Fig. 1. The signal components dominating the signal response in seabed logging application.

In SBL, a horizontal electric dipole (HED) antenna is used that transmit low frequency EM signals in an omni-directional manner in seawater. The antenna is towed over an array of receivers that measure the electric and magnetic responses.

The signal response comprises of the direct wave, airwave, guided and reflected waves. The waves which are considered useful and that gives information about the hydrocarbon presence is the guided and the reflected wave, whilst the rest are considered as noise. The direct wave can be avoided by considering offsets greater than 15 km or more. In shallow water, the airwave dominates the signal response due to many reflections. The airwave transmits from the source vertically upwards towards the seasurface, due to total internal reflection the signals travel along the seasurface and later reflect downwards towards the receivers. In deepwater settings, the signals travelling downward are highly attenuated and become negligible towards the receiver end. These airwave interferes with the signal that comes from sub-surface and due to this, its considered as an unwanted signal.

The airwaves dominate the receiver response collected by the receivers in seabed logging, which hinders the interpretation of the measured data that enables us to determine the presence of Hydrocarbon.

The aim of this research is to filter out these unwanted signals using PCA for varying seawater depths. The tool used to perform the simulation modeling is Computer Simulation Tech (CST) and Matlab for result computations.

The rest of the paper is organized as follows. Section 2 provides illustration of the simulation models used and the detailed description of the proposed algorithm. Section 3 describes the obtained results followed by the conclusion in Sect. 4.

2 Proposed Approach

2.1 Seabed Logging Technique

The Seabed Logging technique implies electromagnetic waves for the detection of hydrocarbon under the seafloor. The SBL technique uses a source electric diploe antenna to transmit low frequency signals to a number of receivers that evaluate the EM waves at the seafloor [5]. The technique takes advantage of the high resistivity value of the hydrocarbon layer, and the surrounding sedimentary which have a very low resistivity. Hydrocarbon has a higher resistivity, around 30–500 Ωm, than compared with the resistivity of the over and underlying sediments. The electric field intensity is dependent upon the resistivity layout of the hydrocarbon beneath the seabed [3].

Due to large resistivity of hydrocarbons, the transmitting source is towed above the receiver array, the effects of the Electric field at different offsets can be determined at varying seawater depths. In [11], Fig. 1, shows the receivers record the received signals which is a amalgamation of various wave components, that is, one transmitted directly within the seawater interface (direct wave), waves reflected by the hydrocarbon layer (reflected wave), waves guided by the hydrocarbon layer (guided wave) and lastly, waves reflected by the seawater surface and back to the receiver (airwave). The frequency taken is 0.125 Hz with current at 1250 A from the source.

2.2 Simulation Model 1

The simulation model as shown in Fig. 2 contains no presence of Hydrocarbon. The E-field containing no Hydrocarbon is determined here. The results are compared with simulation model 2 which has hydrocarbon present in it.

2.3 Simulation Model 2

Model 2 has a layer of Hydrocarbon of about 100 m thick and 100 Ωm resistivity contrast.

The size of the data set is based over an offset of 50 km by 50 km, of the mixed signal response from the receiver. The dataset comprises of the e-field strength in Volts/metres for offset till 50 km.

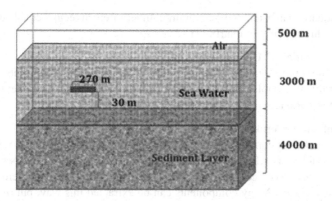

Fig. 2. Simulation Model 1 showing no presence of hydrocarbon reservoir.

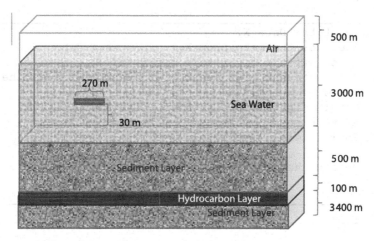

Fig. 3. Simulation Model 2 showing presence of hydrocarbon reservoir of 100 m thickness, at target depth of 1000 m.

2.4   ICA-PCA Algorithm

ICA is a method for seeking patterns within large data sets and transforming the data into knowledgeable information to highlight the similarities and dissimilarities. Since it is an application to Blind Source Separation (BSS), prior knowledge about the data is difficult to assess. Therefore, PCA is a powerful tool for solving this BSS problem. Another advantage PCA has is that data dimensionality reduction or compress can be performed without significant loss of information [14].

The mathematical approach in PCA is the Eigen analysis. We solve for Eigen values and Eigen vectors of a square symmetric matrix with sums of squares and cross products. The Eigen vector with the largest Eigenvalue is considered as the first principal component. The eigenvector associated with the second largest Eigenvalue determines the second principal component. The sum of the Eigenvalues equals the trace of the square matrix and the maximum number of eigenvectors equals the number of rows (or columns) of this matrix [1].

The Basics of Principal Component Analysis

PCA obtains measures for a number of observed variables and determines a reduced number of artificial variables called principal components. These components accounts for most of the variance in the observed variables [2].

Extraction of the Components

In PCA, the number of components to be extracted is usually equivalent to the number of column variables. The first component comprises of majority of the portion of the variance. The successive components after the first, comprise of a mere fractional portion of the variance. Many components can be extracted this way, but only the first few important ones are considered as they comprise most of the variance [14].

An Eigenvalue represents the amount of variance that is accounted for by a given component.

```
1. Input the Data X.
2. Subtract the mean from X.
3. Calculate the covariance matrix of X.
4. Calculate the eigenvectors and Eigenvalues of the
   covariance matrix.
5. Obtain eigenvectors from the covariance matrix,
6. Arrange the Eigenvalue from highest to lowest.
7. Formulate a feature vector
```
$$FeatureVector=(eig_1, eig_2, eig_3,...,eig_n)$$
```
8. Obtain the final data
```
$$FinalData=FeatureVector^T \times MeanData^T$$

Alg.1. Pseudo-code of proposed algorithm

Steps in ICA-PCA

The pseudo code for the algorithm is depicted in Alg. 1 and the illustration of each steps are depicted in Fig. 4.

3 Results and Discussion

In this research, a detailed study and result evaluation has been done over the ICA using PCA algorithm for varying seawater depth from 100 m till 3000 m. Simulation models considered are with and without the hydrocarbon (see Figs. 2 and 3). The ICA-PCA algorithm takes the covariance of the column matrix of the receiver response. The data samples considered are from varying seawater depth, comprising of 100 m, 1000 m, 2000 m and 3000 m. After the covariance matrix is taken, the eigen components are taken and dimensionality reduction is performed based on the eigen value analysis and selection.

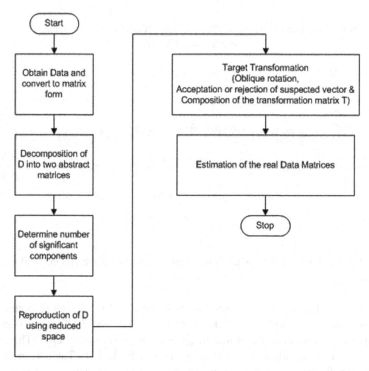

Fig. 4. Flowchart of ICA-PCA algorithm

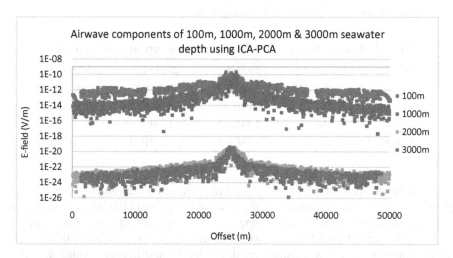

Fig. 5. ICA-PCA results for airwaves of seawater depth 100 m, 1000 m, 2000 m and 3000 m.

Two components are extracted, i.e., representation of the airwave and the presence of hydrocarbon under the seabed floor. These two components are extracted from the algorithm and the results are shown from Figs. 5 and 6.

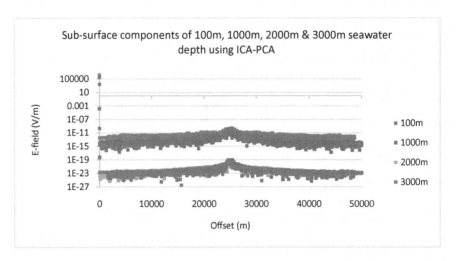

Fig. 6. ICA-PCA results for sub-surface components of seawater depth 100 m, 1000 m, 2000 m and 3000 m.

From Fig. 5, the airwave components are compared for varying seawater depth, from the results. Component of 100 m, 1000 m, 2000 m and 3000 m are decreasing with an indirect relationship according to the increasing seawater depth. The airwave component intensity at different offsets are shown in Table 1. In Table 1, the airwave component for different seawater depths at varying offsets are shown, from zero offset, the airwave shows a very high peak value, however, as we increase the offset, the intensity of the airwave component is decreasing.

Table 1. E-field intensity of airwave component at varying seawater depth.

Offset	100 m	1000 m	2000 m	3000 m
0	0.003126	0.001263	0.000811	0.001005
10 km	2.14E-22	3.01E-23	1.06E-24	6.57E-22
20 km	−1.55E-20	2.73E-22	−1.38E-21	7.84E-21
25 km	−4.10E-19	1.56E-21	8.25E-20	7.01E-19

From Table 2 percentage difference has been obtained for the airwave components, by comparing the e-field intensity of the airwave component (100 m seawater depth) with other airwave components of varying seawater depth (till 3000 m seawater depth).

From the percentage differences, which are mostly positive, indicates that the airwave component of 100 m seawater depth has the highest intensity whilst the other components are gradually decreasing at increasing offset.

$$\alpha \frac{1}{h}$$

Table 2. Percent difference of 100 m airwave component with other components of varying seawater depth

Offset	100–500	100–1000	100–2000	100–3000
0 km	47 %	60 %	74 %	68 %
10 km	64 %	86 %	100 %	–207 %
20 km	106 %	102 %	91 %	151 %
25 km	31 %	100 %	120 %	271 %

So far, from the graphs and tables, the airwave components, obtained from the ICA using PCA algorithm, are obeying the inverse relationship of decreasing intensity of e-field upon increasing seawater depth. However, the only drawback observed so far is that, on increasing seawater depth, the component representing the presence of hydrocarbon is becoming more dispersed and vague and unclear. Therefore the quality of the component showing the presence of the Hydrocarbon is decreasing.

From conclusion, it is evident that the results from the algorithm seems reasonable to a certain extent but the results at greater seawater depth (2500 m and above) are losing its precision, with respect to the component representing the presence of hydrocarbon, which is also significant. Hence this algorithm can offer good results but only at shallow water environments, than compared with deepwater settings. For future work, this algorithm will be considered for pre-processing results for Infomax [6] and Fastica [2] algorithm.

4 Conclusion

In this paper, we have illustrated in detail the ICA using PCA algorithm and it is evident that the results from the algorithm are favorable to a certain extent but the results at greater seawater depth (2500 m and above) are losing its precision and quality, with respect to the component representing the presence of hydrocarbon, which is also significant. Hence this algorithm can offer good results but only at shallow water environments, than compared with deepwater settings.

References

1. Lee, T.: Independent Component Analysis – Theory and Applications. Kluwer Academic Publishers, Hingham (2001). ISBN 0-7923-8261-7
2. Hyvarinen, A., Oja, E.: Independent component analysis: algorithms and applications. Neural Netw. **13**, 411–430 (2000)
3. Andreis, D., MacGregor, L.: Controlled-source electromagnetic sounding in shallow water: principles and applications. Geophy. J. **73**, 21–32 (2008)
4. Amari, S., Cichocki, A.: Adaptive blind signal separation: neural network approaches. Proc. IEEE **86**(10), 2026–2048 (1998)
5. Cardoso, J.F.: Blind signal separation: statistical principles. Proc. IEEE **86**(10), 2009–2047 (1998)

6. Xi, J., Chicharo, J.F., Tsoi, A.C., Siu, W.C.: On the INFOMAX algorithm for blind signal separation. In: 5th International Conference on Signal Processing Proceedings, WCCC-ICSP 2000, vol. 1, pp. 425–428 (2000)
7. Bell, A.J., Sejnowski, T.J.: An information-maximization approach to blind separation and blind deconvolution. Neural Comput. 7, 1129–1159 (1995)
8. Bell, A., Sejnowski, T.: Fast blind separation based on information theory. Neural Comput. 7, 1129–1159 (1995)
9. Hyvarinen, A., Karhunen, J., Oja, E.: Independent Component Analysis. Wiley Interscience Publication, New York (2001). ISBN 0 471 40540-X
10. Nordskag, J.I., Amundsen, L.: Asymptotic airwave modeling for marine con-trolled-source electromagnetic surveying. Geophysics 72(6), F249–F255 (2007)
11. Shaw, A., Al-Shamma'a, A.I., Wylie, S.R., Toal, D.: Experimental investigations of electromagnetic wave propagation in seawater. In: Proceedings of the 36th European Microwave Conference, Manchester, UK (2006)
12. Røsten, T., Amundsen, L.: Generalized electromagnetic seabed logging wavefield decomposition into U/D-going components, 2006 Society of Exploration Geophysicists, SEG Expanded Abstracts, 23, 592 (2004)
13. Løseth, L.O., Amundsen, L., Jenssen, A.: A solution to the airwave-removal problem in shallow-water marine EM. Geophysics 75(5), A37–A42 (2010)
14. Izenman, A.J.: What is Independent Component Analysis?. Temple University, Philadelphia (2003)
15. Zeman, T.: BSS - Preprocessing Steps for Separation Improvement. CTU FEE, Department of Circuit Theory (2000)
16. Biran, A., Breiner, M.: MATLAB For Engineers. Addison-Wesley Publishers Ltd, Reading (1995). ISBN 0-201-56524-2

Finding Survey Papers via Link and Content Analysis

Ali Daud[(⊠)], Aisha Sikandar, and Sameen Mansha

Department of Computer Science and Software Engineering, IIU,
Islamabad 44000, Pakistan
ali.daud@iiu.edu.pk,
{sikandarayesha,sameen_Mansha}@yahoo.com

Abstract. Survey articles provide a comprehensive overview of a specific area of research. Automatic detection of survey articles from huge scientific literature is interesting and useful knowledge discovery task in academic social networks. There are different features which can be exploited to differentiate between survey articles and other research articles. Surveys articles are usually citing many important articles this important feature is used in the past for finding surveys using HITS algorithm in addition to base words, base cues, and article length features. The rank of authors writing the articles and text of articles is not considered. In this paper, two additional features based on Author Rank (author authority score of her papers) and textual feature Entropy (paper disorder score) are introduced. Entropy feature has its special significance as it can be used even when there is no link structure. Empirical results show that proposed enhancements are useful and better results are obtained. Especially for large number of top n papers our proposed methods performance is very stable as compared to existing methods.

Keywords: Survey article finding · HITS · Author rank · Entropy · Academic social networks

1 Introduction

With the emergence of Web online literature is gathered in many repositories such as DBLP1 and Citeseer2 and many academic social network analysis tasks are investigated recently. The co-author and citation based associations between authors and articles, respectively build up these academic social networks. Some interesting tasks are expert finding [12], name disambiguation [17], citation recommendation [13], author interest finding [11] and rising star finding [14]. This work is focused on finding survey articles related to different queries. Survey articles are a type of research articles which provide us detailed literature review about a specific topic in an organized way. They provide researchers a rapid way to jump into new field and save time to first scan and select papers related to a new field. They are useful in grasping the outline of new fields in a short time. Link structure can be exploited to find survey papers.

Previously, automatic detection of survey papers is investigated by [6] using HITS [4] hub scores based on the intuition that survey papers usually cites many important

© Springer International Publishing Switzerland 2014
F.K. Shaikh et al. (Eds.): IMTIC 2013, CCIS 414, pp. 65–75, 2014.
DOI: 10.1007/978-3-319-10987-9_7

papers in return are candidates of achieving high hub scores. In academic literature survey papers are considered as hubs, while papers initiating new problems, ideas and solutions are considered as authorities, respectively. Important papers are first found and then the papers citing important papers are found as possible candidates of survey papers. Namba and Okumura [6] said that HITS considers links but not content as a result papers with high hub scores even they are not surveys will be detected as survey papers. Consequently, an improved content based HITS algorithm named COMB was proposed [6]. The limitations of COMB is to not work well with sparse link structure and not considering the rank of authors writing papers are raised in this paper. The entropy of paper which is independent of link structure and rank of authors of papers is considered by us in this paper. The intuition is based on the fact that when sparse link structure limits the performance of finding survey papers method the content of paper can be better alternative. It is also important to consider the rank of authors as many survey papers are usually written by the experts in that field with high ranks. Experimental results proved that our proposed methods clearly outperform existing methods for automatic survey finding.

The contributions made in this work are as follows. (1) The usage of paper entropy feature, (2) the usage of the Author Rank score and (3) hybridization of entropy and Author Rank based features for survey paper finding. To the best of our knowledge this is the first work of its nature.

The following paper is organized as follows. Section 2 discusses the related work for HITS, PageRank and Entropy. Section 3 provides the details of features and methods used for finding survey papers. In Sect. 4, dataset, baselines, performance measures, and discussions about the results are given. Section 5 finally concludes this work. The word article and papers is used interchangeably in this paper.

2   Related Work

There is not much work done about survey article finding though HITS is used in only one work. Consequently, we provide literature about the PageRank and Entropy which are used in this work for said task, in addition to HITS. First subsection provides some useful work done by using HITS. In second subsection discussions about PageRank algorithm and its applications are made. Finally in Subsect. 3 a very useful work of using entropy for ranking authors is discussed.

2.1   HITS Algorithm

HITS algorithm is applied for autonomous citation indexing on the Citeseer corpus,[1] a full citation index created by Lawrence et al. [5]. A probabilistic extension named PHITS of HITS algorithm is proposed for ranking paper in Cora corpus[2] with full-text citation index [3]. In both previous work, the full-text papers are automatically

---

[1] http://citeseer.ist.psu.edu/

[2] http://www.cs.umass.edu/~mccallum/code-data.html

categorized into different groups and sorted by their hub or authority scores. A useful application of HITS algorithm is shown for automatic detection of surveys by Namba and Okumura [6]. They said that surveys are the papers which usually cite many important papers so that the papers with high hub scores could be strong candidates of survey papers.

PageRank [2] was proposed to rank web pages based on the intuition that the pages linked by many important pages are important. A weakness of PageRank of treating all links equally is raised later and Weighted PageRank algorithm [18] was proposed. It takes both inlinks and outlinks importance into account while calculating the rank of pages and proved effective in retrieving large number of web pages related to a query in comparison to PageRank [6]. Temporal dimension was considered important also in ranking as different events can be popular at different time internals and Time-Weighted PageRank was proposed [16]. It considers page age, event and trend to provide enhanced results.

2.2 PageRank Algorithm

PageRank was also modified as FolkRank [9] which was used to rank users, tags and resources in Folksonomies on the basis of undirected links between them. Biological networks also benefited from a variation of PageRank named Personalized PageRank which was used to rank proteins by using chemical reactions as directed links between them. Results proved that top ranked proteins are playing important part in human body [10].

2.3 Entropy

Entropy is disorder of a system and was recently used as a counter part of citations to measure the quality of the publication venues (journals, conferences), which is used to rank authors in language models. The lower the entropy the higher the quality of publication venue is considered as the venues with lower entropy usually had high number of citations [15].

3 Survey Article Finding

In this section, the features for survey paper finding are first given with their motivation of usage. Later, the methods used for finding survey papers are explained in detail.

3.1 Features

This section provides the details of the features used for finding survey papers.

Base Words
It is based on finding specific words in titles of papers for finding survey papers. These words are called base words. They are: survey, review, overview, state-of-the-art and trend.

Base Cues
It is based on finding specific phrases in the content of papers for finding survey papers. These phrases are called base cues. There are two types of phrases used which are positive and negative. Positive phrases are; this survey, this review, this overview, in this survey and we overview and negative phrases are this thesis, this dissertation and we propose.

Size of Paper
Generally, survey papers are longer than others research papers. This means that the papers with more words or sentences have more chances to become survey papers.

HITS
HITS algorithm [4] is a state-of-the-art algorithm used for ranking web pages by calculating authorities and hub scores. It considers two kinds of pages: hubs, which are valuable sources of good links, and authorities, which are valuable because many pages link to them. It is used to rank papers on the basis of papers as nodes and citations providing the directed links graph. The algorithm determines important hub papers in two stages: (1) Constructing directed graph and (2) computing authority and hub score of each paper iteratively (30 iterations in this work) by using following equations.

$$\text{hub}(p) = \sum_{q=0}^{n} \text{auth}(q)_{q \to p} \tag{1}$$

$$\text{auth}(p) = \sum_{q=0}^{n} \text{hub}(q)_{p \to q} \tag{2}$$

Where, *hub(p)* is hub score of paper p which is the sum of authority scores of all the papers q that links to p, *auth(p)* is authority score of paper p which is sum of hub scores of all the papers q to which p is linked.

PageRank
PageRank [2] is a state-of-the-art algorithm used for ranking web pages by calculating rank scores of web pages. It is a link analysis algorithm that assigns a numerical weighting to each element of a hyperlinked set of documents, with the purpose of measuring its relative importance within the set. The algorithm may be applied to any collection of entities with reciprocal quotations and references. The numerical weight that it assigns to any given element A is referred to as the PageRank of *A* and denoted by *PR (A)*. PageRank is used by us to rank authors of papers on the basis of authors as nodes and papers citing each other are providing the directed link graph in this paper.

The algorithm determines rank of the authors in two steps: (1) Constructing directed graph by using paper citations and (2) by computing the page rank score of each author iteratively (30 iterations in this work) using Eq. 3.

$$\text{PR}(PA) = \frac{1-d}{N} + \sum_{p_j \in M(p_i)} \text{PR}(p_j)/L(p_j) \tag{3}$$

Where, *PR(PA)* is the PageRank score of one paper of author *A*, *d* is damping factor whose value is 0.85, *N* is total number of papers in the data set, *PR(pj)/L(pj)* is the PageRank score of those papers that links to Paper A through citation relationships, divided by number of their out links. One the PageRank score of all paper of an author is calculated, that is summed to get the Author Rank.

Entropy

Entropy is considered as measure of disorder of a system in physics. In this paper, entropy is used to measure the disorder of paper. The unique words in all the papers are noted and term frequency (how many times a single word is present in a paper) and paper frequency (how many times a single word is present in all the documents) is found. And finally entropy is calculated by using Eq. 4.

$$E(\text{Paper}) = \sum_{i=1}^{n} p_i \log_2(p_i) \tag{4}$$

Where, p_i = Term Frequency of word/Document frequency of word.

3.2 Methods

This section provides the existing methods HITS [4] and COMB [6] followed by our proposed methods which are Author Rank Survey Paper Finding, Entropy Survey Article Finding and Three in One Survey Article Finding (3 in 1 SAF), which is combination of all features mentioned in Sect. 3.1.

Existing Methods

In this section an introduction to existing methods HITS and COMB is provided.

HITS. HITS algorithm [4] is applied on the papers to get papers with high hub scores against each query. It is based on the intuition that the survey papers cites many important papers and usually have higher hub scores.

COMB. COMB method [6] is proposed based on five features in combination with HITS which are base words, base cues, size of paper, positional deviation of citations and citation types. Here, for COMB only three features are applied (base words, base cues, and size of paper) in combination with HITS to get top ranked papers against each query by taking into account not only the hub scores of hits as well as the content of papers. The remaining two features are not used as they are shown least significant for survey finding task [6]. The features for COMB are used in a same way they are used for 3 in 1 SAF for comparison purpose.

Proposed Methods

In this section an introduction to our proposed methods Author Rank, Entropy and 3 in 1 SAF are provided.

Author Rank Survey Article Finding. PageRank calculates importance of a page based on the important pages linking to it. Pages are nodes and vertexes represent the links. In case of Author Rank the papers written by authors are the nodes and a paper citing other paper provides directed link to it. The rank for each paper of an author is calculated and then rank of all papers is summed up to get a single value for each author. In this work we have used Author Rank in combination with HITS. Author Rank of an author Ai is compared with the average Author Rank of authors set A, then authority scores are multiplied by 0.5, while the hub scores are doubled to get survey papers against each query.

It is usually thought that the survey papers are written by the highly ranked authors in the field. Conversely, from experiments it is found that the average Author Rank of authors of research papers is greater as compared to Author rank of the authors of survey papers.

Entropy Survey Article Finding. Our proposed entropy feature is merged with HITS in this method. It is usually think that the survey articles are about specific area of research, and then the entropy or disorder in survey paper should have to be less as compared to the research papers. Conversely, form experiments it is found that survey articles have average entropy greater as compared to the research papers. The entropy is calculated using the probabilities of words in papers using standard entropy formula given in Eq. 4.

The entropy E_i of each paper is compared with the average entropy of all papers set E, if entropy of a paper is greater than E; the authority scores are multiplied by 0.5, while the hub scores are doubled to get survey articles against each query.

Three in One Survey Article Finding (3 in 1 SAF). Our proposed method 3 in 1 SAF comprises of five features in combination with HITS which are base words, base cues, size of paper, Author Rank and entropy of papers. The Author Rank and entropy is used in 3 in 1 SAF in a similar way as it is explained in above part of our proposed methods subsection. Base words, base cues and size of paper are used in this method in the following way.

Base Words. If base words are present in the title of paper double (w_{hub}) the hub scores of papers and multiply (w_{auth}) authority scores by 0.5 in the opposite case.

Base Cues. The hub scores of research papers is doubled (w_{hub}) if they contain positive cue phrases, and authority score is multiplied by 0.5 (w_{auth}) in the opposite case.

Size of Paper. The length L_i (the number of sentences) of each paper is compared with the average length L, then authority scores are multiplied by sig (L_i/L) (w_{auth}), while hub scores are multiplied by sig (L/L_i) (w_{hub}).

Using the 5 features explained above, we improve HITS algorithm for survey paper detection by taking into account the hub scores, content of papers, rank of authors and entropy of papers. The authority and hub scores of each paper are calculated by the following equations.

$$x_p = \prod_{j=1}^{5} w_{authj} \times \sum_{q \text{ such that } q \to p} y_p \tag{5}$$

$$y_p = \prod_{j=1}^{5} w_{hubj} \times \sum_{q \text{ such that } p \to q} x_q \tag{6}$$

Where, w_{authj} and w_{hubj} indicate 5 weights for authorities and hubs, respectively.

4   Experiments

This section provides the details of the Citeseer dataset, existing methods and performance measures used for comparison. Finally, results and discussions are provided for existing and our proposed methods.

4.1   Dataset

The sample of data shown in Table 1 is crawled from the Citeseer online computer science publications databases [5]. In total, 20000 papers are taken with 1992 full text papers, 95 survey papers and 32000 unique authors. Papers title or whole text, in-links, out-links, authors and authors in-links and out-links are the used data variables.

Table 1. Queries, number of full text papers and survey papers.

Phrases (Queries)	Full text papers	Survey papers
Bayesian Network	32	1
Support Vector Machine	33	3
Independent Component Analysis	115	4
Data Mining	179	8
AdHoc Network	53	5
Markov Model	88	0
Feature Selection	49	1
Neural Network	434	19
Word Sense Disambiguation	200	4
Information Retrieval	60	4
Image Retrieval	88	12
Machine Learning	144	9
Blind Source Separation	69	0
Fading Channel	38	2
Natural Language Processing	38	0
Object Recognition	29	3
Reinforcement Learning	31	2
Sensor Network	215	13
Speech Recognition	97	5
Average	104.84	5

Statistical n-gram analysis [7] method is applied on titles of all the papers to get frequency of each phrase. We set a value of 2 and 3 for n. Finally 20 most frequent bi-grams and trigram phrases (queries) with meaningful field in computer science and without overlaps are selected. Later, language model [8] is applied on the titles of all papers to get matching percentage of papers against each query. Papers are classified against queries on the basis of their high matching score with the query.

4.2   Baselines

HITS and COMB are taken as baselines to compare the results with our proposed methods Author Rank, Entropy and 3 in 1 SAF.

4.3   Performance Measures

Precision and recall are the most typical evaluation measures in IR community [1]. F-measure, the harmonic mean of precision and recall, has been used to evaluate the overall performance.

$$\text{Precision} = \frac{\text{number of survey papers correctly detected by a system}}{\text{number of survey papers detected by a system}} \quad (7)$$

$$\text{Recall} = \frac{\text{number of survey papers correctly detected by a system}}{\text{number of survey papers that should be detected}} \quad (8)$$

$$\text{F} - \text{Measure} = \frac{2 \times \text{Recall} \times \text{Precision}}{\text{Recall} + \text{Precision}} \quad (9)$$

4.4   Results and Discussions

It is clear from Fig. 1 that for top 5 papers, all methods except Author Rank performs equally well. Though the performance of Author Rank method is poorer for top 5 papers but for different number of top n papers its performance is very stable. For top 10 papers precision for COMB is better as compared to other methods but for greater values of n such as 15, 20 and so on the performance of our proposed methods Author Rank, entropy and 3 in 1 SAF is better as compared to baseline methods.

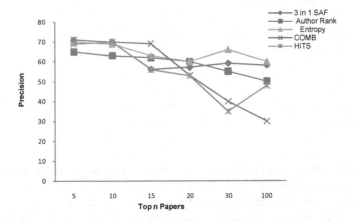

Fig. 1. Precision of top n papers

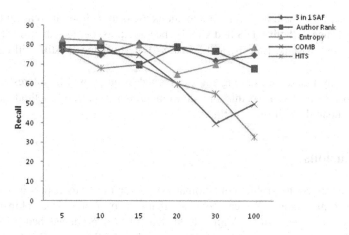

Fig. 2. Recall of top n papers

Table 2. Evaluation by f-measure of top n papers

Top n papers	Our proposed methods			Baselines	
	3 in 1 SAF	Author rank	Entropy	COMB	HITS
5	73.88	71.73	75.95	74.33	73.66
10	72.42	70.49	74.94	72.87	68.98
15	66.22	65.76	70.49	71.87	62.22
20	66.22	68.21	62.40	56.28	56.28
30	64.85	64.16	67.94	40.00	42.77
100	65.42	57.63	68.21	37.50	39.11
Averages	68.17	66.33	69.98	58.81	57.17

One can see from Fig. 2 that for top 5 papers entropy methods performs better as compared to other methods though Author Rank method has also perfumed well. For top 10 papers recall for entropy method is again better though 3 in 1 SAF have comparable performance with it. Just like precision results for greater values of n such as 15, 20 and so on, the performance of our proposed methods Author Rank, entropy and 3 in 1 SAF is better as compared to baseline methods.

From the results shown in Table 2 one can see that by only using HITS the correct results are up to 73.66 % for n = 5 and average results are 57.17 %. When COMB is used which additionally uses three features the results are improved from 73.66 % to 74.33 % for n = 5 and average results are 58.81 %. But by entropy method the correct results are 75.95 % for n = 5 and average results are 69.98, which are much better as compared to the HITS and COMB results. 66 % average accurate results for top ranked papers are found by using Author Rank method are also better as compared to simple HITS and COMB results.

For n = 5, n = 10 and n = 15 all the methods perform well, by increasing the value of n, performance of both HITS and COMB become poor i.e. less than 60 %. On the other hand Author Rank, Entropy and 3 in 1 SAF performance is still well i.e. greater than 60 %.

One can say that a user finding surveys related to query will be interested only in top 5 or 10 papers. Even for this situation our proposed entropy method results are better as compared to all other methods.

5 Conclusions

The paper addressed the problem of automatic detection of survey papers using entropy and Author Rank features. We can conclude that entropy feature in combination with HITS produced better results. Author Rank feature also produced better results for larger number of top n survey papers when merged with HITS. The COMB and HITS fails when papers links are sparse, but entropy can still work well even there is no link structure. In future, classifiers and learning to rank algorithms can be used for automatically finding survey papers.

Acknowledgments.   The work is supported by Higher Education Commission (HEC), Islamabad, Pakistan.

References

1. Azzopardi, L., Girolami, M., van Risjbergen, K.: Investigating the relationship between language model perplexity and IR precision-recall measures. In: Proceedings of the 26th ACM SIGIR International Conference on Research and Development in Information Retrieval (2003)
2. Brin, S., Page, L.: The anatomy of a large-scale hypertextual Web search engine. In: Proceedings of the 7th International Conference on World Wide Web, pp. 107–117 (1998)
3. Cohn, D., Chang, H.: Learning to probabilistically identify authoritative documents. In: Proceedings of the 17th International Conference on Machine Learning, pp. 167–174 (2000)
4. Kleinberg, J.M.: Authoritative sources in a hyperlinked environment. In: Proceedings of the 9th Annual ACM–SIAM Symposium on Discrete Algorithms, pp. 668–677 (1998)
5. Lawrence, S., Giles, L., Bollacker, K.: Digital libraries and autonomous citation indexing. IEEE Comput. **32**(6), 67–71 (1999)
6. Nanba, H., Okumura, M.: Automatic detection of survey articles. In: Rauber, A., Christodoulakis, S., Tjoa, A.M. (eds.) ECDL 2005. LNCS, vol. 3652, pp. 391–401. Springer, Heidelberg (2005)
7. n-gram, http://en.wikipedia.org/wiki/N-gram
8. Zhai, C., Lafferty, J.: A study of smoothing methods for language models applied to ad hoc information retrieval. In: Proceedings of the 24th ACM SIGIR International Conference on Research and Development in Information Retrieval, pp. 334–342 (2001)
9. Hotho, A., Jäschke, R., Schmitz, C., Stumme, G.: Information retrieval in folksonomies: search and ranking. In: Sure, Y., Domingue, J. (eds.) ESWC 2006. LNCS, vol. 4011, pp. 411–426. Springer, Heidelberg (2006)

10. Ivn, G., Grolmusz, V.: When the web meets the cell: using personalized PageRank for analyzing protein interaction networks. Biofinformatics **27**(3), 405–407 (2011)
11. Daud, A.: Using time topic modeling for semantics-based dynamic research interest finding. Knowl.-Based Syst. (KBS) **26**, 154–163 (2012)
12. Daud, A., Li, J., Zhou, L., Muhammad, F.: Temporal expert finding through generalized time topic modeling. Knowl.-Based Syst. (KBS) **23**(6), 615–625 (2010)
13. Daud, A., Shaikh, M.A., Rajpar, A.H.: Scientific reference mining using semantic information through topic modeling. Mehran Univ. Res. J. Eng. Technol. **28**(2), 253–262 (2009)
14. Daud, A., Abbasi, R., Muhammad, F.: Finding rising stars in social networks. In: Meng, W., Feng, L., Bressan, S., Winiwarter, W., Song, W. (eds.) DASFAA 2013, Part I. LNCS, vol. 7825, pp. 13–24. Springer, Heidelberg (2013)
15. Daud, A., Hussain, S.: Publication venue based language modeling for expert finding. In: Proceedings of International Conference on Future Communication and Computer Technology (ICFCCT 2012), 19–20 May 2012
16. Manaskasemsak, B., Rungsawang, A., Yamana, H.: Time-weighted web authoritative ranking. Inf. Retrieval J. **14**(2), 133–157 (2011)
17. Shu, L., Long, B., Meng, W.: A latent topic model for complete entity resolution. In: Proceedings of the International Conference on Data Engineering (ICDE) (2009)
18. Xing, W., Ghorbani, A.: Weighted PageRank algorithm. In: Proceedings of the 2nd Annual Conference on Communication Networks and Services Research, pp. 305–314 (2004)

Dimensionality Reduction of Colored Images Using 2DPCA

Sehar Javaid[✉] and Naveed Rao

Military College of Signals, National University of Sciences and Technology,
Rawalpindi, Pakistan
Sa.Javaid@gmail.com

Abstract. An approach to dimensionality reduction using 2DPCA is presented for colored images. This research also investigates the mechanism of reducing computational complexity for computer vision applications. Since high dimensional data poses various problems like increased computational complexity and increased processing time, there is a dire need of incorporating dimensionality reduction as a preprocessing step in various applications to reduce these factors, which becomes worst for color image processing.

In the first part of this research, key frames are extracted from long video sequences using entropy difference between frames. Afterwards RGB image representing each frame is converted to indexed image and 2DPCA is applied on that image to get its basis vectors. Comparison of uniform quantization and minimum variance quantization techniques for color map approximation from RGB to indexed conversion is presented. Analysis of results obtained by using uniform quantization as a color map approximation technique will be presented in terms of PSNR. Major reduction in overall image dimensions is observed using proposed technique, hence reducing the overall complexity of the required algorithm.

Keywords: PCA · 2DPCA · Approximation technique · Uniform quantization · Minimum variance quantization

1 Introduction

Ever increasing demand on speed and accuracy of image processing applications lead towards development of new techniques for reducing computational complexity of algorithms. As with the increase in computational complexity, processing time also increases, resulting in systems which are inefficient and consume more resources. In real time applications like surveillance systems, this is not desirable because of the time constraints on those systems. At times it is far from practical to increase processing power or storage capacity of existing systems. The problem can be alleviated by reducing dimensions of data.

F.K. Shaikh et al. (Eds.): IMTIC 2013, CCIS 414, pp. 76–85, 2014.
DOI: 10.1007/978-3-319-10987-9_8

Since most of the real world data is high dimensional, there is a strong need to apply dimensionality reduction as a preprocessing step in real world applications to simplify data. This research aims at developing a technique for key frame extraction and dimensionality reduction of colored images which can be incorporated as a preprocessing step in many computer vision algorithms to improve their efficiency. Key frame extraction is done by computing the entropy difference between two consecutive frames and dimensionality reduction is achieved by using 2DPCA.

Traditionally PCA was used for gray scale images which could easily be converted to 1-D vector. In colored image, each image pixel is composed of three color components. Applying PCA on colored image in turn require that each color component must be treated separately. This is a cumbersome process because of overhead involved in further processing. Mostly colored images are converted to gray scale images before applying dimensionality reduction. By doing this color information of that image is lost. Sometimes retaining color information is very important for correct functionality of application. In such kind of situations converting RGB image to indexed image provides a viable solution. This research is based on this conversion. It will be demonstrated that while converting from RGB to indexed image, if quantization technique used is minimum variance quantization than a large amount of noise is seen in reconstructed image.

Rest of the paper is organized as follows: Sect. 2 discusses the existing literature on PCA and its variants. Section 3 contains our proposed methodology followed by experiments and results in Sect. 4. Analysis of results is presented in Sect. 5 and finally Sect. 6 concludes the research.

2   Related Work

PCA is an important statistical technique for analyzing large data sets where we need to find trends or patterns of data. PCA can be employed in many applications including Face Recognition [1] and Image compression [2]. Many variations of PCA have been developed so far. Previously the only way to apply PCA on images is to convert those images to 1 dimensional vectors and combine vectors of all images in database in a single matrix. This results in a large dimensional matrix of image vectors with small number of sample images [3,4]. J. Yang and D. Zhang [5] presented an approach to apply PCA on 2 dimensional image matrices which they called 2DPCA. They showed that 2DPCA is more efficient in terms of computation as compared to 1DPCA because covariance matrix obtained by 2DPCA is much smaller as compared to covariance matrix obtained by 1DPCA. 2DPCA works in a single direction [6] developed 2-Directional 2DPCA in which both column and row directions are considered simultaneously. Experimental results show that for a given data base 2-Directional 2DPCA outperforms PCA and 2DPCA in terms of accuracy and speed. A. Dwivedi [4] makes use of 2DPCA for compression of colored images. In this research author converted image from RGB format to YCbCr format, making use of the fact that three components Y, Cb and Cr are less correlated as compared to R, G and B components of RGB image. Author found that quality of reconstructed image obtained this way is better than that obtained by standard PCA. Another research carried out in this domain is by A. Buchanan and A. Fitzgibbon [7] who implied PCA as a preprocessing step for object tracking. In order to achieve compression, PCA is applied on vector space obtained by incorporating vectors of fixed sized patches of video frames. For standard PCA, the problem of efficiently computing covariance matrix for feature vectors is catered by [8].

3   Proposed Methodology

This section describes the working methodology of our proposed system. The first step is to extract key frames from video sequence which will remove inter frame redundancy and helps achieving compression in long video sequences. For this purpose entropy of each frame is computed as in [9] and entropy difference between two consecutive frames is used for the extraction of key frames. Entropy for each frame is calculated using following formula

$$e_f(k) = p_f(k) * log_2(\frac{1}{p_f(k)})$$ (1)

where $p_f(k)$ is the probability of occurrence of kth color in frame f which can be calculated by dividing its histogram value $h_f(k)$ with total number of pixels as shown in Eq. 2. 'm' is the total number of rows and 'n' is the number of columns in frame f. According to [9], inverse probability of appearance $p_f(k)$ in Eq. 1 indicates the information quantity transmitted by an element.

$$p_f(k) = \frac{h_f(k)}{m * n}$$ (2)

Fig. 1. Key frames

Fig. 2. Original RGB image

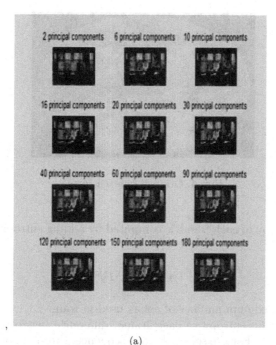

(a)

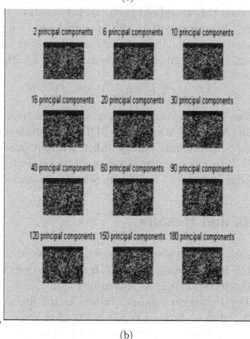

(b)

Fig. 3. Application of 2DPCA on RGB image. Image is reconstructed using variable number of principal components. (a) Results after approximation of color map using uniform quantization. (b) Results after approximation of color map using minimum variance quantization

Fig. 4. Original indexed image

Over all entropy of each frame is computed by adding entropies of individual colors as in Eq. 3

$$E_{Total} = \sum_{k=1}^{b} e_f(k) \tag{3}$$

where b is the maximum number of colors used in frame f.

After computing entropy of each frame, difference between frame (f) and frame (f-1) is taken. For the selected video sequence, threshold of 0.1 is selected. If the difference exceeds this threshold then the information reflected by frame (f) differs significantly from frame (f-1) and is considered as a key frame.

In the second step, dimensionality reduction is achieved by first converting RGB image representing video frame to indexed image I with color map M as shown in Eq. 4

$$M = \{C_k | k = 0, 1, .., N - 1\} \tag{4}$$

For RGB to indexed conversion, color map approximation technique used is uniform quantization. After this conversion, 2DPCA is applied on I. In this way benefit of colored image processing can be taken without processing individual components as in [4]. Image is reconstructed again by retaining variable number of principal components to see the resulting effect of dimensionality reduction.

4   Experiments and Results

Experiments are done on avi video sequence named Wildlife.avi. This video sequence contains 719 frames, out of which 5 frames are detected as key frames (given the threshold selected is 0.1) as shown in Fig. 1.

For dimensionality reduction module, image in tiff format is taken which is than converted to indexed image. While conversion from RGB to indexed, both approximation techniques i.e. uniform quantization and minimum variance quantization are tested. This comparison of both techniques for RGB image in Fig. 2 is presented in Fig. 3a and b. For both techniques, image is reconstructed using variable number of principal components ranging from 2 to 180 PCs. A lot

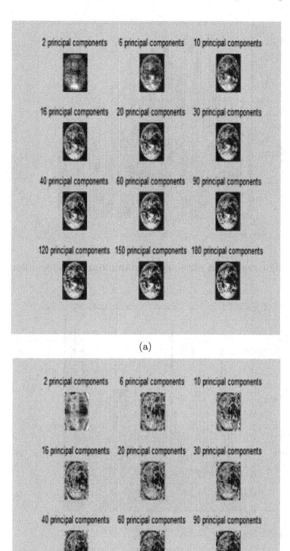

Fig. 5. Application of 2DPCA on indexed image. Image is reconstructed using variable number of principal components. (a) Results after approximation of color map using uniform quantization. (b) Results after approximation of color map using minimum variance quantization

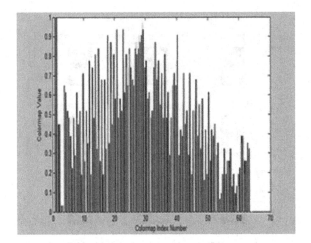

Fig. 6. Color map data obtained by minimum variance quantization

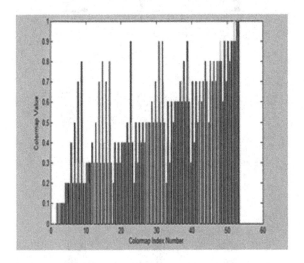

Fig. 7. Color map data obtained by uniform quantization

of noise is seen in the image, reconstructed using minimum variance quantization, as compared to the one reconstructed using uniform quantization. In Fig. 3b image information is lost completely where as in Fig. 3a if 180 PCs are retained than approximately original image is reconstructed again. Another experiment was done on indexed image. Again results of application of both approximation techniques on indexed image in Fig. 4 reveal that UQ is better (Fig. 5a) in terms of image quality than MVQ (Fig. 5b).

Figure 6 shows the graph of color map data obtained by using MVQ. From the graph it is observed that the color map data is in the form of gaussian

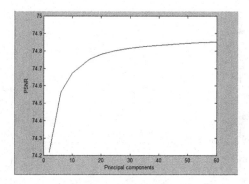

Fig. 8. Plot of principal components Vs their peak signal to noise ratio

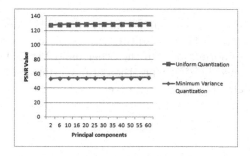

Fig. 9. PSNR comparison of RGB image

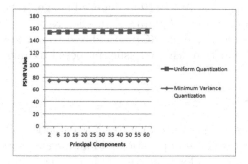

Fig. 10. PSNR comparison of indexed image

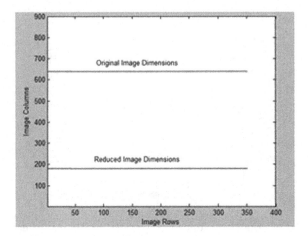

Fig. 11. Plot of dimensionality reduction of original image from 640 dimensions (original image) to 180 dimensions (reduced image)

distribution. Because of non parametric nature of PCA it does not works well with this kind of data and hence resulting reconstructed image becomes noisy and lost most of the information. On the other hand Fig. 7 shows the graph of color map data obtained by UQ. Since the data is in linear form so it produces better results qualitatively and quantitatively.

5   Analysis

This section presents the quantitative comparison in terms of peak signal to noise ratio (PSNR) of reconstructed image. For each reconstructed image, PSNR of that image is computed. Figure 8 shows the PSNR value of reconstructed image against the number of principal components retained of image in Fig. 2.

Comparative analysis of results produced by applying UQ and MVQ is shown in Fig. 9 for RGB image and in Fig. 10 for indexed image. In both cases PSNR is high for UQ as compared to MVQ proving the effectiveness of using UQ as color map approximation technique for RGB to indexed conversion. Figure 11 shows the dimensionality reduction achieved using proposed technique.

6   Conclusion

In this research, a technique for dimensionality reduction of colored images is presented for computer vision applications. Main advantage of this approach is that it takes into account color information of an image while maintaining simplicity of an algorithm. It is fast in terms of computation since it uses 2DPCA in which the size of covariance matrix is much small as compared to the covariance matrix obtained by traditional PCA. For long video sequences, first of all key frames are extracted using entropy difference between video frames. To reduce image dimensions, RGB image was first converted to indexed image and uniform quantization was used as a color map approximation technique. Using proposed approach, if 180 principal components are retained than the compression ratio is more than three times in the reconstructed image. This reduces a great amount of information resulting in processing of more frames per second.

The proposed technique produces best results on RGB images which are converted to indexed image with less number of colors in color map. If the number of colors in color map increases than the quality of reconstructed image is not that much high and effect of noise is seen in the reconstructed image.

In the current part of this research, method for key frame extraction and dimensionality reduction is developed. The extension to this work includes the phase of feature detection and trajectory determination for detecting and tracking objects in object tracking algorithms to perform tracking with minimal time and computational complexity.

Acknowledgment. We would like to thank Dr. Fahim Arif, Dr. Imran Tauqeer and Dr. Adil Masood Siddique of Military College of Signals, for their continuous support and valuable suggestions throughout this research.

References

1. Ebied, H.: Feature extraction using PCA and kernel-PCA for face recognition. In: 2012 8th International Conference on Informatics and Systems (INFOS), p. MM-72. IEEE (2012)
2. Mudrova, M., Prochazka, A.: Principal component analysis in image processing. In: Proceedings of the MATLAB Technical Computing Conference, Prague (2005)
3. Yu, H., Bennamoun, M.: 1D-PCA 2D-PCA to nD-PCA. In: 18th International Conference on Pattern Recognition, 2006, ICPR 2006, vol. 4, pp. 181–184. IEEE (2006)
4. Dwivedi, A., Tolambiya, A., Kandula, P., Bose, N., Kumar, A. Kalra, P.: Color image compression using 2-dimensional principal component analysis (2DPCA). In: 9th International Conference on Asian Symposium on Information Display, 2006, ASID 2006, vol. 2, p. 1 (2006)
5. Yang, J., Zhang, D., Frangi, A., Yang, J.: Two-dimensional PCA: a new approach to appearance-based face representation and recognition. IEEE Trans. Pattern Anal. Mach. Intell. **26**(1), 131–137 (2004)
6. Zhang, D., Zhou, Z.-H.: (2D) 2PCA: Two-directional two-dimensional PCA for efficient face representation and recognition. Neurocomputing **69**(1), 224–231 (2005)
7. Buchanan, A., Fitzgibbon, A.: Interactive feature tracking using kd trees and dynamic programming. In: 2006 IEEE Computer Society Conference on Computer Vision and Pattern Recognition, vol. 1, pp. 626–633. IEEE (2006)
8. Kwatra, V., Han, M.: Fast covariance computation and dimensionality reduction for sub-window features in images. In: Daniilidis, K., Maragos, P., Paragios, N. (eds.) ECCV 2010, Part II. LNCS, vol. 6312, pp. 156–169. Springer, Heidelberg (2010)
9. Mentzelopoulos, M., Psarrou, A.: Key-frame extraction algorithm using entropy difference. In: Proceedings of the 6th ACM SIGMM International Workshop on Multimedia Information Retrieval, pp. 39–45. ACM (2004)

The Performance Enhancement of Inter Relay Cooperative Network Using Amplify-and-Forward Time Division Multiple Access Based Protocol

Imranullah Khan[✉] and Tan Chong Eng

Faculty of Computer Science and Information Technology,
Universiti Malaysia Sarawak, Kota Samarahan, Sarawak, Malaysia
imrankhann0321@gmail.com, cetan@ieee.org

Abstract. Time Division Multiple Access (TDMA) based protocols over Rician fading, have been analyzed and proposed by many researchers. However, these protocols need to be explored further in order to improve diversity order at destination. Therefore, this paper aims to propose TDMA amplify-and-forward based three time slot protocol over Rican fading channel with inter-relay communication. The proposed protocol is further investigated for various relay locations in order to optimize the bit error rate (BER) for different relay locations. It is concluded that the proposed amplify-and-forward (PAFP) three time slots protocol performs better in terms of low bit error rate values, as compared to previously proposed amplify-and-forward (PPAF) two time slot and three time slots protocols. Moreover, the PAFP also shows less BER values, as compared to DF three time slot protocol. Furthermore, the PAFP shows less BER values in case of minimum inter-relay distance.

Keywords: Cooperative inter-relay wireless communication · Amplify-and-forward (AF) protocol · TDMA · BER

1   Introduction

The mobile radio channel suffers due to fading effects during transmission of data from source to destination and undergoes through several signal variations at destination. In order to mitigate fading, diversity communication is used to send the same data over independent fading paths (diversity branches). The most common techniques such as micro diversity, macro diversity, space diversity, frequency diversity and time diversity have been used at the transmitter and receiver to achieve diversity communication [1]. These diversity techniques tend to increase the size, complexity and total power of the wireless network devices. To solve this issue, cooperative diversity communication has been introduced recently.

In cooperative diversity communication, the diversity is achieved due to cooperation among users or relays, for example, in case of two users or relays and one destination, each user or relay transmits their own information signal as well as the information data of their partner user or relay, to the destination, virtually seeking

© Springer International Publishing Switzerland 2014
F.K. Shaikh et al. (Eds.): IMTIC 2013, CCIS 414, pp. 86–97, 2014.
DOI: 10.1007/978-3-319-10987-9_9

the advantages of MIMO spatial diversity [2–5]. Each user in cooperative diversity acts as a relay for another user, using either amplify-and-forward or decode-and-forward protocols, to broadcast the information to destination [3, 6].

Cooperative communication solves the issues of size, cost, and hardware confines of multiple antennas [7]. Moreover, cooperative communication is also used to reduce multi-path fading, increases capacity of wireless channel and achieves high data rates [8, 9].

2 Related Work

Different multiple access techniques such as Time Division Multiple Access, Frequency Division Multiple Access, and Code Division Multiple Access, have been analyzed and proposed by researchers, to achieve high diversity order at destination [10–12]. In 2004, Nabar et al. [13] proposed three different two time slots TDMA based transmission protocols. These protocols have different unstable degree of broadcasting and receive collisions at receiver (destination). In each protocol the relay either AF or DF the received signal from source. A novel scheme of wireless cooperative network using three time slots has been analyzed by Fares et al. [14] in 2008. This scheme is based on data exchange between relays in the third time slot in order to enhance the link performance between relays and destination. In 2012, Tanoli et al. [15] proposed three time slots TDMA-FDMA based protocol, using inter-relay communication, over Nakagami-m fading channel. A TDMA based protocol, using three time slots inter-relay communication, over Nakagami-m and Rician fading channels has been proposed by Tanoli et al. [16] in 2012. The source transmits to both the relays and destination in the first time slot. Moreover, the relays exchange their data over the second time slot. The relays transmit the exchanged data over the third time slot, to destination. The source remains silent in the 2nd and 3rd time slots and does not broadcasts to destination in these slots.

In this work, we have proposed TDMA based three time slots protocol using inter-relay communication. The results obtained from BER analysis, have been compared with the results obtained from previously proposed protocols [13, 16]. It is shown that the proposed protocol performs better in terms of less BER, as compared to the two times slot protocol proposed by Nabar et al. [13] in 2004 and three times slot protocol proposed by Tanoli et al. [16] in 2012.

3 Proposed Methodology

3.1 System Model

We consider wireless cooperative network with two relays, one source and one destination, as shown in Fig. 1. The source (S), relay1 (R1), relay2 (R2) and destination (D), are operational by using single antenna. The h_{SR1}, h_{SR2}, h_{R1D}, h_{R2D}, h_{R1R2} and h_{R2R1} are the path gains of source to relay1, source to relay2, relay1 to destination, relay2 to destination, relay1 to relay2 and relay2 to relay1 channels respectively.

Amplify-and-forward communication is used by the relays. In order to get BER at destination, Maximum Ratio Combining (MRC) is used.

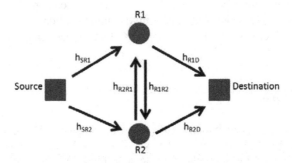

Fig. 1. Inter-relay communication using TDMA based AF three time slots protocol

3.2   Proposed TDMA Based Three Time Slots Protocol

The system model used for three time slots proposed protocol is shown in Fig. 1. The source transmits to destination, relay1 and relay2, over the first time slot. The relay1 and relay2 transmit to destination as well as exchange their data in the second time slot. Over the 3rd time slot, relay1 and relay2 broadcast the previously exchanged data during the second time, to destination. Moreover, the source continuously keeps broadcasting over the second and third time slots, to destination and does not remain silent during these time slots. The summarized form of the proposed protocol is shown in Table 1.

Table 1. Proposed TDMA based protocol with three time slots

Time slot 1	Time slot 2	Time slot 3
$S \rightarrow R_1, S \rightarrow R_2$ $S \rightarrow D$	$R_1 \rightarrow D, R_2 \rightarrow D,$ $R_1 \rightarrow R_2, R_2 \rightarrow R_1$ $S \rightarrow D$	$R_1 \rightarrow D, R_2 \rightarrow D$ $S \rightarrow D$

The signals received at relay1, relay2 and destination over the first time slot are y_{SR1}, y_{SR2} and $y_{SD,1}$ respectively and given by

$$y_{SR1} = E_s h_{SR1} s + n_{SR1} \tag{1}$$

$$y_{SR2} = E_s h_{SR2} s + n_{SR2} \tag{2}$$

$$y_{SD,1} = E_s h_{SD} + n_{SD} \tag{3}$$

where E_S is average transmit energy by the source per symbol. The parameters h_{SR1}, h_{SR2} and h_{SD} are complex fading channels of source to relay1, relay2 and destination links respectively. Similarly, the parameters n_{SR1}, n_{SR2} and n_{SD} are the Additive White Gaussian noises (AWGN's), which are added to the source to relay1, relay2 and destination channels respectively. The Rayleigh and Rician fading models are used as multipath fading models for the entire source to relays and destination channels.

The relay1 and relay2 normalize the received signals and broadcast toward destination. The signals received at destination from relay1, relay2 and source in the second time slot are y_{R1D}, y_{R2D} and $y_{SD,2}$ respectively and given by

$$y_{R1D} = E_1 h_{R1D} \frac{y_{SR1}}{\sqrt{E_s |h_{SR1}|^2 + 1}} + n_{R1D} \tag{4}$$

$$y_{R2D} = E_2 h_{R2D} \frac{y_{SR2}}{\sqrt{E_s |h_{SR2}|^2 + 1}} + n_{R2D} \tag{5}$$

$$y_{SD,2} = E_s h_{SD} + n_{SD} \tag{6}$$

where E1 and E2 are the average transmit energy per symbol by relay1 and relay2 respectively. The parameters h_{R1D} and h_{R2D} are complex fading channels of relay1 to destination and relay2 to destination links respectively. Moreover, the parameters n_{R1D} and n_{R2D} are the AWGN's in the relay1 to destination and relay2 to destination channels respectively. The Rayleigh and Rician fading models are used as multipath fading models for the entire relays to destination channels. In addition, both the relays normalize the received signals from source and exchange their data during second time slot. The signals received at relay2 from relay1 and at relay1 from relay2 are y_{R1R2} and y_{R2R1} respectively and given by

$$y_{R1R2} = E_1 h_{R1R2} \frac{y_{SR1}}{\sqrt{E_s |h_{SR1}|^2 + 1}} + n_{R1R2} \tag{7}$$

$$y_{R2R1} = E_2 h_{R2R1} \frac{y_{SR2}}{\sqrt{E_s |h_{SR2}|^2 + 1}} + n_{R2R1} \tag{8}$$

where h_{R1R2} and h_{R2R1} are complex fading channels of relay1 to relay2 and relay2 to relay1 links respectively. The parameters n_{R1R2} and n_{R2R1} are the AWGN's in the relay1 to relay2 and relay2 to relay1 channels respectively. The Rayleigh and Rician fading models are used as multipath fading models for the relay1 to relay2 and relay2 to relay1 channels.

The relay1 and relay2 normalize the previously exchanged data received during 2nd time slot and transmit to destination, over the 3rd time slot. The signals received at destination from relay1, relay2 and source over the 3rd time slot are y_{R1D}, y_{R2D} and $y_{SD,3}$ respectively and given by

$$y_{R1D} = E_1 h_{R1R2} \frac{y_{R1R2}}{\sqrt{E_1 |h_{R1R2}|^2 + 1}} + n_{R1D} \tag{9}$$

$$y_{R2D} = E_2 h_{R2R1} \frac{y_{R2R1}}{\sqrt{E_2 |h_{R2R1}|^2 + 1}} + n_{R2D} \tag{10}$$

$$y_{SD,3} = E_s h_{SD} + n_{SD} \tag{11}$$

MRC is used at destination, to take out the required information at destination. The received information signal at D using MRC is y_D and given by

$$y_D = y_{R1D} h^*_{R1D} h^*_{SR1} + y_{R2D} h^*_{R2D} h^*_{SR2} + y_{SD} h^*_{SD} + y_{R2D} h^*_{R2D} h^*_{R1R2} h^*_{SR1} +$$
$$y_{R1D} h^*_{R1D} h^*_{R2R1} h^*_{SR2} + y_{SD} h^*_{SD} + y_{SD} h^*_{SD} \tag{12}$$

3.3   Relay Displacement Optimization

This section describes the optimal relay locations for the system model, as shown in Fig. 1. The purpose of relay optimization is to find out the best relay locations in terms of less BER values. The parameters d_{SR1}, d_{R1D}, d_{SR2}, d_{R1D}, d_{R1R2} and d_{R2R1} are distances between source to relay1, relay1 to destination, source to relay2, relay2 to destination, relay1 to relay2 and relay2 to relay1 respectively, as shown in Fig. 2. The source to destination distance is taken d. First, the relay1 is set at fixed location and relay2 is moved along the x-axis. Secondly, the relay2 is set at fix position and relay1 is moved along the x-axis. The system model used for the relay optimization is shown in Fig. 2.

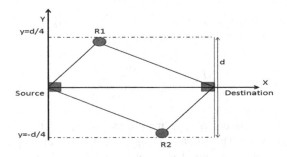

Fig. 2. Optimized relay displacement

The signals received at relay1, relay2 and destination over the 1st time slot are y_{SR1}, y_{SR2} and $y_{SD,1}$ respectively and given by

$$y_{SR1} = (d_{SR1})^{-\alpha} E_s h_{SR1} s + n_{SR1} \tag{13}$$

$$y_{SR2} = (d_{SR2})^{-\alpha} E_s h_{SR2} s + n_{SR2} \tag{14}$$

$$y_{SD,1} = (d_{SD})^{-\alpha} E_s h_{SD} + n_{SD} \tag{15}$$

where d_{SR1}, d_{SR2} and d_{SD} are the distances between source to relay1, source to relay2 and source to destination respectively. The relay relay1 and relay2 receive the signals from the source over the second time slot, normalize the received signals and broadcast towards destination. The signals received at destination from relay1, relay2 and source over the second time slot are y_{R1D}, y_{R2D} and $y_{SD,2}$ respectively and given by

$$y_{R1D} = (d_{R1D})^{-\alpha} E_1 h_{R1D} \frac{y_{SR1}}{\sqrt{E_s|h_{SR1}|^2+1}} + n_{R1D} \tag{16}$$

$$y_{R2D} = (d_{R2D})^{-\alpha} E_2 h_{R2D} \frac{y_{SR2}}{\sqrt{E_s|h_{SR2}|^2+1}} + n_{R2D} \tag{17}$$

$$y_{SD,2} = (d_{SD})^{-\alpha} E_s h_{SD} + n_{SD} \tag{18}$$

where d_{R1D}, d_{R2D} and d_{SD} are the distances between relay1 to destination, relay2 to destination and source to destination respectively. The relay1 and relay2 normalize the received signals from source and exchange their data during second time slot. The signals received at relay2 from relay1 and at relay1 from realy2 are y_{R1R2} and y_{R2R1} respectively and given by

$$y_{R1D} = (d_{R1D})^{-\alpha} E_1 h_{R1R2} \frac{y_{R1R2}}{\sqrt{E_1|h_{R1R2}|^2+1}} + n_{R1D} \tag{19}$$

$$y_{R2D} = (d_{R2D})^{-\alpha} E_2 h_{R2R1} \frac{y_{R2R1}}{\sqrt{E_2|h_{R2R1}|^2+1}} + n_{R2D} \tag{20}$$

$$y_{SD,3} = (d_{SD})^{-\alpha} E_s h_{SD} + n_{SD} \tag{21}$$

MRC is used at destination, to take out the required information at destination. The received information signal at destination using MRC is y_D and given by

$$y_D = y_{R1D} h_{R1D}^* h_{SR1}^* + y_{R2D} h_{R2D}^* h_{SR2}^* + y_{SD} h_{SD}^* + y_{R2D} h_{R2D}^* h_{R1R2}^* h_{SR1}^* + y_{R1D} h_{R1D}^* h_{R2R1}^* h_{SR2}^*$$
$$+ y_{SD} h_{SD}^* + y_{SD} h_{SD}^* \tag{22}$$

4   Simulation Results and Discussion

In this section the performance of proposed three time slots protocol with inter-relay has been evaluated with the comparison of two proposed protocols presented by Nabar et al. [13] and Tanoli et al. [16]. The proposed protocol by Nabar et al. [13] is TDMA based two time slot protocol. The source transmits to relays and destination over the 1st time slot. The relays amplify the signals received from the source and forward to destination, during the 2nd time slot. The proposed protocol by Tanoli et al. [16] is

TDMA based three time slots protocol. The source transmits to relays and destination during the 1st time slot. The relays amplify the signals received from source and forward to destination over the 2nd time slot. The relays also exchange their data, over the second time slot. Similarly, the relays normalize the exchanged data and broadcast to destination over 3rd time slot. Moreover, BER is used as performance metric at destination. MRC is used at destination to merge the signals received in different time slots, from relays as well as destination and to extract information from these received signals.

We have used BER as a performance metric in simulation and calculated BER at destination for proposed TDMA based three time slots cooperative protocol. Similarly, MRC is used at destination to combine the signals received in different time slots. Bipolar Phase Shift Keying modulation scheme is used to modulate the signal at the source. The AWGN's with zero mean and variance together with the Rayleigh and Rician fading are used to make the channels noisy and multipath respectively. To plot the BER vs signal to noise ratio 10^5 symbols are used.

The comparison of amplify-and-forward protocol (AFP) without inter-relay communication by Nabar et al. [13] and proposed amplify-and-forward protocol (PAFP) with inter-relay communication is shown in Fig. 3. It is shown from Fig. 3 that PAFP with inter-relay communication performs better in terms of low BER values and high diversity order as compared to AFP without inter-relay communication. Owing to the fact that the PAFP has one extra time slot during which it exchanges data between the relays. Hence, the destination receives two additional copies of the source signal and increases the diversity order at destination as compared to AFP.

The comparison of previously proposed amplify-and-forward (PPAF) three time slots protocol by Tanoli et al. [16] and proposed amplify-and-forward (PAFP) three time slots protocol is shown in Fig. 4. The PAF three time slots protocol shows less BER values and high diversity order, as compared to PPAF three time slots protocol, as shown in Fig. 4. It is due to the fact that during second and third time slots, the source

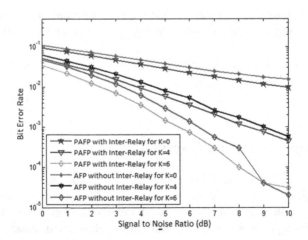

Fig. 3. BER comparison PAFP with inter-relay communication and AFP without inter-relay communication

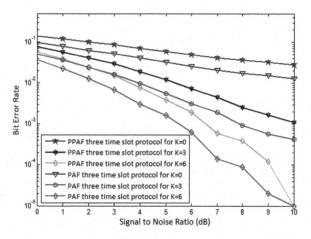

Fig. 4. BER comparison of PAF three time slots and PPAF three time slots protocols

of PPAF protocol remains silent and does not broadcast to destination, where as the PAF protocol source does not remain silent during 2nd and 3rd time slot and continues broadcasting to destination. Hence, the destination of PAF receives extra copies of the source signal during 2nd and 3rd time slots, as compared to PPAF. Due to this phenomenon, the degree of broadcasting at the source as well as diversity order at destination increases, hence the BER decreases at destination.

The PAF three time slots protocol is also evaluated with three time slots decode-and-forward protocol (DFP) as indicated in Fig. 5. The PAF inter-relay protocol performs better in terms of less BER values, as compared to three times slots DFP, as shown in Fig. 5. It is due to the fact that the normalization factors used at the relay for the current simulation environment makes the PAF protocol superior as compared to three time slots DF protocol.

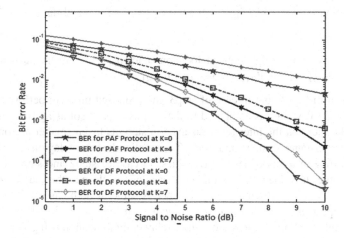

Fig. 5. BER comparison of PAF and DF three time slots protocols

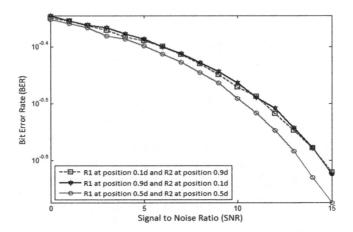

Fig. 6. Comparison of BER values for three different relay1 and relay2 positions

The comparison of BER at three different relay positions using PAF three time slot protocol is shown in Fig. 6. We take d_{SR1}, d_{R1D}, d_{SR2}, d_{R2D}, d_{R1R2} and d_{R2R1} as the distances between source to relay1, relay1 to destination, source to relay2, relay2 to destination, relay1 to relay2 and relay2 to relay1 respectively. The source to destination distance is taken d which is 10 m in the current simulation environment. We use three different steps with respect to the relay positions as shown below.

Step1.
We suppose that relay1 is at location 0.1d and relay2 is at location 0.9d. In this case d_{SR1} = 2.69 m, d_{R1D} = 9.34 m, d_{SR2} = 9.34, d_{R2D} = 2.69, d_{R1R2} = 9.433 m and d_{R2R1} = 9.433 m.

Step2.
By considering relay1 at location 0.9d and relay2 at location 0.1d, the d_{SR1} = 9.34 m, d_{R1D} = 2.69 m, d_{SR2} = 2.69, d_{R2D} = 9.34, d_{R1R2} = 9.433 m and d_{R2R1} = 9.433 m.

Step3.
By taking relay1 and relay2 both at location 0.5d, d_{SR1} = 5.59 m, d_{R1D} = 5.59 m, d_{SR2} = 5.59 d_{R2D} = 5.59, d_{R1R2} = 5 m and d_{R2R1} = 5 m.

It is shown from Fig. 6 that in case of step3, the proposed protocol performs better in terms of less BER values as compared to the proposed protocol using step2 and step1. Owing to the fact that the inter-relay distance in step3 is taken smaller as compared to the inter-relay distance in step1 and step2. The smaller the inter-relay distance the better the performance in terms of less BER values. In case of step2 and step1 the BER is almost the same. It is due to the fact that either relay1 is close to the source or relay2 is close to the source and the inter-relay distance is same in both cases.

The comparison of BER for PAF protocol with inter-relay, PPAF protocol with inter-relay and PPAF protocol without inter-relay communication using step3 is shown in Fig. 7. The PAF protocol with inter-relay communication shows less BER values, as

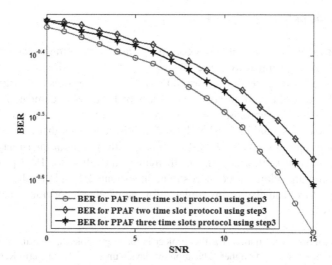

Fig. 7. BER Comparison of PAF three time slots, PPAF two time slots and PPAF three time slots protocols

compared to PPAF protocol with inter-relay and PPAF protocol without inter-relay communication. Owing to the fact that PAF protocol uses exchange of data during 2nd time slot which increases the degree of broadcasting at destination. Furthermore, the PAF protocol does not remain dormant during the 2nd and 3rd time slots and continuously broadcasts to destination. Hence, increases the degrees of broadcasting at source and diversity order at destination.

The BER for PAF protocol with inter-relay using relay1 and relay2 projections is shown in Fig. 8. The PAF protocol indicates minimum BER values, with minimum inter-relay distance. However, with the increase in inter-relay distance, there is an increase in BER values, as shown in Fig. 8.

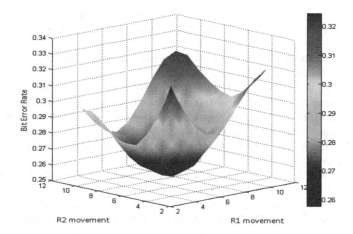

Fig. 8. BER for PAF protocol with inter-relay using relay1 and relay2 projections

5   Conclusions

A TDMA based three time slots protocol, using inter-relay communication, has been investigated. It is concluded from the investigation that the PAF three time slots protocol shows low BER values, as compared to PPAF two time slots and three time slots protocols. Moreover, the PAF protocol shows less BER values as compared to DF three time slots protocol. Furthermore, the PAF protocol has been investigated for BER at various relay locations and inter-relay distances. It is concluded that the PAF protocol shows better results in terms of less BER values, with minimum inter-relay distance.

The channel matrix design using mathematical modeling for PAF protocol with inter-relay communication, further needs to be investigated. Similarly, the performance of the PAF protocol can also be investigated for the wireless cooperative network with multiple relays.

Acknowledgements. The funding for this project is made possible through the research grant obtained from the Ministry of Higher Education, Malaysia under the Long Term Research Grant Scheme 2011 [LRGS grant no: JPT.S (BPKI)2000/09/01/015Jld.4(67)].

References

1. Goldsmith, A.: Wireless Communications. Cambridge University Press, New York (2005)
2. Sendonaris, A., Erkip, E., Aazhang, B.: User cooperation diversity, part I: system description. IEEE Trans. Commun. **51**(11), 1927–1938 (2003)
3. Laneman, J.N., Tse, D.N., Wornell, G.W.: Cooperative diversity in wireless networks: efficient protocols and outage behavior. IEEE Trans. Inf. Theory **50**(12), 3062–3080 (2004)
4. Laneman, J.N., Wornell, G.W.: Energy-efficient antenna sharing and relaying for wireless networks. IEEE Conf. Wirel. Commun. Netw. **1**(1), 7–12 (2000)
5. Laneman, J.N., Wornell, G.W.: Distributed space time coded protocols for exploiting cooperative diversity in wireless networks. IEEE Trans. Inf. Theory **49**(10), 2415–2425 (2003)
6. Kwasinski, A., Liu, K.R.: Source-channel-cooperation tradeoffs for adaptive coded communications [transactions papers]. IEEE Trans. Wirel. Commun. **7**(9), 3347–3358 (2008)
7. Nosratinia, A., Hunter, T.E., Hedayat, A.: Cooperative communication in wireless networks. IEEE Commun. Mag. **42**(10), 74–80 (2004)
8. Anghel, P.A., Kaveh, M.: Exact symbol error probability of a cooperative network in a rayleigh-fading environment. IEEE Transa. Wirel. Commun. **3**(5), 1416–1421 (2004)
9. Pabst, R., et al.: Relay-based deployment concepts for wireless and mobile broadband radio. IEEE Commun. Mag. **42**(9), 80–89 (2004)
10. Mark, J., Zhuang, W.: Wireless Communications and Networking. Prentice Hall, Upper Saddle River (2003)
11. Jiang, H., Waterloo, O.: Quality of service provisioning in future 46 CDMA cellular networks. IEEE Wirel. Commun. **49**, 48–54 (2004)
12. Jiang, H., et al.: Quality of service provisioning and efficient resource utilization in CDMA cellular communications. IEEE J. Sel. Areas in Commun. **24**(1), 4–15 (2006)

13. Nabar, R.U., Bolcskei, H., Kneubuhler, F.W.: Fading relay channels: performance limits and space time signal design. IEEE J. Sel. Areas Commun. **22**(6), 1099–1109 (2004)
14. Fares, S.A., Adachi, F., Kudoh, E.: A novel cooperative relaying network scheme with inter-relay data exchange. IEICE Trans. Commun. **92**(5), 1786–1795 (2009)
15. Tanoli, U.R., et al.: Hybrid TDMA-FDMA based inter-relay communication in cooperative networks over Nakagami-m fading channel. In: IEEE International Conference on Emerging Technologies (ICET), pp. 1–5 (2012)
16. Tanoli, U., et al.: Performance analysis of cooperative networks with inter-relay communication over Nakagami-m and Rician fading channels. Int. J. Multi. Sci. **3**(4), 24–29 (2012)

Automatic Analysis of Affective States: Visual Attention Based Approach

Rizwan Ahmed Khan[1,2]([✉]), Alexandre Meyer[1,2], Hubert Konik[1,3], and Saida Bouakaz[1,2]

[1] CNRS, Université de Lyon, Lyon, France
Rizwan-Ahmed.Khan@liris.cnrs.fr
[2] LIRIS, UMR5205, Université Lyon 1, 69622 Villeurbanne, France
[3] Laboratoire Hubert Curien, UMR5516, Université Jean Monnet,
42000 Saint-Etienne, France
{Alexandre.Meyer,Saida.Bouakaz}@liris.cnrs.fr

Abstract. Computing environment is moving from computer centered designs to human-centered designs. Human's tend to communicate wealth of information through affective states or expressions. Thus automatic analysis of user affective states have become inevitable for computer vision community. In this paper first we focus on understanding human visual system (HVS) when it decodes or recognizes facial expressions. To understand HVS, we have conducted psycho-visual experimental study with an eye-tracker, to find which facial region is perceptually more attractive or salient for a particular expression. Secondly, based on results obtained from psycho-visual experimental study we have proposed a novel framework for automatic analysis of affective states. Framework creates discriminative feature space by processing only salient facial regions to extract Pyramid Histogram of Orientation Gradients (PHOG) features. The proposed framework achieved automatic expression recognition accuracy of 95.3 % on extended Cohn-Kanade (CK+) facial expression database for six universal facial expressions. We have also discussed generalization capabilites of proposed framework on unseen data. In the last paper discusses effectiveness of proposed framework against low resolution image sequences.

Keywords: Facial expression recognition · Human vision · Eye-tracker · Pyramid histogram of oriented gradients · Classification

1 Introduction

Computing environment is moving towards human-centered designs instead of computer centered designs [1], and human's tend to communicate wealth of information through affective states or expressions. Traditional Human Computer Interaction (HCI) based systems ignores bulk of information communicated through those affective states and just caters for user's intentional input. As mentioned that paradigm is shifting towards human-centered designs, thus analysis

© Springer International Publishing Switzerland 2014
F.K. Shaikh et al. (Eds.): IMTIC 2013, CCIS 414, pp. 98–108, 2014.
DOI: 10.1007/978-3-319-10987-9_10

of user affective states becomes inevitable. In near future humans will not interact with machines only through intentional inputs but also through their behavior i.e. affective states [2]. Therefore, computer vision research community has shown a lot of interest in analyzing and automatically recognizing facial expressions. There are lots of application areas that can benefit from a system that can recognize facial expressions i.e. human-computer interaction, entertainment, medical applications e.g. pain detection, social robots, deceit detection, interactive video and behavior monitoring.

Humans have the amazing ability to decode facial expressions across different cultures, in diverse conditions and in a very short time. Human visual system (HVS) has limited neural resources but still it can analyze complex scenes in real-time. As an explanation for such performance, it has been proposed that only some visual inputs are selected by considering "salient regions" [3], where "salient" means most noticeable or most important.

Recently different methods for automatic facial expression recognition [4–7] have been proposed but none of them try to mimic human visual system in recognizing them except [8,9]. Rather all of the methods, spend computational time on whole face image or divides the facial image based on some mathematical or geometrical heuristic for features extraction. We argue that the task of expression analysis and recognition could be done in more conducive manner, if only some regions are selected for further processing (i.e. salient regions) as it happens in human visual system.

To determine which facial region(s) is salient according to human vision, we have conducted psycho-visual experiment. The experiment has been conducted with the help of an eye-tracking system which records the fixations and saccades. It is known that eye gathers most of the information during the fixations [10] as eye fixations describe the way in which visual attention is directed towards silent regions in a given stimuli. We have conducted study on six universal facial expressions as these expressions are proved to be consistent across cultures [11]. These six expressions are anger, disgust, fear, happiness, sadness and surprise.

Rest of the paper is organized as follows: all the details related to psycho-visual experiment is described in the next section. Section 3 presents framework proposed for automatic analysis of facial expression/affect. Results obtained for expression analysis are presented in Sect. 4. This is followed by conclusion.

2 Psycho-Visual Experiment

The aim of the experiment was to record the eye movement data of human observers in free viewing conditions. Data was analyzed in order to find that which component of face is salient for specific displayed expression.

2.1 Participants, Apparatus and Stimuli

Eye movements of fifteen human observers were recorded using video based eye-tracker (EyelinkII system, SR Research), as the subjects watched the collection of 54 videos selected from the extended Cohn-Kanade (CK+) database [12], showing one of the six universal facial expressions [11]. Observers include both male and female aging from 20 to 45 years with normal or corrected to normal vision. All the observers were naïve to the purpose of an experiment. CK+ database contains 593 sequences across 123 subjects. Each video showed a neutral face at the beginning and then gradually developed into one of the six facial expression.

2.2 Eye Movement Recording

Eye position was tracked at 500 Hz with an average noise less than 0.01°. Head mounted eye-tracker allows flexibility to perform experiment in free viewing conditions as the system is designed to compensate for small head movements.

2.3 Psycho-Visual Experiment Results

In order to statistically quantify which region is perceptually more attractive for specific expression, we have calculated the average percentage of trial time observers have fixated their gazes at specific region(s) in a particular time period. As the stimuli used for the experiment is dynamic i.e. video sequences, it would have been incorrect to average all the fixations recorded during trial time (run length of the video) for the data analysis as this could lead to biased analysis of the data. To meaningfully observe and analyze the gaze trend across one video sequence we have divided each video sequence in three mutually exclusive time periods. The first time period correspond to initial frames of the video sequence i.e. neutral face. The last time period encapsulates the frames where the expression is shown with full intensity (apex frames). The second time period is a encapsulation of the frames which has a transition of facial expression i.e. transition from neutral face to the beginning of the desired expression (i.e. neutral to the onset of the expression). Then the fixations recorded for a particular time period are averaged across fifteen observers. For drawing the conclusions we considered second and third time periods as they have the most significant information in terms of specific displayed expression. Conclusions drawn are summarized in Fig. 1. Refer [13] for the detailed explanation of the psycho-visual experimental study.

3   Framework for Affect Analysis

Feature selection along with the region(s) from where these features are going to be extracted is one of the most important step to successfully recognize expressions/affect. As the proposed framework draws its inspiration from the human visual system, it processes only perceptual salient facial region(s) for the feature extraction. The proposed framework creates a novel feature space by extracting Pyramid Histogram of Orientation Gradients (PHOG) [14] features from the perceptually salient facial regions. PHOG features are selected as they have

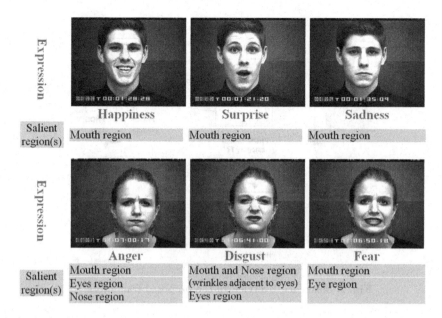

Fig. 1. Summary of the facial regions that emerged as salient for six universal expressions. Salient regions are mentioned according to their importance (for example facial expression of fear has two salient regions but mouth is the most important region according to HVS).

proven to be highly discriminative for FER task [15, 16]. Schematic overview of the proposed framework is illustrated in Fig. 2. Steps of the proposed framework are as follows:

Step 1: The framework initializes with the localization of the mouth region from the input sequence. Then, the PHOG features are extracted from the localized mouth region. The classification ("Classifier-a" in the Fig. 2) is carried out on the basis of extracted features in order to make two groups of facial expressions. First group comprises of those expressions that has one perceptual salient region i.e. happiness, sadness and surprise while the second group is composed of those expressions that have two or more perceptual salient regions i.e. anger, fear and disgust. Purpose of making two groups of expressions is to reduce feature extraction computational time.

Step 2: If the sequence is classified in the first group, then it is classified either as happiness, sadness or surprise by the "Classifier-b". Classification is carried out on the already extracted PHOG features from the salient mouth region.

Step 3: If the input sequence is classified in the second group, then the framework extracts PHOG features from the eyes region and concatenates them with the already extracted PHOG features from the mouth region. Then, the concatenated feature vector is fed to the classifier ("Classifier-c") for the final classification of the sequence.

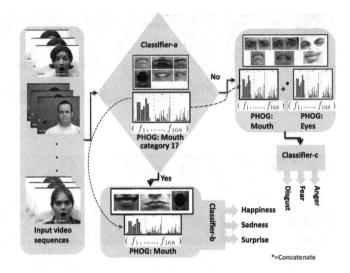

Fig. 2. Schematic overview of the proposed framework

3.1   Feature Extraction Using PHOG

PHOG [14] is a spatial shape descriptor. It first extracts Edge contours of the given stimuli using the Canny edge detector. Then, the image is divided into finer spatial grids by iteratively doubling the number of divisions in each dimension. The grid at level l has 2^l cells along each dimension. Afterwards, a histogram of orientation gradients (HOG) are calculated using 3×3 Sobel mask and the contribution of each edge is weighted according to its magnitude. Within each cell, histogram is quantized into N bins. Each bin represents the accumulation of number of edge orientations within a certain angular range. To obtain the final PHOG descriptor, histograms of gradients (HOG) at the same levels are concatenated. The final PHOG descriptor is a concatenation of HOG at different pyramid levels. Generally, the dimensionality of the PHOG descriptor can be calculated by: $N \sum_l 4^l$. In our experiment we obtained 168 dimensional feature vector $(f_1, ..., f_{168})$ from one facial region, as we created two pyramid levels with 8 bins with the range of [0–360].

4   Affect Recognition Experiment

4.1   First Experiment: High Resolution Image Sequences

To test the effectiveness of the proposed framework on high/full resolution image sequence, we conducted experiment on the CK+ database [12] (which contains six universal facial expressions). The performance of the framework was evaluated using four classifiers i.e. "Support vector machine (SVM)" with χ^2 kernel and $\gamma=1$, "C4.5 Decision Tree" with reduced-error pruning, "Random Forest" of 10 trees and "*2* Nearest Neighbor (2NN)" based on Euclidean distance. The parameters of the classifiers were determined empirically.

For the experiment we used all the 309 sequences from the CK+ database which have FACS coded expression label [17]. The experiment was carried out on the frames which covers the status of onset to apex of the expression, as done by Yang et al. [7]. Region of interest was obtained automatically by using Viola-Jones object detection algorithm [18] and processed to obtain PHOG feature vector. The proposed framework achieved average recognition rate of 95.3%, 95.1%, 96.5% and 96.7% for SVM, C4.5 decision tree, random forest and 2NN respectively. These values were calculated using *10*-fold cross validation. For comparison and reporting results, we have used the classification results obtained by the SVM as it is the most cited method for classification in the literature.

Comparison with the State-of-the-art Methods. Table 1 shows the comparison of the achieved average recognition rate of the proposed framework with the state-of-the-art methods [4–7,19] using the same database (i.e. Cohn-Kanade database). Results from [7] are presented for the two configurations. "[7]a" shows the reported result when the method was evaluated for the last three frames (apex frames) from the sequence while "[7]b" presents the reported result for the frames which encompasses the status from onset to apex of the expression. It can be observed from the Table 1 that the proposed framework is comparable to any other state-of-the-art method in terms of expression recognition accuracy. The method discussed in "[7]b" is directly comparable to our method, as we also employed the same approach. In this configuration, our framework is better in terms of average recognition accuracy.

Behavior of the Classifiers. Figure 3 shows the behavior of the four classifiers used in the experiment. For all the classifiers we have computed the average recognition accuracy using different number of folds (k's) for the k-fold cross validation technique. In k-fold cross validation, features vector set is divided into k equal subsets. k-1 subsets are used for the training while a single set is retained for the testing. The process is repeated k times (k-folds), with each of the k

Table 1. Comparison with the state-of-the-art methods

	Sequence num	Class num	Performance measure	Recog. rate (%)
[4]	313	7	leave-one-out	93.3
[5]	374	6	ten-fold	96.26
[6]	374	6	five-fold	94.5
[19]	375	6	-	93.8
[7]a	352	6	66 % split	92.3
[7]b	352	6	66 % split	80
Ours	**309**	**6**	**ten-fold**	**95.3**

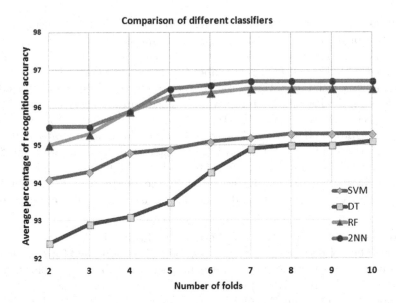

Fig. 3. Evolution of the achieved average recognition accuracy for the six universal facial expressions with the increasing number of folds for the k-fold cross validation technique.

subsets used exactly once for testing. Then, the k estimations from k-folds are averaged to produce final estimated value. Generally, Fig. 3 graphically presents the influence of the size of the training set on the performance of the classifiers. C4.5 decision tree classifier was influenced the most with less training data while 2NN classifier achieved highest recognition rate among the four classifiers with relatively small training set (i.e. 2-folds). This indicates how well our novel feature space was clustered.

4.2 Second Experiment: Generalization on the New Dataset

The aim of the second experiment was to study how well the proposed framework generalizes on the new dataset. According to our knowledge only Valstar et al. [20] have reported such data earlier. Thus, this experiment helps to understand how the framework will behave when it will be used to classify expressions in real life videos.

Experiment was performed in two different scenarios, with the same classifier parameters as the first experiment:

a. In the first scenario samples from the CK+ database were used for the training of different classifiers and samples from FG-NET FEED [21] were used for the testing. Obtained results are presented in Table 2.
b. In the second scenario we used samples from the FG-NET FEED for the training and testing was carried out with the CK+ database samples. Results obtained are presented in Table 3.

Table 2. Average recognition accuracy: training classifier on CK+ database and testing it with FG-NET FEED

	SVM	C4.5 DT	RF	2NN
Training samples	95.3 %	95.1 %	96.5 %	96.7 %
Test samples	80.5 %	72.1 %	71.1 %	80 %

Table 3. Average recognition accuracy: training classifier on FG-NET FEED and testing it with CK+ database

	SVM	C4.5 DT	RF	2NN
Training samples	90.3 %	91.2 %	89.5 %	92.2 %
Test samples	74.4 %	72.2 %	75.4 %	81.9 %

Average recognition accuracies for training phase mentioned in Tables 2 and 3 were calculated using *10*-fold cross validation method.

Second experiment provided a good indication of how accurate the framework will perform in a challenging real life scenario. Results obtained from the second experiment shows that the performance of the framework does not deteriorate significantly even if it is used to classify samples which are different from training samples in terms of lighting conditions, resolution of the video and camera zoom.

4.3   Third Experiment: Low Resolution Image Sequences

There exist many real world applications that require expression recognition system to work amicably on low resolution images. Smart meeting, video conferencing and visual surveillance are some examples of such applications. Ironically most of the existing state-of-the-art methods for expressions recognition report their results only on high resolution images with out reporting results on low resolution images.

We have tested our proposed framework on low resolution images of four different facial resolutions (144×192, 72×96, 36×48, 18×24) based on Cohn-Kanade database as done by Tian [19]. Example of the stimuli with different low resolutions are presented in Fig. 4. Tian's work can be considered as the pioneering work for low resolution image facial expression recognition. Low resolution image sequences were obtained by down sampling the original sequences. All the other experimental parameters are same as the first experiment.

Five different image resolutions (original + four down sampled) were used to evaluate the performance of the proposed framework. For all the classifiers we have computed the average recognition accuracy using *10*-fold cross validation technique. The results are presented in Fig. 5.

It can be observed from the Fig. 5 that the decrease in image spatial resolution is accompanied by the significant decrease in the performance of the proposed framework. Out of all the four tested classifiers, SVM's performance is

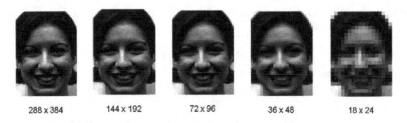

288 x 384   144 x 192   72 x 96   36 x 48   18 x 24

Fig. 4. Example of stimuli with decreasing image resolution. First column shows stimuli in original resolution. Second to fifth column show stimuli in spatial resolution of: 144×192, 72×96, 36×48 and 18×24 respectively.

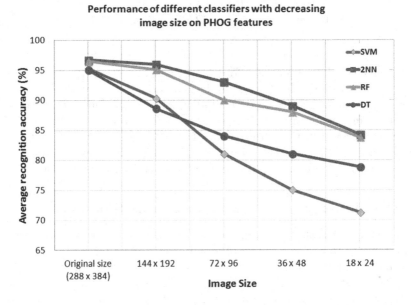

Fig. 5. Robustness of different classifiers for facial expression recognition with decreasing image resolution.

deteriorated the most. The main reason for the drop of performance of the proposed framework is its reliance on the edge/contour based descriptor i.e. PHOG. The first step of the PHOG descriptor is to extract contour information from the given stimuli (for reference see Sect. 3.1) but as the stimuli spatial resoultion gets decreased so does the sharpness of contours. The same can be observed in the Fig. 4. Thus, PHOG fails to extract meaningful information from the low resolution images which explains the cause of bad performance of the framework on low resolution images.

5 Conclusion

Initially, article presented experimental study that provides insight into which facial region(s) emerges as the salient according to human visual attention for the six universal facial expressions. The study provided a evidence that the visual system is mostly attracted towards the mouth region for the expressions of happiness and surprise and it also shows almost the same trend for the expression of sadness. Expressions of disgust, fear and anger shows the interaction of two to three facial regions.

Secondly, article proposed framework for automatic recognition of facial expression/affect. It can be deduced from the presented results that the proposed framework is capable of producing results at par with the other state-of-the-art methods for the stimuli recorded in controlled environment i.e. CK+ database (refer Table 1). By processing only salient regions (based on HVS), proposed framework reduces computational complexity of feature extraction and thus, can be used for real-time applications. Its current unoptimized Matlab implementation runs at 6 frames/second (on windows 7 machine, with i7-2760QM processor and 6 GB RAM) which is enough as facial expressions do not change abruptly.

The proposed framework showed its weakness on low resolution images (refer Sect. 4.3). The proposed framework is unable to cope with stimuli of low resolution or stimuli not having sharp contours. The reason for this weakness is its reliance on the edge/contour based descriptor i.e. PHOG.

Acknowledgment. This project is supported by the Région Rhône-Alpes, France.

References

1. Pantic, M., Pentland, A., Nijholt, A., Huang, T.S.: Human computing and machine understanding of human behavior: a survey. In: Huang, T.S., Nijholt, A., Pantic, M., Pentland, A. (eds.) AI for Human Computing. LNCS (LNAI), vol. 4451, pp. 47–71. Springer, Heidelberg (2007)
2. Zeng, Z., Pantic, M., Roisman, G., Huang, T.: A survey of affect recognition methods: audio, visual, and spontaneous expressions. IEEE Trans. Pattern Anal. Mach. Intell. **31**, 39–58 (2009)
3. Zhaoping, L.: Theoretical understanding of the early visual processes by data compression and data selection. Netw. Comput. Neural Syst. **17**, 301–334 (2006)
4. Littlewort, G., Bartlett, M.S., Fasel, I., Susskind, J., Movellan, J.: Dynamics of facial expression extracted automatically from video. Image Vis. Comput. **24**, 615–625 (2006)
5. Zhao, G., Pietikäinen, M.: Dynamic texture recognition using local binary patterns with an application to facial expressions. IEEE Trans. Pattern Anal. Mach. Intell. **29**, 915–928 (2007)
6. Kotsia, I., Zafeiriou, S., Pitas, I.: Texture and shape information fusion for facial expression and facial action unit recognition. Pattern Recogn. **41**, 833–851 (2008)
7. Yang, P., Liu, Q., Metaxas, D.N.: Exploring facial expressions with compositional features. In: IEEE Conference on Computer Vision and Pattern Recognition (2010)

8. Khan, R.A., Meyer, A., Konik, H., Bouakaz, S.: Framework for reliable, real-time facial expression recognition for low resolution images. Pattern Recogn. Lett. **34**(10), 1159–1168 (2013)
9. Khan, R.A., Meyer, A., Konik, H., Bouakaz, S.: Human vision inspired framework for facial expressions recognition. In: IEEE International Conference on Image Processing (2012)
10. Rajashekar, U., Cormack, L.K., Bovik, A.: Visual search: Structure from noise. In: Eye Tracking Research & Applications Symposium, pp. 119–123 (2002)
11. Ekman, P.: Universals and cultural differences in facial expressions of emotion. In: Cole, J. (ed.) Nebraska Symposium on Motivation, pp. 207–283. Lincoln University of Nebraska Press, Lincoln (1971)
12. Lucey, P., Cohn, J.F., Kanade, T., Saragih, J., Ambadar, Z., Matthews, I.: The extended cohn-kande dataset (CK+): a complete facial expression dataset for action unit and emotion-specified expression. In: IEEE Conference on Computer Vision and Pattern Recognition Workshops (2010)
13. Khan, R.A., Meyer, A., Konik, H., Bouakaz, S.: Exploring human visual system: study to aid the development of automatic facial expression recognition framework. In: Computer Vision and Pattern Recognition Workshop (2012)
14. Dalal, N., Triggs, B.: Histograms of oriented gradients for human detection. In: IEEE Conference on Computer Vision and Pattern Recognition (2005)
15. Bai, Y., Guo, L., Jin, L., Huang, Q.: A novel feature extraction method using pyramid histogram of orientation gradients for smile recognition. In: International Conference on Image Processing (2009)
16. Dhall, A., Asthana, A., Goecke, R., Gedeon, T.: Emotion recognition using PHOG and LPQ features. In: IEEE Automatic Face and Gesture Recognition Conference FG2011, Workshop on Facial Expression Recognition and Analysis Challenge FERA (2011)
17. Ekman, P., Friesen, W.: The Facial Action Coding System: A Technique for the Measurement of Facial Movements. Consulting Psychologist, Palo Alto (1978)
18. Viola, P., Jones, M.: Rapid object detection using a boosted cascade of simple features. In: IEEE Conference on Computer Vision and Pattern Recognition (2001)
19. Tian, Y.: Evaluation of face resolution for expression analysis. In: Computer Vision and Pattern Recognition Workshop (2004)
20. Valstar, M., Patras, I., Pantic, M.: Facial action unit detection using probabilistic actively learned support vector machines on tracked facial point data. In: IEEE Conference on Computer Vision and Pattern Recognition Workshop, pp. 76–84 (2005)
21. Wallhoff, F.: Facial expressions and emotion database (2006), www.mmk.ei.tum.de/waf/fgnet/feedtum.html

Extending Network Life Time of WSN Through an Optimal Number of Aggregator Nodes for Data Aggregation Protocols

Sander Ali Khowaja, Iqra Kanwal Lakho[✉],
and Lachhman Das Dhomeja

Institute of Information and Communication Technology,
University of Sindh, Jamshoro, Pakistan
{sandar.ali,lachhman}@usindh.edu.pk,
iqrakanwallakho@gmail.com

Abstract. Maximization of life of Wireless Sensor Network (WSN) is a challenging task. As WSNs are energy-constraint networks, it is very important for them to use their energy in an efficient manner so that their network life is prolonged. This aspect has attracted many researchers to work on different parameters for determining the method for increasing the efficient energy utilization in WSN. One approach is to choose an optimal number of cluster heads or aggregator nodes for data aggregation. For every protocol in a multi-hop environment an average energy per round is calculated and optimal probability of node becoming the aggregator node is determined and hence a selection of an optimal number of aggregator nodes. This leads to the minimization of the average energy per round for the network in question. In this paper, we carry out the comparative analysis of variants of Distributed Energy Efficient Clustering (DEEC) protocol by following probabilistic approach for calculating the number of cluster heads to analyze the network life time and number of packets transmitted to the base station. The results from comparative analysis provide the basis for further investigating the use of probability factor to extend network life time. We propose a method to dynamically calculate the probability for selecting the optimal number of aggregator nodes to maximize the network lifetime as well as to maximize the number of packets sent to the base station.

Keywords: Wireless sensor networks (WSN) · Aggregator nodes · Data aggregation protocols · Energy consumption in Wireless sensor network (WSN) · Distributed Energy Efficient Clustering (DEEC)

1 Introduction

Wireless Sensor Networks consist of wireless sensor nodes having limited signal processing capability, which sense the data from the environment and send it to the sink (base station) for further processing [4]. Sensor networks can provide several applications including habitants monitoring, collecting information of construction sites, health care monitoring, monitoring directions of enemy, their identity, and observing the field and borders. Since sensors are resource-constrained devices

© Springer International Publishing Switzerland 2014
F.K. Shaikh et al. (Eds.): IMTIC 2013, CCIS 414, pp. 109–120, 2014.
DOI: 10.1007/978-3-319-10987-9_11

(e.g. low CPU power, the development of scalable, robust Wireless Sensor Network) is a challenging task. This area has got focus in research and resulted in various research efforts to address these issues. In wireless sensor networks, different nodes may sense the same data and send it to base station, although it is not required or is already sent by another node. This increases the load on the network. To cope with this issue, data aggregation is used that reduces the packet transmission and hence decreases the energy consumption and redundancy.

Data aggregation protocols provide an opportunity to each sensor node for becoming an aggregator node; it will then be the job of the aggregator node to reduce the communication and to balance the load of the system. Aggregator nodes receive the packets from the members of the sensor network, perform aggregation and forward them to the sink node. Various aggregation protocols, such as Distributed Energy Efficient Clustering (DEEC), Developed Distributed Energy-Efficient Clustering (DDEEC), Enhanced Distributed Energy Efficient Clustering (EDEEC) and Threshold Distributed Energy Efficient Clustering (TDEEC) have been proposed in the literature, which choose or select the aggregator node from sensor network on the basis of the left-over battery power of the sensor nodes – the one which has the highest battery power will be selected as an aggregator node.

Our research adopts the same energy calculation algorithm which has been used by other research efforts focusing on data aggregation. However, we propose our method for selection of an optimal number of cluster nodes. The proposed method calculates the probability dynamically for an optimal selection of aggregator nodes to both maximize the network lifetime and the number of packets sent to the base station.

2   Optimal Clustering Analysis for Data Aggregation Protocols

Optimal number of data aggregator nodes is an important factor in data aggregation protocols and have great significance in extending network life. It is because of these protocols that we have a basis to research on optimizing different parameters to extend the network lifetime. These protocols provide us room for selecting optimal number of aggregator nodes which can gather the data from all sensor nodes and communicate them to the base station when necessary. Following are some data aggregation protocols which are used mostly in sensor networks.

2.1   DEEC (Distributed Energy Efficient Clustering)

Initial and residual energy level is used to select a cluster head [7] in DEEC. DEEC uses ideal lifetime to compute the reference energy that each node should expand during each round [4]. Nodes with high initial and residual energy will have more chances to be the cluster-heads than the nodes with low energy. DEEC achieves longer lifetime and more effective messages than current important clustering protocols in heterogeneous environments [8]. We can have probability threshold with which every node (si) needs to decide either it to be a cluster head in each round as in Eq. 1.

$$T(si) = \begin{cases} \dfrac{pi}{1 - pi\left[rmod\left(1/pi\right)\right]} & si \in G \\ 0 & otherwise \end{cases} \tag{1}$$

pi = 1/ni, which is average probability to be a cluster-head during ni rounds, ni denote the number of rounds to be a cluster head for the node si, G is the set of nodes that have eligibility to be a cluster head. If node si has not got chance to become cluster head in the ni rounds we have $si \in G$ in every r round. Whenever node si itself has eligibility to become cluster head, it chooses a random number between 0 and 1. If the number is smaller than threshold T(si), the node si becomes a cluster-head in the current round [8].

2.2   DDEEC (Developed Distributed Energy-Efficient Clustering)

DDEEC is based on DEEC algorithm where both energy levels i.e. an initial and residual energy is used to select an aggregator. It also estimates the ideal value of network lifetime which is used in computation of reference energy that each node should expand during each round [9].

Difference between DEEC and DDEEC is available in Eq. 2 to become a cluster head, probability is defined to become a cluster head for normal and advance node.

$$pi = \begin{cases} \dfrac{poptEi(r)}{(1+am)\bar{E}(r)} for\ normal\ nodes \\ \dfrac{(1+a)poptEi(r)}{(1+am)\bar{E}(r)} for\ advanced\ nodes \end{cases} \tag{2}$$

It is observed in this expression that nodes having greater residual energy $\bar{E}(r)$ at round r having more probability to be selected as a cluster head. There is a possibility that at some point the energy of advanced nodes will possess same residual energy as normal nodes. As DEEC continues to select these advance nodes but this is not an optimal strategy, because they will always be the cluster head, their energy will start decreasing and will die soon ultimately.

To balance this problem the DDEEC has made some changes in Eq. 1. It is done by using threshold residual energy value ThREV [4].

Here EdisNN is Energy dissipated by a Normal Node in a round and EdisAN is Energy dissipated by an Advanced Node in a round [4].

$$Th_{REV} = Eo\left(1 + \frac{aEdisNN}{EdisNNEdisAN}\right) \tag{3}$$

It can be written as:

$$Th_{REV} = bEo \tag{4}$$

Where:

$$b = \left(1 + \frac{aEdisNN}{EdisNNEdisAN}\right) \tag{5}$$

According to different simulations by researchers the perfect value of b = 0.7 [4].

$$Th_{REV} \simeq \left(\frac{7}{10}\right)Eo \tag{6}$$

The idea behind this is that the normal nodes must also be having the same probability to become aggregator node. Now the average probability p_i will be:

$$pi = \begin{cases} \frac{poptEi(r)}{(1+am)\bar{E}(r)} & for\ Nml\ nodes, Ei(r) > ThREV \\ \frac{(1+a)poptEi(r)}{(1+am)\bar{E}(r)} & for\ adv\ nodes, Ei(r) > ThREV \\ c\frac{(1+a)poptEi(r)}{(1+am)\bar{E}(r)} & for\ Adv, Nml\ nodes, Ei(r) \leq ThREV \end{cases} \tag{7}$$

Where $b \in [0; 1]$ and if b = 0, then we'll be having the traditional DEEC. In Eq. 7, c is a real positive variable which is responsible to control directly the cluster heads [4]. If we increase the c number of cluster heads is increased and if c has value equal to 0 the probability of becoming cluster heads will be 0. In case c = 0; the nodes will send information directly to the base station.

It is observed that the best value of c = 0.2 [4], it increases the network performance.

2.3   EDEEC (Enhanced Distributed Energy Efficient Clustering)

EDEEC is following the same concept (using initial and residual energy) for selection of a cluster head as in of DEEC. Additionally, it includes another node which is known as super node to increase the heterogeneity [11]. Probability of super, advanced and normal nodes will be:

$$p_i = \begin{cases} \frac{p_{opt}E_i(r)}{(1+m.(a+mo.b))\bar{E}(r)} & if\ Si\ is\ normal\ node \\ \frac{(1+a)p_{opt}E_i(r)}{(1+am)\bar{E}(r)} & if\ Si\ is\ advanced\ node \\ c\frac{(1+a)p_{opt}E_i(r)}{(1+am)\bar{E}(r)} & if\ Si\ is\ the\ super\ node \end{cases} \tag{8}$$

Threshold to select cluster head is calculated for normal, super and normal node by:

$$
T_{(si)} =
\begin{cases}
\dfrac{p_i}{1-p_i\left(r\,mod\frac{1}{p_i}\right)} & if\ p_i \in G' \\[2ex]
\dfrac{p_i}{1-p_i\left(r\,mod\frac{1}{p_i}\right)} & if\ p_i \in G'' \\[2ex]
\dfrac{p_i}{1-p_i\left(r\,mod\frac{1}{p_i}\right)} & if\ p_i \in G''' \\[2ex]
0 & otherwise
\end{cases}
\tag{9}
$$

Here, G' is the set of normal nodes which have not got a chance to be cluster head in previous $1/p$ rounds of epoch [5] and si is normal node, G'' is the set of advanced nodes which have not got a chance to be cluster head in previous $1/p$ rounds of epoch and si is advanced node, G''' is the set of super nodes which have not got a chance to be cluster head in previous $1/p$ rounds of epoch and si is super node [11].

Probabilities will be calculated depending on the e average energy of the network at round r, the average energy will be:

$$
\bar{E}(r) = \frac{1}{N} E_{total}\left(1 - \frac{r}{R}\right)
\tag{10}
$$

R = total number of Network lifetime. It can be calculated as:

$$
R = \frac{E_{total}}{E_{round}}
\tag{11}
$$

If we calculate the derivative of E_{round} with respect to k to zero, we can have the optimal number of aggregator node.

$$
k_{opt} = \sqrt{\frac{N}{2\pi}} \frac{M}{d^2_{toBS}} \sqrt{\frac{E_{fs}}{E_{amp}}}
\tag{12}
$$

2.4   TDEEC (Threshold Distributed Energy Efficient Clustering)

TDEEC use the same approach to select an aggregator node and for average estimated energy as in DEEC. On every round, the node will make decision to be an aggregator node or not by selecting a random number from 0 and 1. When number is lower than threshold Ts then the node decides to be an aggregator node for that particular round. Threshold value in TDEEC is adjusted and on the basis of that value, node makes the decision to be an aggregator node by taking residual energy and average energy of the round with respect to optimal number of aggregator nodes [12].

According to TDEEC the threshold value is proposed as:

$$
T_{(s)} =
\begin{cases}
\dfrac{p}{1-p\left(r\,mod\frac{1}{p}\right)} * \dfrac{residual\ energy\ of\ anode * kopt}{average\ energy\ of\ the\ network}
\end{cases}
\tag{13}
$$

3 Simulation Results

In this paper we have simulated the above mentioned clustering protocols and with varying probability of a node for becoming the aggregator node. Initial values have been mentioned in Table 1. While simulating these results we have ignored any energy losses caused by collision of packets and interference caused by channel conditions between different nodes [12]. These simulation results take into consideration the varying probability i.e. 0.5, 0.05, 0.1 for the results shown in Figs. 1, 2, 3 and 4.

Table 1. Initial value parameters

Parameter	Values
Network field	100 m, 100 m
E_o	0.5 J
E_{elec}	50 nJ/bit
E_{fs}	10 nJ/bit/m^2
E_{amp}	0.0013 pJ/bit/m^4
EDA	5 nJ/bit/signal
Message size	4000 bits
d_o (threshold distance)	70 m

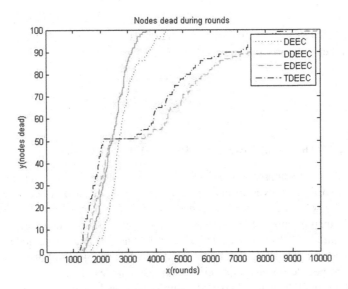

Fig. 1. No. of Dead nodes, Pr = 0.5, No. of nodes = 100

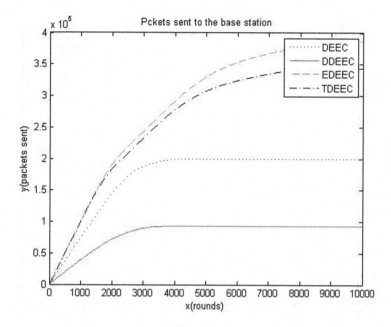

Fig. 2. Packets sent to B.S Pr = 0.5, No. of nodes = 100

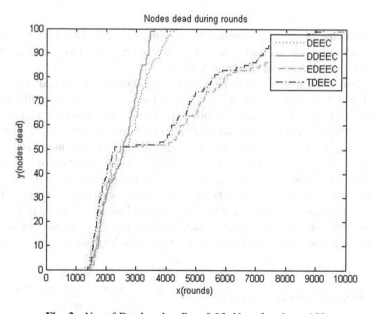

Fig. 3. No. of Dead nodes, Pr = 0.05, No. of nodes = 100

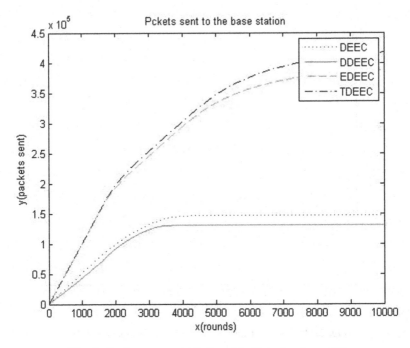

Fig. 4. Packets sent to B.S, Pr = 0.1, No. of nodes = 100

The following results are compiled by varying the probability with four specific values i.e. 0.5, 0.1, 0.05 and 0.01 from simulation for 100 and 50 wireless sensor nodes respectively and tabulated as shown in Table 2.

These results are analyzed from the above figures but are represented in a tabulated form in Table 2 to have a clear image of how the network varies its life time and packets sent to Base station when varying the probability accordingly with the number of nodes deployed in the sensor networks. Though it is difficult to suggest which probability factor to use to extend the network lifetime with a minor change but as suggesting that we should calculate the probability as per the function of initial energy of the sensor nodes and the number of nodes we can propose a method for the optimal probability selection for the nodes being aggregator nodes in the sensor networks. The proposed formula is expressed in Eq. 14. Keeping Figs. 1, 2, 3 and 4 as a reference where we are varying the probabilities manually this equation would give us a clear idea whether the proposed method can yield better results from the results shown in Table 2.

$$Probability\ of\ being\ the\ aggregator\ node = \frac{0.1 * Initial\ Energy\ of\ Sensor}{No.of\ nodes} \tag{14}$$

Table 2. Results for various probabilities and different number of nodes

S. no	Protocol	Probability	No. of nodes	Network Lifetime in terms of (Dead nodes/round)	Packets sent to B.S	Packets sent to Aggregator nodes
1	DEEC	0.5	100	4747	174779	84074
2	DDEEC	0.5	100	3535	90222	140133
3	EDEEC	0.5	100	9264	376751	0
4	TDEEC	0.5	100	9250	378754	0
5	DEEC	0.1	100	4123	117451	137634
6	DDEEC	0.1	100	3454	85001	156776
7	EDEEC	0.1	100	8928	395077	0
8	TDEEC	0.1	100	8898	395478	0
9	DEEC	0.05	100	4467	150324	109607
10	DDEEC	0.05	100	3594	130461	120823
11	EDEEC	0.05	100	9281	382647	0
12	TDEEC	0.05	100	9245	382857	0
13	DEEC	0.01	100	4833	259421	52550
14	DDEEC	0.01	100	4715	263096	50288
15	EDEEC	0.01	100	9342	400447	0
16	TDEEC	0.01	100	9305	401457	0
17	DEEC	0.5	50	4596	92094	41420
18	DDEEC	0.5	50	3633	52594	6665
19	EDEEC	0.5	50	9139	187632	0
20	TDEEC	0.5	50	9130	187750	0
21	DEEC	0.1	50	4946	77458	52130
22	DDEEC	0.1	50	3789	61248	61570
23	EDEEC	0.1	50	9249	195506	0
24	TDEEC	0.1	50	9236	195639	0
25	DEEC	0.05	50	4464	93958	42037
26	DDEEC	0.05	50	4007	88063	45389
27	EDEEC	0.05	50	9221	190563	0
28	TDEEC	0.05	50	9215	190760	0
29	DEEC	0.01	50	5293	145158	14520
30	DDEEC	0.01	50	5252	145767	14164
31	EDEEC	0.01	50	9392	198012	0
32	TDEEC	0.01	50	9364	198236	0

Again simulating the network on the same parameters but with the proposed probability we will get the results shown in Figs. 5 and 6 (Table 3).

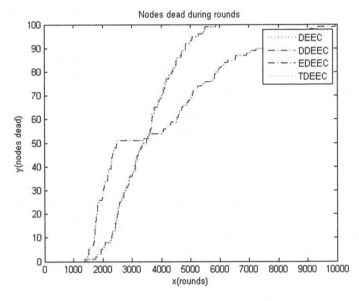

Fig. 5. Dead nodes per round with proposed probability for 100 nodes

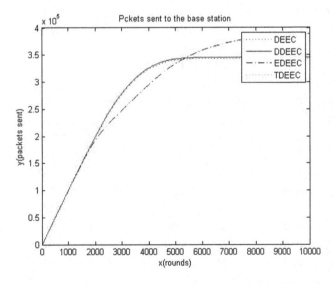

Fig. 6. Packets sent to BS with proposed probability for 100 nodes

Table 3. Results by optimization of probability values

S. no	Protocol	No. of nodes	Network Lifetime in terms of (Dead nodes/round)	Packets sent to B.S	Packets sent to Aggregator nodes
1	DEEC	100	5835	342861	4153
2	DDEEC	100	5877	345215	2392
3	EDEEC	100	9940	389137	0
4	TDEEC	100	9940	389137	0
5	DEEC	50	5672	162445	1961
6	DDEEC	50	5755	162905	1961
7	EDEEC	50	9845	193208	0
8	TDEEC	50	9845	193208	0

4 Conclusions

In this paper we have proposed a Probability Density Function (PDF) that dynamically calculates the probability of each node for being an aggregator node in WSN. Experiments have been conducted using MATLAB to compare existing aggregation protocols for their capability of extending network life time with our proposed approach. Results presented in Figs. 5 and 6 clearly shows that probability of selecting the aggregator nodes using our proposed method not only extends the network life time but also increases the transmission of packets to the base station. The parameters used in the analysis are the same that have been used in existing research works. We have analyzed the results by varying the probability of the node for becoming an aggregator node only while keeping the other parameters constant, whereas existing approaches keep probability constant and vary other parameters.

References

1. Renjith, P.N., Baburaj, E.: An analysis on data aggregation in wireless sensor networks. In: International Conference on Radar Communication and Computing (ICRCC) (2012)
2. Al-Juboori, F.A., Ismaili, S.F.: Performance analysis of variable energy, levels of clustering protocols, for wireless sensor networks. Int. J. Comput. Sci. Issues (IJCSI) (2013)
3. Chen, G., Zhang, X., Yu, J., Wang, M.: An improved LEACH algorithm based on heterogeneous energy on nodes in wireless sensor network. In: International Conference on Computing Management Control and Sensor Network (2012)
4. Elbhiri, B., Saadane, R., El Fkihi, S., Aboutajdine, D.: Developed distributed energy efficient clustering (DDEEC) for heterogeneous wireless sensor networks. In: 5th International Symposium on I/V Communication and Mobile Networks (2010)
5. Qin, Z., Zhou, Z., Zhao, X.: Research on optimal number of cluster heads of wireless sensor networks based on Multi-HOP LEACH. In: IEEE, International Conference on Communications (ICC) (2012)

6. Maraiya, K., et al.: Architectural based data aggregation techniques in wireless sensor networks, a comparative study. Int. J. Comput. Sci. Eng. (2011). ISSN: 09753397, 20110301

7. Pal, V., Singh, G., Yadav, R.P.: Smart cluster head selection scheme for clustering algorithms in wireless sensor networks. Wirel. Sensor Netw. **4**, 273–280 (2012)

8. Qing, L., et al.: Design of a distributed energy efficient, clustering algorithm for heterogeneous wireless sensor networks. Comput. Commun. **29**, 2230–2237 (2006). 20060804

9. Elbhiri, B., et al.: Stochastic and equitable distributed energy efficient clustering for heterogeneous wireless sensor networks. Int. J. Adhoc Ubiq. Comput. **7**, 4–11 (2011)

10. Sheikhpour, R., et al.: Comparison of energy efficient clustering protocols in heterogeneous wireless sensor networks. Int. J. Adv. Sci. Technol. **36**, 27 (2011). ISSN: 20054238, 20111101

11. Saini, P., Sharma, A.K.: Enhanced distributed energy efficient clustering scheme for heterogeneous WSN. In: First International Conference on Parallel Distributed and Grid Computing (PDGC) (2010)

12. Qureshi, T.N., Javaid, N., Malik, M., Qasim, U., Khan, Z.A.: On performance evaluation of variants of DEEC in WSNs. In: 7th International Conference on Broadband Wireless Computing Communication and Applications (2012)

Frequency, Voltage and Temperature Sensor Design for Fire Detection in VLSI Circuit on FPGA

Tanesh Kumar[1(✉)], B. Pandey[1], Teerath Das[1], Sujit Kumar Thakur[1], and Bhavani Shankar Chowdhry[2]

[1] Department of Computer Science, South Asian University, New Delhi, India
tanesh.sitani@hotmail.com, gyancity@gyancity.com,
{teerath.sitani,thakursujitkumar}@gmail.com
[2] Faculty of Electrical and Computer Engineering, MUET, Jamshoro, Pakistan
c.bhawani@ieee.org

Abstract. Fire has both destructive and beneficent qualities. According to Rig Veda, The sacrifices made to Agni (lord of fire) go to the deities because Agni is a messenger from and to the other gods, it is his beneficent quality. Our concern in this work is to control destructive qualities of Fire by airflow, ambient temperature, and the mantra of frequency and voltage. Our target FPGA is 28 nm Kintex-7 FPGA. Xilinx XPower 14.4 is in use to calculate junction temperature with variation in ambient temperature, airflow, voltage and frequency. Kintex-7 is operable until or unless temperature of device is less than 125 °C. Beyond 125 °C temperature, it is destined to burn. To verify Sensor functionality, simple Image Inverter is target design. FPGA caught fire when either frequency reaches 125 GHz or voltage reaches 1.7 V or ambient temperature reaches 45 °C with 250 LFM airflow. When airflow is 500 LFM, frequency threshold is 160 GHz, voltage threshold is 2.1 V and ambient temperature threshold is 60 °C. Therefore, frequency, ambient temperature and voltage sensor is placed to prohibit voltage, ambient temperature and frequency beyond the permissible range to save FPGA from fire.

Keywords: Fire · Ignition temperature · Heat dissipation · Power consumption · Device operating frequency · Voltage supply

1 Introduction

The reason of fire is a temperature beyond the ignition temperature. The ignition temperature is a temperature at which something catches fire and burns on its own. In order to avoid fire, temperature is controlled: by improving the accuracy and performance of sampled thermal simulation at the architectural level [1], by switching off some cores using per-core power gates in [2], by using balance power gradient across vertical stacks based on the assumption of strong thermal correlation among processing cores within a stack [3], by decreasing the oxygen supply for under-ventilated rooms [4], by Light Weight VthHopping (LW-VH) technique to tackle the energy overhead (for performing mode transition) problem [5], by investigating dynamic thermal

© Springer International Publishing Switzerland 2014
F.K. Shaikh et al. (Eds.): IMTIC 2013, CCIS 414, pp. 121–133, 2014.
DOI: 10.1007/978-3-319-10987-9_12

management (DTM) policies under soft thermal constraint that allow the thermal constraint to be violated occasionally for boosting system performance [7], by dynamic thermal management systems track the hot spots during runtime and adjust the performance and the cooling system of the processor when necessary [8]. Close interdependence between temperature and leakage current is discussed in [6], temperature has become a major issue to be considered for power-aware system level design techniques. We are extending the idea of power-aware system level design into fire-aware system level design. In [9] three important factors are discussed regarding Optical Network on Chip (ONoC) power efficiency under temperature variations, and proposed several techniques to reduce the temperature sensitivity of ONoCs. There is thermal compact modeling of integrated optical devices in [10] and their use in an optical circuit level simulator is also demonstrated. A novel waveform sensitivity method for timing evaluation under any body bias and temperature condition is under discussion in [11], which gives us idea to incorporate timing evaluation in our three sensors. In order to control temperature, traditional heat sinks are expected to quickly reach their limits for meeting the cooling needs of 3D ICs. Therefore, a new parameterized dynamic thermal modeling algorithm for emerging thermal-aware design and optimization for high-performance microprocessor design at architecture and package levels [12]. Process variations impose statistical behavior on the temperature and leakage current [14]. A fast circuit simulation technique based on the latency insertion method (LIM) is proposed in [15] for the electro-thermal analysis of circuits and high-performance systems.

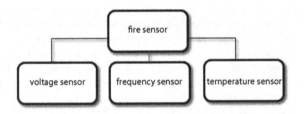

Fig. 1. Fire sensor and its components

The reason of temperature is continuous heat dissipation. More heat means more temperature and less heat means cool device. The reason behind heat is power dissipation in form of heat energy. Power is directly proportional to the frequency and voltage. Therefore, junction temperature of a chip is dependent on the supply voltage and device operating frequency of circuit of FPGA. Temperature of a chip also depends on the temperature of the neighbor chip, ambient temperature and Airflow. Using the above concept, we are designing three internal sensors (voltage sensor, frequency sensor and ambient temperature sensor) in a fire sensor. These three sensors are shown in Fig. 1. Two different Air velocity (distance traveled per unit of time) which is usually expressed in 250 and 500 Linear Feet per Minute (LFM) is under consideration for these entire three sensor. A unique model Wireless Sensor Networks for Intelligent Spaces (WIS), for Smart Civil Structures, which aims to cover utility of WSN in Intelligent Structures, is proposed in [16]. WIS uses smoke detectors that monitor different parts of the building and communicate to track the spread of the fire [16]. We are extending the idea of sensing smoke to sensing frequency, voltage and temperature. We are also extending our base from building to FPGA. References [13, 17, 18] deals with dynamic thermal modeling algorithm for thermal aware design, which gives us idea to tackle temperature in order to control fire and detect fire with the help of temperature. Reference [19] describe working of 40nm FPGA and power dissipation on it, that can be again controlled by clock gating [20].

2   Architecture

There are three types of independent sensor in Fire Sensor as shown in Fig. 2. All are independent of rest two sensors and independently sense the respective Frequency, Voltage and Junction Temperature in Frequency Sensor, Voltage Sensor and Temperature Sensor. All of these 3 sensor invoke two signal one Ring_Fire_Alarm and other No_Fire. Ring_Fire_Alarm is fed to a Fire Alarm, which start ringing when it receive Ring_Fire_Alarm signal from any of these 3 sensors. The main motive to design fire sensor to control voltage, frequency and ambient temperature till it reach their respective fire threshold limit.

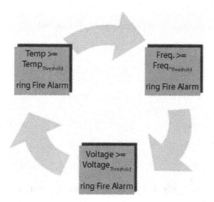

Fig. 2. Control flow in fire sensor

2.1   Frequency Sensor (FS)

FS assumes voltage is default 1.0 V and ambient temperature is default 25 °C and continuously senses only variation in frequency as shown in Fig. 3. It has four inputs and two outputs. These are: Additional Airflow, Frequency Threshold1, Frequency Threshold2, and Operating Frequency. When we varying the device operating frequency of Image Inverter in range of 1 GHz–1 THz, we observed that beyond 125 GHz (i.e. FrequencyThreshold1) with 250 LFM (without additional air flow), FPGA will burn because Junction Temperature will reach 125 °C.

Fig. 3. Top level schematic of frequency sensor

When we provide additional air flow, i.e. to make equivalent airflow of 500 LFM then FrequencyThreshold2 is 160 GHz for this image inverter design. The algorithm of frequency sensor is shown in Algorithm 1 which also explains the working of Fig. 3.

```
module FrequencySensor(
        input   OperatingFrequency,
        input   FrequencyThreshold1,
        input   FrequencyThreshold2,
        input   AdditionalAirFlow,
        output  NoFire,
        output  RingFireAlarm
        );
reg  NoFire;
reg  RingFireAlarm;
always   @ (OperateingFrequency or FrequencyThreshold1 or Frequen-
cyThreshold2 or AdditionalAirFlow)
begin
   if (~AdditionalAirFlow)
      begin
      if (OperateingFrequency<=FrequencyThreshold1)
           NoFire=1;
      else
           RingFireAlarm=1;
   end
   if (AdditionalAirFlow)
      begin
      if(OperateingFrequency<=FrequencyThreshold2)
        NoFire=1;
      else
        RingFireAlarm=1;

      end
   end
endmodule
```

Alg. 1. Frequency Sensor Algorithm

FrequencyThreshold1 is 125 GHz and FrequencyThreshold2 is 160 GHz for this image inverter design. If Additional Airflow is set then it means airflow is 500 LFM and otherwise 250 LFM. The algorithm of frequency sensor is depicted in Algorithm 1.

2.2   Voltage Sensor (VS)

Power is directly proportional to square of voltage. Therefore, temperature also depends on square of voltage. Therefore, x unit change in voltage reflect in x^2 unit change in overall power and somewhat overall temperature. Therefore, voltage may be the primary responsible element to cause fire. Whereas, frequency and ambient temperature play secondary role in order to cause Fire. VS as shown in Fig. 4 assumes frequency is 100 GHz and senses only variation in voltage for two cases. In one case A, Airflow is 250 LFM. In other case B, Airflow is 500 LFM.

Fig. 4. Top level schematic of voltage sensor

When we vary the supply voltage of Image Inverter in range of 0.5 V–2.0 V with step size of 0.1 V, we observed that beyond 1.7 V in case A and 2.1 V in case B, FPGA will burn because Junction Temperature will reach 125 °C. VoltageThreshold1 is 1.7 V and VoltageThreshold2 is 2.1 V for this image inverter design. The functioning of Fig. 4 is further explained in algorithm given in Algorithm 2.

```
module VoltageSensor(
        input SupplyVoltage,
        input VoltageThreshold1,
        input VoltageThreshold2,
        input AdditionalAirFlow,
        output NoFire,
        output RingFireAlarm,
        );
reg NoFire;
reg RingFireAlarm;
always @(SupplyVoltage or VoltageThreshold1 or VoltageThreshold2or Addi-
tionalAirFlow)
begin
    if (~AdditionalAirFlow)
    begin
      if (SupplyVoltage<=VoltageThreshold1)
        NoFire=1;
      else
        RingFireAlarm=1;
    end
    if (AdditionalAirFlow)
      begin
      if (SupplyVoltage<=VoltageThreshold2)
        NoFire=1;
      else
        RingFireAlarm=1;
      end
    end
endmodule
```

Alg. 2. Voltage Sensor Algorithm

2.3   Ambient Temperature Sensor (ATS)

Ambient Temperature is also called Room Temperature. Room Temperature sensor sense the variance of ambient temperature. In Fig. 5, it has four input Additional Airflow, Room Temperature, RoomTemperatureThreshold1 and RoomTemperature-Threshold2. Outputs are No_Fire and Ring_Fire_Alarm Signal.

ATS assumes frequency is 100 GHz and Voltage is 1.0 V and senses only variation in ambient temp for two cases. In one case A, Airflow is 250 LFM. In other case B, Airflow is 500 LFM. The working of Fig. 5 is elaborated in algorithm mentioned in Algorithm 3.

Fig. 5. Top level schematic of ambient temperature sensor

```
`timescale 1ns / 1ps
// Ambient Temperature is also called Room Temperature
module RoomTempSensor(
        input RoomTemperature,
        input RoomTempThreshold1,
        input RoomTempThreshold2,
        input AdditionalAirFlow,
        output NoFire,
        output RingFireAlarm,
        );
reg NoFire;
reg RingFireAlarm;
always @(RoomTemperature or RoomTempThreshold1 or RoomTempThreshold2 or
AdditionalAirFlow)
begin
   if (~AdditionalAirFlow)
   begin
      if (RoomTemperature<=RoomTempThreshold1)
         NoFire=1;
      else
         RingFireAlarm=1;
   end
   if (AdditionalAirFlow)
   begin
      if (RoomTemperature<=RoomTempThreshold2)
         NoFire=1;
      else
         RingFireAlarm=1;
      end
   end
endmodule
```

Alg. 3. Ambient Temperature Sensor Algorithm

In Algorithm 3, algorithm of Ambient Temperature Sensor is shown. When we vary the ambient temperature of Image Inverter in range of 25 °C–60 °C with step size of 5 °C, we observed that beyond 40 °C in case A and 60 °C in case B, FPGA will burn because Junction Temperature will reach 125 °C. Ambient Temperature Threshold1 is 40 °C and Ambient Temperature Threshold2 is 60 °C for this image inverter design. In some case, It is possible that FPGA caught Fire even if Frequency is less than 125 GHz and Voltage is also less than 1.7 V. It may happen due to other factor like airflow, hit sink and room temperature. Therefore, we are using global temperature sensor to sense that temperature is less than 125 °C or not.

2.4 Image Inverter - A Target Design

Image Inverter is Verilog implementation of Invert function in context of Image, which takes a binary or gray level image as input and produces its photographic negative, i.e. dark areas in the input image become light and light areas become dark.

This Image Inverter has 4 inputs and 3 outputs as shown IN Fig. 6. It has 67 basic elements. Out of 67 basic elements, 1 is ground, 8 is inverter, 8 is 2-input LUTs, 9 is

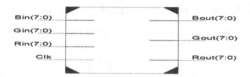

Fig. 6. Image inverter used to verify fire sensor algorithm

3-input LUTs, 8 is 4-input LUTs, 17 are Multiplexer, 16 are XOR with Carry. There are 24 Flip Flops are in use in Image Inverter. There are 48 Input and Output buffers.

3 Evaluation

3.1 Effect of Frequency on Temperature

Since, Power dissipation is directly proportional to the Frequency. Therefore, temperature is directly affected by operating frequency of the device. Here, voltage is taken as constant, i.e., 1.0 V.

Table 1. Frequency versus temperature in FPGA

Period (ns)	Frequency (GHz)	Temperature (°C)
1	1	26.0
0.1	10	33.2
0.001	100	105.8
0.008	125	FIRE ALARM

We are varying frequency in range of 1 GHz–125 GHz on 250 LFM airflow as shown in Table 1 and Fig. 7.

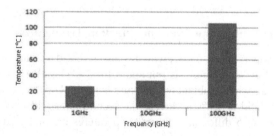

Fig. 7. Comparison of temperature with change in frequency

3.2 Effect of Voltage on Temperature

We know that power dissipation is directly proportional to supply voltage. The dissipation in power creates heat. The heat dissipation contributes in increase of junction temperature, which ultimately contributes for fire.

Here, frequency is constant i.e. 100 GHz. We are varying Voltage in range of 0.5 V–2.0 V as shown in Table 2 and Fig. 8.

Table 2. Effect of voltage on junction temperature of FPGA

Supply voltage (V)	Temperature on 250 LFM air flow (°C)
1.0	105.8
1.1	106.9
1.2	108.2
13	109.8
1.4	111.9
1.5	114.6
1.6	118.4
1.7	124.1
1.8	FIRE ALARM
1.9	FIRE ALARM
2.0	FIRE ALARM

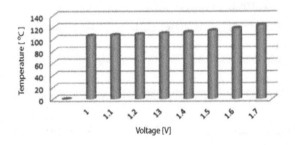

Fig. 8. Comparison of temperature with change in voltage

3.3 Effect of Ambient Temperature on Junction Temperature

Default ambient temperature is 25 °C, which is also referred as Standard Normal Room Temperature. Junction temperature is minimum for 25 °C ambient temperatures. Fire Alarm started ringing when ambient temperature is beyond 45 °C as shown in Table 3. Here, the first threshold is 45 °C, whereas the second threshold is 60 °C.

In Fig. 9, there are 5 different ambient temperatures are under consideration.

3.4 Effect of 500 LFM Air Flow on Temperature

Air velocity (distance traveled per unit of time) is usually expressed in Linear Feet per Minute (LFM). In our consideration we are taking two different airflows, i.e., 250 LFM and 500 LFM.

Table 3. Effect of ambient temperature on junction temperature of FPGA

Ambient temperature (°C)	Junction temperature on 250 LFM air flow (°C)
25	105.8
30	106.9
35	108.2
40	109.8
45	111.9
50	FIRE ALARM

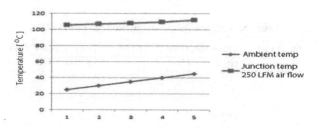

Fig. 9. Comparison of temperature with change in ambient temperature

Table 4. Airflow versus frequency in FPGA

Frequency (GHz)	On 250 LFM (°C)	On 500 LFM (°C)
1	26.0	25.7
10	33.2	31.3
100	105.8	87.3
125	FIRE ALARM	103.1
150	FIRE ALARM	119.1
155	FIRE ALARM	122.3
160	FIRE ALARM	FIRE ALARM

In Table 4 and Fig. 10, voltage is constant i.e. 1.0 V. We are varying frequency in range of 1 GHz–125 GHz for both 250 LFM and 500 LFM. Air velocity (distance traveled per unit of time) is usually expressed in Linear Feet per Minute (LFM).

In Table 5 and Fig. 11, frequency is constant i.e. 100 GHz. We are varying Voltage in range of 05 V–2.0 V for both 250 LFM and 500 LFM. Air velocity (distance traveled per unit of time) is usually expressed in Linear Feet per Minute (LFM).

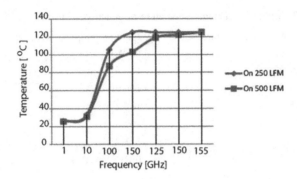

Fig. 10. Relation between airflow, frequency and junction temperature

Table 5. Airflow versus supply voltage in FPGA

Supply voltage (V)	Temperature on 250 LFM air flow (°C)	Temperature on 500 LFM air flow (°C)
0.5	102.1	84.7
0.6	102.7	85.2
0.7	103.4	85.7
0.8	104.1	86.2
0.9	104.9	86.7
1.0	105.8	87.3
1.1	106.9	88.0
1.2	108.2	88.8
1.3	109.8	89.6
1.4	111.9	90.7
1.5	114.6	91.9
1.6	118.4	93.6
1.7	124.1	95.7
1.8	FIRE ALARM	98.5
1.9	FIRE ALARM	102.6
2.0	FIRE ALARM	108.6
2.1	FIRE ALARM	118.7
2.2	FIRE ALARM	FIRE ALARM

In Table 6 and Fig. 12, frequency and voltage is constant i.e. 100 GHz, 1.0 V respectively. We are varying ambient temperature in range of 25 °C–60 °C for both 250 LFM and 500 LFM. We assume that when junction temperature reaches 125 °C, fire alarm start ringing.

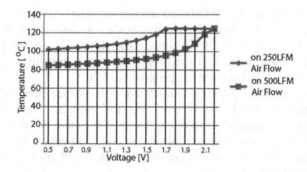

Fig. 11. Relation between airflow, voltage and junction temperature

Table 6. Airflow versus ambient temperature in FPGA

Ambient temperature (°C)	Junction temperature on 250 LFM air flow (°C)	Junction temperature on 250 LFM air flow (°C)
25	105.8	87.3
30	106.9	92.4
35	108.2	97.5
40	109.8	102.7
45	111.9	107.8
50	FIRE ALARM	113.0
55	FIRE ALARM	118.1
60	FIRE ALARM	123.4
Beyond 60 °C	FIRE ALARM	FIRE ALARM

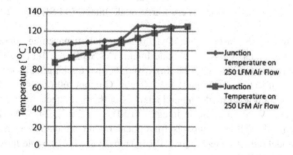

Fig. 12. Relation between airflow, ambient and junction temperature

4   Conclusion and Future Directions

For 250 LFM airflow, there is 125 GHz frequency threshold, when voltage is 1.0 V and ambient temperature is 25 °C. There is 1.7 V voltage thresholds, when frequency is 100 GHz and ambient temperature is 25 °C. There is 45 °C ambient temperature threshold, when frequency is 100 GHz and ambient temperature is 25 °C. For 500 LFM airflow, there is 160 GHz frequency threshold, when voltage is 1.0 V and ambient temperature is 25 °C. There is 2.1 V voltage thresholds, when frequency is 100 GHz and ambient temperature is 25 °C. There is 60 °C ambient temperature threshold, when frequency is 100 GHz and ambient temperature is 25 °C.

In this work, we are calculating frequency threshold, voltage threshold and ambient temperature threshold for Image Inverter. We can calculate frequency threshold, voltage threshold and ambient temperature threshold for more complex design ALU, microprocessor. We are implementing this design on 28 nm FPGA. Therefore, there is open scope to redesign and re-implement this work on 16 nm future ultra scale FPGA in order to get wide threshold.

References

1. Ardestani, E.K., Martinez, F.J., Southern, G., Ebrahimi, E., Renau, J.: Sampling in thermal simulation of processors: measurement, characterization, and evaluation. IEEE Trans. Comput. Aided Des. Integr. Circuits Syst. **32**(8), 1187–1200 (2013)
2. Lee, J., Kim, N.S.: Analyzing potential throughput improvement of power- and thermal-constrained multicore processors by exploiting DVFS and PCPG. IEEE Trans. Very Large Scale Integr. (VLSI) Syst. **20**(2), 225–235 (2012)
3. Cheng, Y., Zhang, L., Han, Y., Li, X.: Thermal-constrained task allocation for interconnect energy reduction in 3-D homogeneous MPSoCs. IEEE Trans. Very Large Scale Integr. (VLSI) Syst. **20**(2), 239–249 (2013)
4. Quintiere, J.G.: Fundamentals of Fire Phenomena. Wiley, West Sussex (2006)
5. Xu, H., Jone, W.B., Vemuri, R.: Aggressive runtime leakage control through adaptive light-weight V_{th} hopping with temperature and process variation. IEEE Trans. Very Large Scale Integr. (VLSI) Syst. **19**(7), 1319–1323 (2011)
6. Bao, M., Andrei, A., Eles, P., Peng, Z.: Temperature-aware idle time distribution for leakage energy optimization. IEEE Trans. Very Large Scale Integr. (VLSI) Syst. **20**(7), 1187–1200 (2012)
7. Shi, B., Zhang, Y., Srivastava, A.: Dynamic thermal management under soft thermal constraints. IEEE Trans. Very Large Scale Integr. (VLSI) Syst. **21**(11), 2045–2054 (2013)
8. Reda, S., Cochran, R.J., Nowroz, A.N.: Improved thermal tracking for processors using hard and soft sensor allocation techniques. IEEE Trans. Comput. **60**(6), 841–851 (2011)
9. Ye, Y., et al.: System-level modeling and analysis of thermal effects in optical networks-on-chip. IEEE Trans. Very Large Scale Integr. (VLSI) Syst. **21**(2), 292–305 (2013)
10. Burke, D., Smy, T.: Thermal models for optical circuit simulation using a finite cloud method and model reduction techniques. IEEE Trans. Very Large Scale Integr. (VLSI) Syst. **32**(8), 1177–1186 (2013)
11. Gupta, S., Sapatnekar, S.S.: Compact current source models for timing analysis under temperature and body bias variations. IEEE Trans. Very Large Scale Integr. (VLSI) Syst. **20**(11), 2104–2117 (2012)
12. Feng, Z., Li, P.: Fast thermal analysis on GPU for 3D ICs with integrated micro channel cooling. IEEE Trans. Very Large Scale Integr. (VLSI) Syst. **21**(8), 1526–1539 (2013)
13. Eguia, T.J.: General parameterized thermal modeling for high-performance microprocessor design. IEEE Trans. Very Large Scale Integr. (VLSI) Syst. **20**(2), 211–224 (2012)

14. Haghdad, K., Anis, M.: Power yield analysis under process and temperature variations. IEEE Trans. Very Large Scale Integr. (VLSI) Syst. **20**(10), 1794–1803 (2012)
15. Klokotov, D., Schutt, J.E.: Latency insertion method (LIM) for electro-thermal analysis of 3-D integrated systems at pre layout design stages. Compon. Packag. Manuf. Technol. **3**(7), 1138–1147 (2013)
16. Chowdhry, B.S., Shardha, K.K., Naeem, U., Rajput, A.Q.: Development of wireless sensor networks for smart civil structures and highway safety. In: IEEE International Conference on Signal Processing and Communications, pp. 420–423 (2007)
17. Hassan, Z.: Full spectrum spatial temporal dynamic thermal analysis for nanometer scale integrated circuits. IEEE Trans. Very Large Scale Integr. (VLSI) Syst. **19**(12), 2276–2289 (2012)
18. Long, J., Dawei, L., Memik, S.O., Ulgen, S.: Theory and analysis for optimization of on-chip thermoelectric cooling systems. IEEE Trans. Comput. Aided Des. Integr. Circuits Syst. **32**(10), 1628–1632 (2013)
19. Pandey, B., Yadav, J., Singh, Y., Kumar, R., Patel, S.: Energy efficient design and implementation of ALU on 40-nm FPGA. In: IEEE International Conference on Energy Efficient Technologies for Sustainability-(ICEETs), Nagercoil, Tamilnadu, 10–12 April 2013
20. Li, L., Choi, K.: Activity driven optimised bus specific clock gating for ultra low power smart space application. IET Commun. **5**(17), 2501–2508 (2011). ISSN:1751-8628

Energy Hole Minimization Technique for Energy Efficient Routing in Under Water Sensor Networks

Kamran Latif[1,2], Malik Najmus Saqib[1,2], Safdar H. Bouk[1,2], and Nadeem Javaid[1,2(✉)]

[1] National Institute of Electronics, Islamabad, Pakistan
[2] COMSATS Institute of Information Technology, Islamabad, Pakistan
nadeemjavaid@comsats.edu.pk

Abstract. Energy conservation is one of the challenging tasks in Wireless Sensor Networks (WSNs) whether deployed on ground or underwater. Applications of Underwater Sensor Networks (UWSNs) are gradually increasing due to the remote nature of control and automatic data transmission to onshore base stations. However, this automatic mechanism of WSNs is totally based on their built-in battery, which can not be replaced during network operation. Depth based routing is a popular routing technique which, do not needs full dimensional location information. However, consideration of depth and residual energy information for selection of next hop are not enough for balanced energy consumption of WSNs. In this research work, we identified the areas where energy is consumed most in depth based routing techniques. Due to which energy hole may be created. In addition we introduced Receive Signal Strength Indicator (RSSI) based location identification and multilevel power transmission in depth based routing technique. Simulation result shows that the proposed technique gives better results than its counterparts.

Keywords: Underwater wireless sensor networks · Routing protocols · Depth based routing

1 Introduction

Importance of WSNs is increasing day by day. Whether it is a defence application or medical application or industrial application, WSNs play an important role in data collection. Now WSNs are getting attention in oceanographic data collection. A variety of applications in oceanography need WSNs assistance. For example underwater pollution monitoring, disaster management, tsunami and seaquake predilections etc. Traditional data collection techniques such as remote telemetry and sequential local sensing are insufficient to full fill the needs of different applications [1] mentioned earlier. In UWSNs, sensor nodes are deployed in certain area of under water.

In this paper, the convention WSNs is used for terrestrial WSNs. UWSNs differ in characteristics from WSNs. For example deployment of nodes in WSNs

© Springer International Publishing Switzerland 2014
F.K. Shaikh et al. (Eds.): IMTIC 2013, CCIS 414, pp. 134–148, 2014.
DOI: 10.1007/978-3-319-10987-9_13

is generally in 2-dimensions while nodes in UWSNs are mostly deployed in 3-dimensions. WSNs use radio modems for communication while UWSNs use acoustic modems for communication. Acoustic modems consumes more energy as compared to radio modems although communication range of acoustic modem is greater than radio modem. Many factors like multi path, path loss, doppler spread, and noise effect acoustic communication channels [2].

Routing techniques of UWSNs are generally categorized into location based protocol and localization free protocol. In location based protocols, it is assumed that each node knows, its own location, location of the node to which data is to be forwarded and the location of the sink. Different routing protocols use different techniques to find the location of the nodes. As GPS signal can not propagate deep through underwater therefore different localization schemes [2–4] have been proposed in the literature. However, in general accurate localization is possible only through some sort of assistance from GPS. That is surface node (sink) equipped with GPS and underwater nodes may take relative position from surface nodes. Although localization improves the efficiency and help to design efficient algorithms, but at a higher cost. On the other hand location free algorithms use some sort of existing information for direction finding or selection of next hop node. Each node knows its depth with the help of a depth sensor.

In this article we formulate a mathematical model of energy consumption analysis of Depth Based Routing (DBR) protocol [5] and Energy Efficient Dept Based Routing (EEDBR) protocol [6]. From the analysis we found, how energy is consumed in the protocols and how energy holes are created during network operation. Then we introduces a new energy efficient technique for UWSNs. In our technique we used RSSI as location finder of the destination node. Depth and residual energy information are used to select the next hop node. Multiple power levels are used for transmitting data from source to next hop node. We also used pickaback technique for information sharing instead of frequent execution of Knowledge Acquisition Phase (KAP). Our work is supported with MATLAB simulations.

Rest of this article is organised as follows: in Sect. 2, a brief related research work is presented. Section 3 presents motivation. In Sect. 4, energy hole analysis of the close related work is performed. Section 5 presents the proposed technique. In Sect. 6 simulations in MATLAB are performed, results are discussed and compared with existing techniques. Conclusion and future directions are presented in Sect. 7.

2   Related Work

Energy conservation is a hot issue, whether it is WSNs or UWSNs. However due to different communication devices in WSNs and UWSNs, energy consumes differently in these networks. In this section we little elaborate our previous research efforts regarding energy conservation and then we briefly discuss efforts of research community in this regard.

In our previous work [7,8], we have identified energy holes in traditional famous WSNs scheme. In this work, we found that how energy is consumed in clustered WSNs and formulated a mathematical model for energy consumption of WSNs. We also introduced an energy efficient routing technique based on our mathematical formulation.

S. Ahmed, *et.al.*, presents a detailed survey on UWSNs routing techniques in [9]. The comparative analysis of UWSNs protocol provide assistance in selection of a specific protocol for certain network environment.

In UWSNs, not much work is done on energy hole detection however, different energy efficient routing techniques have been introduced in the literature. Due to unique characteristics of UWSNs communication these techniques are categorized on the bases of depth, location and trajectory etc.

In [5], authors proposed depth based routing strategy for UWSNs. Sensor nodes forward data to nodes, which are at minimum depth. In this protocol energy is conserved up to some extent. Only depth factor is considered for next hop selection due to which unbalanced energy consumption distribution is created in the network. This unbalanced energy consumption distribution causes creation of energy holes. Due to creation of energy hole end-to-end delay also increases.

A. Wahid and D. Kim in [6] introduces localization free protocol for UWSNs. To balance energy consumption in the network authors considered residual energy of sensor node along with depth as next hop selection parameters. Although the objective of balanced energy consumption is achieved up to some extent, but tradeoff is made on frequent execution of KAP. The consequence of which is creation of energy holes and larger end-to-end delay.

To improve the performance of their previous technique, A. Wahid, *et.al* in [10], introduces a new routing technique for UWSNs. In this work, authors calculated physical distances between sensor nodes and sink nodes on the bases of Time of Arrival (ToA) and Time Difference of Arrival (TDoA). Author uses physical distance instead of depth as selection parameter for next hop. Although the performance of their protocol is improved from previous version however, the problem of frequent execution of KAP is not addressed.

Vector Based Forwarding (VBF) is introduced in [2]. VBF is location based protocol. In VBF a directional path is formed from source to sink to forward the data. Nodes along this path forward their data through nodes with in this path only which is a kind of controlled flooding. Although authors succeeded in saving energy through controlled flooding however, localization in UWSNs is a difficult task and in case of sparse network when relay nodes start dying in a path then live nodes can not forward their data.

Hop-by-Hop Vector Based Forwarding (HHVBF) is another location based routing protocol introduced in [11]. In HHVBF, path calculation is made on per hop bases. HHVBF improves its performance over VBF by removing the limitation of limited radius of the path however, this improvement do not remove the possibility of dead nodes in the path which restricts forwarder to forward data.

Focussed Beam Routing (FBR) [12] is proposed by N. Nicolaou, A. See and P. Xie. In FBR, a range of transmission power levels are used to identify the relay nodes. If RTS and CTS exchange mechanism between source and relay node in a certain power level is successful then source node record it as relay node. FBR is also a location based routing protocol. In FBR RTS/CTS mechanism consumes energy which deterred its performance from energy consumption perspective.

Threshold-optimized Depth-based routing (AMCTD) scheme is proposed in [13]. This scheme explores the different variations of depth threshold and implements an optimal weight function to enhance network lifetime. Author also introduces adaptive mobility of courier nodes in this scheme. However introduction of courier nodes is an expensive solution in terms of cost and end to end delay of packets.

3   Motivation

In this research article, our objective is to propose an energy efficient routing protocol for UWSNs keeping in view the harsh conditions of underwater environment and available technology. A detailed literature review elaborated the gaps in existing research work which, motivated us to improve them. We focused our research work by analysing two famous depth based routing protocols; DBR and EEDBR. We analysed these protocols and found following gaps.

- DBR and EEDBR assume nodes in the bottom of ocean surface can sense data only, all other nodes act as relay nodes. However, there are many applications, e.g., in monitoring missions, in which ocean column sensing is required. Therefore in such applications all nodes have sensing and relaying capabilities. Which needs improved routing strategy.
- DBR and EEDBR executes KAP for information sharing and knowledge up-dation. Frequency of Execution of KAP is a trade-off between node's knowledge up-dation about residual energy and energy consumption. Therefore we can say that if F is the frequency of execution of KAP and E_c is the energy consumption then, we can establish the following relation.

$$F \propto E_c \tag{1}$$

On the other hand if frequency of execution of KAP is reduced to conserve energy then nodes remain unaware about the residual energy status. Consequence of which is same node will be selected as relay node again and again. Which ultimately depletes the node energy quickly and energy hole is created.
- In DBR and EEDBR data is transmitted from source to relay node at fixed power level. In the initial phase of the network it may seems fine, but as the network evolves, residual energy of the nodes change. In this case sending data to relay node which is in the near vicinity of forwarder node at fix transmission power is a waste of energy.

4   Energy Hole Analysis in DBR and EEDBR

In DBR and EEDBR protocols, data is routed through multi-hop communication strategy. Originator node broadcasts data. Nodes in the communication radius of originator node receive data and the node which is at the highest level in the communication radius again broadcasts data and so on. This process repeats until data reaches from source to sink. In rest of this section, we analyse how energy is consumed in this process. We have divided energy consumption analysis in two major portions: energy consumption in reception and energy consumption in transmission.

4.1   Energy Consumption in Reception

Generally there are two types of nodes in UWSNs; originator nodes and forwarder nodes. If there are $totaln$-number of nodes in 3-dimensional cube of surface area $6a^2$ and we assume that p-number of nodes broadcast data simultaneously from uniform distant sensing areas then energy consumption in reception of receiving nodes is given by Eq. 2

$$Rx_{En\_all} = (n - p)R_{energy} \tag{2}$$

Receive energy of forwarder node consumes differently. The communication hierarchy of UWSNs nodes' is like a directed tree graph as shown in Fig. 1, in which data travels from leaf to root node. Therefore, amount of data received at forwarder node depends on the number of children (c) of forwarder node and the hierarchical level (i) at which forwarder node exists. Higher the hierarchical level of forwarder node more data will be received. Equation 4 gives the energy consumption of forwarder node at ith hierarchical level.

$$D_i = \sum_{k=1}^{c} \ell_k + \ell, \quad 2 <= i <= n, \tag{3}$$

where D_i is the amount of data gathered at i^{th} hierarchical level, and ℓ is the amount of data of kth child.

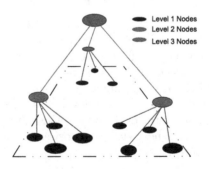

Fig. 1. Data receive hierarchy

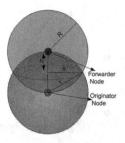

Fig. 2. Area of nodes affected due to overhearing

$$Rx_{En\_all}^{F} = D_i R_{energy} \tag{4}$$

To avoid retransmissions of same packets, depth based routing protocols use over-hearing mechanism. An originator node when transmit a packet all the nodes in range receive packet and calculate holding time. The minimum depth node due to its shortest holding time forward the packet and nodes in common vicinity of forwarder and originator node receive same packet again thus, avoiding retransmission of the same packet. This phenomena is called overhearing. However, nodes in common vicinity of forwarder and originator node expand receive energy. Figure 2 shows the common region of the two spheres. Volume of the common spherical region V_{com} is given by Eq. 5 and receive energy consumption of the nodes in this common spherical region is given by Eq. 6.

$$V_{com} = \pi h/6(3a^2 + h^2) \tag{5}$$

Receive energy consumption of nodes in common region:

$$R_x^{com} = \rho V_{com} \ell R_{energy} \tag{6}$$

Total energy consumed in reception of entire network is given by Eq. 7.

$$Rx_{En}^{Total} = Rx_{En\_all} + Rx_{En\_all}^{F} + R_x com \tag{7}$$

4.2 Energy Consumption in Transmission

Figure 3 shows the broadcast scheme of depth based routing protocols. Originator node transmits fixed amount of data while forwarder node has to relay the traffic. In order to find the energy consumption of forwarder node it is necessary to find the volume of traffic forwarder node has to relay. Equation 3 computes the amount of data gathers at forwarder node at any hierarchical level. if (Φ) is data aggregation energy then transmit energy of forwarder node is given by Eq. 8.

$$Tx_{En}^{F} = D_i \Phi T_{energy} \tag{8}$$

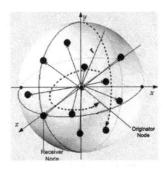

Fig. 3. Broadcast message received by nodes within transmission radius of originator node

If there are m number of forwarder nodes then total energy consumption of all forwarder nodes is calculated in Eq. 9

$$Tx^F_{En\_all} = mD_i \Phi T_{energy} \qquad (9)$$

If there are n number of nodes out of which m numbers are forwarder nodes then transmit energy of all originator nodes can be calculated from Eq. 10

$$Tx^N_{En\_all} = (n - m)T_{energy} \qquad (10)$$

By adding transmission energy of originator and forwarder nodes in Eq. 11, we can get the total energy consumption in transmission of entire network.

$$Tx^{Total}_{En} = Tx^N_{En\_all} + Tx^F_{En\_all} \qquad (11)$$

4.3   Analysis

In DBR and EEDBR, originator node transmits data and all nodes in communication range receive data as shown in Fig. 3. If ρ is the node density per unit area and ℓ bits data is transmitted then Eq. 13 gives the energy consumption of nodes in radius (r).

$$Number\ of\ nodes\ in\ radius\ (r) = 4\pi r^2 \rho \qquad (12)$$

$$Rx^{sphere}_{En} = (4\pi r^2 \rho - 1)\ell R_{energy} \qquad (13)$$

Node density plays an important role in the energy consumption. As nodes are randomly deployed therefore, if in certain area nodes become dense, so energy consumption in dense area becomes higher. The reason is: nodes are in near vicinity to each other therefore, more nodes receive broadcast message and deplete.

5   Proposed Protocol

This section describes detail design of our proposed protocol; Pick a Back Depth Based Routing (PB-DBR). First we describe network architecture adopted for our proposed protocol and then, we describe detail operation of proposed technique.

5.1   Network Model

Due to strong signal attenuation, multi-path propagation, time variation of the channel and limited bandwidth in under water communication [14], underwater data communication is feasible through acoustic waves only. Therefore, sensor nodes are equipped with acoustic modems. Characteristics of acoustic modems varies according to the nature of application. However, the basic characteristics needed for almost all of the application are transmission range, transmission power levels, lifetime of battery. It is also important from energy conservation perspective that how much energy an acoustic modem consumes during transmission, receive and idle modes and in different transmission power levels. Characteristics of acoustic modem used in our simulations are: 2.5 mW power consumption in stand-by mode, 5-285 mW power consumption in listening mode, and 1.1 mW power consumed in receive mode. In transmission mode, modem consumes power for three different ranges: for 250 m power consumption is 5.5 W, for 500 m power consumption is 8 W, and for 1000 m power consumption is 18 W. We also assume variable gain characteristic embedded in the acoustic modem [15]. This feature is like RSSI in RF modems. With the help of this characteristics we can identify the distance between two sensor nodes. The deployment of the nodes in UWSNs is in three dimension. In our protocol we have assumed three dimensional architecture. Sensor nodes are floating in different depths to monitor ocean columns. Radius r of sphere determines the communication range of a sensor node. Three dimensional deployment of nodes is shown in Fig. 4. Movement of the sensor node is almost negligible. Nodes are anchored to the bottom of the ocean and depth is controlled with the length of the wire that connects sensor with anchor [16]. The floating capability of sensor node is created with the help of floating buoy attached with sensor node. We have deployed five sinks at the ocean surface. Sinks are equipped with acoustic and radio modems. Onshore communication is performed with radio link and under water communication through acoustic modem. Sinks are assumed to be free of energy problem.

5.2   KAP in PB-DBR

In KAP, sensor nodes exchange depth, location and residual energy information. We have used RSSI as location finder. Although Electromagnetic (EM) Waves are highly attenuated in water, but their reducing trend is very clear [17]. Therefore EM waves can be used for distance measurement in underwater sensor networks. In this research work we have used MoteTrack [18] localization scheme

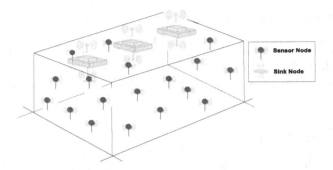

Fig. 4. Deployment of sensor nodes and sink nodes

to identify the nodes location. MoteTrack uses RSSI signature for location finger-printing. The location of the node once identified is permanently stored because the movement of water currents is horizontal and vertical movement is almost negligible [11].

After identification of node locations next step in KAP is to share depth and residual energy information. Each node broadcasts hello packet containing depth, residual energy, node id and node location. Each node maintain a sorted list of those nodes which are with in the communication range of maximum power level and pre-set threshold value. List is sorted on the basis of depth parameter.

In our proposed technique KAP is executed only once in startup to save energy. Hello packet is broadcasted by each node. Hello packet contains information about node depth, location, residual energy and node ID. Nodes with in the transmission range of broadcast node receive information and maintain a list of nodes in neighbouring vicinity of pre-set threshold value. KAP is an important phase in actual protocol operation. Nodes on the basis of these information select next hop node. However, execution of KAP costs transmission and receive energy of nodes. In energy analysis phase we identified the energy cost of transmission and receive operation.

5.3 Steady State Phase

This section describes actual data transmission from originator node to sink node. In ocean column sensing application all nodes have the sensing capability unlike bottom sensing applications where, only bottom sensors have the sensing capability and other nodes act as relay nodes. Therefore, in column sensing applications all nodes sense data and all nodes except bottom nodes relay data therefore, data aggregation is required at relay nodes. In UWSNs finding the best possible next hop from energy conservation perspective is a challenging task. As mentioned in related work section different protocols uses different parameters like depth, residual energy, distance, etc., for next hop selection.

After initiation of data from originator node next step is to find forwarder node. As originator node broadcasts data, all nodes in the communication range of originator node receive data packet. All nodes in communication range calculate holding time. Holding time calculation is adopted from [6]. However, a new parameter d is added in Eq. 14 to resolve the issue of selection of forwarder node among nodes with same residual energy. Equation 14 calculates holding time.

$$H_t = (1 - \frac{C_e}{I_e \times d}) \times Max_{H_t} + p \qquad (14)$$

Where C_e is current energy, I_e is initial energy, p is the priority value of packet in the list, d is the depth of the node and Max_{H_t} is the maximum time a node can hold a packet, after expiry of Max_{H_t} and no over hearing, packet is broadcasted.

Holding time is inversely proportional to C_e. Greater the C_e, smaller will be the holding time. However, there may arise a case when two nodes have same C_e. In such a case decision is made on the basis of depth, that is, node with smaller depth have minimum holding time. There is a possibility that when both C_e and d are same, in such a case the node ID which appear first in the list is selected as forwarder node.

After selection of forwarder node next step is to select transmission power level. Each node knows the location information of all its neighbouring nodes with in transmission range. Originator node calculate its distance from the forwarder node and selects transmission power level accordingly. As the network evolves energy of nodes decreases therefore, it is possible that a node x has energy information about node y as $m - joules$ at time (t_1) which is highest in the list. At time (t_2) the energy of node y changes from $m - joules$ to $n - joules$, where $(m > n)$. In this case if node x is not aware about the new energy status of node y at time (t_2) then node y is again selected as forwarder node which may lead to wrong selection of forwarder node and imbalance consumption of energy. Therefore, it is necessary to update the knowledge about residual energy of the nodes to avoid creation of energy holes. Frequent execution of KAP solves this problem, but frequent execution of KAP costs energy and delayed execution of KAP cause energy holes. To avoid this problem we introduced pickaback technique in our protocol to save energy and regular update of energy information. The depth and location of the nodes are almost fixed, residual energy changes with the passage of time. On broadcast of data packet broadcast node also embed residual energy information in the data packet. All receiving nodes update residual energy information and discard rest of data, only node with matching ID forward data.

6   Simulation Results and Discussions

This section presents the simulations of the proposed protocol. As our research focuses on depth based routing protocols therefore, we have selected the most widely used routing protocols; DBR and EEDBR for comparison.

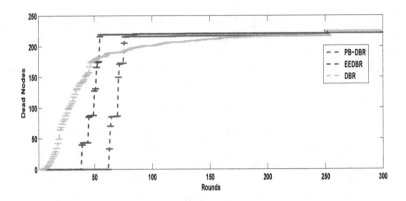

Fig. 5. Dead nodes comparison

6.1 Simulation Environment

MATLAB v7.8.0.347 R2009a is selected as a simulator. Area of 500 m depth by 500 m length by 500 m width is taken as sensing field. Initially 225 sensor nodes are deployed with poisson random distribution. Transmission range of each sensor node is scale down to 100 m, 50 m and 25 m according to acoustic modem's different transmission power levels. Data packet size is taken as 65 bytes. One byte is reserved for current energy status of sensor node. Initially all sensor nodes are homogenously energised. Average results are taken from five time simulations performed. Confidence interval shows the range of best results obtained.

6.2 Number of Dead Nodes

From Fig. 5, it is clear that PB-DBR leads in network life time. Figure 5 shows that first node dead time of PB-DBR is remarkably increased. This is because their distance with sink fall in the lowest transmission power level therefore, their energy is remarkably conserved and they are still alive although rest of the nodes has been died. The major issue that is faced in EEDBR and DBR is that nodes near sink are overloaded of relaying traffic. Due to over load of traffic their energy deplete quickly and energy holes created near sink.

6.3 Number of Packets Received at Sink

Due to enhanced network life time and balanced energy consumption of all nodes ratio of packets received at sink of PB-DBR is also increased as shown in Fig. 6. Reason behind increase in delivery ratio is that the chance of path loss is minimized due to balanced energy consumption and nodes are timely updated about residual energy of their next forwarder node. Therefore, in PB-DBR there is a minimum chance that a node selected as forwarder node is live in forwarder list, but actually it is died. Which is the main problem in EEDBR that if KAP is not

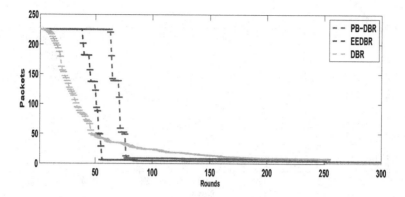

Fig. 6. Packets received at sink

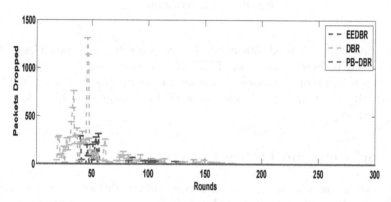

Fig. 7. Packets dropped

executed frequently nodes are not well aware about the real status of residual energy of their neighboring nodes and frequent execution of KAP costs energy.

6.4 Number of Packets Dropped in Network

Packet drop is another useful metric of network performance evaluation. Packets drop of PB-DBR is remarkably decreased as shown in Fig. 7. Uniform energy consumption of nodes create less energy holes. If a hole is created at any location then packet may take another path to reach at sink. Although it is at the cost of end-to-end delay because when a packet stuck into energy hole it is rebroadcasted by another neighboring node when its holding time elapse.

6.5 Energy Consumption(joules)

Main goal of this technique is how to save energy. Figure 8 shows that PB-DBR consumes less energy than its counterparts. The reason behind less energy

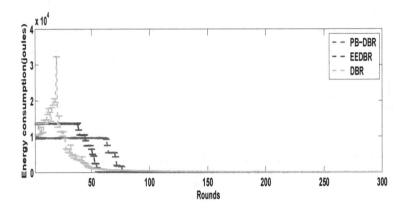

Fig. 8. Energy consumption

consumption is that we used transmission power levels for data transmission from source to relay node while DBR and EEDBR uses fixed transmission power level. Other reason is use of pickaback technique for information sharing while DBR and EEDBR uses frequent execution of KAP for information up-dation which consumes energy.

7   Conclusion and Future Directions

In this research article, we presented a new energy efficient routing technique for UWSNs. We mathematically analysed depth based routing protocols. From the analysis we found how energy is consumed during network operation. The processes which consume more energy become the reason for creation of energy holes. Pickaback technique is introduced to overcome the creation of energy holes. We also introduced RSSI based location identification mechanism in our technique. Once nodes become aware about location of other nodes then it become easy to find the distance between source node and destination node. Identification of location is also helpful in using multilevel power transmission mechanism. This helps to conserve energy remarkably.

Research work is always a trade-off between gain and loss. Although in this research work we have used multilevel power transmission acoustic modems which ultimately increases the cost of overall system. Secondly, change of transmission power level is an energy consumption process although it is less than transmit or receive energy. Third switching of transmission power level is time consuming job which may create delay in packet transmissions. As these issues are majorally related with physical or MAC layer therefore, we are interested to integrate MAC protocols like [19–21] with our routing scheme in future.

References

1. Pompili, D., Melodia, T., Akyildiz, I.F.: Three-dimensional and two-dimensional deployment analysis for underwater acoustic sensor networks. Ad Hoc Netw. **7**(4), 778–790 (2009)
2. Xie, P., Cui, J.-H., Lao, L.: VBF: vector-based forwarding protocol for underwater sensor networks. In: Boavida, F., Plagemann, T., Stiller, B., Westphal, C., Monteiro, E. (eds.) NETWORKING 2006. LNCS, vol. 3976, pp. 1216–1221. Springer, Heidelberg (2006)
3. Zhou, Z., Cui, J.-H., Zhou, S.: Localization for large-scale underwater sensor networks. In: Akyildiz, I.F., Sivakumar, R., Ekici, E., Oliveira, J.C., McNair, J. (eds.) NETWORKING 2007. LNCS, vol. 4479, pp. 108–119. Springer, Heidelberg (2007)
4. Chandrasekhar, V., Seah, W.: An area localization scheme for underwater sensor networks. In: OCEANS 2006-Asia Pacific, pp. 1–8. IEEE (2007)
5. Yan, H., Shi, Z.J., Cui, J.-H.: DBR: depth-based routing for underwater sensor networks. In: Das, A., Pung, H.K., Lee, F.B.S., Wong, L.W.C. (eds.) NETWORKING 2008. LNCS, vol. 4982, pp. 72–86. Springer, Heidelberg (2008)
6. Wahid, A., Kim, D.: An energy efficient localization-free routing protocol for underwater wireless sensor networks. Int. J. Distrib. Sens. Netw. 2012 (2012)
7. Latif, K., Ahmad, A., Javaid, N., Khan, Z., Alrajeh, N.: Divide-and-rule scheme for energy efficient routing in wireless sensor networks, arXiv preprint arXiv:1303.5268 (2013)
8. Ahmad, A., Latif, K., Javaid, N., Khan, Z., Qasim, U.: Density controlled divide-and-rule scheme for energy efficient routing in wireless sensor networks, arXiv preprint arXiv:1303.6573 (2013)
9. Ahmed, S., Khan, I., Rasheed, M., Ilahi, M., Khan, R., Bouk, S., Javaid, N.: Comparative analysis of routing protocols for under water wireless sensor networks, arXiv preprint arXiv:1306.1148 (2013)
10. Wahid, A., Lee, S., Kim, D.: A reliable and energy-efficient routing protocol for underwater wireless sensor networks. Int. J. Commun. Syst. (2012)
11. Nicolaou, N., See, A., Xie, P., Cui, J.-H., Maggiorini, D.: Improving the robustness of location-based routing for underwater sensor networks. In: OCEANS 2007-Europe, pp. 1–6. IEEE (2007)
12. Jornet, J.M., Stojanovic, M., Zorzi, M.: Focused beam routing protocol for underwater acoustic networks. In: Proceedings of the Third ACM International Workshop on Underwater Networks, pp. 75–82. ACM (2008)
13. Jafri, M., Ahmed, S., Javaid, N., Ahmad, Z., Qureshi, R.: Amctd: Adaptive mobility of courier nodes in threshold-optimized dbr protocol for underwater wireless sensor networks, arXiv preprint arXiv:1307.7009 (2013)
14. Akyildiz, I.F., Pompili, D., Melodia, T.: State-of-the-art in protocol research for underwater acoustic sensor networks. In: Proceedings of the 1st ACM International Workshop on Underwater Networks, pp. 7–16. ACM (2006)
15. Sanchez, A., Blanc, S., Yuste, P., Serrano, J.: A low cost and high efficient acoustic modem for underwater sensor networks. In: 2011 IEEE-Spain OCEANS, pp. 1–10. IEEE (2011)
16. Cayirci, E., Tezcan, H., Dogan, Y., Coskun, V.: Wireless sensor networks for underwater survelliance systems. Ad Hoc Netw. **4**(4), 431–446 (2006)
17. Kwak, Min, K., Kim, Jinhyun.: Development of 3-dimensional sensor nodes using electro-magnetic waves for underwater localization. J. Inst. Control, Rob. Syst. (2013)

18. Lorincz, K., Welsh, M.: MoteTrack: a robust, decentralized approach to RF-based location tracking. In: Strang, T., Linnhoff-Popien, C. (eds.) LoCA 2005. LNCS, vol. 3479, pp. 63–82. Springer, Heidelberg (2005)
19. Rahim, A., Javaid, N., Aslam, M., Rahman, Z., Qasim, U., Khan, Z.: A comprehensive survey of mac protocols for wireless body area networks. In: 2012 Seventh International Conference on Broadband, Wireless Computing, Communication and Applications (BWCCA), pp. 434–439. IEEE (2012)
20. Rahim, A., Javaid, N., Aslam, M., Qasim, U., Khan, Z.: Adaptive-reliable medium access control protocol for wireless body area networks. In: 2012 9th Annual IEEE Communications Society Conference on Sensor, Mesh and Ad Hoc Communications and Networks (SECON), pp. 56–58. IEEE (2012)
21. Alvi, A., Naqvi, S., Bouk, S.H., Javaid, N., Qasim, U., Khan, Z.: Evaluation of slotted CSMA/CA of IEEE 802.15. 4. In: 2012 Seventh International Conference on Broadband, Wireless Computing, Communication and Applications (BWCCA), pp. 391–396. IEEE (2012)

Association Rule Mining in Social Network Data

Naeem A. Mahoto[(✉)], Anoud Shaikh, and Shahzad Nizamani

Department of Software Engineering, Mehran University of Engineering
and Technology Jamshoro, Sindh 76062, Pakistan
{naeemmahoto,anoudmajid85,shahzad.nizamani}@gmail.com

Abstract. The use of social networks has significantly altered the way of life of online community since last decade. The user-generated contents help to investigate various aspects of the online communities. This paper presents an approach of extracting associations between contents and contextual features of social network data. The aim is to discover the hidden correlations among the contents posted on social networking website, and detect trends of online users. The proposed approach uses association rule mining technique to uncover correlations and build taxonomy based on their corresponding relationships to deeply analyse the social network data contents. The obtained results show the efficiency of the proposed framework in mining association rules and analysing behaviours and trends of online users.

Keywords: Knowledge discovery · Social network analysis · User-generated contents · Association rule mining

1 Introduction

The birth of social networking has greatly taken attention of researchers to address the significant and effective use of social web data. The social networking has rapidly increased data on the web as well as have altered lives of online community [1]. The recent research investigates the use of social data in academic applications, e-commerce and discovers the user habits and interests of different geographical online communities to support analysts in decision-making and optimal resource management in business as well as web maintenance [2]. For example, analysis of clickstream data that provides information about user interactions and the frequently with which the user connects to social networks is addressed in [3]. The sentimental analysis of users from twitter data is reported in [4]. The contextualized semantic meaning of individual twitter posts from strategies, which connects tweets with related news articles to yield semantics is presented in [5]. The privacy protection algorithm is proposed in [2], which protects users' identification and selected profile features.

The social networks, such as Facebook, Twitter, Orkut and Digg etc., help its users to find people of common interests, facilitate them to exchange their

© Springer International Publishing Switzerland 2014
F.K. Shaikh et al. (Eds.): IMTIC 2013, CCIS 414, pp. 149–160, 2014.
DOI: 10.1007/978-3-319-10987-9_14

ideas [6], and provide them a platform to share news, articles, and multimedia contents [7]. The data of these websites is referred to as user-generated contents (UGC), which is one of the powerful sources of data to get knowledge about social communities, and investigate the behavior and other different aspects of the online communities.

The data mining techniques are greatly adopted in order to retrieve valuable and interesting knowledge from a huge amount of data posted every day on micro-blogging websites. Recently, the research on user-generated contents is carried out for many applications to help online organizations to enhance their services based on users perspectives. For example, TwitterMonitor [8] detects common trends from twitter streams and clickstream data is analyzed in [3]. The study in [9] highlights the twitter as conversational tool for the user to interact and collaborate. The search engines and social sciences could increasingly get fruits from user-generated contents. The approach in [10] aims at exploring the most useful and informative messages about events. The real-time summaries of events from twitter tweets are addressed in [11], which learns hidden state of events by means of Hidden Markov Models and provides help in summarizing tweets. The data mining techniques are effectively exploited to discover hidden, interested and meaningful knowledge from the social data published on social networking websites. The detected knowledge allows getting deep insight of information about user behaviors and trends, and providing web services to support management and decision making strategies.

This paper presents an approach of discovery of hidden knowledge from messages (i.e. user-generated contents or tweets) published on social web that will be helpful for investigation of tweet contents, analysis of their correlations and trend detections of users in social communities. The proposed framework helps to understand the behavior of the users. To this aim, it exploits the use of data mining technique i.e., association rule mining [12] to find out the hidden correlations between social network data (i.e., tweets). Since, this technique fits the concept of finding implications between several sparse items contained in tweets. Unlike other data mining techniques, association rule mining discovers the dependability of items among them, which is the theme of this paper. Moreover, the taxonomies are built from the detected correlations to identify the combinations and relations among various items contained in tweets. The framework extracts strong association rules among tweet contents and generates automatic taxonomies, helping to investigate trends of social networking users based on geographical locations.

The rest of the paper is organized as Sect. 2 presents the related work carried out in social network data. The proposed framework is discussed in Sect. 3. The experimental evaluation and application of the proposed approach are reported in Sects. 4 and 5 respectively; and finally conclusions are drawn in Sect. 6.

2   Related Work

The birth of social networking has greatly taken attention of researchers to address the significant and effective use of social web data. For instance, TwitterEcho crawler [13] is introduced for distributed architecture to collect data on Portuguese Twittosphere. The work in [14] reported the use of micro-blogging as the means to predict the political sentiment. Some researchers are active in the analysis of product marketing based on twitter posts, for instance, the work in [15] claimed the customer sentiments derived from their tweets regarding branding of the products as the opinion of the customers for the brand. The even extraction in one-domain from twitter (TwiCALL) is proposed in [16], which discovers important events and it categorizes and classifies them. TwiCALL extracts entities and event phrases from raw twitter data, then events are categorized into appropriate types. The significance of the event, finally, is measured based on the occurrence of tweets. A tool named Navigating Information Facets on Twitter (NIF-T) is introduced in [17] for exploring data published on micro-blogging website (i.e., Twitter). The NIF-T is web-based system and exploits client-sever architecture; the system utilizes HTML5, CSS, and Javascript as client side and PHP along with MySQL storage database at the server side. Furthermore, it offers three facet search interfaces: Geo Facet - allows to view different regions, Topic Facet - allows selection of one or more topics to view corresponding checkpoints, and Time Facet - allows to view corresponding results in accordance with time selection. An approach to summarize data from Twitter is developed in [18].

In recent years, the usage and understanding of the micro-blogging has remained in focus. For example, the work performed in [9] highlights the twitter as conversational tool for user to interact and collaborate. The search engines and social sciences could increasingly get fruits from user- generated contents. Becker et al. [10] reports approach about finding highly relevant and informative messages from vast variety of Twitter messages. The approach in [10] aims at exploring the most useful and informative messages about events. The real-time summaries of events from twitter tweets are addressed in [11], which learns hidden state of events by means of Hidden Markov Models and the provide help in summarizing tweets. The mechanism of extracting association rules and automatic generation of taxonomy from tweets is presented in this paper. The discovered correlations and generated taxonomy help to understand the behavior of the users.

3   The Proposed Framework

The proposed framework as illustrated in Fig. 1 presents an environment for the association rule mining, a popular and well-established data mining technique, to discover hidden patterns from tweets. It mainly comprises of four main blocks.

3.1   Collecting and Preprocessing of Tweets

Though the tweets are easily available from Twitter website[1] and can be collected by means of Application Programming Interfaces (APIs) allowed for the

---

[1] http://www.twitter.com

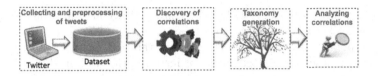

Fig. 1. Block diagram of the proposed framework

social network data. However, the received tweets are unsuitable for the subsequent processes, for example, due to their format and containing additional information, which is not required for problem under consideration. Therefore, the collected tweets that are publicly available on the micro-blogging website (i.e., Twitter) are preprocessed to remove unnecessary information and transform them into a suitable format for the mining process. The tweets are collected containing few hundreds to thousand posts for specific keywords, for instance, popular personalities i.e., "Barack Obama", "Einstein" etc.

The preprocessing phase transforms tweet data into items and their related contextual (i.e. location, date and time) features. Especially, stopwards, numbers, hyperlinks and non-ASCII characters are eliminated using stemming algorithm. The transformed tweets are then mapped into a transactional database composed of set of stems, which is formally defined in the Definition 1. For example, consider a tweet message "Imagination is more important than knowledge" may be mapped into corresponding transaction {imagination, important, knowledge} composed of three distinct terms.

Definition 1. *Transactional dataset. Let $\perp$ be a tweet set. The transactional dataset T associated with $\perp$ is a set of transactions T_i, such that each tweet $tw_i \epsilon T$. Whilst each transaction $T_i = \{t_1, t_2, \ldots, t_n\}$ is a set of terms (i.e., stemmed words) relative to tw_i.*

The transactional dataset is exploited further in the data mining process for the generation of high-level correlations among the tweet terms.

3.2   Discovery of Correlations

Discovery of correlations phase addresses mining of high level correlations from the transactional dataset created in the previous phase. The association mining technique [12] has been exploited, which applies apriori level-wise method to extract frequent itemset mining of an arbitrary size of the set of terms present in the transactional dataset. An association rule (see Definition 3) is usually represented as: If *Body* then *Head*, where *body* (also antecedent) and *head* (also consequence) are disjoint subsets of a large set of frequent patterns/items/terms (see Definition 2). This does not mean that if *antecedent* happens then *consequence* must also happen; instead, it is a relationship between them. Precisely, if *antecedent* happens then there are more chances that *consequence* may also happen depending upon the strength of the rule. The strength and reliability of the correlation (also association rule) are measured by association rule support and confidence described in Definitions 4 and 5 respectively for extracting frequent correlations. The rule confidence describes the conditional probability of the consequence of the association rule, given the antecedent of the association rule, which ensures the correlation between them. The higher the strength of the rule, higher the association is between the terms (i.e., rule antecedent and consequence).

Definition 2. *Frequent item/itemset. Let X be a set of items such that $X \epsilon \tau$, where τ is an enumeration of all items. An item/itemset I is a frequent itemset, if the support of I is higher than a given minimum support threshold (misupp), where $I \subseteq X \subseteq \tau$.*

Definition 3. *Association rule. Let X and Y be two frequent itemsets such that $X \cap Y = \phi$. An association rule is represented in the form $X \Rightarrow Y$, where X and Y are the antecedent and the consequence of the rule respectively.*

Definition 4. *Association rule support. Let T be a transactional dataset of tweets and $X \Rightarrow Y$ be an association rule. The support of $X \Rightarrow Y$, denoted as $sup(X \Rightarrow Y)$ in T is defined as the support $X \bigcup Y$ in T.*

Definition 5. *Association rule confidence. Let T be a transactional dataset of tweets and $X \Rightarrow Y$ an association rule. The confidence of the rule $X \Rightarrow Y$, donated as $conf(X \Rightarrow Y)$ is given by*

$$\text{conf}(X \Rightarrow Y) = \frac{\text{supp}(X \cup Y)}{\text{supp}(X)} \tag{1}$$

where $sup(X \bigcup Y)$ is the number of the occurrence of both terms X and Y together, and $sup(X)$ is the number of its occurrence in the transactional dataset T.

For example: consider an association rule (i.e., correlation) between terms *imagination* and *knowledge* as in the following.

$$imagination \Rightarrow knowledge$$

Here *imagination* is antecedent and *knowledge* is the consequent of the rule, having rule support equals to 40 % and confidence to 70 %. The rule support indicates that 40 % of the total transactional dataset contains this correlation (i.e., relationship) and 70 % confidence means that among the records which posses this relationship, there are 70 % records, which validates this relationship. The discovered association rules satisfy the minimum threshold values of support and confidence for the given set of frequent terms in transactional dataset.

3.3   Taxonomy Generation

The representation of hierarchical knowledge, defining $< is - a >$, $< is - part - of >$, $< is - type - of >$ relationships among concepts and its data items, is taxonomy that can be used to categorize objects and its additional information. Generalized rule mining approaches as discussed in [19,20] deal with user-generated taxonomies as a general purpose. These general-purpose taxonomies may not portrait the real information, which lays in the data collection. *Taxonomy Generation* block automatically generates taxonomy based on tweet attributes, in particular, frequent keywords from the association rules (i.e., correlations) that are generated in the previous phase of the framework. The generated taxonomy represents taxonomy over set of terms present in the transactional dataset and is composed of mostly frequent keywords present in the transactional dataset. The taxonomy addresses the categorical representation of tweet terms. For example, consider three keywords: *society, country, World.* The generalized concept is *World* and its lower level items are *country* then *society* both as specific items. The more generalized or high-level concepts or correlations can be extracted provided that there have been more features and higher levels in the transactional dataset. The taxonomy nodes represent distinct terms extracted from tweet contents, and it is built by two-step procedures: (1) *Graph extraction* and (2) *Graph partitioning and pruning.*

The tweet contents transformed into transactional dataset contain social network data contents i.e., keywords (see details in Sect. 3.1). The use of Apriori algorithm [21] allows the discovery of hidden correlations among the set of terms of arbitrary size available in the transactional dataset. The association rule graph is built for the set of terms, which satisfy the given minimum support and confidence thresholds. Thus, strong correlations among set of tweet terms are detected. The generated correlations are represented in graph format, the edges of the graph represent the implications present in the rule and vertices are the items of tweet contents.

Consider for instance the rules, which are extracted during *graph extraction* step: (country ⇒ World), ([*society, people*] ⇒ country), (peace ⇒ World), (society ⇒ World) and (society ⇒ country).

The *graph extraction* step builds the association rule graph as shown in Fig. 2 from the generated association rules (i.e., correlations). The association rule graph vertices may have more than one out-going edges. In order to reduce graph

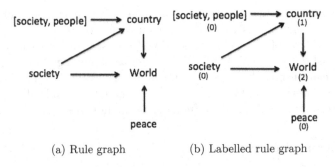

(a) Rule graph   (b) Labelled rule graph

Fig. 2. An example - graphs of the generated rules.

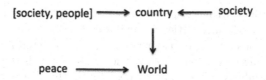

Fig. 3. An example - generated taxonomy.

size and make it compact and comprehensive *graph partitioning and pruning* step is performed.

The *graph partitioning and pruning* step makes the graph compact and represents the taxonomy according to tweet contents. Further, it prunes edges, which do not have string relevant relationship by performing vertex labeling and edge pruning. Vertex labeling processes each vertex and assigns them a label that represents level of taxonomy. The two vertices, which are disconnected are assigned zero label. Whilst, the label shows the number of maximum nodes between the two vertices. The graph after this step is shown in Fig. 2. The vertices labeled zero are considered as leaf nodes i.e. *peace* and *society*. *Country* is level 1, where as node *World* has level 2 in Fig. 3.

3.4   Analyzing Correlations

The selection and ranking of the significant correlations in order to better understand the analysis are addressed at this step. The selection is made having either a rule schema (i.e. some attributes that must appear in the rule body or head) or given interesting rule items. For instance a rule schema may be like $< (keyword, *) \Rightarrow (Place, *) >$, this will produce all the length-2 rules along with having attributes *Keyword* in body and *Place* in head of the rule. Similarly, given items can also be used such as $< (Keword, School) \Rightarrow (Place, London) >$, this produces the *School* keyword in the body and *London* in the head satisfying both rule schema and specific item constraints. The results of the query are placed based on their support and confidence quality indexes.

4   Experimental Evaluation

This section discusses the experiments carried out on tweets using proposed framework as well as their evaluation. Firstly, the collected tweet textual contents highlight the famous topical subjects and events of the world such as European Union. Experiments are performed on different datasets crawled from social networking website (i.e., Twitter). For barvity, the results of Dataset-1 are presented, which comprises of 58 transaction with 209 distinct items (i.e., keywords). The effectiveness of the proposed framework is presented in two scenarios: *User behavior analysis* and *Topic trend analysis*.

User behavior analysis: The extracted correlations from the dataset allow the experts to highlight hidden and potentially interesting user behaviors.

For example, consider the rules $peace \Rightarrow World$, $society \Rightarrow country$ and $country \Rightarrow World$. The framework automatically generates the taxonomy from the mined rules (i.e., correlations among items or keywords) as depicted in Fig. 3. The taxonomy clearly highlights the behaviour of the people towards the peace.

Topic trend analysis: The scenario deals with the discovery and analysis of the topics, which are currently matter of contention on Twitter (i.e., tweets). Consider, for instance, a domain expert wants to discover from the Social dataset the subjects of topical interest for Twitter users. Figure 3, which is the generated taxonomy from the proposed framework, suggests the expert that society as a general and people in particular are concerns with peacein the World. Hence, Twitter users are currently interested in peace throughout the World.

Secondly, Quality of generated taxonomies built from tweets data and the performance of the framework is discussed. The results achieved from the proposed approach are compared with the approach addressed in [22]. In particular, effectiveness of taxonomy generation at high level of specialization is evaluated. The evaluation of taxonomy generation is measured with three quality measures: global and local quality indexes, which are proposed in [22], considered as measures of categorical goodness and spread quality measure. The global quality addresses information regarding generality of the root of taxonomy. It is given by:

$$GloablQuality = [\prod_{i \epsilon R} supp(t_i)]^{\frac{1}{|R|}} \qquad (2)$$

where t_i is the keyword in the taxonomy and $|R|$ is the number of root notes.

The local quality is the degree of correlation between not-leaf and leaf nodes of the taxonomy. It is the product of confidence of rules in association graph with edges from a given edge to root note in taxonomy. The third quality measure is *spread*, which is the measure of number of nodes across the taxonomy to move from a given node to its root node in the association graph.

Figure 4 reports the results of Dataset-1 with minimum support threshold 1 % and varying the confidence value. The Fig. 4a and b respectively summarize global and local quality achieved. For the considered dataset (i.e., Dataset-1), the proposed framework outperforms comparing with the ones defined in [22]. The same behavior is observed for the spread values are shown in Fig. 4c for the association rule graph built. The global quality measure remained same in both approaches: the one described in [22] and the one proposed in this paper.

Furthermore, the proposed approach produced pretty balanced local quality versus spread measurement indexes, as shown in Fig. 4d. Almost at every confidence value global quality measure results remain pretty similar, ensuring the fact that less frequent are ignored during the taxonomy generation.

Figure 5 reports the time taken by the proposed and the approach defined in [22] for the analyzed dataset. The proposed approach takes slightly less time comparing with the approach reported in [22]. It indicates the fact that the sparse dataset is directly proportional to the time required for generating taxonomy. The reason behind the more time consumption is the inherited nature of user-generated contents (i.e., high dimensionality and sparse nature). The

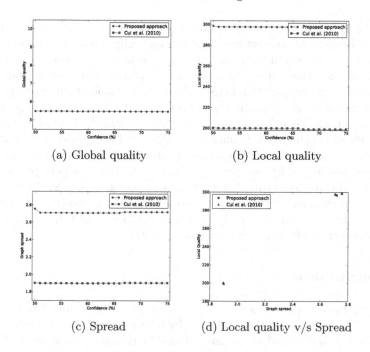

(a) Global quality

(b) Local quality

(c) Spread

(d) Local quality v/s Spread

Fig. 4. Quality indexes with minsupp = 1 %.

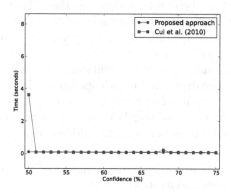

Fig. 5. Execution time when minsupp = 1 %.

experiments are carried out on a Pentium 4 having 2.26 GHz Intel Core 2 Duo processor with 4 Giga Bytes of RAM.

5   Applications

The proposed framework would be effective and beneficial for the analysts to investigate Twitter users behavior and tend of their discussions based on twitter postings. We report some examples as the possible applications for the proposed framework to investigate user-generated contents: *Analysis of content propagation* and *Analysis of correlations*. The content propagation analysis needs to carry on some procedural steps such as selection of set of tweets to be investigated, association rule mining, taxonomy development, and querying rules for a given criteria. The propagation helps to have insight look at the propagation of messages. For instance, if some news is posted in UK, the same is propagated in other countries. Therefore it may help to understand the level of propagation and its spreading rate in other countries or regions of the World. The analysis of correlations helps to extract most relevant and highly associated twitter posts from tweet postings. The analysis helps to provide the user perceptions based on their tweets to infer certain knowledge about social, economical and political concerns. For example, if there exists a correlation among posts about economical growth in a certain region, the strong correlations will help to understand the typical user behavior for the economical growth.

6   Conclusions

This paper presented the mechanism of extracting hidden correlations among the terms available in the tweet contents by means of proposed framework. The twitter data provides analysts to understand the trends and behaviors of online community as well as novel knowledge from data available on social media. The generated correlations are helpful to understand the hidden associations among the textual contents and contextual features of the user- generated content. The proposed approach generates automatic taxonomy generation instead of modeling from user provided ones.

The experimental results validate the efficiency as well as effectiveness of the proposed framework. The discovered knowledge from twitter data helps analysts to understand insight meaning of user contents and is applicable in real scenarios.

Future work will focus on mining large-scale contents of social media, and considering generation of rules based on user driven constraints.

Acknowledgement. The authors would like to thank Dr. Alessandro Fiori of Politecnico di Torino for providing specifications.

References

1. Bakshy, E., Rosenn, I., Marlow, C., Adamic, L.: The role of social networks in information diffusion. In: Proceedings of the 21st International Conference on World Wide Web, pp. 519–528. ACM (2012)
2. Song, Y., Karras, P., Xiao, Q., Bressan, S.: Sensitive label privacy protection on social network data. In: Ailamaki, A., Bowers, S. (eds.) SSDBM 2012. LNCS, vol. 7338, pp. 562–571. Springer, Heidelberg (2012)
3. Benevenuto, F., Rodrigues, T., Cha, M., Almeida, V.: Characterizing user behavior in online social networks. In: Proceedings of the 9th ACM SIGCOMM Conference on Internet Measurement Conference, IMC '09, pp. 49–62. ACM, New York (2009)

4. Bollen, J., Pepe, A., Mao, H.: Modeling public mood and emotion: twitter sentiment and socio-economic phenomena. In: Proceedings of the Fifth International
   AAAI Conference on Weblogs and Social Media, pp. 450–453 (2011)
5. Abel, F., Gao, Q., Houben, G.-J., Tao, K.: Semantic enrichment of twitter posts
   for user profile construction on the social web. In: Antoniou, G., Grobelnik, M.,
   Simperl, E., Parsia, B., Plexousakis, D., De Leenheer, P., Pan, J. (eds.) ESWC
   2011, Part II. LNCS, vol. 6644, pp. 375–389. Springer, Heidelberg (2011)
6. Aljomai, S.D.H.J.R., Sarhan, A., Alhajj, W.A.R.: Integrating social network analysis and data mining techniques into effective e-market framework. In: The 6th
   International Conference on Information Technology (2013)
7. Nancy, P., Geetha Ramani, R., Jacob, S.G.: Mining of association patterns in
   social network data (Face book 100 universities) through data mining techniques
   and methods. In: Meghanathan, N., Nagamalai, D., Chaki, N. (eds.) Advances in
   Computing & Inf. Technology. AISC, vol. 178, pp. 107–117. Springer, Heidelberg
   (2012)
8. Mathioudakis, M., Koudas, N.: Twittermonitor: trend detection over the twitter
   stream. In: Proceedings of the 2010 ACM SIGMOD International Conference on
   Management of Data, SIGMOD '10, pp. 1155–1158. ACM, New York (2010)
9. Honey, C., Herring, S.: Beyond microblogging: conversation and collaboration via
   twitter. In: 42nd Hawaii International Conference on System Sciences, HICSS'09,
   pp. 1–10. IEEE (2009)
10. Becker, H., Naaman, M., Gravano, L.: Selecting quality twitter content for events.
    In: Proceedings of the Fifth International AAAI Conference on Weblogs and Social
    Media (ICWSM'11) (2011)
11. Chakrabarti, D., Punera, K.: Event summarization using tweets. In: Proceedings of
    the Fifth International AAAI Conference on Weblogs and Social Media, pp. 66–73
    (2011)
12. Agrawal, R., Imieliński, T., Swami, A.: Mining association rules between sets of
    items in large databases. In: Proceedings of the 1993 ACM SIGMOD International
    Conference on Management of Data, SIGMOD '93, pp. 207–216. ACM, New York
    (1993)
13. Boanjak, M., Oliveira, E., Martins, J., Mendes Rodrigues, E., Sarmento, L.: Twit-
    terecho: a distributed focused crawler to support open research with twitter data.
    In: Proceedings of the 21st International Conference Companion on World Wide
    Web, WWW '12 Companion, pp. 1233–1240. ACM, New York (2012)
14. Tumasjan, A., Sprenger, T., Sandner, P., Welpe, I.: Predicting elections with twit-
    ter: what 140 characters reveal about political sentiment. In: Proceedings of the
    Fourth International AAAI Conference on Weblogs and Social Media, pp. 178–185
    (2010)
15. Jansen, B.J., Zhang, M., Sobel, K., Chowdury, A.: Twitter power: tweets as elec-
    tronic word of mouth. J. Am. Soc. Inf. Sci. Technol. 60(11), 2169–2188 (2009)
16. Ritter, A., Mausam, Etzioni, O., Clark, S.: Open domain event extraction from
    twitter. In: Proceedings of the 18th ACM SIGKDD International Conference on
    Knowledge Discovery and Data Mining, KDD '12, pp. 1104–1112. ACM, New York
    (2012)
17. Kumar, S., Morstatter, F., Marshall, G., Liu, H., Nambiar, U.: Navigating infor-
    mation facets on twitter (nif-t). In: Proceedings of the 18th ACM SIGKDD
    International Conference on Knowledge Discovery and Data Mining, KDD '12,
    pp. 1548–1551. ACM, New York (2012)

18. Yang, X., Ghoting, A., Ruan, Y., Parthasarathy, S.: A framework for summarizing and analyzing twitter feeds. In: Proceedings of the 18th ACM SIGKDD International Conference on Knowledge Discovery and Data Mining, KDD '12, pp. 370–378. ACM, New York (2012)
19. Srikant, R., Agrawal, R.: Mining generalized association rules. In: Proceedings of the 21th International Conference on Very Large Data Bases, VLDB '95, pp. 407–419. Morgan Kaufmann Publishers Inc., San Francisco (1995)
20. Han, J., Fu, Y.: Mining multiple-level association rules in large databases. IEEE Trans. Knowl. Data Eng. 11(5), 798–805 (1999)
21. Agrawal, R., Srikant, R.: Fast algorithms for mining association rules in large databases. In: Proceedings of the 20th International Conference on Very Large Data Bases, VLDB '94, pp. 487–499. Morgan Kaufmann Publishers Inc., San Francisco (1994)
22. Cui, B., Yao, J., Cong, G., Huang, Y.: Evolutionary taxonomy construction from dynamic tag space. In: Chen, L., Triantafillou, P., Suel, T. (eds.) WISE 2010. LNCS, vol. 6488, pp. 105–119. Springer, Heidelberg (2010)

Relational Factors of EHR Database in Visual Analytic Systems for Public Health Care Units

Muhammad Sheraz Arshad Malik[1(✉)], Suziah Sulaiman[1],
and Muhammad Faraz Arshad Malik[2]

[1] Department of Computer and Information Sciences,
Universiti Teknologi PETRONAS, Bandar Seri Iskandar,
31750 Tronoh, Perak, Malaysia
sheraz_awan@hotmail.com, suziah@petronas.com.my
[2] Department of Biosciences, COMSATS Institute of Information Technology,
Islamabad, Pakistan
famalik@comsats.edu.pk

Abstract. Information Visualization (IV) in Electronic Health Records (EHR) is a significant source of patient knowledge using available medical data set(s). Although IV applications most focus on demands of doctors as considering primary stake holders for this use but unavailability of simplified, ease to use and a user friendly application is due to non-consideration and absence of database contextual factors in EHR tools development. Efficient query handling and data retrieval is carried out using various visual health data related queries based on structure and hierarchical flow of event based information. Conventional visual EHR applications ignore the fact of heterogeneity within the different data entities, i.e., text, number, figure and other form of data and more focus on presentation of data rather than considering the pre alignment and configuration of database affecting results. This research work is carried out solely for highlighting the needs of database professional and influencing factors affecting the efficacy of query based visualization results in EHR. More emphasis is on future needs of database professionals point of view in context of developing a Visual Analytic System that can address the needs of doctors and other stake holders based on capacity and performance ability of given database based on encoupled factors. It also represents the gaps areas of databases within visualizations and determines the solution by providing highly demanded scope areas for visualization in EHR. This will yield to a contribution to formulate database model within ongoing research for CARE1.0 as a complete EHR visualization model.

Keywords: Visual interfaces · EHR · Information visualization · Patient data visualization · IV knowlededge areas · CARE

1 Introduction

Different important patient history events in Electronic Health Records (EHR) are represented by using Visual Analytic Systems (VAS) in a very intricate and user friendly format. Information Visualization (IV) systems always revealed this fact that design of such graphic applications should always consider human sensory capabilities

© Springer International Publishing Switzerland 2014
F.K. Shaikh et al. (Eds.): IMTIC 2013, CCIS 414, pp. 161–172, 2014.
DOI: 10.1007/978-3-319-10987-9_15

in a perceivable fashion for important data elements and data patterns [1, 2]. Primary objective of IV in EHR is to facilitate the end users such as doctors, physicians and hospital management bodies for clear knowledge about the patient history and data trends user friendly format by the help of different colors and pictorial shapes. Perception of such knowledge is primarily made dependent on the doctor's requirements while ignoring the important factors that are coming as other constituent components from other stake holders, e.g., EHR database, Data Base Administrators (DBA) and Visual designers. DBA play a backbone role as an IT professional for EHR database and considered as potential secondary stake holder [2–5].

Existing IV applications pay lesser attention to the derivation of these results from the database and highly focus on the role of easy understanding of pictures, more knowledge sharing and handoff and user friendly interfaces. Absence of unified standard interfaces due to multi format databases results in incomplete transformation of the EHR details on screens in the form visualizations [3–7]. Still a number of hospitals in various countries do not have a common EHR database that creates multiple interpretations due to multiple data representations even for the same disease and symptoms. This leads in failure and non-adaptation of EHR systems and hinders IV frequent use in health care units due to variance in data base entities, difference in data formats from one data base of one hospital to other and varied data retrieval mechanism on tool basis.

Different kind of database systems are used to input, store, retrieve and process patient data at each clinic and hospital based on their financial, geographical and management perspective uses. They also use different technologies to accumulate data from different locations such as Intensive Care Unit (ICU), operation theatre, laboratories and other facilities to represent it in a single location. These applications fail in information sharing due to different data formats or locations.

Active Notes [4], SOAP [8], Problem Oriented Medical Record (POMR) [9], Event Flow [10] and many other applications try to address the IV issues in EHR databases. These tools address the less highlighted factors and areas by designers in IV applications but still they did not meet the complete knowledge requirements of DBAs. Most of applications fail to provide the desired result as due to not understanding the query structure development with reference to database architecture. This can only be resolved if requirements of DBAs pertaining to EHRs are properly understood and given a proper highlight to better demonstrate within the existing systems. Conventionally more time is used on understanding the requirements of doctors and lesser attention is given to the knowledge sharing gap between doctors and DBAs. The incomplete information retrieval, multiple formats for same results and the complicated process of IV makes it difficult to understand the EHR. More time consumption and difficult application interface are resulting side effects of such results representations. Except few states of USA and CANADA rest of hospitals in the world face the difficulty of existence of unified, same format and single source of uniform EHR database and this leads as the biggest challenge at the moment [11–13].

This research work highlights the core DBA's perception areas in improvement of IV in an EHR system. To highlight the areas of DBA's belief, EHR data knowledge set, Data set assessment and individual future expectation for data base areas related to EHR visualizations for its potential benefit to doctors and allied stake holders.

This work is a continual phase of our ongoing project as CARE 1.0 model for designing of an EHR visualization solution [2, 13, 14].

The rest of the paper is organized as follows. Section 2 presents the relevant work and EHR database issues with reference to database administrators and gaps previously addressed by different researchers. Section 3 highlight the motivation for this work. Section 4 presents the details of the case study and its different areas. Section 5 describes the results and Sect. 6 highlights the conclusion and future work areas.

2 Related Work

DBA's normally design and formulate database and its queries based on the health care professionals demands and requirements in EHR. Each hospital normally uses different database systems, design and architecture based on their budget availability, number and amount of resources and complexity of data. But base format is same just like patient chart structure in nearly all EHR queries returning patient ID, name, location, doctor's name, disease, symptoms, doctor's comments/notes, test reports and medicine recommendations. But the query structure and demand of stake holder requirements changes the structure and results of query in representation from simple to complex data scenarios.

Representation could be in any format but the results are based on the structure of query developed some times merely on the bases of doctor's demand. These results in visualization that is not sometimes completely fulfilling the demand of doctor as due to many factors like DBAs are from IT field and doctors are from medicine with different set of requirements, lesser attention towards the limitations of database, sparse entities distribution in complex dataset etc. To address these issues, more work is done towards the visualization side but lesser work is done to standardize DBA's perception in past. Few approaches like in the form of active notes, temporal querying, data mapping and ontological based semantics [9, 10, 15, 16].

Temporal queries are developed by extracting different approaches either using time stamp sorting of data like Life Flow, or event based division like Event Flow, in some applications on the bases of case context approach and few are addressed using grouping on based of different work groups like mental disorders or other associated medical division terms [7, 10, 17–19]. Event based or temporal queries bring the results and those results formulate in such diagrams that are complex enough to understand or explore much from other stake holders' point of view.

Different database systems from different vendors also have different limitations based on the SQL queries as well as transformation of those results into an organized format for a comprehensive visualization. The main reasons behind such complexities are non-understanding of DBA's requirements and involvement within the dataflow transformation for a resulting visualization. Although data is present but retrieval techniques and exploration of data from complex to simpler form is another challenge. For instance, to visualize medication results used by similar group of patients against intestinal infection in hospital may be easier till determining patient chart. But in case patients are diabetic or hyper tension associated then to measure affect with reference to side effects monitoring on other body parts is more complex query within given data set. This scenario can be only solved if a unified and understandable format is available from DBAs for query development as well this requirement is understandable by them as well.

Couple of applications also tried to solve this challenge by segregating the expertise, level of navigation and information in addition to perception of stake holders about queries in different groups. Aligning, filtering, regrouping, temporal based queries, formulation of single patient and later on multiple patient, information granularity, command on retrieval procedures and comparing the results are different research interest areas in similar data set or heterogeneous data sets [1, 5, 12, 17, 19, 20].

Most efficient and very well formulate databases cannot bring results itself till they are properly operated and mechanized by DBAs based on end user requirements IV majorly depends upon the results based on the queries and level of complexity in the queries addressed. But only best results can be obtained related to the information required only. This is very important that if IT professionals like DBAs requirements as well as influencing factors should be identified and considered a valid importance for designing and utilizing such applications. As doctors, information is primary goal but for DBAs the goal is to understand the demand based on the system and then to present the results. But if there is no alignment and proper flow of information between these stake holders, it will result only complex or incomplete visualization to waste resources. To solve this problem, it is utmost important to group the requirements of DBAs and their expectations from the database systems as well as future exploration procedures clarification. This work is carried out in the similar ICT procedures followed in previous tools and development process based on survey and close interview based study with DBAs of different government hospitals using different available databases [3, 9, 20, 21].

3 Motivation

The basic purpose for this research work is to identify the gap areas within use and knowledge set for the stake holders especially DBAs and their interaction with others, i.e., Doctors and Visual designers. This will help to improve the application use as well as strengthen the flow of only required information upon demand process. Data base administrators from different domains and from different databases back ground handling experience usually encounter with the situation of less understanding about deriving the real time information from EHR data set due to lesser information provisions and poor coordination. Returning results from different forms of queries like temporal, event, phase oriented or entity based does not merely fulfil the demands of a desired visualization. Although from a database, results are deducted but they are not the completely related or not fulfilling the requirements of doctors due to lesser knowledge [13, 16].

Complex dataset and most intricated database solutions by different vendors can handle the data efficiently but techniques and way to handle the data by and for users is the real key solution. Currently there are different EHR applications like Amalga [6] by Microsoft and couple of others at different hospitals are being used within different states of US and CANADA that try to fulfill the query based requirements of its stake holders but still they are not widely adopted due to complex understanding procedures and differentiation in data set structure. Database professionals may possess excellent knowledge and expertise in EHR data retrieval queries but till the time requirements and proper goal for that query is not understood, it is not viable to extract complete insight of results. Data set sometimes does not contain the required information and if it does sometimes even complete previous notes are not able to be retrieved based in multiple patients records due to various factors like lesser understanding of requirement explanation, limitations of onsite data availability, increasing demand of doctors with complexity of past data analysis.

Main objective of this paper is to focus on the difficulties pertaining to DBA's related to a dataset that can help them to improve the doctor's requirements. In this way, results can be retrieved in more articulated format and query development process will be more standardized for future research as well for current applications. This will help to measure the level of information navigation, requirements understanding and their future expectation with the dataset and the areas where they need to work more based on their expertise.

Normally the date retrieval, information updation and deletion processes are similar in EHR like any other heterogeneous databases like weather forecast or stock exchange etc. but the format change and information representation is different than prior ones. So although DBA has knowledge and expertise but training and knowledge sharing are important facts that are widely ignored has been presented with the results of this work.

4   DBA Case Study

This piece of research work is an effort to represent the knowledge of DBAs with reference to already implemented EHR visualization systems, applications and tools in different hospitals using survey based questionnaire approach. It will also highlight, in its later parts about the weak areas within the understanding of EHR systems that should be more significant in future oncoming research for DBA and data management professionals. The study has been carried out involving 20 DBAs working in different general and teaching hospitals with the help of questionnaire and short interview based approach [4, 5, 8, 9]. These factors have been divided into four major categories entitled as DBA's belief, Data set knowledge for visualization, Assessment of EHR database and DBA's individual & future perspective. Likert scale has been used for choice of expertise from 1–5 based on 1 for less or no knowledge and 5 for expert and proficient rank. This section is going to highlight the details of each category intrinsically.

4.1   DBA's Belief

DBA's belief is the primary portion within this study showing the basic expertise level of database administrators about understanding and operating existing EHR database, IV tools and medical dataset of patients. As study was carried out in third world country hospitals where DBA performs the role of administration and development of hospital database with smaller or bigger IT team. Nominated factors in this study are sorted out based on previous studies, tools and applications in IV and are aggregated at single core for different stake holders to emerge aligned and standardized requirements for EHR users. X-axis is representing the names of factors that are segregated in this part and Y-axis is representing the response rate of participants in the Fig. 1. Graph is representing that most of DBA professionals have EHR application knowledge, Dataset Information, Multiple Patients data comparison and EHR tools expertise level at medium level showing with scale 3 and 4. Overall working in different hospitals, DBA can contribute to IV development information and entities field applicability as well to a minimized level in EHR tools feature knowledge. But there are also facts lacking their attention or requiring more expertise from them.

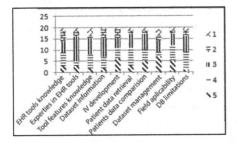

Fig. 1. Comparison of factors in DBA's belief for IV

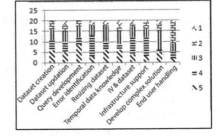

Fig. 2. Comparison of factors in DBA knowledge set for IV

Results for factors within this category represents that even DBAs have prior knowledge but still majority of them feels difficulty in understanding the complete information about features in tools and database, lesser number are marked to higher or maximum level of expertise in existing EHR tools. Most participants fall at level 3 and level 4 for multiple patients data retrieval, single patient history retrieval and database architecture information. But still the graph shows lack of dataset management techniques that are highly demanded for query development and complex IV formulation. These techniques are quite highly desired from DBAs particularly when an unorganized dataset from various sources is updating on daily basis.

4.2 Data Set Knowledge for Visualization

Data set provides a base line for developing visualization that results in easier understanding of single of multiple patient histories. As multiple patients history always contain difficult data entities constructing complicated dataset, so complete information to handle and understand such data set is the key for a useful visualization. 10 different factors within this category were selected based on previous work in IV tools and studies. They are also quite much related with their titles for use of different stake holders, i.e., doctors and visual designers. They are also considered important at similar grounds for DBA as well [4, 9, 11, 19, 20]. Figure 2 represents the analytical comparison of these factors with reference to DBA expertise level.

Dataset creation and End user requirements handling are significant areas where DBA needs more expertise with reference to above mentioned Fig. 2 as most of them are falling at level 2. Results show interesting fact that database professionals working in different hospitals are very less in numbers which are confident in handling dataset updation, query development process, IV & dataset relationship and Infra structure link with database support. The graph is also showing that majority of database professionals are falling at level 2 to 3 for complex solution development from complex dataset that is one of the leading requirements for IV in various scenarios. This is mentioning the deficiency provoking areas that are still need to be addressed.

4.3 Assessment of EHR Data Set

Development of Visualization, Strength & weakness of data base and data set, Information extraction on demand, Results interpretation easiness and Complete solution to end user requirements are key factors within the category of assessment of EHR dataset(s). These factors try to determine the capabilities of a database professional about assessing the data set and database system that is going to be operated. It also helps to understand the short comings and future enhancement milestones for oncoming challenges.

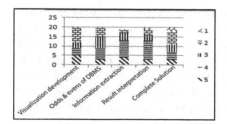 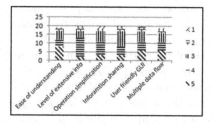

Fig. 3. Comparison of data set assessment factors for IV

Fig. 4. Analysis of future perspective areas for DBAs

Very few number of DBAs lack the ability of driving a complete solution for other stake holders like doctors and visual designers based on their requirements as mentioned in Fig. 3. But still there are about 25 % of population in database professionals who still lack the ability of results interpretation and solution derivation. 65 % professionals are comfortable at average level of scale 3 with information extraction features and techniques based on requirements in addition to results interpretation. Number of participants who are expert in identifying the strength and weakness of Database management systems, driving complete solution is also very less. So these are more areas of interest for junior and fresh database professionals in EHR visualization domain. Mostly other stake holders in IV are very much interested in finding insights of information and additional details [7, 10, 19]. These features are actually the supply line for providing a useful visualization within EHR and help to under fold different facts. Most of the researchers are quite much interested to follow the past information and alignment of information in a way so that it can help to improvise the functionality and adaptability of IV systems. This is also highlighting, that real task behind the colored pattern is development of a smart query system to better solve the user problem with the help of database professional that only be achieved with expertise in these factors.

4.4   Individual and Future Perspective

The fourth category particularly constitutes the factors that apprehend the DBA's personal perception as well future expectations from a dataset, DBMS and data base operations for interaction with other stake holders. Ease in understanding of information retrieved, Level of depth of information, Operational simplification, Information sharing with other users, contribution towards friendly GUI and multiple data flow from different sources or sets at single place are different factors present within this area. These factors are being narrow down here based on already existing applications proposed future work and areas of research, short comings and other related areas that are not being attended or put in the future work section [3, 5, 7, 15, 16, 21]. Database professionals work for information digging, retrieval, management and updation processes. The information retrieved will be the base source for developing a useful and easily understandable IV. So their input has a vital role for helping in boosting efficiency and improvement of IV applications as future work. DBA's feedback is as mentioned in Fig. 4 about such factors.

Majority of database professionals are highly interested in increasing the information sharing and expect the systems should help in underfolding more level of information with other stake holders. As other stake holders are highly interested in level of information by going in more depth of information about patient history. So this feature in database systems will not only help database professionals but also facilitate others using IV. Up to 45 % of DBAs are also in the favor of simplification of processes in data retrieval and data mining steps as it facilitate in better understanding. Also they tried to highlight the importance of friendly GUI.

5   Results

EHR database and dataset play a vital role in developing a useful Information visualization for medical professionals and associated stake holders. Single to multiple patients record retrieval, patient history on demand and different formats of results reports and development of queries for such functions are routine job of database professionals. Most of database professionals are interested in operating and deriving results based on IT query set but sometimes these queries are not as same as desired by other stake holders of visual analytic systems of EHR. Although it looks simple task to say but complicated as in scenarios to different patients suffering from same disease but with different physical background, suffering from different side effects and having different history status.

Different formats of EHR dataset and different operational procedures and set up of EHR database management systems result in retrieving different type and quality of results. This reflects a tremendous change in resulting visualizations that are end product for any visual analytic systems for efficient analysis and problem understanding. Different visualizations with similar results will result in different interpretations and in complete information not only to end users but also to database professionals. This increases more time consumption for results finding, facts gathering and poor perception of inferences from such systems resulting in failure or their lesser adaptability in public hospitals.

Primary objective of this paper is to streamline those difficulties that are faced both professionally and technically by DBAs with EHR database management systems and datasets. DBA's skills, knowledge and understanding to develop a simple query is very much directly linked for an effective and efficient user friendly visualization. Although finding information about single patient or multiple patients are just to compare the patient daily chart or hospital file from cabinet or record branch. But when comparing the results in hundreds on single screen or sheet then it becomes difficult and complex. Different vendors like Microsoft, ORACLE, IBM etc. provide different DBMS solutions for information retrieval, recording, query development and reports generation. The records are kept in different hospitals in different formats like MS word, Excel, Fox Pro or Fortran based programs or SQL based modern data storage tools. The real job is to bring the records in front in a useful format in a transparent and understandable fashion to visualize that is directly related to DBAs.

Patient dataset format is although quite much similar with reference to name, address, basic disease and doctor's notes structure in various databases widely used in the public hospitals around the world. But with latest diseases, complicated lab reports, extensive and exhaustive and temporal events in patient health results in driving more information granularity that was not possible couple of years before. This leads to theoretically a better and efficient health care system but based on scarce resources, minimum technology change patterns and latest training trends unavailability at public hospitals also result in poor knowledge provision results, in complete query oriented schemas and complex visualizations for doctors and stake holders. This results in overall lower efficiency of DBMS system supporting to visualize results as well as also lesser orientation towards the systems updation. As different DBMS varies from hospital to hospital that also effect on bringing uniformity among the visualization that can only be achieved by updating the skills of DBAs as mentioned with the above results.

Temporal patient data representation is main focus in visualization for presenting data by DBAs. As different events and health status reports of single or multiple patients becomes difficult for various database professionals. Main reasons behind this fact are incomplete information understanding about requirements of other stake holders due to poor information sharing, complicated data set with different DBMS formats as well mal functioning of one scenario query set in other scenarios. This piece of work also depicts about the weakness areas of DBAs particularly in organizing, managing and replicating the results in an understandable format.

A general comparison of all four categories of factors bring forward very interesting facts related to data retrieval, dataset basic knowledge information, management of database and comparison of future trends within different patients records. Most of DBAs are expert in developing and running basic queries to bring out the single patient data and multiple patient general records but when it comes to retrieve complex data in easy form it becomes difficult. The reasons behind these facts are less training on multiple database management systems for health care units in public hospital and lesser exposure to the real understanding about objectives of other stake holders. Different vendors and IT solution providers in different countries are providing different solutions about EHR management and its organization. But the format and structure of database nearly in each medical and teaching hospital in developing countries is varying from to another as due to non-standardization in data keeping act, availability of budget and resources and other social influences. This result in sparse and dis integrated form of EHR data, that is replicated many times and complex in segregation for query development at multiple sources.

Results also focus on the less interaction of database professionals and other stake holders. Normally doctors expect more from IV applications without considering the limitation of the available DBMS. While DBAs develop queries that bring maximum amount of results and information with a poor and not well defined filter. This results in bringing the information but that information is not to the point and thus results in extra information with non-interesting facts or unrelated insights of patient history. Thus results are representing a continuous upgrade in technical knowledge and information retrieval techniques update in DBAs as well as a standardized information flow cycle by aligning the requirements of all EHR stake holders at single junction to avoid confusion and complications in data retrieval. As data retrieval and formulation into visualization is not as much time taking process as to analytically understand that visualization. If it is not up to the mark its rejection rates are high, thus, causing frustration and time wasting for different stake holders.

As requirements and future needs of medical domain professionals will change in a particular span of time that is not identified or clarified yet. There could also be change in requirements based on some events like some disease outbreak or some natural disaster activity that will result the data retrieval of multiple patients at single or multiple places. So the DBMS and DBA both should be well acquainted with these facts to have a flexibility mode and ease in data set to facilitate such changes that are both timely intimated or unintimated. Although DBMS for EHR from different solution providers try to encompass the future needs but still the requirements of medical professionals at public hospitals as due to vitality as well as for more research mode, thus also change the requirements for DBAs.

A brief analysis of all results represent a four key areas improvement note for DBAs in which first one is making more knowledge improvement with temporal dynamic query set structure, i.e., live multiple patients data from multiple sources at different or similar time zones have similarity like diabetic B patients heart beat rate at morning time before eating any food in different age groups etc. Second area is understanding the limitation of EHR DBMS and visualization format and with different data set of previous years and current years in an agreeable format. Third is availability of level of information depth based on doctor's demand in public hospitals both for research and day to day operational needs. Fourth is understanding and standardization in dataset information not only for junior level DBAs but also for other IT and non IT professionals associated with EHE visual analytic systems by trainings, workshops as well as update in bringing the implementation of novel ideas in front.

This piece of work is an integral part of our ongoing research work on EHR visualization model based on integration of studies carried out on needs, gaps and requirements all three stake holders associated with it, i.e., doctors, DBAs and visual designers. So this is a step forward to integrate our under process work as CARE 1.0 a future EHR model as an analytic base for patient history records.

6   Conclusion and Future Work

IV in EHR is direct proportional in context of its means to the results of patient database management system and personals working on it. More granular results would be, more simplified and understandable visualization format GUI in the EHR tool will be obtained. Although within this work, the best efforts were focused on the needs, gaps and working requirements influencing factors of DBAs but still there is more extensive and in depth work is still pending to be done specifically on the EHR database standardization and temporal query format uniformity sides. A lot of applications and tools will be emulating the results in visible and colored format from different EHR database systems but still there is no uniformity is obtained even at the structure of basic patient record and history setup. Each vendor is producing different format supporting but at the user end, due to unavailability and lesser attention to the features identification very less implementation is observed. The more knowledge exploration about EHR database systems should be disseminated not only in developed countries hospitals but also in under developed countries. Currently most of public hospitals having DBAs with minimized qualification and lesser expertise at future trends and innovation lines in future EHR visualization tools for alarming situation. Information filtration and development of efficient temporal queries containing numbers, events, status or any other divisional category based are the areas of future exploration. Although previous related work covers need of physicians in public hospitals, as in our ongoing research project of CARE 1.0, and this work encompassed the interaction of same needs in DBAs. But we feel more input is required from different geographical regions and from different hospitals to improve the IV applications in patient's records both from DBAs as well as other stake holders. Aligning the needs of all stake holders with proper information filter and perceptual design patters are future research goals in this area of domain.

Acknowledgement. The authors would like to thank Universiti Teknologi PETRONAS for providing technical and financial supports for this research work. Special thanks to The MediaSol Pakistan for providing feedback and active participation in conducting this study with the help of Database administrators working in EHR domain.

References

1. Ware, C.: Information Visualization Perception for Design, 3rd edn., p. 14. Morgan Kaufmann Publishers, San Francisco (2013)
2. Malik, M.S.A., Sulaiman, S.: Towards the development of an interface model for information visualization in multiple electronic health records. Presented at the IEEE International Conference on Computer Medical Applications (ICCMA) (2013)

3. Mane, K.K., Bizon, C., Schmitt, C., Owen, P., Burchett, B., Pietrobon, R., Gersing, K.: VisualDecisionLinc: a visual analytics approach for comparative effectiveness-based clinical decision support in psychiatry. J. Biomed. Inf. **45**, 101–106 (2012)

4. Wilcox, L., Lu, J., Lai, J., Feiner, S., Jordan, D.: Physician-driven management of patient progress notes in an intensive care unit. Presented at the Proceedings of the 28th International Conference on Human Factors in Computing Systems, Atlanta, Georgia, USA (2010)

5. Krist, W., Monroe, M., Plaisant, C., Shneiderman, B., Millstein, J., Gold, S.: Exploring Point and Interval Event Patterns: Display Methods and Interactive Visual Query (2012). http://www.cs.umd.edu/hcil/eventflow/

6. Microsoft Amalga. http://www.microsoft.com/Amalga/

7. Hirsch, M.D.: Lack of standardized EHR interface delaying interoperability (2012). http://www.fierceemr.com/story/lack-standardized-ehr-interface-delaying-interoperability/2012-02-14

8. Schaefbauer, C.L., Siek, K.A.: Cautious, but optimistic: an ethnographic study on location and content of primary care providers using electronic medical records. In: 2011 5th International Conference on Pervasive Computing Technologies for Healthcare (PervasiveHealth), pp. 63–70 (2011)

9. Nair, V., Kaduskar, M., Bhaskaran, P., Bhaumik, S., Hodong, L.: Preserving narratives in electronic health records. In: 2011 IEEE International Conference on Bioinformatics and Biomedicine (BIBM), pp. 418–421 (2011)

10. Megan Monroe, K.W., Plaisant, C., Shneiderman, B., Millstein, J., Gold, S.: Exploring Point and Interval Event Patterns: Display Methods and Interactive Visual Query (2012). http://www.cs.umd.edu/hcil/eventflow/

11. Wilcox, L., Morris, D., Tan, D., Gatewood, J.: Designing patient-centric information displays for hospitals. Presented at the Proceedings of the 28th International Conference on Human Factors in Computing Systems, Atlanta, Georgia, USA (2010)

12. Wang, X., Wenwen, D., Butkiewicz, T., Bier, E.A., Ribarsky, W.: A two-stage framework for designing visual analytics system in organizational environments. In: 2011 IEEE Conference on Visual Analytics and Technology Visual Analytics Science and Technology (VAST), pp. 251–260 (2011)

13. Malik, M.S.A., Sulaiman, S.: An integrated modular approach for visual analytic systems in electronic health records. Int. J. Adv. Comput. Sci. Appl. **3**, 246–250 (2012)

14. Malik, M.S.A., Sulaiman, S.: Evaluation framework for interface usability in visualization of electronic health records. Int. J. Enhanced Res. Manage. Comput. Appl. **1** (2012)

15. Bui, A.A.T., Aberle, D.R., Hooshang, K.: TimeLine: visualizing integrated patient records. IEEE Trans. Inf. Technol. Biomed. **11**, 462–473 (2007)

16. Wang, H.-Q., Li, J.Z., Yi, F.S., Muneou, A.K.: Creating personalised clinical pathways by semantic interoperability with electronic health records. Artif. Intell. Med. **58**, 81–89 (2013)

17. U.K. National Health Service, NHS datamodel and dictionary service (2013). http://www.connectingforhealth.nhs.uk/systemsandservices/data/nhsdmds

18. Health and Social Care Information Center: Quality of dataset report in various groups (2012). http://www.hscic.gov.uk/catalogue/PUB08687

19. Maldonado, J.A., Costa, C.M., David, M., Marcos, M., Diego, B., José Antonio, M., Jesualdo, T.F., Montserrat, R.: Using the ResearchEHR platform to facilitate the practical application of the EHR standards. J. Biomed. Inf. **45**, 746–762 (2012)

20. Viitanen, J., Hannele, H., Tinja, L., Jukka, V., Jarmo, R., Ilkka, W.: National questionnaire study on clinical ICT systems proofs: physicians suffer from poor usability. Int. J. Med. Inf. **80**, 708–725 (2011)

21. Bum Chul, K., Fisher, B., Ji, S.: Visual analytic roadblocks for novice investigators. In: 2011 IEEE Conference on Visual Analytics Science and Technology (VAST), pp. 3–11 (2011)

Dual Watermarking of CT Scan Medical Images for Content Authentication and Copyright Protection

Nisar Ahmed Memon[1(✉)], Zulfiqar Ali Keerio[2], and Fatima Abbasi[2]

[1] Department of Computer Systems Engineering, QUEST Nawabshah,
Nawabshah, Pakistan
drnisar@quest.edu.pk
[2] Department of Information Technology, QUEST Nawabshah,
Nawabshah, Pakistan
{zakhalai,fatimaabbasi29}@gmail.com

Abstract. Digital CT Scan images are exchanged among the medical practitioners for consultative purposes or discussing diagnostic and therapeutic measures. This exchange of medical images imposes two main constraints for medical information: (i) the Content Authentication and (ii) Copyright protection. To address these two issues, we have proposed a technique of watermarking for medical images which embeds two watermarks in the CT scan image. The binary pattern is embedded in region of interest (ROI) for content authentication and the composite watermark is embedded in the region of non interest (RONI) for copyright protection. Initially CT Scan image is divided in ROI and RONI by segmentation process. The segmented ROI contains some holes which are first filled. The image morphology is then used and closing operation is applied on the resultant image which eliminates small holes and fills gaps in the contour. Thus binary mask is obtained which is used to separate ROI from RONI. Before embedding the binary pattern in ROI for data authentication purpose, the Least Significant Bit (LSB) information of ROI is extracted first and is saved in separate store. Also, before embedding the composite watermark, pixels in RONI are scrambled for providing the further security. The payload in both ROI and RONI is embedded with simple LSB substitution technique. The extraction procedure is the reverse of embedding process. However few steps of extraction procedure are same as embedding procedure. We have used CT scan image database obtained from Radiology Department, Ackron University Ohio USA. The experimental results show that the proposed algorithm provides better security of medical information during transmission by addressing both issues of data authentication and copyright protection.

Keywords: Medical image watermarking · Least significant bit technique · Image morphology · Image segmentation · Data authentication · Copyright protection · Region of interest (ROI) · Region of non interest (RONI)

1 Introduction

Millions of radiological images are produced daily in the radiology departments of the hospitals through the globe. These medical images are exchanged between the hospitals

© Springer International Publishing Switzerland 2014
F.K. Shaikh et al. (Eds.): IMTIC 2013, CCIS 414, pp. 173–183, 2014.
DOI: 10.1007/978-3-319-10987-9_16

by the medical practitioners for number of reasons. One main reason of these is the second opinion of doctor from another hospital on the same case under consideration [1]. This exchange of medical images imposes two main constraints for medical information (i) Content Authentication means image content has not been modified or tampered with during transmission from one hospital to another. (ii) Copyright protection means only authorized persons have access to the information [2]. Recently digital image watermarking has proven to facilitate remote handling of medical images in a secure manner [3]. The number of watermarking techniques are used for protection of digital images. For example Robust watermarking [4], Fragile watermarking [1], Semi-Fragile watermarking [5], and Hybrid Watermarking [6] and Reversible watermarking [7]. We have used the Hybrid watermarking technique for authentication and copyright protection of CT Scan medical Images. We have performed dual watermarking. One watermark named as binary pattern, is embedded in Region of Interest (ROI) and other watermark named as Composite Watermark (CW) is embedded in Region of Non-interest (RONI). By embedding the binary pattern in ROI part of the input image, we are much concerned with the integrity of ROI [8], while by embedding, CW watermark in RONI part of image, we are much concerned with the image security and confidentiality [1].

2 Literature Review

A large number of authors has reported watermarking techniques for medical images. Wakatani [9] has reported a medical image watermarking technique that avoids ROI watermarking and embeds watermark in the RONI. Although it preserves the image quality in ROI, the major drawback is the ease of introducing copy attack on the non-watermarked image. Giakoumaki et al. [6] have reported a wavelet-based multiple watermarking scheme which embeds different watermarks in the medical images. The results show that scheme offers better confidentiality and record integrity of medical image. The drawback is the integrity of medical image. The watermarking of the image is done on permanent basis. Thus the watermarking in the ROI of image is not undo which results in compromising on the diagnosis value of medical image. Woo et al. [10] have proposed a multiple watermarking technique for medical images. Encrypted patient data are embedded as annotation watermark for achieving privacy control and tiled binary pattern is embedded as fragile watermark for tamper localization.

All these techniques have one common limitation, that is, watermark embedding procedure introduces the distortion in the input image. This distortion is produced due to quantization, bit replacement or truncation, which is not completely removed from the input image. Thus diagnosis value of image is compromised which can results in wrong diagnosis. The proposed scheme undo the watermarking process after the image is declared authentic by the system. This is done by replacing the first bit plane of ROI with the LBS information extracted from RONI which restores the ROI in its original state. Thus in this way the diagnosis value of medical images is not compromised and medical practitioner can diagnosis the image without having any fear of loss of information due to the watermarking.

3 Proposed Scheme

We have proposed a simple watermarking scheme based on image segmentation, digital image morphology and LSB technique. The scheme embeds two different types of watermarks, the binary pattern and composite watermark, into the CT Scan medical images of the patient. The binary pattern detects changes in the ROI if it were tampered with during the transmission from one hospital to another. Thus it serves for the purpose of data authentication. The composite watermark which is comprised of four different watermarks named as patient information (history of patient), hospital logo, doctor's ID (who produced the image) and LSB information of ROI (The first bit plane of ROI) is embedded in RONI for copyright protection. On the detection side, the embedded watermarks from the both ROI and RONI are extracted and are compared with reference watermarks for checking the image integrity and ownership of image.

3.1 Generation of Watermarks

For checking the data integrity of ROI, a binary pattern comprised of ones and zeros is first created as shown in Fig. 1. The image was created using Microsoft Paint. Then a composite watermark is produced by concatenating 4 different watermarks as shown in the Fig. 2. The concatenated watermark is further combined with pseudo generated binary vector by using EX-OR operator in order to create more secure watermark.

About 1 K bits of patient information is embedded. The patient information contains the patient name, age, sex, and the history of his/her disease. We first have converted the alphabetic characters of patient information into ASCII codes. Later each ASCII code is converted into binary. The binary vector, thus created is concatenated with other watermarks. The Hospital logo of size 64×64 as shown in Fig. 3 is used for ownership purpose by the hospital. The binary matrix of size 64×64 pixels is first converted into binary vector and is then concatenated with other vectors to create CW watermark. Next pseudo binary vector of size 1024 bits based on user define key is generated and is referred as Doctor's ID. This code serves for the copyright claim for the medical image. Through this code it can be verified, that who is the producer of the image under examination. Finally LSB information of ROI is extracted and is concatenated with other watermarks to create CW watermark.

3.2 Segmentation of Input Image into ROI and RONI

For embedding the payload, the input image is divided into ROI and RONI. Geneally in image diagnosis applications, the ROI is selected by medical practitioner.

Different methods are applied, for example polygon, ellipse, rectangle, and even freehand is used for selecting ROI [11]. The medical practitioner defines ROI in a medical image that he would like to process and retrieve information from. For our proposed method we have selected the segmentation method as proposed in [12] with some further post processing by using region filling and image morphology. A structured element of shape 'disk' having radius of 5 pixels is used for closing operation.

```
1010101010101010101010101
0101010101010101010101010
1010101010101010101010101
0101010101010101010101010
1010101010101010101010101
0101010101010101010101010
1010101010101010101010101
0101010101010101010101010
1010101010101010101010101
0101010101010101010101010
1010101010101010101010101
0101010101010101010101010
```

Fig. 1. The binary pattern embedded in ROI

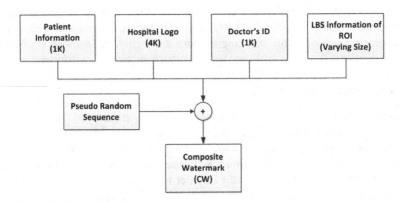

Fig. 2. The four different watermarks concatenated in single composite watermark (*CW*)

Fig. 3. The hospital logo

The closing operation generally smoothes section of contours, fuses narrow breaks and long thin gulfs, eliminates small holes and fill gaps in the contour [13]. In our case closing operation eliminates small holes and fills gaps in the contour. The binary mask obtained in this way is applied on the original image and ROI is easily obtained.

3.3   Watermark Embedding Procedure

Before starting the watermark embedding process first the segmentation process is performed as described in Sect. 3.2 above. After separating the ROI and RONI, the different steps are separately performed on both ROI and RONI regions. The complete embedding procedure is shown in Fig. 4. Each step of block diagram is explained in detail as given below.

1. Generate the Binary pattern and *CW* watermarks as explained in Sect. 3.1.
2. Divide the input image *f* into ROI and RONI as described in Sect. 3.2.
3. Extract the LSBs of ROI and store this information in separate store.
4. Set the LSBs of ROI to zeros.
5. Now embed the binary pattern as shown in Fig. 1 into the first bit plane of ROI part of image by LSB substitution method.
6. Scramble the pixels in RONI part as shown in Fig. 5(c) and embed the *CW* into the first bit plane of pixels using LSB substitution method.
7. De-scramble the pixels in RONI part after embedding *CW* watermark.
8. Reconstruct the image by combining watermarked ROI and RONI to get the complete watermarked image *f'*.

3.4 Watermark Extraction Procedure

The few steps of extraction procedure are exactly same as embedding procedure. The overall scheme of extraction procedure is shown in Fig. 6. We have developed the blind watermarking scheme, therefore there is no need of original image for extraction procedure. The watermark extraction procedure is explained as follows:

1. Segment the watermark image *f'* into ROI and RONI as described in Sect. 3.2.
2. Extract the binary pattern from the first bit plane of ROI which will later be examined for checking the integrity of ROI.
3. Scramble the pixels in RONI and extract the *CW* watermark from the pixels by getting the LSBs from first bit plane of RONI.
4. Decrypt the extracted *CW'* with the same pseudo generated vector using the same key as was used at the time of encryption using EX-OR operation.
5. Divide the *CW'* into Patient Information, Hospital Logo, Doctor's ID, and LSB information.
6. Compare the extracted watermarks with the reference watermarks to check the image authentication and copyright protection claim of the image.
7. After checking the authenticity of received image, replace the received LSB information with the first bit plane of ROI to get the exact original ROI part of image.

4 Results

The experiments are performed using the dataset as shown in Table 1. The medical images were received from the Radiology Department, Ackron University Ohio, USA. All images used in the experiments are of size 256 × 256 and 8-bit gray level images.

4.1 Results of Watermark Embedding

First the watermarks are embedded in ROI and RONI regions of the input image as shown in Fig. 5(a). Figure 7(a) shows the difference between the original and the watermarked ROI, whereas, Fig. 7(b) shows the difference between original and watermarked RONI. Figure 7(c) shows the difference between the original input image

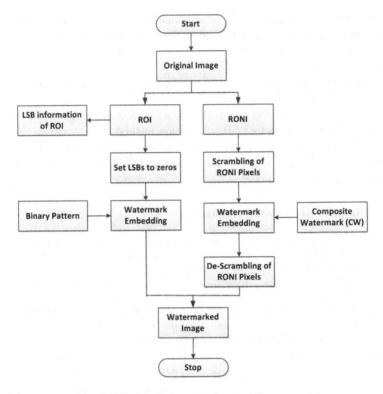

Fig. 4. The block diagram of embedding process

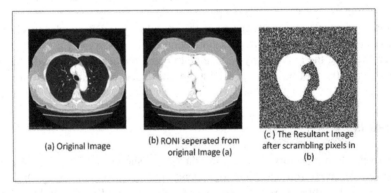

(a) Original Image

(b) RONI seperated from original Image (a)

(c) The Resultant Image after scrambling pixels in (b)

Fig. 5. The original image, the RONI and pixels scrambled in RONI

and watermarked image. The size of binary pattern to be embedded in ROI region depends on the area of ROI in the input image. For the CT scan image shown in Fig. 5 (a) having the size of 256 × 256 or 65536 pixels, the size of ROI was 16,463 pixels and the size of RONI was 49073 pixels. Thus binary pattern of size 16,463 pixels are embedded in ROI. Whereas, 1024 bits (1 Kb) of patient information, 4096 bits (4 Kb)

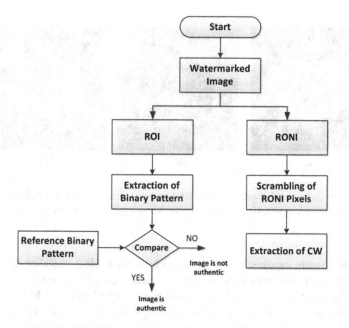

Fig. 6. The block diagram of watermark extraction procedure

Table 1. The dataset used in experiments

S. No.	Patient-ID	Total no. of slices	Slice thickness (mm)
1	110010A	99	2.0
2	110011A	60	3.0
3	110012A	56	5.0
4	110013A	30	2.0
5	110014A	81	4.0
6	110015A	78	4.0
7	110016A	64	3.0
8	110017A	55	3.0
9	110018A	67	3.0
10	110019A	120	4.0

of hospital logo, 1024 bits (1 Kb) of doctor's ID and 16,463 bits of LSB information are embedded in RONI. Thus the payload of 16.463 Kbits is embedded in ROI and 22.643 Kbits are embedded in RONI. The total payload for whole image was about 39 K bits. The noise introduced in the watermarked image is measured through *PSNR* and was found 53.33 dB. This is much higher than bench mark 38 dB.

The total time required for complete embedding procedure was 31.17 s. We have used MATLAB version R2007b on Intel Core i-5-2430 M CPU 2.4 GHz machine. The Table 2 shows the dataset of patient of age 50 years. The slice thickness was 0.3 mm.

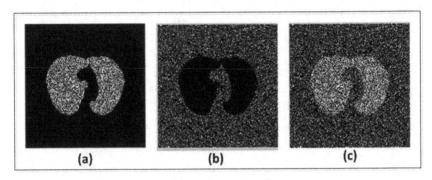

Fig. 7. (a) The difference between original ROI and watermarked ROI (b) Difference between RONI and watermarked RONI (c) Difference between original input image and watermarked image

Total 64 slices were captured on CT scan machine. In Table 2, the slice number, total area of ROI, total time consumed in both segmentation and embedding process and *PNSR* for each slice is shown. The embedding capacity of ROI and RONI is actually adaptive. Because in starting and end part of lung CT images, the area of ROI is small thus having low embedding capacity, whereas in the middle part of lung the embedding capacity of ROI is high thus resulting in higher embedding capacity as shown in column 2 of Table 2.

Table 2. Simulation results for model patient

Slice #	ROI (pixels)	Segmentation time (s)	Total embedding time (s)	PSNR (dB)
1	0	12.04	23.07	61.26
5	0	11.76	23.60	61.33
10	7599	12.03	20.70	55.99
15	13023	11.97	19.40	54.19
20	15041	12.09	18.88	53.66
25	15136	12.04	18.96	53.65
30	14204	11.82	18.97	53.88
35	12831	12.30	19.54	54.27
40	12104	12.43	19.84	54.46
45	7858	11.87	20.60	55.85
50	1738	11.51	21.85	59.47
55	0	11.35	22.41	61.33
60	0	11.46	22.36	61.28
64	0	11.56	22.69	64.01

Due to less area of ROI, the less bits of binary pattern are embedded in ROI and consequently less number of bits of LSB information is embedded in RONI. Due to this fact, the early slices and end slices report high values of *PSNR*, whereas middle slices report low values of *PNSR*. The column 5 of Table 2 reveals this fact.

4.2 Watermark Extraction

After segmenting the watermarked image into ROI and RONI, the binary pattern was extracted from ROI. For this purpose, the LSB of each pixle of ROI portion was extracted. Figure 8 shows the binary pattern extracted from ROI when no attack was performed on watermarked image.

Fig. 8. Extracted watermark from ROI without attack

The composite watermark was then extracted from RONI area of watermarked image. The extracted watermark was first combined with pseudo random vector using the EX-OR operator. The pseudo generated vector was created with the same key as was used at the time of embedding. The *CW* was then divided in the four different watermarks. Both subjective and objective measures are used. The Hospital logo was checked visually and found the same, thus copyright protection of image was ensured. However the Doctor's ID was compared with the reference pattern by using the Normalized Hamming Distance (*NHD*) [14]. The distance of zero was found between both the reference and the extracted doctor's IDs. This ensured the authenticity of image. The binary vector of patient information was passed under the reverse procedure of creating the patient information watermark as described in Sect. 3.1 to find the English alphabet characters of Patient information. The LSB information found from the *CW'* vector was used to replace the first bit plane of ROI to reconstruct the original image. This ensures the integrity of ROI. Thus our scheme does not compromise on the diagnosis value of ROI.

For checking the integrity of ROI, different types of attacks were performed. Here also both subjective and objective measures are used. In case of subjective measure, the visual inspection of watermarked images and images after attacked showed that those were looking same. However using the objective measure such as Normalized Hamming Distance, the results were different. Table 3 shows the different attacks performed on the watermarked images and the corresponding *NHD* for each attack. It can easily be observed that in case of no attack, hamming distance of 0 (zero) was found for both

Hospital Logo and Doctor's ID. However for other attacks the values of *NHD* are different and greater than zero, which helps in conclusion that that the received image is not authentic and has been tamped with during transmission.

Table 3. The various attacks applied on watermarked images and *NHD* for extracted watermarks from attacked images

S. No.	Type of attack	Strength of attack	Status of binary pattern extracted from ROI	Normalized Hamming Distance (*NHD*)	
				Hospital logo	Doctor's ID
1	No attack	–	Extracted exactly	0.000	0.000
2	JPEG compression	Q.F = 90 %	Completely destroyed	0.5349	0.5293
3	Median filtering	Window size = 3 x 3	Mostly blurred	0.4927	0.4326
4	Gaussian noise	Mean = 0, variance = 0.0001	Completely destroyed	0.5251	0.5156
5	Geometric attack	1 degree clock-wise	Marginally destroyed	0.5371	0.4844

5 Conclusions

We have reported a blind watermarking scheme which do not require original unwatermarked image for extraction of watermark. The scheme two types of watermarks namely binary watermark and composite watermark for data authentication and copyright protection. The scheme can be used for transmission of medical images from one hospital to another by carrying medical record of patient. Usually medical record of patient is sent through separate file along with the image The proposed scheme do the same in single image. Thus it saves the bandwidth and memory storage by watermarking the patient record in the image by sending the one file instead of one. Number of attacks are performed to show the validity of scheme. Almost all attacks are detected. Thus scheme can easily be implemented in medical applications, where medical practitioners send images from one hospital to another hospital for second opinion.

Acknowledgements. The authors are very thankful to R&D Lab, of Department of Information Technology, and Networking Lab of Department of Computer Systems Engineering, Quaide-Awam University of Engineering, Science and Technology, Nawabshah, District Shaheed Benazirabad for providing the resources for carrying out this research work and Radiological Department of Ackron University, Ohio, USA for providing the medical database for simulations.

References

1. Memon, N.A., Gilani, S.A.M.: NROI watermarking of medical images for content authentication. In: Proceedings of 12th IEEE International Multitopic Conference (INMIC-2008), Karachi, Pakistan, pp. 106−110 (2008)
2. Coatrieux, G., Montagner, J., Huang, H., Roux, C.: Mixed reversible and RONI watermarking for medical image reliability protection. In: 29th IEEE International Conference of EMBS, Cite Internationale, Lyon, France (2007)
3. Coatrieux, G., Lecornu, L., Sankur, B., Roux, C.: A review of image watermarking application in Healthcare. In: Proceedings of IEEE-EMBC Conference, New York, pp. 4691−4694 (2006)
4. Eggers, J.J., Bauml, R., Tzschoppe, R., Girod, B.: Scalar SOSTA scheme for information hiding. IEEE Trans. Sig. Process. 5(151), 1003–1019 (2003)
5. Delong, C.: A semi-fragile watermarking for ROI image authentication. In: MMIT International Conference on Multimedia and Information Technology, pp. 302−305 (2008)
6. Giakoumaki, A., Pavlopulos, S., Koutouris, D.: Multiple image watermarking applied to health information management. IEEE Trans. Inf. Technol. Biomed. 10(4), 722–732 (2006)
7. Nilanjan, D., Shouvik, B., Bardhan Roy, B.: Analysis of photoplethysmographic signals modified by reversible watermarking technique using prediction-error in wireless telecardiology. In: First International Conference on Intelligent Infrastructure the 47th Annual National Convention at COMPUTER SOCIETY of INDIA CSI − 2013 (2013)
8. Chang-Ri, P., Wong Min, W., Dhong Chul, P., Seung Soo, H.: Medical Image authentication using hash function and integer wavelet transform. In: IEEE 2008, Congress on Image and Signal Processing, Snaya, Hainan, China, pp. 7−10 (2008)
9. Wakatani, A.: Digital Watermarking for ROI medical images by using compressed signature image. In: Proceedings of the Annual Hawaii International Conference on Systems Sciences (HICCS), pp. 2043−2048 (2002)
10. Woo, C.S., Du, J., Pham, B.: Multiple watermarking method for privacy control and tamer detection in medical images. In: Lovell, G.C., Maeder, A.J. (eds.) Proceedings of APRS Workshop on Digital Image Computing (WDIC2005), Australia, Brisbane, South Bank, pp. 59−64 (2005)
11. http://desperate-engineers.com/blog/2011/05/06/matlab-multiple-roimask-editor-class/. Accessed August 2013
12. Memon, N.A., Mirza, A.M., Gilani, S.A.M.: Segmentation of Lungs from CT Scan images for early diagnosis of Lung Cancer. In: Proceedings of 2006 Enformatika, XIV International Conference, Prague, Czech Republic, 25−27 August (2006)
13. Gonzalez, R.C., Woods, R.E.: Digital Image Processing, 2nd edn. Pearson Education Incorporation, Singapore (2004)
14. Memon, N.A., Chaudhary, A., Ahmed, M., Keerio, Z.A.: Hybrid watermarking of medical images for ROI authentication and recovery. Int. J. Comput. Mathemtatics, Taylor and Francis 88(10), 2057–2071 (2011)

A Quality-Aware Computational Cloud
Service for Computational Modellers

Shahzad Nizamani[(✉)] and Amirita Kumari

Department of Software Engineering,
Mehran University of Engineering and Technology, Jamshoro, Sindh, Pakistan
{shahzad.nizamani,amirita}@faculty.muet.edu.pk

Abstract. Cloud computing, a relatively recent term, builds on decades of research in virtualization, distributed computing, utility computing, and more
recently networking. It is an emerging paradigm for large scale infrastructures
and there is a growing use of Cloud computing as it provides on-demand High
performance computing (HPC) resources. On the other end a Cloud service
provides a predictable and flexible on-demand pay-per-use ac-cess to a shared
pool of computing resources (e.g. networks, servers, storage, applications and
services). This research has been conducted to help computational modellers, to
select the most cost effective Cloud service provider. In this paper a novel
quality aware computational cloud selection service (QaCompPSS) is proposed
and evaluated. This selects the best (cheapest) cloud provider's service. After
selection, it automatically sets up and runs selected services. QaCompPSS
includes an integrated ontology that makes use of OWL- 2 features. The
ontology provides a standard specification and a common vocabulary for
describing cloud provider's services. The semantic descriptions are processed by
QaCompPSS information management service and the non-semantic selection
and run services.

Keywords: Cloud computing · Computational modellers · QOS

1 Introduction

Computational modellers in physical, financial management and life sciences organi-
sations need access to High Performance Computing (HPC). However computational
modellers are frustrated. Professor Peter Jimack, Leeds University states, *"Computational modellers have been experiencing frustrations in two areas. Firstly, they feel
disadvantaged by the way local HPC facilities schedule jobs with a run-time of twelve
hours or more. The turnaround time of these jobs can be unpredictable. Secondly, they
find the price and reliability of the service. These are inflexible and do not cater very
well for their computational service needs as they vary throughout the model development process."*

There is a growing use of Cloud computing [1] because it provides on-demand
HPC resources rather than using centrally managed large HPC facilities. On the other
end a Cloud service provides a predictable and flexible on-demand pay-per-use access
to a shared pool of computing resources. In this research we were concerned solely
with IaaS (Infrastructure as a Service) cloud service providers. Each cloud computing

© Springer International Publishing Switzerland 2014
F.K. Shaikh et al. (Eds.): IMTIC 2013, CCIS 414, pp. 184–194, 2014.
DOI: 10.1007/978-3-319-10987-9_17

service provider offers the user a choice of different VMs (Virtual Machines). Each VM has processor, memory, storage and other resources. Price of a VM depends on the allocated resources (e.g. the amount of run-time memory and the number of CPU cycles). An advantage of Cloud computing to an organization (e.g. University) is that it avoids having to make lumping, large capital investments thus improving their cash flow. Computational modellers benefit because there are more on-demand service options than the "one-size-fits-all" service provided by the in-house HPC facilities. Running large computational model is expensive. So quality of the service (QoS) is an important concern for users [6]. This is particularly important for a user who wishes to run large computation jobs particularly if they have to meet strict time constraints. However it is very difficult to enforce QoS guarantees without human involvement so the current public Cloud providers offer only "best-efforts". This is referred to as *Quality-awareness*. The service provider can: (1) just drop the service in the case of overload; and (2) provide no guarantees concerning the response time, job throughput etc.).

To address this problem a novel Quality-aware Computational Cloud Service (QAComPMS) service, that is a Software-as-a-Service (SaaS), is proposed. This is described in the following section. The key underlining service is a quality aware *federated computational semantic Web service* (QAComPSS). Its main features are (1) A federated cloud provider's ontology service to integrate the information on the QoS and cloud provider's resources with associated costs, (2) automatic (agent) selection process to discover the best VM that meets the computational modellers QoS and resources requirements, and (3) A semantic annotation for web service description language (SAWSDL) interface between the Broker information and QAComPSS service, for example, to update the QoS metrics [8, 9].

The rest of the paper is organized as follows. Section 2 states the background and related work. Section 3 elaborates the Webs service QoS selection. In Sect. 4 the QoS based framework is proposed. Section 5 evaluates the framework and discusses the results. The paper is concluded in Sect. 6.

2 Background and Related Work

Godse [2] points out that for any Web Service architecture (including Cloud services) there are two aspects: functional and QoS. He points out that in the case when there are many providers offering same function then: QoS becomes a service-differentiating criterion of selection.

In case of computational Clouds there are many providers offering a variety of VMs providing computation recourses. For example in this paper they are classified as Small, Medium, Large and Extra Large (High CPU) levels. At each level there are many providers having the capability of delivering the computational resources. Therefore, the QoS becomes a service-differentiating criterion of selection. Hence, our problem is provide a service that can, by mediating across a number of commercial computational Cloud providers, select and run (transparently) the best (e.g. cheapest) computational provider's virtual machine that meets the user's computational resources and QoS requirements (e.g. Cost, Risk and Trust).

In this paper a novel Software-as-a-Service (SaaS) *Quality-aware Computational Cloud Service (QAComPMS)* is proposed to address this problem. An overview of the service is shown in Fig. 1.

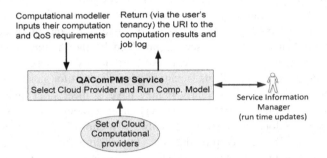

Fig. 1. Overview of the service

The external services are, (1) *Pubic Computational Web* Services which enables a modeller to input their computational and QoS requirements and then the service returns the results of the job and its log via URIs, (2) *Private Information Management Web Service* which is an internal, private Information Management Web service to automatically update the dynamic QoS ratings after each run service has executed and terminated, and (3) *Private Computational Cloud service:* to manage the service the set of public IaaS computational providers are selected from the available on the Internet.

3   Web Service QoS Selection

Web service is an example of a service oriented computing that are widely used to significantly reduce the development times and cost. Then there are a number of providers offering the same functionality then QoS is the service-differentiating criterion of selection [3]. They point out that:

Selecting the service with the best match service of QoS requirements is a multi-criteria decision problem that needs a thorough understanding of the QoS.

The purpose of this research is to provide a service that can by mediating across a number of commercial computational Cloud providers to select and run (transparently) the best (e.g. cheapest) computational provider's virtual machine that meets the user's computational resources and QoS requirements (e.g. Cost, Risk and Trust). Underpinning the QAComPMS is an important semantics Web Service called QAComPSS. It is a quality aware *federated computational semantic Web service.*

3.1   QoS/Cost Selection Model

The selection of the best Cloud provider's VM has two dimensions i.e. the Cost (functional) and QoS which is used to select the cheapest VM. An example is shown in Fig. 2 and is the case study used in this paper.

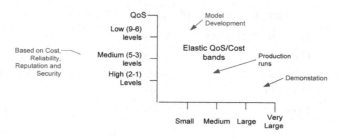

Fig. 2. QoS/Cost selection

The Cloud provider's VMs are organised according to a cost model which relates the cost to the resources required (e.g. memory, cores). This is classified into cost bands (e.g. Small, Medium, Larger and Very large). The other dimension is the QoS ratings using a scale 1-Q Rate (e.g. 1-9 is often used). The ratings are grouped into QoS levels (1-Levels) where each Level has number ratings this is shown in Fig. 3 using High, Medium and Low. The levels are used to filter the provider's VM to speed up the selection process. User can prioritise the importance of each QoS metric. An important difference from existing selection of Web Services is QAComPSS the treatment of the Cost QoS metrics. This is derived the Cost model that is used to mediate the actual Cloud providers. Because the goal is to select the cheapest provider's VM the QoS Cost is always of 1 rating. However in other situations one may use other rating points.

As it can be or the user to specify the exact QoS they require they are asked to indicate whether they desire a high, medium or low QoS. They are also required to state the relative importance of the each QoS metric for a job. The QAComPMS can be adapted to incorporate additional levels.

3.2   Cost Model

The cost element of the QoS model is derived from a separate Cost model. This maps cost against the computational resources purchased for example RAM (GB), virtual core (integer), Disk space (GB), price per hour, communication and storage services. The cost model can be expressed as:

$$Cost = (\alpha \times C_l + \beta \times Dt)/(\alpha + \beta)$$

where C_l is made up of memory (GB), processor (virtual cores), and non-persistent storage. D_t is the data transfer rate and α, β are constants chosen by the Service Information Manager. The computational resource size is in four bands: Small, Medium, Large and Very Large. Table 1 shows the actual cost values used in our evaluation study. Here the model does not include long term storage costs that may also be important.

Four cloud providers were considered: Amazon, Rackspace, GoGrid and FlexiScale as a representative sample of computational cloud services. These providers were used to specify a logical cost model and associated resources (see Table 1). As said above the Cost model was also used to define the cost QoS rating. In our evaluation study we

Table 1. QAComPMS *Cost Model RUN Service*

	MaxCost US $/month	Memory GB	#Cores	Storage GB
Small	Upto 100	2.00	1	160
Medium	Upto 350	4.00	4	500
Large	Upto 500	8.00	8	800
Very large	Upto 1000	16.00	16	1700

used three cost bands: Low (1–4) equates to high cost VMs (the most expensive for the computational resources they provide); medium (5–7) represents intermediate value for money and high (8–9) represents excellent value for money (the lowest cost). Cost bands are the main linkage between the actual costs (what the user pays) and the Cost QoS ratings.

Amazon and FlexiScale [7] explicitly offer HPC VMs. These are clustered and support applications using MPI (the message passing interface) and running very computationally intense jobs. As these services are ideal for running HPC applications the QAComPMS Run service can be restricted to considering only computational clouds that offer this type of service.

3.3 QoS Metrics

All the Cloud providers currently offer "best effort" so the QoS cost, risks and trust are particularly important when running large computational jobs. The QoS considered in this paper are Cost, Risk and Trust. These are measured by four QoS metrics: Cost C (p), Reputation R_p (p), Reliability $R_l(p)$ and Security S(p), where p is a provider and each rating is on a rating scale of 1–9 with 1 equating to highest quality and 9 to lowest quality. For each QoS:

Reliability: R_l is probability that the provider's services fails to complete the execution of a RUN job and return the URI to the results of the RUN. The value of the success rate is computed from data on past invocations using the expression $R_l = N(p)/K$ where N is the number of times that the provider' services has been successfully completed within the maximum expected time frame, and K is the total number of invocations. Closely related to reliability is the availability determined by the probability of a SLA violations which are likely to incur a penalty cost. This can be mapped uniformly into a 9 point. To limit the size of the history a sliding window of, say, the last 100 RUNs is used. A more sophisticated statistic measure of reliability is given in [5].

Reputation: R_p is the reputation of the provider's service measure of the trustworthiness of the provider. It's a posterior estimation based on historic end-user experiences either directly or indirectly. The reputation, in part, is measured using user feedback collected from the user's experience in using the service. Security: This is a soft QoS metric and is the rating for security which is regularly monitored and updated as required.

3.4 QAComPMS User Client Service

The QAComPMS client is shown in Fig. 3. There are three parts:

(1) Pubic Computational Web Services. The modeller inputs their computational and QoS requirements and the service returns the results of the job and its log via URIs. Before running the run service the user downloads their code and selects the type of service (e.g. general service or HPC only service).

(2) Private Information Management Web Services. This is an internal, private Information Management Web service. Service automatically updates the dynamic QoS ratings after each run service has executed and terminated. The information manager is responsible for updating the static QoS rating. It can activate or deactivate a provider's VM. Periodically the QAComp software is updated and the re-compiled (e.g. to update the cost model, add/subtract/modify Cloud providers and associated VMs).

(3) Other Services. Also need to provide (a) SLA description of the QAComPMS and (b) User feedback (reputation). These are not considered further in this paper because these are business issues that are outside the scope of this paper.

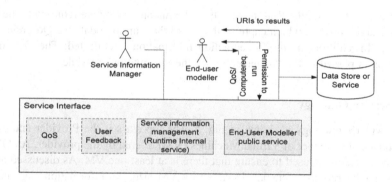

Fig. 3. QAComPMS client

3.5 Service Side

The service side of the QAComPMS is shown in Fig. 4. The QAComPMS is embedded within a commercial Cloud provider hosting service to access the standard Cloud services (like billing etc.). The main modules are:

(1) The service information manager will select the set of public computational Clouds (at run time) and can dynamically mark activate or deactivate.

(2) Management of the dynamic (run time activities) information service to manage updates about the QoS of each VM (either automatically at the end of each run or periodically by the service manager). For each VM image there are the two services: QAComPSS which mediates the Cloud providers to select the "best" Cloud provider's VM; and the selected VM is passed to the Run process (note the user's code

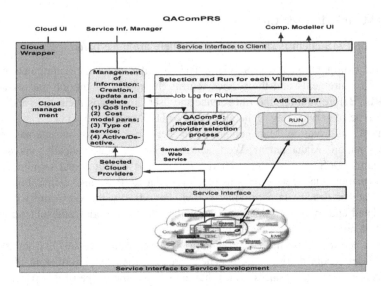

Fig. 4. Service side

is preloaded). After the Run the results of the run and its log are returned to the QoS information process which captures the log of the Run to update the QoS reliability value. In addition the user's reputation information is collected. The QoS information is passed to the "management of the information" module.

3.6   Service Ontology

The Provider's ontology is shown in Fig. 5. The top class is the Provider and a subclass models the number of Virtual Machines (VM) offered by the provider. An OWL2 property restriction is used to ensure that there is at least one VM. As discussed above the cost model provides four levels varied by VM size. An information class is provided that handles information associated with a provider. The VMProvider class models the type of VM and whether it's active or inactive. A UpDateProvider class

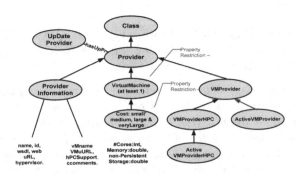

Fig. 5. Provider's ontology

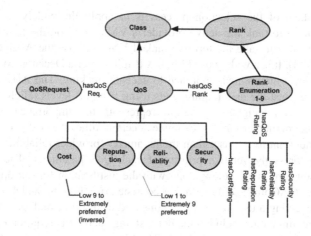

Fig. 6. QoS ontology

enables the information on the selected Provider's VM to be transferred to RUN service using SAWSDL annotations [8].

The QoS ontology is based on the QoS model as shown in Fig. 6. It uses an OWL2 Rank Enumeration giving the meaning to the ranking. The data properties enable the user to access each QoS data property.

4   System Architecture

The QAComPSS architecture has three main functions as shown in Fig. 7. (1) The management of the selected providers, (2) The matchmaker, and (3) The selection of the best cloud provider. The service ontology federates across the active cloud providers and logically filters the providers' VMs into High, Medium or Low quality services. This filter improves the performance of the selection process.

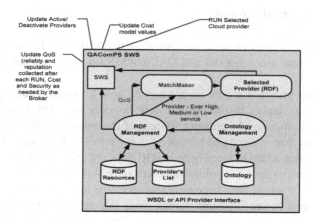

Fig. 7. System architecture

The first stage of the selection process is to apply the widely used Euclidean distance algorithm to rank the active provider's VMs based on the four QoS ratings. The second phase is to take the top five ranked VMs and use the Analytic Hierarchy Process (AHP) [4]. It is a widely used MCDA (Multi Criteria Decision Analysis) based method that uses a hierarchical approach to decision making. The AHP process matches the VMs against the user requirements using the QoS levels (High, Medium and Low) together with weights. A weight represents the importance of each QoS parameter for the particular job. For example at certain times the cost parameter may be much more important to the user than the parameter 'provider reliability'. QoS levels and weights express the relative priority of each QoS parameter. The performance evaluation results are given below along with the justification for our approach.

Alternative: QAComPSS MatchMaker consisted of a ranking and selection step. It starts off by receiving a user request that consisted of resource and QoS requirements. The resource requirements included memory, storage and CPU requirements. The QoS requirements were low, medium and high. The request was passed on to the Euclidean Distance based ranker that ranked the list of available providers. The top five providers were passed on to the AHP-based matchmaker that selected the "best" provider. At the top of the AHP hierarchy the goal was setup to identify the best provider. This was followed by the QoS criteria parameters and their associated weights. These were inputted by the user to reflect their relative priorities. At the bottom of the hierarchy there were alternatives that represented available VM options.

SAWSDL is used to communicate with other services. SAWSDL annotations included a model reference, and lifting and lowering schema mapping data. The model references represented entities that form part of the ontology while the lifting and lowering schema mapping formed the communication channel between QAComPSS and other web services. The lifting schema mapping was used for transferring data from a non-semantic source, such as XML to QAComPSS. For the lowering schema mapping QAComPSS used a SPARQL query to extract information from RDF and pass it to a non-semantic web service.

5 Evaluation and Results

The experiment consisted of the development of two services: QAComPSS (responsible for processing user requests) and QAComPMS (used for updating the provider information).

QAComPMS provided a light weight service used for creating and updating provider information. Inputs to the service were provider and VM information. This information was processed by creating a model of the ontology with the inputted data values. This was than inferred and reasoned for any errors. If there were no errors than the information was added to a newly created RDF record and an entry was made in the index file. For this experiment public providers such as Amazon were considered but were not used as it would have been too expensive. The results from this research will provide assurance before investing further with this research. Instead twenty five simulated providers were created each offered a different set of QoS metrics while all of them offered the same computational resources. The simulated providers offered small, medium, large VMs.

The experiment was performed by creating twenty five simulated providers and twenty four user requests. There were eight user requests each for low, medium and high QoS. They were controlled requests whose output was previously calculated beforehand to identify the progress of each service. Each user request was passed to AHP, QMP, QAComPSS and QAComPSS (filter).

The horizontal axis shows the user request whilst the vertical axis shows the logical cost. The logical cost is measured on a scale of one to nine (with nine showing the best option).

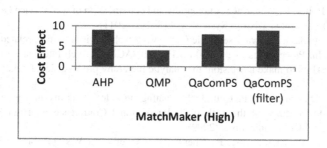

Fig. 8. MatchMaker comparisons (High QoS)

The selection was dependent on the user requests and provider's QoS. While providers with higher QoS service and lower costs were selected more than once there were other providers which were not selected at all as they offered higher costs and lower QoS.

Figure 8 shows the results for high QoS. This means that each of the QoS rating (Cost, Reliability, Reputation and Security), for the selected providers, were high. It can be observed that AHP, QAComPSS with and without the filter produced good results. However QAComPSS had some inconsistencies and QMP was not very effective. It was observed that QAComPSS and QAComPSS (with filter) were very effective when the selected providers had a medium level of QoS for all four ratings. Overall QMP performed well for low QoS ratings but was not very good for the higher QoS level. This is due to the way QMP operates as it may prioritize for providers offering lower QoS.

Overall the results showed that the QAComPSS (with filter) performs best for all the three levels of QoS. Another advantage of the filter was that the performance was enhanced as it reduces the set of relevant providers which results in less processing.

6   Conclusion and Future Work

This paper has presented a novel quality-aware federated computational semantic Web service (QAComPSS). This service enabled automatic selection of cloud providers. QAComPSS is the key service for the envisioned cloud broker. The evaluation results have potentially shown that QAComPSS service can successfully select the best computational cloud provider that meets the user's resource and QoS requirements. For the future this research needs to ground the simulated results to actual computational cloud providers. The next stage is to fully integrate QAComPSS service into to QA-CommPMS service.

References

1. Mell, P., Grance, T.: The NIST definition of cloud computing (draft). NIST special publication 800.145, p. 7 (2011)
2. Godse, M., Bellur, U., Sonar, R.: A taxonomy and classification of web service QoS elements. Int. J. Commun. Netw. Distrib. Syst. **6**(2), 118–141 (2011)
3. Zhou, J., Niemela, E.: Toward semantic QOS aware web services: issues, related studies and experience. In: Proceedings of the 2006 IEEE/WIC/ACM on Web Intelligence (2006)
4. Saaty, T.L.: How to make a decision: the analytic hierarchy process. Eur. J. Oper. Res. **48**(1), 9–26 (1990)
5. Gourlay, I., Djemame, K., Padgett, J.: Evaluating provider reliability in grid resource brokering. In: Proceedings of the 11th IEEE International Conference on High Performance Computing and Communications (2009)
6. Rajendran, T., Balasubramanie, P., Cherian, R.: An efficient WS-QoS broker based architecture for web services selection. Int. J. Comput. Appl. **1**(9), 79–84 (2010)
7. Ferraris, F.L., et al.: Evaluating the auto scaling performance of Flexiscale and Amazon EC2 clouds. In: 14th International Symposium on Symbolic and Numeric Algorithms for Scientific Computing. IEEE (2012)
8. Vitvar, T., Kopecký, J., Viskov, J., Fensel, D.: WSMO-lite annotations for web services. In: Proceedings of the 5th European Semantic Web Conference (2008)
9. Kopecky, J., Vitvar, T., Bournez, C., Farrell, J.: SAWSDL: semantic annotations for WSDL and XML schema. IEEE Internet Comput. **11**(6), 60–67 (2007)

Logically Optimized Smallest FPGA Architecture for SHA- 3 Core

Muzaffar Rao[1(✉)], Thomas Newe[1], and Arshad Aziz[2]

[1] University of Limerick, Limerick, Ireland
{muhammad.rao,thomas.newe}@ul.ie
[2] National University of Sciences and Technology, Islamabad, Pakistan
arshad@nust.edu.pk

Abstract. This work proposes a logically optimized smallest arithmetic architecture for the new Secure Hash Algorithm-3 (SHA-3) core using the Look-Up-Table (LUT) resources of FPGA. In this work a novel technique for compact implementation of SHA-3 core is discussed. The Logical operations of the SHA-3 core are optimized using Boolean equations and the result is saved in LUT_6 primitives available in modern Xilinx FPGAs. The proposed architecture consists of 64 LUT_6 primitives and these LUTs are used throughout the compression function operation. Work is still in progress on control circuitry in which we are trying to access internal resources of FPGA. So results of only Core implantation are discussed now and will be updated after designing of control circuitry.

Keywords: SHA-3 · High speed hardware · FPGA

1 Introduction

Secure cryptographic hash functions are one of the main components in many applications like authentication systems or digital signature schemes. Commonly used Hash functions are SHA-0, SHA-1, SHA-256, SHA-512, RIPEMD, MD4 and MD5. In previous years Cryptanalysis of these algorithms has found serious vulnerabilities [1–3]. Although no attacks have yet been reported on the SHA-2 variants, but given to their algorithmically similarities to SHA-1 there are fears that SHA-2 could also be cracked in the near future. The National Institute of Standards and Technology (NIST), USA announced the SHA-3 Contest in Nov 2007 [4]. This contest was to result in a new and secure cryptographic hash algorithm. This competition ended on 2nd October 2012 with the announcement of Keccak, one of the finalists of SHA-3 competition, as the winner for the title of SHA-3 [5].

For many secure systems, hardware implementations of cryptographic algorithms are needed to provide high speed and real time results. ASIC and FPGA are the two hardware platforms that can be used for these implementations. A lot of work has been done on high speed implementation of SHA-3 using the dedicated resources of FPGA like LUTs, DSP Slices etc. [6–8] but few results are available for compact implementation. This work proposes a low resource and compact implementation of SHA-3 on an FPGA. FPGA is seen as the best leading platform of the modern era in terms of flexibility, reliability and re-configurability.

© Springer International Publishing Switzerland 2014
F.K. Shaikh et al. (Eds.): IMTIC 2013, CCIS 414, pp. 195–203, 2014.
DOI: 10.1007/978-3-319-10987-9_18

Conventional coding techniques and synthesis tools are often not intelligent enough and do not utilize FPGA resources efficiently [9]. This results in inefficient designs both in terms of area and speed and can lead to some fast and dedicated areas on the chip remaining unutilized. To avoid the extra utilization of FPGA resources (due to unintelligent synthesis tools) and to implement the SHA-3 compression function with minimum hardware resources, the logical operations of the compression function have been manually computed and directly saved as an INIT value in the dedicated LUT_6 primitives of Xilinx FPGAs (Virtex-6 & Virtex-7). The manually created and implemented look-up-table has proven to be more effective and provides flexibility to implement the logic efficiently with respect to the designer's requirements. Without this manual implementation the synthesis tools can generate inefficient designs which can use extra hardware resources. For example, a synthesis tool may only use 1 input of a LUT in a particular slice (A slice consist of 4-LUTs and each LUT consist of 6-inputs in case of Virtex-6, 7) and then count the whole slice in the final results. This can be prevented by manually shifting this input to any other slice that is already in use but has free inputs. Although this can result in frequency compromise, for compact implementations our main concerned is to save area.

2 Secure Hash Algorithm-3

SHA-3 [10] comprises of a family of sponge functions characterized by two parameters [r, c], where r is the bitrate and c is the capacity. The sponge function is a generalization of the concept of cryptographic hash function with infinite output and can perform quasi all symmetric cryptographic functions, from hashing to pseudo-random number generation to authenticated encryption. The sum of r + c determines the width of the SHA-3 function permutation used in the sponge construction and is restricted to values of 1600 bits with different r and c values for each desired length of hash output. The 1600-bit state of SHA-3 consists of a 5×5 matrix of 64-bit words. There are 24 rounds in the compression function of SHA-3 and each round consists of 5 steps, Theta (θ), Rho (ρ), Pi(π) Chi (χ) and Iota (i) as shown in (1) to (6) below.

Theta (θ) Step: $(0 \leq x, \ y \leq 4)$

$$C[x] = A[x, 0] \oplus A[x, 1] \oplus A[x, 2] \oplus A[x, 3] \oplus A[x, 4]; \tag{1}$$

$$D[x] = C[x-1] \oplus ROT(C[x + 1, 1); \tag{2}$$

$$A'[x, y] = A[x, y] \oplus D[x]; \tag{3}$$

Rho (ρ) and Pi (π) Step: $(0 \leq x, y \leq 4)$

$$B[y, 2x + 3y] = ROT \ (A'[x, y], r[x, y]); \tag{4}$$

Chi (χ) Step: $(0 \le x, y \le 4)$

$$F[x,y] = B[x,y] \oplus ((NOTB[x+1,y])ANDB[x+2,y]); \qquad (5)$$

Iota (i):

$$F'[0,0] = F[0,0] \oplus RC; \qquad \text{Where } RC \text{ is the Round Constant} \qquad (6)$$

In Eqs. (1) to (6) above all operations within indices are done modulo 5. A denotes a 5×5 matrix of 1600-bit state and A[x, y] denotes a particular 64-bit word in that state. B[x, y], C[x] and D[x] are intermediate variables. The θ step consists of a 5 and 2 input XOR logical operation where each input is a 64-bit word. ρ is simply rotation of A'[x, y] bits according to the cyclic shift offset (r[x, y]) and π step change the position of rotated bits of A'[x, y] according to the given scheme of [y, 2x + 3y]. The χ step involves χ logic that is the combination of XOR, NOT and AND logical operation. In i step only 64-bits of F[0, 0] are updated by using XOR operation with 64-bit RC that is unique for each round. RC and r[x, y] are given in the specification sheet of SHA-3.

3   Novel Arithmetic Architecture for Compact Implementation of a SHA-3 Core

This novel architecture uses LUT_6 primitives. LUTs are the basic logic building blocks of an FPGA and are used to implement most logic functions of a design. LUT_6 as shown in Fig. 1, is a 6-input, 1-output look-up table (LUT) that can either act as an asynchronous 64-bit ROM (with 6-bit addressing) or implement any 6-input logic function. The INIT parameter for the FPGA LUT primitive provides the logical value of the LUT and consists of a 64-bit Hexadecimal value.

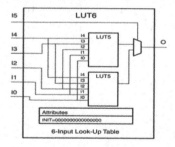

Fig. 1. LUT_6 primitive

It is obvious from the compression function steps that there are two types of logical operations throughout the compression function (a) XOR logic (b) χ logic. In this design we have stored the result of these logics manually in a single LUT_6 primitive as an INIT value. The MSB of the LUT_6 input is used as a control bit for the selection between XOR and χ logic. If the control bit is '0' then XOR logic is selected and in the case of the control bit being a '1', χ logic is selected. The INIT value of the LUT_6 primitive is derived by using the truth table for all possible combinations of LUT inputs as shown in Tables 1 and 2.

Table 1. Truth table for INIT value of LUT_6 (Control bit = 0)

Inputs						O1	O1('h)	Inputs						O1	O1('h)
I5	I4	I3	I2	I1	I0			I5	I4	I3	I2	I1	I0		
0	0	0	0	0	0	**0**	6	0	1	0	0	0	0	**1**	9
0	0	0	0	0	1	**1**		0	1	0	0	0	1	**0**	
0	0	0	0	1	0	**1**		0	1	0	0	1	0	**0**	
0	0	0	0	1	1	**0**		0	1	0	0	1	1	**1**	
0	0	0	1	0	0	**1**	9	0	1	0	1	0	0	**0**	6
0	0	0	1	0	1	**0**		0	1	0	1	0	1	**1**	
0	0	0	1	1	0	**0**		0	1	0	1	1	0	**1**	
0	0	0	1	1	1	**1**		0	1	0	1	1	1	**0**	
0	0	1	0	0	0	**1**	9	0	1	1	0	0	0	**0**	6
0	0	1	0	0	1	**0**		0	1	1	0	0	1	**1**	
0	0	1	0	1	0	**0**		0	1	1	0	1	0	**1**	
0	0	1	0	1	1	**1**		0	1	1	0	1	1	**0**	
0	0	1	1	0	0	**0**	6	0	1	1	1	0	0	**1**	9
0	0	1	1	0	1	**1**		0	1	1	1	0	1	**0**	
0	0	1	1	1	0	**1**		0	1	1	1	1	0	**0**	
0	0	1	1	1	1	**0**		0	1	1	1	1	1	**1**	

Table 2. Truth table for INIT value of LUT_6 (Control bit = 1)

Inputs						O2	O2('h)	Inputs						O2	O2('h)
I5	I4	I3	I2	I1	I0			I5	I4	I3	I2	I1	I0		
1	0	0	0	0	0	**0**	2	1	1	0	0	0	0	**0**	2
1	0	0	0	0	1	**1**		1	1	0	0	0	1	**1**	
1	0	0	0	1	0	**0**		1	1	0	0	1	0	**0**	
1	0	0	0	1	1	**0**		1	1	0	0	1	1	**0**	
1	0	0	1	0	0	**1**	D	1	1	0	1	0	0	**1**	D
1	0	0	1	0	1	**0**		1	1	0	1	0	1	**0**	
1	0	0	1	1	0	**1**		1	1	0	1	1	0	**1**	
1	0	0	1	1	1	**1**		1	1	0	1	1	1	**1**	
1	0	1	0	0	0	**0**	2	1	1	1	0	0	0	**0**	2
1	0	1	0	0	1	**1**		1	1	1	0	0	1	**1**	
1	0	1	0	1	0	**0**		1	1	1	0	1	0	**0**	
1	0	1	0	1	1	**0**		1	1	1	0	1	1	**0**	
1	0	1	1	0	0	**1**	D	1	1	1	1	0	0	**1**	D
1	0	1	1	0	1	**0**		1	1	1	1	0	1	**0**	
1	0	1	1	1	0	**1**		1	1	1	1	1	0	**1**	
1	0	1	1	1	1	**1**		1	1	1	1	1	1	**1**	

In Table 1 output of O1 is used to represent XOR logic and in Table 2 output of O2 is used to represent χ logic as shown in (7) & (8). The outputs of O1 and O2 provide INIT value of LUT_6 that is 64'h D2D2D2D296696996.

$$O1 = I0 \oplus I1 \oplus I2 \oplus I3 \oplus I4 \oplus I5 \tag{7}$$

$$O2 = I0 \oplus (\sim I1\&I2) \tag{8}$$

The 1600- bit of compression function is divided into a 5 × 5 matrix in such a way that each position of the matrix contains a 64-bit word. All the bitwise logical operations are performed between these 64-bit words. Because of this we have instantiated the 64 LUT_6 primitives with the same INIT value as shown in Fig. 2. These 64 LUTs are used throughout the completion of the compression function.

Figure 2 represents 64 LUTs with different sets of inputs. The sequence of input bits is taken, keeping in mind the bitwise logical operation between a 64-bit word of state matrix A. This architecture is used throughout the compression function. Intermediate values are stored in temporary register. Implementation of each step of the SHA-3 compression function shown in Fig. 2 is given in detail below.

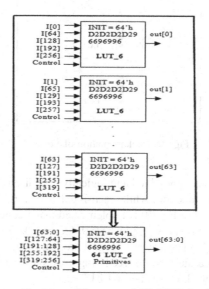

Fig. 2. Proposed smallest arithmetic architecture of 64 LUT_6 primitives for SHA-3 Core (compression function)

3.1 Theta (θ) Step

Equation (1) of the θ step involves a logical operation of a 5-input XOR function between a 64-bit word of each row of matrix A. For example C[0] is the XOR output of a 64-bit word of each row of the 1st column of matrix A i.e. C[0] = A[0, 0] ⊕ A[0, 1] ⊕ A[0, 2] ⊗ A[0, 3] ⊕ A[0, 4]. So, 64 LUT_6 primitives of Fig. 2 are used with the control bit tied to '0' because of XOR logic. One clock cycle is required to find C [0]. In the next clock cycle a 64-bit word of each row of the 2nd column of matrix A is applied as input to the previously used 64 LUT_6 primitives to find C[1] and the same process is repeated for C[2], C[3] and C[4] with respective sets of inputs. So, Eq. (1) is implemented using 5 clock cycles and at each clock cycle the same hardware resources of 64 LUTs are used as shown in Fig. 3.

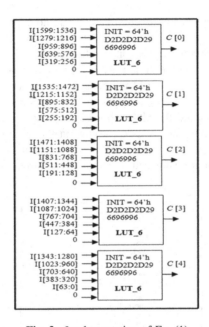

Fig. 3. Implementation of Eq. (1)

Equations (2) and (3) are combined and logically optimized as shown in Eq. (9) and becomes a 3-input XOR function, while each input is of a 64-bit word size. One bit rotation in the last operand of Eq. (9) is implemented using concatenation. Twenty five clock cycles are required to find A'[x, y] where $0 \leq x$, $y \leq 4$ and at each clock cycle the previously used 64 LUT_6 primitives of Fig. 2 are used with different inputs and the control bit tied to '0' because of the XOR logic as shown in Fig. 4. So, θ step is implemented using 30-clock cycles and 64 LUTs.

$$A'[x, y] = A[x, y] \oplus C[x-1] \oplus ROT(C[x+1], 1) \qquad (9)$$

3.2   Rho (ρ), Pi (π) and Chi (χ) Step

ρ is a simply bit rotation of A'[x, y] and π changes the position of the rotated bits of A' [x, y]. These permutation steps are performed in advance and directly applied to the χ step. The χ step uses χ logic that is a combination of XOR, NOT and AND logical

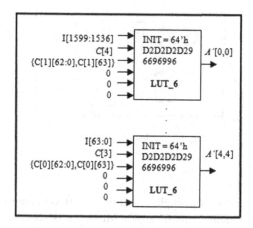

Fig. 4. Implementation of Eq. (9)

operations as shown in Eq. (8). In this step the previously used LUTs of Fig. 2 are used with the output of the θ step as input as shown in Fig. 5. Now the control bit is tied to '1' because of χ logic. To find F[x, y] where $0 \leq x$, $y \leq 4$ twenty five clock cycles are required.

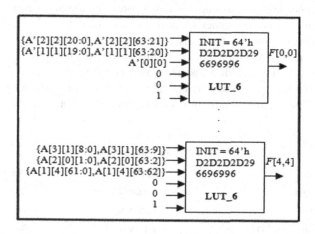

Fig. 5. Implementation of ρ, π and χ step

3.3   Iota (I)

This step involves a 2-input XOR function between a 64-bit RC and 64-bits of F[0, 0]. It has been implemented using the 64 LUTs of Fig. 2 as shown in Fig. 6 with the control bit tied to '0'. One clock is required to implement this step.

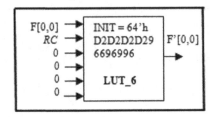

Fig. 6. Implementation of *i* step

3.4 Summary

Therefore, implementation of a single round of the SHA-3 compression function that consists of five steps requires only 64 LUTs. Multiplexers are used for the selection of LUTs. The remaining 23 rounds of the compression functions are completed in the same way using the same hardware resources of Fig. 2 sequentially.

4 Results

Table 3 shows the results of SHA-3 core implementation in terms of area and shows that SHA-3 core implementation utilizes only 16 slices and we have proved it in Sect. 3 by discussing architecture of each step of SHA-3 core. The routing was performed manually by the authors as the synthesis tool required extra slices to be used for routing. Previous implementation results are also shown in Table 3. We can see that previous design used a lot of slices. Although our results are intermediate but we can see that in previous work utilization of slice resources are more from the slice utilization of our proposed architecture and we can say that after completion of work on control circuitry our results will be much better as compare to previously reported results.

Table 3. SHA-3 Core implementation results

Author(s)	Device	Area(Slices)
This work	**Virtex-7**	**16**
This work	**Virtex-6**	**16**
Kris Gaj *et al.* [11]	Virtex-6	365
J.P.kaps *et al.* [12]	Virtex-6	106
Bernhard Jungk [13]	Virtex-6	397

5 Conclusion

In this work a smallest arithmetically and logically optimized FPGA architecture for the newly selected SHA-3 core was proposed. Low resource implementations of hash functions are very important because they are needed for constrained application environments such as smart cards, RFID tags, Sensors and portable devices like cell phones, IPads etc. The authors argue that the architecture proposed here is best suited for these applications as it utilizes minimum area as far as core implementation is concerned. Work on Control circuitry is still in progress and results presented in this paper are intermediate.

References

1. Wang, X., Feng, D., Lai, X., Yu, H.: Collisions for hash functions MD4, MD5, HAVAL-128 and RIPEMD. Cryptology ePrint Archive, Report 2004/199, pp. 1–4 (2004). http://eprint.iacr.org/2004/199

2. Szydlo, M.: SHA-1 collisions can be found in 2^{63} operations. CryptoBytes, Technical Newsletter (2005). http://www.rsa.com/rsalabs/node.asp?id=2927

3. Stevens, M.: Fast collision attack on MD5. ePrint-2006-104, pp. 1–13 (2006). http://eprint.iacr.org/2006/104.pdf

4. Federal Register, Vol. 72, No. 212, Friday, November 2 (2007), Notices. http://csrc.nist.gov/groups/ST/hash/documents/FR_Notice_Nov07.pdf

5. National Institute of Standards and Technology (NIST): SHA-3 Winner announcement. http://www.nist.gov/itl/csd/sha-100212.cfm

6. Latif, K., Rao, M., Aziz, A., Mahboob, A.: Efficient hardware implementations and hardware performance evaluation of SHA-3 finalists. In: NIST third SHA-3 Candidate Conference, Washington D.C., 22–23 March 2012

7. Provelengios, G., Kitsos, P., Sklavos, N., Koulamas, C.: FPGA-based design approaches of Keccak hash function. In: 2012 15th Euromicro Conference on Digital System Design (DSD), pp. 648, 653, 5–8 Sept 2012. doi:10.1109/DSD.2012.63

8. Homsirikamol, E., Rogawsk, M., Gaj, K.: Comparing hardware performance of round 3 SHA-3 candidates using multiple hardware architectures in Xilinx and Altera FPGAs. In: ECRYPT II Hash Workshop 2011, Tallinn, Estonia, 19–20 May, pp. 1–15 (2011)

9. Latif, K., Aziz, A., Mahboob, A.: Optimal utilization of available reconfigurable hardware resources. Elsevier's Comput. Electr. Eng. **37**(6), 1043–1057 (2011)

10. Bertoni, G., Daemen, J., Peeters, M., Assche, G.: The Keccak SHA-3 submission version 3, pp. 1–14, (2011). http://keccak.noekeon.org/Keccak-reference-3.0.pdf

11. Gaj, K., Homsirikamol, E., Rogawsk, M., Shahid, R., Sharif, M.: Comprehensive evaluation of high speed and medium speed implementations of five SHA-3 finalist using Xilinx and Altera FPGAs. In: SHA-3 Conference (2012)

12. Kaps, J., Yalla, P., Surapathi, K., Habib, B., Vadlamudi, S., Gurung, S.: Lightweight implementations of SHA-3 finalists on FPGAs. In: SHA-3 Conference (2012)

13. Jungk, B.: Evaluation of compact FPGA implementations for all SHA-3 finalists. In: SHA-3 Conference 2012

Hybrid Guided Artificial Bee Colony Algorithm for Earthquake Time Series Data Prediction

Habib Shah[1(✉)], Rozaida Ghazali[1], Tutut Herawan[2], Nawsher Khan[2],
and Muhammad Sadiq Khan[2]

[1] Faculty of Computer Science and Information Technology,
Universiti Tun Hussein Onn Malaysia, Parit Raja,
86400 Batu Pahat, Johor, Malaysia
habibshah.uthm@gmail.com, rozaida@uthm.edu.my
[2] Department of Information Systems,
Faculty of Computer Science and Information Technology,
University of Malaya, Lembah Pantai,
50603 Kuala Lumpur, Malaysia
{tutut,nawsher}@um.edu.my, sadiq571@gmail.com

Abstract. Backpropagation is a well-known learning algorithm used to train Multilayer Perceptron (MLP) with the iterative process. However, one of the critical shortcomings with the BP learning strategy is that it can sometimes trapped in the local minima with suboptimal weights due to the existence of many local optima in the solution space. To remove the above drawbacks of BP algorithm, researchers interested in naturally swarm intelligence algorithm. Here Guided Artificial Bee Colony (GABC) and Gbest Guided Artificial Bee Colony (GGABC) algorithms are hybrid called Hybrid Guided ABC algorithm. The HGABC algorithm used to train MLP for earthquake time-series data for the prediction task. The performance of proposed Hybrid Guided ABC compared with ordinary BP, GGABC and ABC learning algorithms. The simulation results show that proposed learning algorithm HGGABC has outstanding prediction performance than BP, GGABC and ABC algorithms.

Keywords: Back propagation · Gbest Guided Artificial Bee Colony · Multilayer Perceptron · Hybrid Guided Artificial Bee Colony algorithm

1 Introduction

Though the rapid developments in various applications, existence became easy and world is becoming virtually a global town. Systems are happening more and more complex, whether it is science, engineering, transportation, communication resources, diseases, foods, power, water distribution and land division. These complexities may be due to the increase in number of components, increased interdependencies among various components, and population. The complexities further increases when these communications are subjected to natural or man-made disasters like earthquake, tsunami and so on.

© Springer International Publishing Switzerland 2014
F.K. Shaikh et al. (Eds.): IMTIC 2013, CCIS 414, pp. 204–215, 2014.
DOI: 10.1007/978-3-319-10987-9_19

In the past decade, the fracture of earth, flow of rocks, movements of tectonic plates, heat waves temperature and the high range of sea waves has been the focus by geologists, geophysics and engineers. These sources may be the most important rule in earthquake, weather temperature water level height and tsunami occurrence called seismic signals and natural hazards. The strength of these seismic event's occurrence creates disasters and can change human life as well as animals and other social swarms [1].

The disaster caused by non made actions was beyond compute, position, moment in time and concentration of a future seismic events occurrence are accurately predicted, and some appropriate precautionary measures can be carried out in advance. The numerous lives in seismic activity risk regions can be saved, and the human and economic sufferers caused by these events can be reduced. Each natural hazard is related to a different source process, its instance and spatial distribution could be used as elements seismic for early warning system [2–4]. The predictions of earthquake seismic event incidents are really crucial, to our continuation. The data of an earthquake occurring events are depending on geographical areas in real time series form. The behavior of seismic time-series data is quite different among the other data, so the prediction of these nature data is quite challenging for a scientist. In this regard, to predict earthquake events the scientist used to study the grounds of these trials.

ANN has great data modeling and predictor means that can able to confine and characterize complex input/output connections. NN is known to have the ability to solve both linear and nonlinear relationships and to learn these associations openly from the time series data. The application of ANN to simulation and/or forecasting problems can now be found in various disciplines. The application of ANN in time-series data prediction has shown improved performance in comparison to statistical methods because of their nonlinear and training capability and universal approximators ability for complex mapping [5, 6]. ANN approach has been applied to the comprehensive seismic signal such as earthquake forecasting and obtained satisfying results.

Here, to increase and balance the exploration, exploitation procedures of the standard ABC algorithm, and at the same time for getting high efficiency for time series prediction, the two global algorithms namely: Guided Artificial Bee Colony (GABC) and Gbest Guided Artificial Bee Colony (GGABC) are hybrid called HGABC algorithm [7]. In this research, the proposed HGABC algorithm and standard algorithm's ABC, GGABC and BP are used to train and test ANN for the prediction task.

2 Earthquake Time Series Data and Neural Networks

Time series data is a collection of observations of well-defined data items obtained through repeated measurements over time [8, 9]. It is a sequence of data points, measure typically at successive time instance spaced at uniform time intervals [10]. ANNs can solve nonlinear problems which are difficult to be solved by traditional techniques. Often, time series processes have temporal and spatial variability, and are influenced by issues of nonlinearity of physical processes [11]. Subsequently, ANNs have the capability of extracting the relationship between the inputs and outputs of a process. These properties of ANNs make them appropriate for the problem of time series forecasting.

3   The Learning Algorithms

Artificial Neural Networks is based on human brain processing techniques and gets decision using neuron, and it is connection values to find better results. The most significant aspect of ANN is its ability to learn from its environment, and to improve its performance through learning. ANN learns about its environment or a dynamic system through an iterative process of adjustments applied to its weights and biases. One of the most important characteristics in ANN is its knowledge ability, which makes it generally suitable for the computational purpose whose organization is known or unknown. The decision is based on the synapse's learning strategy. The network becomes more "knowledgeable" about its environment after each iteration of the learning process.

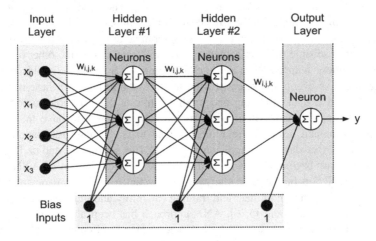

Fig. 1. Multilayer Perceptron Neural Network [12]

Figure 1 shows the multilayer perceptron (MLP), where the connections are called synapses or weight [12]. Every weight has an assigned scaling coefficient, by which the data propagated through the synapse is multiplied. These scaling coefficients are called weights w (i, j, k). Global ABC is also one of the famous learning algorithm for training MLP [13, 14]. Here three meta heuristic learning algorithms namely Gbest Guided Artificial Bee Colony (GGABC), Guided GABC and proposed Hybrid Guided Artificial Bee Colony algorithm (HGABC) detailed in the subsections.

3.1   Gbest Guided Artificial Bee Colony Algorithm

Artificial Bee Colony (ABC) also called meta heuristic algorithm, was proposed in 2007 for optimization, classification, and NNs problem solution based on the intelligent foraging behaviour of honey bee swarms [15, 16]. In the standard ABC algorithm, the explore space stands for an background and each point in the search space corresponds to best solution that the employed and Onlooker's bees can exploit specific food sources [17]. However, there is still an insufficiency in standard ABC algorithm regarding its solution search procedure, which is good at exploration but poor in exploitation. The performance of the population-based algorithm can be improved by increasing and balancing the exploration and exploitation properties.

Here also, to improve the exploitation properties and balance with exploration, this section will explain the proposed, modified and improved ABC algorithms by the Gbest Guided Artificial Bee Colony (GGABC) technique by incorporating the information of global best (gbest) solution into the solution search equation proposed for training MLP [18]. The new candidate solution of both agent are generated by moving the old solution towards (or away from) another solution selected randomly from the population. The probability Eqs. (1) and (2) that the randomly selected solution for employed and onlookers' bee are given below as:

$$V_{ij} = x_{ij} + \theta_{ij}(x_{ij} - x_{kj}) + Gbest \tag{1}$$

$$Gbest = \psi_{ij}(y_j - x_{i,j}) \tag{2}$$

where, ψ_{ij} is a uniform random number in the range of [0, C], C shows nonnegative constant and y_j represents the jth element of the global best solution.

3.2 Guided Artificial Bee Colony (GABC) Algorithm

How to improve the exploration and exploration procedure with balance quantity is the challenge for swarm based algorithm, especially for standard ABC. In standard ABC algorithm, the process of replacing the abandoned food resource is replicated by randomly producing a new solution, through the employed and onlooker bee's section with same strategy as in Eq. (3) as;

$$v_{ij} = x_{ij} + \phi_{ij}(x_{ij} - x_{kj}) \tag{3}$$

The new solutions in scout bee of standard ABC algorithm are not based on the information of previous best solutions. Researchers used different advance searching strategies like hybridization, improvement, global, gbest and so on, with standard ABC. Guided ABC is one of the proposed algorithm [19]. The new modify solution search equation by applying the global best solution to guide the search of scout in order to improve the exploration procedure of standard ABC. In the standard ABC in scout bee new solution is generated by using a random approach, thus it is very difficult to generate a new solution that could be placed in the promising region of the search space.

$$x_{ij}^{rand} = x_{ij}^{min} + rand(0, 1)(x_j^{max} - x_j^{min}) \tag{4}$$

Thus, the Guided Artificial Bee Colony (GABC) algorithm proposed for improving the exploration procedure within scout bee searching strategy [19]. In GABC algorithm, the scout will generate a new solution through global knowledge information $(x_{best,j})$ the best global food source to Eq. (3). The global best experience will modify the equation with the following best guided strategy as:

$$v_{ij} = x_{ij} + \phi^*(x_{ij} - x_{kj}) + (1 - \phi)^*(x_{ij} - x_{best,j}) \tag{5}$$

The guided ABC will increase the capabilities of the usual ABC algorithm performance to produce new best solutions located near the sufficient area of exploration.

4 Hybrid Guided Artificial Bee Colony (HGABC) Algorithm

The Gbest Guided Artificial Bee Colony (GGABC) [21] algorithm and Guided Artificial Bee Colony are swarm based meta-heuristic algorithm, applied to different problems like engineering optimization problems and to Artificial Neural Network for training purpose and other tasks, using inspired intelligent foraging behavior of global artificial honey bees [14, 20]. GABC algorithm has outstanding performance from standard ABC algorithm in terms of exploration procedures [19]. Furthermore, GGABC has great achievements for increasing exploitation procedure than standard ABC [18]. Taking the advantage of the GABC and GGABC algorithms, to improve and balance the exploitation and exploration procedures, are hybrid called HGABC algorithm. The proposed hybrid approach HGABC has the following modification in employed, onlooker and scout bees phases are:

(1) Gbest Guided Employed Bee Phase:

$$v_{ij} = x_{ij} + \phi_{ij}(x_{ij} - x_{kj}) + \Psi_{ij}(y_j - x_{i,j}) \tag{6}$$

(2) Gbest Guided Onlookers Bees Phase:

$$v_{ij} = x_{ij} + \phi_{ij}(x_{ij} - x_{kj}) + \Psi_{ij}(y_j - x_{i,j}) \tag{7}$$

where y_j is the j_{th} element of the global best solution, w_{ij} is a uniform random number in [0, C], where C is a nonnegative constant. The value of C can balance the exploitation ability.

(3) Guided Scout Bee Phase:

$$v_{ij} = x_{ij} + \phi^*(x_{ij} - x_{kj}) + (1 - \phi)^*(x_{ij} - x_{best,j}) \tag{8}$$

The exploitation process will be increase through the neighbour agents gbest guided employed and gbest guided onlooker bees phase, are given in Eqs. (6) and (7). Furthermore, the exploration procedure will be increase through guided scout bee phase as given in Eq. (8). The guided scout will generate a new solution by adding the global experience information ($x_{best,j}$-the best global food source). A new solution will be generated by using information about the food source that is abandoned, the optimal global food resource and a randomly chosen as given in Eq (8). The proposed flow chart of HGABC algorithm is given in Fig. 2.

HGABC algorithm as a hybrid optimization tool provides a population-based search procedure in which individuals called foods positions are modified by guided

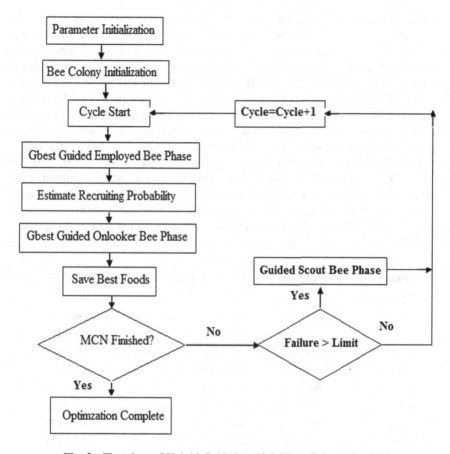

Fig. 2. Flowchart of Hybrid Guided Artificial Bee Colony algorithm

and gbest artificial bees with time, and the bee's aim is to discover the places of best food sources with high nectar amount and finally the one with the highest nectar. The HGABC algorithm will update the solution step and will convert to best solution based on neighborhood values for ANN, through hybridization strategy.

5   Simulation Results and Discussion

In this research, the earthquake significant parameter called magnitude is time-series data used for prediction of same parameter using MLP by the proposed and standard algorithms. The data used from the Southern California Earthquake Data Center (SCEDC) holdings for 2010 [22]. The data include local, regional, and quarry-blast events with epicenters between latitudes 32.0S and 37.0N and longitudes between −122.0W and −114.0E. The earthquake Data from the past are provided to the inputs of ANN and it is expected data from future from the outputs of the network.

Here, GGABC, ABC, BP and HGABC algorithms are used to train MLP. To evaluate the time series prediction performance of the GGABC, ABC, BP and proposed HGABC algorithms by Mean Square Error (MSE), Normalized Mean Square Error and SNR, using Matlab 2010a software. The stopping criterion of BP is minimum error set to 0.0001 while ABC, GGABC and HGABC stopped on Maximum Cycle Number (MCN) 2000. During the experimentation, 10 trials performed for training with sigmoid function for network production. During the simulation, when the number of input's signals, hidden nodes, output node and running time varies, performing training algorithms were stable, which is important for delegation NNs in the current state. The best average simulation results are given in Tables 1 and 2, with MSE and NMSE. Meanwhile from the best average simulation, when the MSE calculated, it can be seen from the Table 1, HGABC outperforms from all learning algorithms. Here it can be noted that the standard ABC also reached to minimum NMSE compare to standard BP and GGABC algorithms. HGABC has outstanding NMSE compared to BP, GGABC and also from ABC, given in Table 2.

Table 1. Average MSE out of sample for Earthquake Magnitude Prediction

NN structure	ABC	BP	GGABC	HGABC
2-2-1	0.000871	0.020654	0.000792	**0.000321**
2-3-1	0.000533	0.021648	0.000641	**0.000491**
3-3-1	0.006812	0.020022	0.000954	**0.000754**
4-4-1	0.010071	0.028219	0.003850	**0.000261**
4-6-1	0.000759	0.020523	0.000790	**0.000773**
5-5-1	0.002362	0.022091	0.000791	**0.000401**
5-6-1	0.000292	0.014776	0.0013291	**0.000493**
7-9-1	0.013012	0.011032	0.001231	**0.000729**

Table 2. Average NMSE for Earthquake Magnitude Prediction

NN structure	ABC	BP	GGABC	HGABC
2-2-1	0.032181	0.941482	0.031031	**0.021011**
2-3-1	0.023951	0.891633	0.022012	**0.022432**
3-3-1	0.022002	1.012614	0.119332	**0.101326**
4-4-1	0.045182	1.223243	0.290818	**0.210319**
4-6-1	0.033892	1.198244	0.031822	**0.021124**
5-5-1	0.012178	0.912315	0.099823	**0.069724**
5-6-1	0.013553	0.924346	0.109282	**0.069652**
7-9-1	0.088191	0.803237	0.234454	**0.105382**

The maximum SNR for Earthquake magnitude prediction with best average simulation results by using the ABC, BP, GGABC and HGABC algorithms are 36.2846, 17.0971, 38.2846 and 39.9023 respectively. Here the ANN output with the proposed HGABC algorithms is much closer to the original index data. The BP algorithm fails to predict the earthquake magnitude signals as presented. Also, the testing and learning curves of BP is fails to provide less prediction error for earthquake magnitude signals and MSE for earthquake magnitude. The comparative simulation studies have been presented to show the effectiveness of our new algorithms. The predicted signal is pretty close to original signal during training phase of HGABC algorithm at Fig. 3.

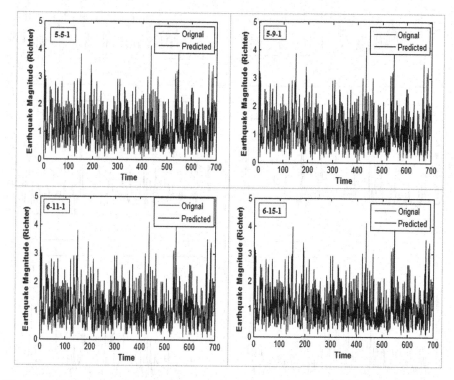

Fig. 3. Prediction of earthquake magnitude using HGABC during training phase with different NN topologies

Using the above learning techniques adjusts the optimal weights of each synapsis in order to decrease the training/testing error for seismic time series prediction task. After replicating these procedures for a sufficiently big number of learning series the network will generally converge to some position where the calculations error is too small with outstanding performance. In this case, the network has learned a particular target function. For properly adjusting weights, one applies a general method for time series prediction. Figure 4 shows the prediction for earthquake magnitude time series with proposed learning algorithm has outstanding performance. The black signal represents actual and blue predicted signal for earthquake time series at Fig. 4.

The proposed HGGABC algorithm has small MSE value on out of samples. The convergence speed of HGGABC is fast for earthquake's time series from standard BP, GGABC and ABC. The MSE is continuously decreasing using HGABC on earthquake's time-series, where the BP fails to decrease MSE for earthquake magnitude. From comparison, BP fails to converge until 2000 epochs, while the rest of the

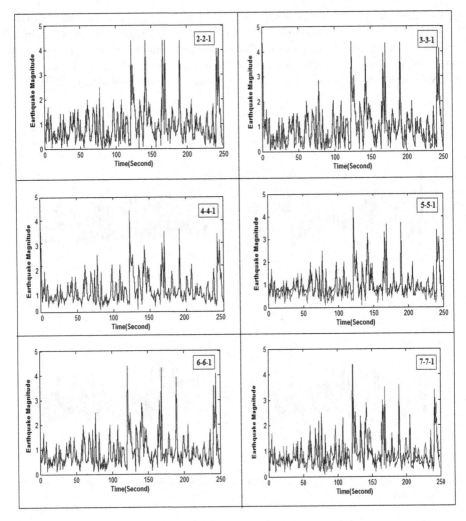

Fig. 4. Prediction results for earthquake out of samples using HGABC algorithm with different network topologies.

proposed algorithms converged in the range of 2000 MCN. The proposed HGABC has a faster convergence speed for the earthquake time-series data. The comparative simulation studies have been presented to show the effectiveness of our new hybrid algorithms.

From the comparison convergence curve Fig. 5 shows that proposed HGABC algorithm has small MSE and fast convergence than standard learning approaches. The MSE is continuously decreasing using HGABC on earthquake's time-series, where the BP fails to decrease. For Earthquake time-series data with proposed HGABC technique the MSE is stable for all network structure and decreased continuously in every iteration as depicted in Fig. 6.

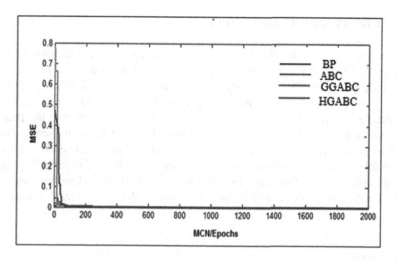

Fig. 5. Convergence comparison of BP, ABC, GGABC and HGABC algorithms

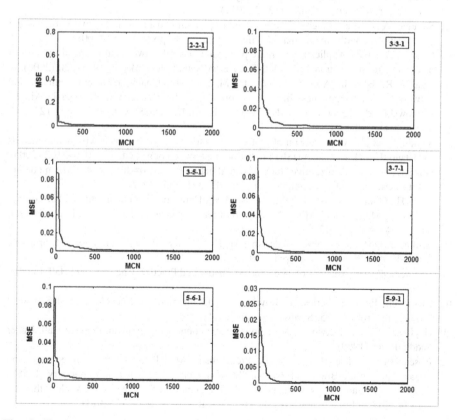

Fig. 6. Convergence curves of HGABC algorithm for earthquake magnitude prediction with different NN topologies

6 Conclusion and Future Work

The proposed HGABC algorithm collects the exploration and exploitation processes successfully through hybrid guided methods of employed, Onlookers bee and scout bees, which proves the high performance of training and testing of NN for earthquake magnitude time series. It has the powerful ability of searching global optimal solution with suitable synapses values. The above simulation results show that the proposed Hybrid Guided ABC algorithm can successfully train and test time series data for prediction task. In future research work, different kind of multivariate time series will be used for prediction, clustering, forecasting and classification tasks with proposed learning algorithm. Furthermore, hybridization of HGGABC algorithm with local search or with global search will be investigated for solving optimization problems.

References

1. Shah, H., et al.: Using artificial bee colony algorithm for MLP training on earthquake time series data prediction. J. Comput. **3**, 7 (2011)
2. Suratgar, A.A., et al.: Magnitude of earthquake prediction using neural network. In: Natural Computation, Fourth International Conference on, 2008, pp. 448–452 (2008)
3. Ghazali, R., et al.: Application of ridge polynomial neural networks to financial time series prediction. In: International Joint Conference on Neural Networks, pp. 913–920 (2006)
4. Ghazali, R., Hussain, A.J., Al-Jumeily, D., Merabti, M.: Dynamic ridge polynomial neural networks in exchange rates time series forecasting. In: Beliczynski, B., Dzielinski, A., Iwanowski, M., Ribeiro, B. (eds.) ICANNGA 2007. LNCS, vol. 4432, pp. 123–132. Springer, Heidelberg (2007)
5. Yümlü, S., et al.: A comparison of global, recurrent and smoothed-piecewise neural models for Istanbul stock exchange (ISE) prediction. Pattern Recogn. Lett. **26**, 2093–2103 (2005)
6. Ho, S.L., et al.: A comparative study of neural network and Box-Jenkins ARIMA modeling in time series prediction. Comput. Ind. Eng. **42**, 371–375 (2002)
7. Shah, H., Ghazali, R., Nawi, N.M., Deris, M.M., Herawan, T.: Global artificial bee colony-Levenberq-Marquardt (GABC-LM) algorithm for classification. Int. J. Appl. Evol. Comput. (IJAEC) **4**, 58–74 (2013)
8. Brillinger, D.R.: Time Series: Data Analysis and Theory. SIAM: Society for Industrial and Applied Mathematics, Philadelphia (2001)
9. Chatfield, C.: The Analysis of Time Series: Theory and Practice. Chapman and Hall, London (1975)
10. Brockwell, P.: Time Series. In: Lovric, M. (ed.) International Encyclopedia of Statistical Science, pp. 1601–1605. Springer, Berlin (2011)
11. Haykin, S.: Neural Networks: A Comprehensive Foundation, 2nd edn. Prentice-Hall, Upper Saddle River (1999)
12. Rosenblatt, F.: The Perceptron: A Probabilistic Model for Information Storage and Organization in the Brain, vol. 65, pp. 386–408. Cornell Aeronautical Laboratory (1958)
13. Shah, H., Ghazali, R., Nawim, N.M.: Hybrid global artificial bee colony algorithm for classification and prediction tasks. J. Appl. Sci. Res. **9**, 3328–3337 (2013)

14. Shah, H., Ghazali, R., Nawi, N.M.: Global artificial bee colony algorithm for boolean function classification. In: Selamat, A., Nguyen, N.T., Haron, H. (eds.) ACIIDS 2013, Part I. LNCS (LNAI), vol. 7802, pp. 12–20. Springer, Heidelberg (2013)

15. Karaboga, D., Akay, B.: Artificial bee colony (ABC) algorithm on training artificial neural networks. In: IEEE 15th Signal Processing and Communications Applications, pp. 1–4 (2007)

16. Karaboga, D., Akay, B., Ozturk, C.: Artificial bee colony (ABC) optimization algorithm for training feed-forward neural networks. In: Torra, V., Narukawa, Y., Yoshida, Y. (eds.) MDAI 2007. LNCS (LNAI), vol. 4617, pp. 318–329. Springer, Heidelberg (2007)

17. Ozturk, C., Ozturk, D.: Hybrid artificial bee colony algorithm for neural network training. In: IEEE Congress on Evolutionary Computation (CEC), pp. 84–88 (2011)

18. Zhu, G., Kwong, S.: Gbest-guided artificial bee colony algorithm for numerical function optimization. Appl. Math. Comput. **217**, 3166–3173 (2010)

19. Tuba, M., et al.: Guided artificial bee colony algorithm. In: Proceedings of the 5th European Conference on European Computing Conference, Paris, France (2011)

20. Peng, G., et al.: Global artificial bee colony search algorithm for numerical function optimization. In: Seventh International Conference on Natural Computation (ICNC), pp. 1280–1283 (2011)

21. Shah, H., Ghazali, R., Mohmad Hassim, Y.M.: Honey bees inspired learning algorithm: nature intelligence can predict natural disaster. In: Herawan, T., Ghazali, R., Deris, M.M. (eds.) Recent Advances on Soft Computing and Data Mining SCDM 2014. AISC, vol. 287, pp. 215–225. Springer, Heidelberg (2014)

22. SCEDC.: Southern California Earthquake Data Center (SCEDC), 12 Jan 2010. http://www. data.scec.org/ftp/catalogs/SCSN/2010.catalog

An Enhanced Procedure for Mobile IPv6 Route Optimization to Reduce Handover Delay and Signaling Overhead

Peer Azmat Shah[1,3]($\boxtimes$), Halabi B. Hasbullah[1], Syeda Adila Afghan[2], Low Tang Jung[1], Ibrahim A. Lawal[1], and Abubakar Aminu Mu'azu[1]

[1] Department of Computer and Information Sciences (CIS),
Universiti Teknologi PETRONAS, Seri Iskandar, 31750 Tronoh,
Perak, Malaysia
{halabi,lowtanjung}@petronas.com.my,
{pshah_g01944,ibrahim_g01867,
abuaminu_g01797}@utp.edu.my
[2] Department of Computer Systems Engineering (CSE),
Mehran University of Engineering and Technology, Jamshoro, Pakistan
syedaafghan137@gmail.com
[3] Department of Computer Science,
COMSATS Institute of Information Technology, Islamabad, Pakistan

Abstract. Mobile IPv6 was proposed to provide mobility support to IPv6 based mobile nodes for continuous communication when they roam across different networks. As mobile nodes are dependent on a central entity home agent, hence due to mobility the path from mobile node to correspondent node via the home agent might be longer as compared to the direct path between them and results in triangular routing. Route Optimization in Mobile IPv6 using Return Routability provides the opportunity to eliminate the inefficient triangular routing between mobile and corresponding nodes and therefore, greatly improves the network performance. However, this Return Routability based route optimization involves the verification of mobile node's reachability at home address and at care-of address (home test and care-of test) that results in higher handover delays and signalling overhead. This article presents an enhanced procedure for Mobile IPv6 Route Optimization that uses the concepts of shared secret Token and one time password along-with verification of mobile node via direct communication. The new solution was implemented in NS-2 making changes in the implementation of Mobile IPv6. Results show that the new solution provides lower handover delays and signalling overhead in comparison to the Return Routability based Mobile IPv6.

Keywords: Component · Mobile IPv6 · Shared secret token · One-time password · Route optimization · Handover delay · Signalling overhead

1 Introduction

Due to an increase in the variety of mobile devices like Personal Digital Assistants (PDAs), laptops and digital phones, the classical opinion on the Internet is now beginning to change and new scenarios of the mobile applications have emerged.

© Springer International Publishing Switzerland 2014
F.K. Shaikh et al. (Eds.): IMTIC 2013, CCIS 414, pp. 216–226, 2014.
DOI: 10.1007/978-3-319-10987-9_20

In the near future, more and more Internet services of both conventional and novel types can be smoothly accessed with various mobile devices through the wide deployed wireless networks. The Internet is extending its coverage area into a more spacious and attractive field, which brings more opportunities for service providers and network operators to expand their network. To users, this means more benefits and conveniences in their work and daily life.

Mobile Internet applications have become popular and are being widely used. With the evolution of 4G wireless heterogeneous networks, all time access and seamless mobility across different networks, like WLAN, WiMAX, UMTS and WWAN etc., is desirable. On the other hand, Internet users want to use the best access network according to the network characteristics or their own preferences. Whenever a Mobile Node (MN) moves from one access network to another, the already established communication with Correspondent Node (CN) remains no longer active. Hence, some mobility management procedure is required [1]. In wireless networks, mobility management can be defined as changing the point of attachment without losing ability to communicate with other nodes in the network. Whenever, MN changes its point of attachment, its Internet Protocol (IP) address changes. As communication between communicating nodes in the Internet is associated with IP addresses, thus whenever one of the communicating node changes its IP address due to mobility and location change, all on-going communications remain no more active [1]. Hence, end user suffers.

To solve the above mentioned problem, research community has worked on mobility management solutions for seamless continuation of service for mobile users when they are moving across heterogeneous networks.

The remainder of the paper is organized as follows. Section 2 explains the Mobile IPv6 and its limitations. Section 3 highlights the need for IPv6 route optimizations. Section 4 depicts the proposed enhanced route optimization scheme. Section 5 explains experimental results and discussion on results. Finally, conclusions are drawn in Sect. 6.

2   Mobile IPv6 and It's Limitations

Mobility management for IPv6 based nodes, or Mobile IPv6 [2], facilitates the mobile nodes to move from one IPv6 address to another by migrating active transport layer connections and application sessions. As per Mobile IPv6's specification [2], the concept of home agent (HA) is used that proxies the mobile node to a fixed permanent address, called home address (HoA). In case of roaming, mobile node establishes a bidirectional tunnel with it's HA using a local care-of address (CoA). HA makes a binding between MN's HoA and its CoA and forwards the packets to mobile node's new IPv6 address (which is CoA), which were actually destined to MN's HoA. Hence, MN becomes reachable at the new location and can so communicate with the correspondent node.

In the case of bidirectional tunneling, propagation delay is observed as MN and CN do not communicate directly and have to communicate via the HA. To overcome this problem, Mobile IPv6 proposed Route Optimization [2] procedure that permits the two end nodes for communication using the direct path without tunneling packets through HA. Route Optimization requires that CN should maintain a binding between MN's HoA and CoA, just like one maintained at the HA. For this purpose control signaling is done between MN and CN directly. The problem is how can the two end nodes (mobile and correspondent) authenticate and authorize the control messages that they exchange? From security perspective, to establish a binding entry at the CN requires the verification of the MN for claiming of both the addresses (HoA and the CoA). If this compulsion is compromised, then security threats like impersonation and flooding will arise [3].

To solve this problem, Mobile IPv6 proposed the Return Routability [2] procedure for the authentication of MNs. In this procedure two different tests (home address test and care-of address test) are performed. Reachability of MN at the HoA and CoA is checked in these two tests. Home address test involves Home Test Init (HoTI) and Home Test (HoT) messages to be exchanged between MN and CN directly and care-of test involves Care-of-Test Init (CoTI) and Care-of Test (CoT) messages to be exchanged between mobile and CN via the HA. In case of successful verification at both addresses, legitimacy of binding between the HoA and the CoA is proved and MN sends Binding Update (BU) message to CN which is acknowledged with Binding Acknowledgement (BA). The sequence of message flow for the Mobile IPv6 Route Optimization with Return Routability is shown in Fig. 1.

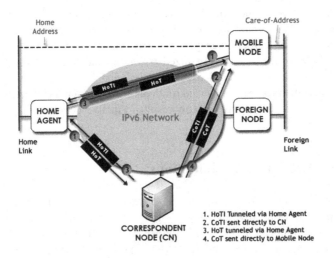

Fig. 1. Mobile IPv6 Route Optimization with Return Routability sequence flow

Return Routability has an advantage that it is a lightweight procedure and has no requirements of pre shared authentication keys [4]. Also, it does not maintain states at the CN. On the negative side, this process has an undesirable impact on handover delay and results in longer handover delay and increased overhead [13] as it involves signaling among all the three nodes (MN, HA and CN) involved in the mobility management process. It is because, the home address test and the care-of address test involve message exchange between the MN and the CN, between MN and HA and between the HA and CN. The delay of home address test is high as compared to the care-of address test, as it routes the messages through the HA. The delay caused by these two reachability tests (home address test and care-of address test) might be undesirable for different real time applications or interactive applications e.g. applications like Voice over IP (VoIP) and video conferencing [4].

Another problem of Return Routability procedure with respect to security is that, the security assured by this procedure might not be enough for applications that are security sensitive. The reason is that, Return Routability is vulnerable where attackers can interject in the home or care-of address test.

Finally, this procedure requires periodic signaling exchange in an interval of at most 7 minutes, even in the case when there is no movement for MN and no change in IP connectivity [4]. This periodic refresh of binding registration at CN involves additional signaling overhead.

Keeping in mind the above points, this article proposes an enhancement to Mobile IPv6 Route Optimization through a CN compatibility option and shared secret Token. In the proposed solution, MN keeps record of Mobile IPv6 compatible CNs and in case of mobility, MN communicates only with those CNs that have active Mobile IPv6 implementation. Also, the new proposed mechanism does not route the signaling messages via the HA (rather signaling is done directly) and does not involve the communication between the HA and CN, that results in further performance improvement. To achieve security, shared secret Token is used to compute One Time Password (OTP) hence to authenticate the MN.

The organization of this paper is as follows: In Sect. 3, needs for the improvement of route optimization have been discussed. Section 4 presents the enhancements proposed for the Mobile IPv6. In Sect. 5, simulation and results have been discussed and finally conclusion along-with future work is presented in Sect. 6.

3 Need for Improvement of Mobile IPv6 Route Optimization

As wireless networks with frequent movements of nodes have many salient features that differentiate them from networks with static nodes or with nodes having very occasional movements, hence efficiency is an important aspect of mobility management in these environments. Enhancements that are needed to be made for Mobile IPv6 Route Optimization include, reducing the handover delay, increasing the security level, lowering the signaling overhead and increasing the protocol robustness.

3.1 Delay Optimizations

One of the main objectives of the Route Optimization improvement is the reduction of handover delays. Mobile IPv6's care-of address test has lower delay as compared to the home address test, but MNs can not resume communication until both tests (HoA test and CoA test) are completed. Hence, the delay caused by the home address test will be considered for the overall handover delay. The first data packet that is to be sent to MN's new care-of address, at new location, takes additional one-way time for propagation from the CN to the MN. The communication is resumed at the MN right after Binding Update message has been sent. In case, MN has requested a Binding Acknowledgment message from CN, then communications may not be resumed until acknowledgement message is received. These delays are additive do not include other delays of the lower layers (Network and Link).

The long handover delays can cause significant quality degradation for applications that run in real-time environments. Similarly, TCP data transfers in bulk form are also affected. The reason is that, due to long handover delays in TCP retransmission timeouts can occur which will eventually degrade the throughput.

3.2 Security Optimizations

The objective of Mobile IPv6's Return Routability procedure was to provide a certain level of security that may be compared with the security level of today's static Internet [3]. The assumption of Return Routability is that, mobile Internet cannot be as safe as the non mobile Internet. Hence, it protects against certain attacks like impersonation, denial of service, redirection and flooding. It is recommended for the applications which require much more security than provided by the Return Routability that they may use some end-to-end protection mechanisms like IPSec [5] etc. But still these applications are susceptible to denial of service (DoS) attacks. This problem motivates the research community to develop more efficient security solutions for Route Optimization.

As HoA and CoA are carried in plaintext form in route optimized packets, hence an important concern of Route Optimization is location privacy. To overcome this problem, one standard way is to go back and use Bidirectional Tunneling whenever location privacy is desirable. Thus, packets which carry CoA are then transferred only between MN and the HA and can be encrypted using IPsec Encapsulating Security Payload (ESP) [5]. Even in the case of Bidirectional Tunneling, MN needs to re-establish the IPsec security associations with HA periodically.

3.3 Signaling Optimizations

The process of Route Optimization in Mobile IPv6 exchanges periodic signaling messages even in the absence of MN's movement. This signaling overhead is calculated as 7.16 bps if the MN is communicating with a static CN [6]. These periodic refresh messages consume some part of the wireless bandwidth that is already limited and can be used more efficiently in the absence of these periodic messages. The amount of this overhead will be doubled in case both the communicating nodes are mobile. Optimizations are required to reduce signaling overhead that could overcome these problems.

3.4 Robustness Optimizations

Home agent failure may happen or may become temporarily unavailable; hence Route Optimization should enable the communicating nodes to continue communications during such periods. This independence is not achieved by the Mobile IPv6 defined in [2]. It is because, the HA has an active role to execute home-test in the Return Routability procedure. Proper optimizations could result is a solution that is independent from HA and is more robust.

4   Proposed Enhanced Route Optimization

In the proposed route optimization, two functionalities are used. At the start of communication, signaling is done between mobile node and corresponding node to check the compatibility of correspondent node for Mobile IPv6 implementation, and in the second phase mobile node does not perform signaling like home test and correspondent test performed in the Return Routability procedure of route optimized Mobile IPv6. To secure the communication, concept of shared secret Token is used. Figure 2 shows the sequence of message flow for the proposed enhanced Route Optimization.

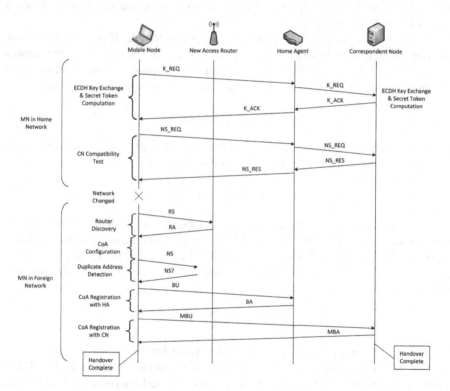

Fig. 2. Proposed Route Optimization sequence flow

4.1   Shared Secret Token Computation

In the proposed route optimization scheme, a shared secret identifier (Token) is used to achieve the security. This Token is computed through the use of an Elliptic Curve Diffie Hellman (ECDH) key exchange [7] at the start of communication between two end nodes. The proposed mechanism does not depend upon any third party to authenticate the Binding Update messages that are sent to the correspondent node, thus permitting the end nodes to use the authentication method which they prefer for the establishment of trust relationship.

The computation of shared secret token is achieved as done in [8]. For any node i, which is initiating the communication (initiator), the generation of its ECDH public key ki is done by selecting a random number and then encoding using the complex conversion routine encoding (CCRE) [9]. The random number is $Xi = \{1,2,3,\ldots, n-1\}$, where n is the order of a, a is a number for which $a^n = 1(mod\ p)$ and p is a prime number. Now computing the ECDH public key for node i as:

$$ki = 136\text{Lsb}\ [CCRE(Xi * a)] \tag{1}$$

The $*$ is the traditional mathematical multiplication operator and *136Lsb* means 136 least significant bits. The security of *Token* depends upon the value of Xi, hence it should be randomly generated.

When the respondent node j, with a compliant Mobile IPv6 implementation, receives message from initiator node i with ECDH information, it selects the random number $Xj = \{1,2,3,\ldots, n-1\}$ in the similar manner as done by node i and uses it to construct its own ECDH public key kj, and sends back to node initiator node.

$$kj = 136\text{Lsb}\ [CCRE(Xj * a)] \tag{2}$$

Now both nodes have the same set of public keys and can compute the *Token*. First they compute the shared secret key K, as discussed in [7].

$$K = k_i * X_j = k_j * X_i \tag{3}$$

Now the shared secret Token can be computed from K that will be used for authentication and validation in case of route optimization during mobility management. The computation of Token is accomplished by concatenating the key (K) and the random numbers Xi and Xj and then computing the hash using Secure Hash Algorithm (SHA-1) [10].

$$Token = SHA(X_i, X_j, K) \tag{4}$$

SHA-1 algorithm produces a unique Token value for the particular node.

Now both nodes have computed the same Token and make an entry in their Token Cache. Token Cache is a list, maintained at all the Mobile IPv6 compatible nodes, that keeps record of the home addresses and Tokens for the nodes which are communicating to this particular node.

4.2 Correspondent Node's Compatibility Test

At the start of communication on initiator side, node sends a message which we call as Node's Status Request, to check whether correspondent node has support for Mobile IPv6 or not. This message requests from responder (correspondent node) whether it has any support for Mobile IPv6 or not. Node's Status Request also contains public key information to compute the Token and then to secure the control communication between MN and CN. The mechanism of secure private key computation is explained in previous sub section. When correspondent node (responder) receives this message, it can process it in two different ways:

1. Correspondent node also supports Mobile IPv6, computes the Token and responds back to initiator by sending the Node's Status Response message informing the mobile node that correspondent node also supports Mobile IPv6. When initiator receives Node's Status Response from correspondent node (responder) with public key information, it also computes the Token and recordss the CN's status as having support for Mobile IPv6. The Token that is computed at both ends is same and will be used to secure the future communication between MN and CN. Details are explained in Secret Token Computation Subsection.
2. If correspondent node (responder) has no support for Mobile IPv6, then it does not know Node's Status Request message. CN discards the message and an ICMP error message is returned. When ICMP error message is received, then mobile node (initiator) records the correspondent node's status as it has no support for Mobile IPv6.

This correspondent node's status which is maintained at the mobile node is used for route optimization during handover management. Details are discussed in Optimized Route Optimization sub-section.

4.3 Enhanced Route Optimization

When MN receives a new router advertisement message and it acquires a new IPv6 address, then it detects that it has moved into a new network using movement detection mechanism discussed in [2]. Now mobile node checks the CN's compatibility for Mobile IPv6, means whether CN has support for Mobile IPv6 or not.

In case, CN also supports Mobile IPv6 then MN interacts with correspondent node directly and sends Binding Update message. The Binding Update message contains the authentication information as well. A one time token (OTT) is generated using the one time password (OTP) technique [12] by concatenating the Token, MN's home address and the timestamp as below:

$$OTT = OTP(MD5(Token \,|\, HoA \,|\, Timestamp)) \qquad (5)$$

Correspondent node upon receiving Binding Update message from MN, computes the OTT taking the Token value from local Token Cache and verifies the message by comparing the computed OTT value with the received OTT value. In case both OTT vales matched, correspondent node sends Binding ACK and sends data to mobile node's new location (new IPv6 address) directly using Type 2 routing header [2]. This procedure decreases the handover control signaling as compared to Mobile IPv6, where control signaling is also performed between HA and CN for home test (HoTi and HoT) [2].

In case, correspondent node has no support for Mobile IPv6, then route optimization will not work and mobile node has to continue communication through bidirectional tunneling via the HA. In this case, incoming data from the Internet for MN will be received by HA, which is then forwarded to the MN's new location using care-of address in a tunnel. This optimization mechanism once again reduces the control traffic by not performing any control signaling with the correspondent node.

To achieve signaling optimization, proposed scheme does not send periodic Binding Update messages, thus reducing the overall signaling overhead.

5   Simulation and Results

Proposed solution for Mobile IPv6 Route Optimization was simulated in network simulator 2 (NS-2.33) by making changes in the Mobile IPv6 implementation of RFC 3775 in the mobiwan patch [11].

Simulations were performed with different number of mobile nodes communicating with a single correspondent node with following settings: Channel type: Wireless, Propagation model: Two Ray Ground, Network interface type: Phy/Wireless Phy, Mac type: Mac/802.11, Interface queue type: Drop Tail/Priority Queue, Link layer type: LL, Antenna model: Antenna/Omni Antenna, Interface queue length: 70 and Adhoc routing protocol: AODV.

Figure 3 shows the signaling overhead comparison for Mobile IPv6 and the proposed scheme. Result shows that the overhead produced by the proposed idea is high at the startup point. This high overhead is due to the CN compatibility test and shared secret Token computation. At time $t = 30sec$, $100sec$ and $190sec$ handovers were initiated that generated the control signalling, so overhead for both of the protocols increased at these times. The signalling overhead of Mobile IPv6 is increasing with time as the binding lifetime for Mobile IPv6 was set to $10sec$, so every 10 seconds it exchaged binding refresh messages resulting in increased overhead. In case of proposed solution, the overhead remained constant as long as there was no movement of mobile node. When mobile node moved and performed some signaling for handover then the overhead was increased.

Figure 4 shows the handover delay comparison of Mobile IPv6 with the proposed technique. Handover delay has been computed with varying number of MNs. Result show that the handover delay of Mobile IPv6 increased too much in comparison with the proposed technique as the number of MNs increased. The reason for this reduced handover delay of the proposed technique is that, proposed idea does not perform signaling like home test and careof test as they are performed in the Mobile IPv6 that results in higher handover delay.

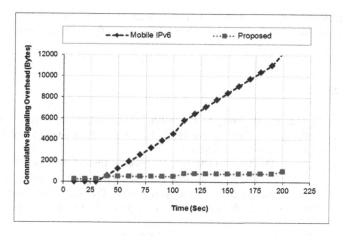

Fig. 3. Signaling overhead comparison

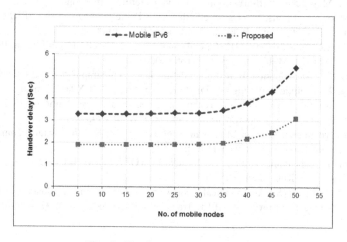

Fig. 4. Handover delay comparison

6   Conclusion and Future Work

In this paper a new solution has been proposed for the Mobile IPv6 Route Optimization, to decrease the handover delay and signaling overhead. Simulations were performed in network simulator-2 (ns-2). Results showed that the proposed enhancement has significantly improved the performance with respect to handover delay and signaling overhead. In future, our intention is to extend this solution for time-based one time password based authentication and to perform the security analysis of the solution. Research community can use this enhanced solution for other variants of Mobile IPv6 as well to improve their performance.

Acknowledgement. Authors would like to acknowledge the managemnt of Universiti Teknologi PETRONAS, Malaysia for providing financial support to this research work.

References

1. Shah, P.A., Yousaf, M., Qayyum, A., Hasbullah, H.B.: Performance comparison of end-to-end mobility management protocols for TCP. Elsevier J. Netw. Comput. Appl. (JNCA). **35** (6), 1657–1673 (2012). ISSN: 1084-8045
2. Perkins, C., Johnson, D., Arkko, J.: Mobility Support in IPv6. IETF RFC 6275, July 2011
3. Nikander, P., Arkko, J., Aura, T., Montenegro, G., Nordmark, E.: Mobile IP Version 6 Route Optimization Security Design Background. IETF RFC 4225, December 2005
4. Arkko, J., Vogt, C., Haddad, W.: Enhanced Route Optimization for Mobile IPv6. IETF RFC 4866, May 2007
5. Kent, S.: IP Encapsulating Security Payload (ESP). IETF RFC 4303, December 2005
6. Arkko, J., Vogt, C.: Credit-Based Authorization for Binding Lifetime Extension. Work in Progress, May 2004. draft-arkko-mipv6-binding-lifetime-extension-00
7. Zuccherato, R., Adams, C.: Using elliptic curve Diffie-Hellman in the SPKM GSS-API. Internet Draft, IETF, Aug. 1999. draft-ietf-cat-ecdh-spkm-00.txt
8. Snoeren, A.C., Balakrishnan, H.: An end-to-end approach to host mobility. In: Proceedings of 6th ACM/IEEE MobiCom, pp. 155–166 (2000)
9. American National Standards Institute: Public key cryptography for the financial service industry: The elliptic curve digital signature algorithm, ANSI X9.62, January 1998
10. National Institute of Standards and Technology: The Secure Hash Algorithm (SHA-1), NIST FIPS PUB 180-1, U.S. Department of Commerce, April 1995
11. Mobile IPv6 implementation MobiWan patch on ns2.33, http://www.nicta.com.au/people/mehanio/nsmisc/ns-233-mobiwan-1.patch
12. M'Raihi, D., Machani, S., Pei, M., Rydell, J.: TOTP: Time-Based One-Time Password Algorithm. IETF RFC 6238, May 2011
13. Makaya, C., Pierre, S.: An analytical framework for performance evaluation of ipv6-based mobility management protocols. IEEE Trans. Wirel. Commun. **7**(3), 972–983 (2008)

Implementation and Evaluation of Vehicle-to-Vehicle Traffic Congestion Detection

Faisal Karim Shaikh[1(✉)], Mohsin Shah[1], Bushra Shaikh[1],
and Roshan Ahmed Shaikh[2]

[1] Department of Telecommunication,
Mehran University of Engineering and Technology, Jamshoro 76062, Pakistan
{faisal.shaikh,mohsin.shah,bushra.shaikh}@tl.muet.edu.pk
http://www.tl.muet.edu.pk
[2] Aisoft Inc., New York, USA
ras@aisft.com
http://www.aisft.com

Abstract. With the growing population worldwide the traffic problems such as traffic congestion is increasing day by day. By using the technology offered by Vehicular Ad-hoc Networks it is possible that the traffic congestion can be avoided. Existing transportation systems rely on fixed infrastructure to monitor traffic conditions resulting in costly solutions. This paper presents an implementation and evaluation of distributed traffic congestion detection mechanism using the vehicle to vehicle communications without requiring fixed infrastructure. Each vehicle keeps track of its speed and the speed of the surrounding vehicles to detect the congestion. If the speed of the nearby vehicles is not up to the desired threshold than congestion message is created which is transmitted in a multi-hop manner to the vehicles at the rear end of the congestion and even to the vehicles approaching the congestion. We implement the approach on IRIS motes and evaluate its performance on a testbed.

Keywords: Vehicular communications · Vehicle-to-Vehicle (V2V) communications · Traffic congestion detection

1 Introduction

In order to make roads cleaner, safer and smarter Wireless Sensor Network (WSN) technologies are increasingly considered in research, standardization and development. Vehicular Ad-Hoc Networks (VANETs) provide communications between nearby vehicles and considered as most special application of WSNs.

This research was partially supported by Mehran University of Engineering and Technology, Jamshoro, Pakistan and National ICT R&D Fund, Ministry of Information Technology, Pakistan under National Grassroots ICT Research Initiative.

© Springer International Publishing Switzerland 2014
F.K. Shaikh et al. (Eds.): IMTIC 2013, CCIS 414, pp. 227–238, 2014.
DOI: 10.1007/978-3-319-10987-9_21

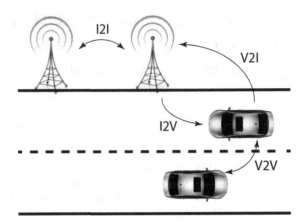

Fig. 1. Communication in distributed intelligent transportation system [1,2]

Today's vehicles are already able to sense the surrounding environment and communicate with a roadside communication infrastructure and with each other. Vehicles create a fundamental building block of Intelligent Transport Systems (ITS) and can provide several application services to improve safety and comfort of driving. Every participating vehicle in VANETs becomes a wireless router, allowing nearby vehicles to exchange data. VANETs primary goals are to provide safety, security and comfort to passengers and drivers. To avoid accidents, roadside and in-vehicle sensor nodes measure the road conditions at various positions on the surface, aggregate the measured values and communicate them to central location and among other vehicles.

Congestion detection is one of the main applications of VANETs and it is not designed to be used as a means for automated driving but rather as a tool to deliver information to the driver that will help him to make decisions to avoid heavy traffic jams. Implementing a traffic congestion detection system will have tremendous impact on the economy, allowing us to spend less time stuck in traffic and more time doing dynamic and enjoyable activities.

There are three types of communications in VANETs (Fig. 1), i.e., Vehicle-to-Vehicle (V2V), Vehicle-to-Infrastructure (V2I)/Infrastructure-to-Vehicle (I2V) and Infrastructure-to-Infrastructure (I2I) [1,2]. In V2I/I2V paradigm the vehicles are supported by fixed infrastructure which is termed as a base station to offer increased range of access and mobility. Generally, these base stations are installed along the roadside. The infrastructure is also equipped with the same short range wireless devices that will provide the communication between the vehicle and itself. Generally, these fixed infrastructures are deployed at certain intervals along the roads. Therefore, it is hard to have realtime congestion and lane occupancy information. Furthermore, the two base stations will communicate with each other (I2I paradigm) and disseminate the information regarding different road conditions to the approaching vehicles and the central control room of ITS. The design of infrastructure based traffic monitoring solutions are characterized by a trade-off between the traffic estimates accuracy and the number of deployed infrastructure points.

In V2V mode of communication, the vehicles themselves are capable to continuously propagate information about the traffic conditions along the road. The vehicles are equipped with short range wireless devices (such as Wifi or Zigbee devices such as sensor motes) which enable communication across vehicles. By enabling vehicles with the communication capabilities, the traffic safety and efficiency can be improved and controlled. Accordingly, the vehicles continuously exchange theirs information, i.e., location, speed and vehicles around it, to identify the traffic conditions in a distributed manner. In particular, this paper makes the following contributions.

- We extended an existing mechanism [3] to detect traffic congestion using V2V communication paradigm and make it working for various congestion scenarios.
- We provide evaluation of the extended algorithm on real testbed using IRIS motes and radio controlled (RC) vehicles.

The rest of the paper is organized as follows. We present related work in Sect. 2. Section 3 provide description of the Congestion Detection Mechanism and the scenarios that are considered in this paper. Section 4 elaborates the conducted experiments, provides the results and other factors that were observed during the experiments. Finally, Sect. 6 concludes the paper.

2 Related Work

VANETs focus on simulating vehicular traffic [4–9] and multi-hop routing [10–13]. Congestion or Collision avoidance systems [1, 14] are designed to avoid collisions between traffic and distribute the real time information among other vehicles. Controlling and safety applications of traffic systems [15–17] are designed to avoid accidents. In [18], an algorithm of real time estimation of truck traffic in multi-lane freeway is proposed. A peer-to-peer overlay over the Internet, using cellular Internet access [19] eliminates problems which are caused by direct communication of cars like capacity constraints and limited initial deployment of the technology.

TrafficView [20] proposes an aggregation mechanism combining information from different vehicles in the vicinity. In [21], digital road maps are used to efficiently combine the information generated by multiple vehicles in distributed manner. Differently from [21], in [22], a cluster head is chosen in a segment of road for collecting and aggregating road traffic data and disseminating it to other cluster heads. The drawback of this approach is that the selection of the cluster head usually generates additional signaling overhead. In [23], in order to reduce the communications overhead, the exchange of information is limited and done only when situation arises, e.g., traffic jams. In [24], a different approach is adopted where each vehicle continuously estimates a congestion index in the area it is located and other vehicles which are interested to know the information will request it. A pattern matching technique is exploited in [25] to reduce the communication overhead. An efficient road congestion detection scheme is proposed in [26] using multi-hop communication and geocast principles to gather and analyze the information. In [3,27] fuzzy logic is used to estimate and detect the congestion on roads. The messages are exchanged locally to save the overhead of information dissemination.

All the above discussed techniques are evaluated through simulations only in the literature. One of the major reasons is the lack of real testbeds. Furthermore, to have large scale testbeds require lot of expenses. Therefore, majority of existing work depend on simulations. In this paper, we have developed a small scale VANET testbed using IRIS motes and radio controlled cars. We have implemented and evaluated the congestion detection mechanism on this testbed.

3   DVCD: Distributed V2V Congestion Detection

The traffic congestion detection mechanism is based on [3,27] and is carefully extended to suit the intelligent and low power sensors to tackle the congestion scenarios as depicted in Fig. 2. The mechanism detects the traffic congestion locally and broadcast the messages across the approaching vehicles to make them aware of the congestion situation of the road before they reach and get stuck into it. The algorithm uses the Co-operative Awareness Messages (Co-AM) or beacon messages that vehicles periodically broadcast, mainly for safety purposes, to updating the nearby vehicles with theirs own speed or the road traffic conditions. These conditions are monitored locally by every vehicle using fuzzy logic. When a congestion situation is detected, the individual estimations made locally by different vehicles are shared among other vehicles to collectively and accurately detect and characterize the road traffic congestion.

The possible fuzzy sets for the speed are slow, medium and fast. For traffic density, the defined fuzzy sets are low, medium and high. Table 1 defines the fuzzy sets including the input (speed and density) and the output sets (congestion levels).

The proposed distributed approach (Fig. 3) is based on multi-hop communication to achieve a collective decision on the traffic congestion situation. This approach allows evaluation of the individual estimations locally made by the different participating vehicles. Every vehicle is continuously monitoring the road traffic conditions and estimates through the fuzzy logic-based detection system

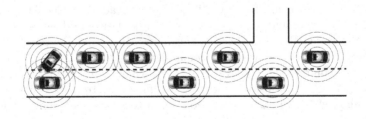

Fig. 2. Traffic congestion scenario

Table 1. Defined fuzzy sets for the algorithm [3]

		Traffic density		
		Low	*Medium*	*High*
Speed	*Slow*	Minor	Medium	Severe
	Medium	Free flow	Minor	Medium
	Fast	Free flow	Minor	Minor

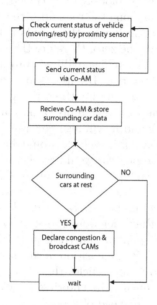

Fig. 3. DVCD flow diagram

about the current level of road congestion. The method adopted in the approach is based on the comparison of the speeds of the surrounding vehicles with the predefined threshold [3]. Each vehicle calculates its speed and surrounding number of vehicles, and broadcast this information via Co-AMs periodically. Upon reception of Co-AM the other vehicles will update their status, i.e., number of vehicles surrounding them and their speeds. The congestion alert messages (CAM) are broadcasted only when the vehicle locally estimate that there is minimal threshold congestion (C_{TH}) on the road. The value of C_{TH} can vary depending upon the local traffic department policies. The CAM message includes speed of the vehicle, number of surrounding vehicles and their minimum speed, and the hop count. The hop count parameter is utilized to find the length of the traffic congestion. Accordingly, vehicles located at the front end of the traffic jam are responsible for the periodic generation of the CAM which is forwarded via multi-hop (at each hop the hop count is incremented) towards the rear end of the jam. Every vehicle relaying a CAM updates the traffic information included in the packet based on its own traffic estimation. Finally, vehicles situated in the rear end of the traffic jam that receive CAM will get a complete picture of the level of road congestion. There can be two basic congestion scenarios to this proposition. These scenarios are discussed below.

3.1   Scenario A: Single Lane Traffic Congestion

In this scenario (Fig. 4), a traffic congestion occurs on a single lane road. The vehicles that passed before the blockage are considered free from congestion. However, the vehicles moving along the road after the blockage will have to slow down and eventually stop. In such case, the speed of the vehicle which is immediate next to the blockage will be zero, therefore this zero value is considered as threshold value for CAMs. The vehicle will generate the CAM after the speed becomes zero at some fixed interval. Let us assume this message starts at time t_0, which acts as the reference time for the series of CAMs. The next vehicle that stops after the first one will then apply brakes and its speed also becomes zero. Hence, its timer starts and it will also generate its CAM after some fixed interval. During this time the first vehicle would have transmitted its CAM, which we assume that the second car would receive without error. After receiving this CAM, the second car updates its table of CAMs and would calculate that it is the second in line in the congestion. The timer of the second car has a time t_1. This vehicle would update its table based on the fact that $t_0 > t_1$. For the third vehicle in queue, the timer would start at t_2 and during that time the second vehicle would have updated and transmitted its table of CAMs to the third which would easily identify its position in the queue as $t_0 > t_1 > t_2$. The same procedure would be applied to all vehicles that enter the congested lane and in this way by the end of the queue, the entering vehicles would have a complete picture of the congestion state ahead of them.

In this scenario some vehicles which are ahead of the blockage also receive the CAMs. In such a case, the CAMs will be ignored as the speed of the vehicles is greater than the threshold and they are moving in the same direction, i.e., away from the congestion. This way the vehicles out of the congestion will not have to update the information.

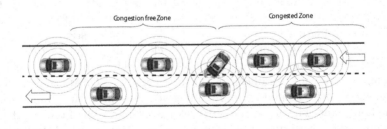

Fig. 4. Single lane traffic congestion

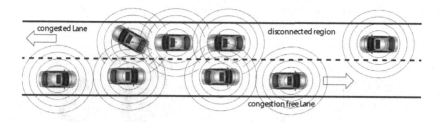

Fig. 5. Single lane traffic congestion on two way road

3.2 Scenario B: Single Lane Traffic Congestion on Two Way Road

In this scenario, we have assumed scenario A in one direction (congested lane) and the other direction is assumed congestion-free. On the other lane which does not have congestion, the CAMs timers are not initiated as the speed threshold is not approached. However, as they are moving in opposite direction, i.e., towards congestion, the vehicles will carry the CAM messages and broadcast them in other direction of the congested lane. In such a way the information will be propagated faster and also to the disconnected segment of vehicles which are approaching towards the congested area as shown in Fig. 5.

4 Experimental Testbed Setup

In order to create a VANET scenario, we have selected radio controlled (RC) car as a prototype of vehicle. Generally, in RC cars we can not get the speed of the vehicle directly. Thus, in order to find the speed of RC car we have embedded the proximity sensor along the wheel of a RC car to monitor a small metallic strip on the wheel. The proximity sensor is basically used to count the number of revolutions per minute of the wheel at various speeds. For the RC cars to communicate with each other we have used IRIS motes [28]. The proximity sensor used in the testbed works between 6–36 volts and consumes 300 mA when working whereas the IRIS mote works on 3 V. Therefore, interfacing of the proximity sensor with the IRIS mote requires a hardware circuit that will enable proximity sensor to communicate with the IRIS mote. Figure 6(a) depicts the schematic diagram for interfacing the sensor with the mote. For a testbed we have made five RC cars as stated above. Figure 6(b) shows the complete working model of RC car. Two cars are used to emulate the congestion for scenario A (Sect. 3.1). The remaining RC cars are moving on the same track towards the congestion point in such a way that they create multi-hop scenario. For scenario B, similarly two cars will create traffic congestion and two cars will approach to the congestion point in such a way that they can not communicate with each other. One RC car will be moving in opposite direction from the congestion point. The RC cars were deployed in a 50 m long corridor of Telecommunication Department, Mehran University, Jamshoro. The speed of RC cars was approximately 0.75 m/s on congested lane and 1.5 m/s on non-congested lane. In order to listen

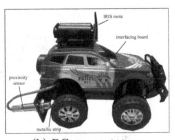

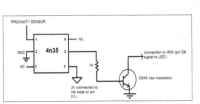

(a) Circuit interfacing proximity sensor with IRIS

(b) RC car prototype

Fig. 6. Testbed vehicle

the communication among the cars we have deployed four base stations across the corridor. The base station is essentially an IRIS mote connected with the laptop and only listen to the ongoing communication.

Algorithm 1 shows the implementation of one fuzzy logic of DVCD approach for IRIS motes, i.e., when the speed of car is slow or at the rest. When the speed of the car (S_{car}) becomes zero or less than the predefined slow speed threshold $S_{s_{TH}}$, the CAM timer (t_{CAM}) starts. This is to avoid any circumstance where the car has to stop or slow down for a while, which is not an indication of traffic congestion. When the CAM timer expires, the speed of the car is checked again and if it is still less than $S_{s_{TH}}$ or zero and there are threshold number of cars (V_{TH}) in surrounding (calculated from received Co-AM and CAM messages), then the CAM is broadcasted by the car. In the meantime if a CAM of another car is received by the car then its CAM is updated before broadcasting it. Upon receiving the CAM by a car moving in opposite direction on other lane where the congestion is not occurring, it will continue Co-AM till congestion queue length. After waiting for congestion queue length time (t_q) the car will broadcast threshold amount of CAM (B_{TH}) in order to disseminate the information to cars approaching the congestion spot.

5   Evaluation

In this section we discuss the various results obtained from the testbed. Figure 7 shows the total number of messages transmitted by the RC Cars during the execution of the scenarios as discussed in Sect. 3. The total number of messages directly impact the reliability of the system, i.e., more messages mean more collisions and contention, and the energy efficiency of the DVCD. We observe that for scenario A the total number of messages by each car is more or less similar. The cars which are part of congestion itself (i.e., car ID = 1 and 2) and cars near to the congestion (i.e., car ID = 3) transmit relatively higher number of messages compared to the cars approaching to the congestion point. On the other hand, for scenario B we observe that the nodes approaching to the congestion transmit

---

Algorithm 1. Algorithm for RC car

Input: $S_{s_{TH}} = 0$, $V_{TH} = 2$, $t_q = 5$, $B_{TH} = 3$

1 **if** $(S_{car} < S_{s_{TH}})$ || $(S_{car} = 0)$ && $(vehicles >= V_{TH})$ **then**
2   start(t_{CAM})

3 **if** $expires(t_{CAM})$ **then**
4   **if** $(S_{car} < S_{s_{TH}})$ || $(S_{car} = 0)$ && $(vehicles >= V_{TH})$ **then**
5   broadcast(CAM)

6 **begin**
7   receive(CAM)
   //CAM is received from other cars
8   **if** $CAM.direction == this.direction$ **then**
9   update(this.CAM)

10   **else**
11   **begin**
12   wait (t_q)\{ //wait till congestion queue length
13   **for** $i=1$; $i<= B_{TH}$; $i++$ **do**
14   broadcast(CAM)

15   \}

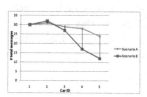

Fig. 7. Total messages

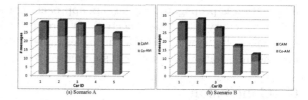

Fig. 8. Number of Co-AM and CAM messages

less number of messages. It should be noted that the car ID = 5 in scenario B is a node moving in opposite direction on non-congested lane. This shows the clear benefit corresponding to number of messages exchanged to propagate the congestion information.

Figure 8 classifies the total number of messages into number of Co-AM and CAM messages to show the overhead of the messages generated due to congestion detection. Figure 8(a) and (b) show that in general, the overhead of CAM for both scenarios is less. Furthermore, for scenario B, car ID = 5 we observe that the number of Co-AM is also less. This is because on the non-congested lane, the speed of car is faster than on the congested lane.

Figure 9 depicts the reliability achieved to successfully detect the congestion at all the cars. For scenario B it is evident that the achieved reliability is less than the scenario A due to fact of high mobility on non-congested lane where sometimes the CAM was not received. Thus, the car ID = 4 is also not able to

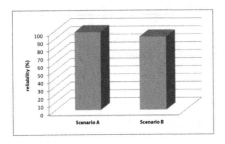

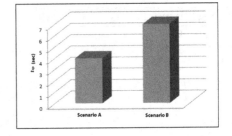

Fig. 9. Congestion detection reliability   **Fig. 10.** Congestion propagation delay

get the CAM alert. Figure 10 shows the delay incurred on sending the CAM message from the congestion point to the last known car on the congested lane. For scenario B the delay is higher as the congestion information traveled via the car on non-congested lane to the car approaching the congestion (from scenario A's point of view the approaching car is disconnected and the message can not be transmitted to it).

The results show a tradeoff between the delay, disconnected regions, the achieved reliability and the number of messages. For scenario B we acquire less number of messages (which is desired), high delay and less reliability but the information is propagated to the cars approaching the congestion which are not in close vicinity (i.e., disconnected). Whereas, for scenario A the number of messages is high (which is not much desirable), high reliability and less delay but the information can not be disseminated to disconnected cars.

6   Conclusion

In this paper we evaluate an enhanced fuzzy rule based approach for road traffic congestion detection in a distributed manner for two different scenarios. The proposed Distributed V2V Congestion Detection approach is implemented and evaluated on a testbed comprising of RC cars equipped with IRIS motes. The number of messages broadcasted, the delay occurred and the reliability of both scenarios are compared and statistically defined. The results show that generally DVCD has less overhead and can reliably detect the congestion. This work can further be extended for more complex traffic scenarios.

Acknowledgement. We would like to thank Wahaj Khan, Shahzoob Bilal, Nimra Anjum, Batool Pirah, Murad Ali and Himat Kumar (students of Telecommunication Department) for conducting the initial experiments.

References

1. Rawashdeh, Z.Y., Mahmud, S.M.: Intersection collision avoidance system architecture. In: 5th IEEE Consumer Communications and Networking Conference, CCNC 2008, pp. 493–494. IEEE (2008)

2. Santa, J., Tsukada, M., Ernst, T., Mehani, O.: Assessment of vanet multi-hop routing over an experimental platform. Int. J. Internet Protoc. Technol. **4**(3), 158–172 (2009)
3. Bauza, R., Gozalvez, J., Sanchez-Soriano, J.: Road traffic congestion detection through cooperative vehicle-to-vehicle communications. In: 2010 IEEE 35th Conference on Local Computer Networks (LCN), pp. 606–612. IEEE (2010)
4. Bana, S.V.: Coordinating Automated Vehicles via Communication. Ph.D. thesis, University of California at Berkeley (2000)
5. Härri, J., Filali, F., Bonnet, C., Fiore, M.: Vanetmobisim: generating realistic mobility patterns for vanets. In: Proceedings of the 3rd International Workshop on Vehicular Ad Hoc Networks, pp. 96–97. ACM (2006)
6. Karnadi, F.K., Mo, Z.H., Lan, K.-C.: Rapid generation of realistic mobility models for vanet. In: IEEE Wireless Communications and Networking Conference, WCNC 2007, pp. 2506–2511. IEEE (2007)
7. Potnis, N., Mahajan, A.: Mobility models for vehicular ad hoc network simulations. In: Proceedings of the 44th Annual Southeast Regional Conference, pp. 746–747. ACM (2006)
8. Sommer, C., Dietrich, I., Dressler, F.: Realistic simulation of network protocols in vanet scenarios. In: 2007 Mobile Networking for Vehicular Environments, pp. 139–143. IEEE (2007)
9. Zhang, H.M., Kim, T.: Understanding and modeling driver behavior in dense traffic. Final report University of California Transportation Center (2002)
10. Dikaiakos, M.D., Iqbal, S., Nadeem, T., Iftode, L.: Vitp: an information transfer protocol for vehicular computing. In: Proceedings of the 2nd ACM International Workshop on Vehicular Ad Hoc Networks, pp. 30–39. ACM (2005)
11. Eichler, S., Schroth, C., Kosch, T., Strassberger, M.: Strategies for context-adaptive message dissemination in vehicular ad hoc networks. In: 2006 Third Annual International Conference on Mobile and Ubiquitous Systems: Networking & Services, pp. 1–9. IEEE (2006)
12. Tonguz, O., Wisitpongphan, N., Bai, F., Mudalige, P., Sadekar, V.: Broadcasting in vanet. In: Mobile Networking for Vehicular Environments, pp. 7–12. IEEE (2007)
13. Wischhof, L., Rohling, H.: Congestion control in vehicular ad hoc networks. In: International Conference on Vehicular Electronics and Safety, pp. 58–63 (2005)
14. Mak, T.K., Laberteaux, K.P., Sengupta, R.: A multi-channel vanet providing concurrent safety and commercial services. In: Proceedings of the 2nd ACM International Workshop on Vehicular Ad Hoc Networks, pp. 1–9. ACM (2005)
15. Lu, X.-Y., Varaiya, P.P., Horowitz, R.: An equivalent second order model with application to traffic control. In: Control in Transportation Systems, pp. 375–382 (2009)
16. Haas, J.J., Hu, Y.-C.: Communication requirements for crash avoidance. In: Proceedings of the Seventh ACM International Workshop on VehiculAr InterNETworking, pp. 1–10 (2010)
17. Lee, S.-H., Lee, S., Youngtae, O.: New loop detector installation guidelines for real-time adaptive signal installation. J. Eastern Asia Soc. Transp. Stud. **6**, 2337–2348 (2005)
18. Kwon, J., Varaiya, P., Skabardonis, A.: Estimation of truck traffic volume from single loop detectors with lane-to-lane speed correlation. Transp. Res. Rec. J. Transp. Res. Board **1856**(1), 106–117 (2003)
19. Rybicki, J., Scheuermann, B., Koegel, M., Mauve, M.: Peer ITS- a peer-to-peer traffic information system. In: The Sixth ACM International Workshop on VehiculAr Inter-NETworking (2009)

20. Nadeem, T., Dashtinezhad, S., Liao, C., Iftode, L.: Trafficview: traffic data dissemination using car-to-car communication. ACM SIGMOBILE Mob. Comput. Commun. Rev. **8**(3), 6–19 (2004)
21. Wischhof, L., Ebner, A., Rohling, H.: Information dissemination in self-organizing intervehicle networks. IEEE Trans. Intel. Transp. Syst. **6**(1), 90–101 (2005)
22. Miller, J.: Vehicle-to-vehicle-to-infrastructure (v2v2i) intelligent transportation system architecture. In: 2008 IEEE Intelligent Vehicles Symposium, pp. 715–720. IEEE (2008)
23. Dornbush, S., Joshi, A.: Streetsmart traffic: Discovering and disseminating automobile congestion using vanet's. In: IEEE 65th Vehicular Technology Conference, VTC2007-Spring, pp. 11–15. IEEE (2007)
24. Lakas, A., Cheqfah, M.: Detection and dissipation of road traffic congestion using vehicular communication. In: 2009 Mediterrannean Microwave Symposium (MMS), pp. 1–6. IEEE (2009)
25. Vaqar, S.A., Basir, O.: Traffic pattern detection in a partially deployed vehicular ad hoc network of vehicles. IEEE Wirel. Commun. **16**(6), 40–46 (2009)
26. Younes, M.B., Boukerche, A.: Efficient traffic congestion detection protocol for next generation vanets. In: 2013 IEEE International Conference on Communications (ICC), pp. 3764–3768. IEEE (2013)
27. Bauza, R., Gozálvez, J.: Traffic congestion detection in large-scale scenarios using vehicle-to-vehicle communications. J. Netw. Comput. Appl. **36**(5), 1295–1307 (2013)
28. IRIS Mote Datasheet. Wireless measurement system. Document Part Number: 6020–0124-01 Rev A. http://www.xbow.com. Accessed on 5 August 2013

Photovoltaic System in Progress: A Survey of Recent Development

Ghulam Mustafa Shoro[✉], Dil Muhammad Akbar Hussain[✉], and Dezso Sera[✉]

Aalborg University Denmark, Aalborg, Denmark
{gms,akh,des}@et.aau.dk

Abstract. This paper provides a comprehensive update on photovoltaic (PV) technologies and the materials. In recent years, targeted research advancement has been made in the photovoltaic cell technologies to reduce cost and increase efficiency. Presently, several types of PV solar panels are commercially utilized and playing an important role in the market. Three generations of photovoltaic technologies are investigated and discussed; Crystalline Silicon Technology categorized as first generation of PV technology, Thin Film Technologies are second generation of PV technologies and Multi-junction Cells falls in the third generation PV technologies. However, Multi-junction Cells are still considered new and have not yet achieved commercialization status. The fundamental change observed among all generations has been how the semiconductor material is employed and the development associated with crystal structure. Silicon remains the prominent semiconductor within photovoltaic.

Keywords: Solar cell technologies · Photovoltaic technologies · PV technologies

1 Introduction

Energy is such an important component without which our modern world will not be operational. Increasing global energy demand is one of the greatest challenges experienced by modern society. Today, main share of the energy generated worldwide is obtained from fossil fuels. Due to the reported decline in world reserve of such fossil energy sources, as well as the environmental impacts associated with their use, alternatively energy sources are the only solution. Solar energy is an affordable, abundant and clean technology and one of the renewable energy sources which could eliminate impending energy crises associated with rising oil prices, global warming, environment and others energy issues. Solar energy technologies consist of photovoltaic, solar thermal electricity, solar architecture and solar heating. Due to the climbing efficiencies in Table 1 coupled with lower PV module prices in Fig. 1, the production of photovoltaic cells and arrays have advanced greatly and penetration in photovoltaic system has observed to be growing. Table 1 and Fig. 1 is taken from reference [3], it can be seen that

© Springer International Publishing Switzerland 2014
F.K. Shaikh et al. (Eds.): IMTIC 2013, CCIS 414, pp. 239–250, 2014.
DOI: 10.1007/978-3-319-10987-9_22

Table 1. Module Efficiency [3]

Technologies	Module efficiency	Surface area needed for 1 kwp
Mono-crystalline Silicon	13 %–19 %	5–8 m^2
Poly-crystalline Silicon	11 %–15 %	7–9 m^2
Copper Indium Gallium Selenide CIGS	10 %–12 %	8–10 m^2
Cadmium Telluride (CdTe)	9 %–12 %	9–11 m^2
Amorphous Silicon (a-Si)	5 %–8 %	13–20 m^2

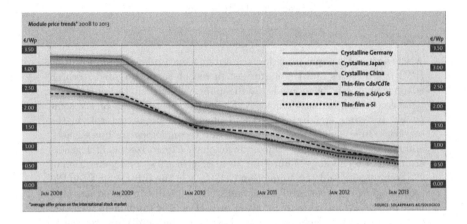

Fig. 1. Module price trend [3]

how efficiency for these different technologies varies with the surface area (to get 1 kwp) and it can also be seen that the price variations in all the technologies as modules have approximately similar downhill slope.

Photovoltaic system is comprised of PV cells assembled into modules, which are connected into arrays, and the so called balance of system (BOS) components [2]. A PV system can produce outputs from microwatt to megawatt. Global focus has increasingly shifted from using conventional methods of generating electricity to photovoltaic system and large investments have been made with the testing and installation of large PV power plants [3]. Currently, the use of photovoltaic system placed after the use of wind and hydro power, as the biggest renewable power source with regards to globally installed capacity. Considering the cost and the fact that PV systems is limited in generating any power during night periods demands that the highest possible efficiency during day light hours should be achieved which is very critical for solar power viability. So, the trend is going in a right direction, so that the reduction in the cost of PV systems will be accomplished through improved materials usage and higher efficiencies. In this context the paper reviews the current status of three generations of photovoltaic technologies and investigates their reliability, efficiency and cost. Furthermore, developments and future potentials with these systems will also be summarized.

2   Solar Resource and Worlds Energy Consumption

2.1   The Solar Potential

The Sun is the main source (directly or indirectly) of almost all power, used on earth. The Sun is center of our solar system and 150 million kilometers away from the earth [4]. Solar energy is the radiant heat and light from the sun. This energy supports life and can be converted to other forms of energy that are useful to humans. The radiation emitted by the sun is estimated to be about $63\,MW/m^2$ of this huge solar potential, the energy that reaches the earths surface without any significant absorption is measured to be 1353–$1366\,W/m^2$; this is referred as the solar constant [5]. A normal quantity of solar radiation reaching the surface of Earth is 1.05×10^5 terawatts (TW) in a year, even though global electricity need averages 1.99 (TW) in a year [6].

2.2   History of Solar Cells

Solar energy has been used to produce electrical power for a couple of centuries using a range of constantly evolving technologies. The Table 2 shows a summary on the progress of the PV cells with time [7]. Solar cells were developed during the 1950s, primarily at the Bell Telephone laboratories. These cells proved to be the best power sources for extra-terrestrial missions, and more than 1000 satellites using solar cells were launched between 1960 and 1970. In mid-seventies, efforts were initiated to make solar cells for terrestrial applications. Last three decades saw newer device technologies enabling reduction in cost and hence opening new horizons for commercial applications of solar cells.

Table 2. Dates of relevance to photovoltaic solar energy conversion [7]

Scientists and innovations	Year
Edmond Becquerel discovered the photovoltaic effect	1839
W.G. Adams and R.E. Day observed photovoltaic in selenium	1876
Max Planck claimed the quantum nature of light	1900
Alan Wilson proposed quantum theory of solids	1930
Mott and Schottky develop the theory of solid-state rectifier diode	1940
Schottky, Bardeen and Brattain invented the transistor	1949
Pearson, Charpin and Fuller announced 6 % efficient silicon solar cell	1954
Reynolds et al. highlight solar cell based on cadmium sulphide	1954
First use of solar cells on an orbiting satellite Vanguard 1	1958

3   Basics of Photovoltaic

3.1   Photovoltaic Effects

Photovoltaic effect can be observed when certain semiconductor materials exposed to sunlight. Using this technique, semiconductors which have the photovoltaic effect can then be used to convert solar rays into direct current electricity.

3.2   Principle of Solar Cell Operation

A solar cell is a semiconductor electrical junction device which is usually made up of element silicon. Sunlight is composed of energy packets called photons. These photons consist of energy packets corresponding to the different wavelengths associated with light [8]. When a solar cell is struck by photons with appropriate energy, the photons are consumed through the space charge region of the p-n junction of cell, this leads to transfer of the photons energy to an electron. The electron thus becomes excited to knock free from its atoms and electron hole pairs formed in the junction. In order to generate electricity, the electrons and holes need to be separated. When a load is connected at the terminals that causes an electron current flow and electrical power is available at the load. The free electron movement from one layer to the next generates electricity. Due to well-designed structure of photovoltaic cell, the electrons are permitted to go in one way. An array of solar cells converts solar power into direct current (DC) electrical power.

4   Photovoltaic Technologies

Photovoltaic power generation uses solar panels and these panels are composed of an array of packaged solar cells, constructed from semiconductor material. At present, materials used for photovoltaic cells are consists of monocrystalline silicon, polycrystalline silicon, amorphous silicon cadmium telluride and copper indium gallium selenide. Figure 2 provides how different types of solar cells are constructed; this figure has been taken from reference [1]. The following subsections will provide the brief description of these materials.

4.1   Crystalline Silicon Cell Technologies

Solar cells constructed with crystalline silicon (Si) semiconductor are most efficient [1]. Silicon is currently predominating solar cell material and is expected to remain dominant until a more inexpensive material and higher efficiency PV technologies are developed [7]. As outlined by NREL, throughout 2011, 90 % of market sales were from Silicon based photovoltaic (PV) products and the annual production of Si-based PV was reported to reach 15 GW [9]. However, crystalline silicon solar cells achieved the highest efficiency on the expense of high manufacturing cost.

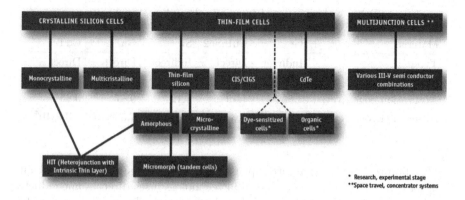

Fig. 2. Types of solar cell [1]

4.1.1 Monocrystalline and Multicrystalline

A crystalline silicon solar cell could be designed with distinct techniques such as the industry dominating single-crystalline/monocrystalline and polycrystalline/multi-crystalline techniques. Commercial manufacture of standard monocrystalline silicon cells has obtained a good efficiency of 17–18 % [1], although multicrystalline silicon cells currently have achieved 16–17 % efficiencies. Technological developments are currently in progress to develop cells with higher efficiencies [1]. Crystalline cells are made from silicon wafers simply by cleaning as well as doping the particular wafer and in a separate manufacturing process; several cells are then wired up to form a module.

4.1.2 Hetrojunction with Intrinsic Thin Layer (HIT)

HIT (Hetrojunction with Intrinsic Thin-layer) solar cells are attracting a growing number of interests after appearing in 1992. When compared to a-Si solar cells, the efficiency of HIT solar cells is much higher [10]. On the other hand, the low temperature technology of HIT solar cells makes it possible to reduce cost by the application of low quality Si materials and high temperature performance is improved a lot compared to the c-Si solar cells. HIT Cell design processes involve an ultra-thin layer of amorphous silicon that is deposited on both faces of textured or thin single-crystal wafer [1]. Efficiency of HIT cells can be improved using both crystalline and amorphous silicon layers to efficiencies over 22 %.

4.2 Thin Film Cells Technologies

Silicon as a solar cell material has many advantages; however, it also conveys disadvantages. Table 3 from reference [13] describes that silicon is an indirect semiconductor and its absorption coefficient near to band edge is low. Thus, a fairly thick substrate is required for crystalline silicon cell manufacturing. This leads to substantial material and mechanical processing costs.

Table 3. Properties of common solar cell material [13]

Material	Ge	CuInSe2	Si	Ga	CdTe
Type	Indirect	Direct	Indirect	Direct	Direct
Band gap (eV)	0.67	1.04	1.11	1.43	1.49
Absorption edge (μm)	1.85	1.19	1.12	0.87	0.83
Absorption coef. (cm^{-1})	5.0×10^4	1.0×10^5	1.0×10^3	1.5×10^4	3.0×10^4

Thin-film technology is an attempt to reduce the cost and maintain the efficiency of crystalline solar cells. Thin-film technology uses direct semiconductor materials which has absorption coefficient higher than silicon. This means that fewer micrometers of thickness of semiconductor material are sufficient for the development of solar cells. Thin film solar cells could therefore be manufactured with small amount of semiconductor material leading to decreases in price ranges. The cost of raw material is much lower than the capital equipment and processing since thin film production unit requires more space. Thin film cells are prepared by depositing layers of semiconductor material barely 0.3–2 μm thick onto glass or stainless steel substrates [11]. This provides roll-to-roll layer that gives positive aspects with reference to manufacturing and current carrying capability. Efficiencies of 11–14 % have been achieved with this construction [12].

Thin film technologies including amorphous silicon/microcrystalline silicon (a-Si/c-Si), Copper Indium Selenide (CIS), Cadmium telluride (CdTe) absorb the solar spectrum and are much more efficiently than c-Si or mc-Si [14]. Presently, the thin film technologies a-Si/c-Si, CIS, CdTe have included integrated adjustments to help size fabrication and enjoy good commercial results. Overall, thin film solar panels are less efficient but widely used in PV industry due to its affordability. Figures 3 and 4 shows the relative efficiency of these technologies and the market share by them respectively [15].

4.2.1 Amorphous Silicon/Microcrystalline (a-Si/c-Si)

Amorphous silicon was developed in the early days of thin film technologies. It is a non-crystalline form of silicon. It requires small quantity of active material and has considerably better light absorption capability i.e. 1 μm thick film will absorb light significantly better when compared with crystalline silicon. Thin film a-Si solar cell provides an advantage since cells can be manufactured onto rigid (glass) or flexible substrates and could potentially offer lower costs. However, the disordered nature of the amorphous silicon results in dangling bonds and lattice defects. Consequently this produces less charge carriers as a result of the lower efficiency i.e. 4–8 %. In spite of low reported efficiencies, amorphous silicon is mass produced for applications where efficiency is not crucial and can be tolerated.

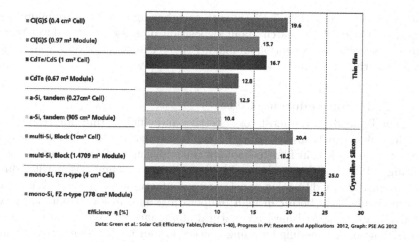

Fig. 3. Efficiency comparison of technologies [15]

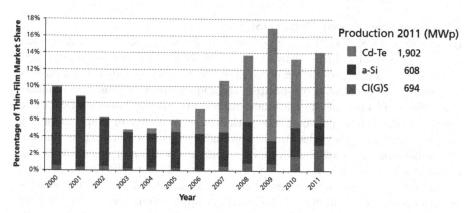

Fig. 4. Market share of thin-film technologies related to total worldwide PV production [15]

4.2.2 Copper Indium Selenium (CIS) or Copper Indium Gallium Diselenide (CIGS)

Copper Indium Selenium (CIS) is designed to obtain higher optical absorption coefficients along with electrical characteristics enabling device tuning [7]. Among all thin-film modules, CIGS and CIS technologies have the maximum efficiencies. 20 % efficiency has been recorded under laboratory conditions. Commercially available modules possess 7–12% efficiency [1]. A long-term issue with CIS technology is however the available resources. All known reserves of indium would only produce enough solar cells to provide a capacity equal to all present wind generators [16]. The main problem associated with CIGS modules has been the limited capability to scale up the procedure regarding large throughput, large yield along with low-cost. Several deposition methods are used: sputtering, ink printing and electroplating [7,17,18] with each having different throughput and efficiencies. Currently, research about deposition processes is at a development stage with specific concentration on making this technology cheaper from a business perspective to compete with Silicon modules [19].

4.2.3   Cadmium Telluride (CdTe)

Cadmium Telluride is the most cost-effective and efficient thin film technology. CdTe modules usually are low-priced compared to c-Si, with a higher efficiency with regard to a-Si thin film technology. The efficiency of CdTe modules is in the range of 7–11% (lower than c-Si), but greater in comparison with single junction a-Si [20]. CdTe solar panels are manufactured on glass. CdTe panels perform significantly better in high temperatures and in low irradiation levels [21]. CdTe are toxic and have low natural abundance [22] but various research reports showed that module recycling is necessary for CdTe to solve toxicity and the future availability problem of Tellurium.

4.2.4   Dye-Sensitized Cells (DSC)

Dye-Sensitized Cell (DSC) is a successful thin-film photovoltaic cell with demonstrated good results. Inspired by the principle of natural photosynthesis, Dye-Sensitized Solar cells have become a credible alternative to solid-state pn junction devices [22]. Conventional roll-printing techniques are widely-used to manufacture DSCs and most of the materials utilized are usually low-cost. DSCs offer the possibilities to design solar cells with a large flexibility in shape, color, and transparency [23]. They absorb more sunlight per surface area than standard silicon-based solar panels. Its efficiency is comparable to amorphous silicon solar cells but with a much lower cost [24]. Dye-sensitized solar cells can be potential replacements for silicon-based solar cells. Uncomplicated processing, low-cost material resources along with broad range of applications are reasons supporting DSCs. A limitation issue of the dye-sensitized cells is its stability over the time and the temperature range which occurs under outdoor conditions [25].

4.2.5   Organic Solar Cell

High efficiency Photovoltaic technologies are usually produced from inorganic materials, which often require higher material price together with manufacturing price. In recent years, organic solar cells have attracted scientific and economic interest. This was mainly triggered by growing demand for cost-effective production of photovoltaic modules. Organic semiconductors represent promising approaches as they use plastic which have low production costs in high volumes and can be processed into large-areas. The optical absorption coefficient of organic molecules is higher; consequently a substantial amount light might be consumed with a small amount of materials. The drawback related with organic photovoltaic cells is reduced efficiency, low stability and low strength when compared with inorganic photovoltaic cells [26]. Significant challenges related to organic cells are low efficiency, low stability, and low strength to protection against environmental influences compared to inorganic photovoltaic cells.

4.3 Multi-junctions Cells Technologies

The efficiency of solar cells can be significantly enhanced by stacking several p-n junctions in a cell [25]. Alloys of semiconductors with various band gap energies are layered on top of one another. The band gap energy indicates the wave length until which a semiconductor may process light and convert it into electricity [1]. This makes best possible use of the energy contained in the solar spectrum. Although solar cells designed with one semiconductor material have achieved theoretical efficiencies of 33 % and solar cells using two semiconductors with different band gaps have shown 42 % efficiencies [1]. Multijunction cells constructed from alloys merging the elements of group III and group V semiconductor materials in the periodic table, showed higher efficiencies matched by simply no other existing photovoltaic technology. Multijunction cells are composed off 3 layers of material which have different band gap while the bottom layer has the smallest band gap. This design allows less energetic photons to pass through the upper layers and be absorbed by lower layers which boost the overall efficiency of solar cells [27].

5 Current Status of PV System

5.1 PV Modules and Balance of System (BOS)

Photovoltaic systems have two key subsystems, PV modules and Balance of System (BOS). A PV module is a grid of PV cells. It has 72 cells wired in several parallel circuit packaged in metal frame for strength. Modules are protected from weather with lamination on front and back surfaces. Under standard conditions, commercial solar modules produce power capacity of 175–300 W. A PV array is a group of modules attached serially and strongly affixed to a firm structure. BOS are secondary components which are required to install PV modules and arrays. It contain wires for connecting modules in series, junction boxes for merging the circuits, power electronics for managing the PV arrays output and mounting hardware. BOS requirements differ caused by reliability, environmental conditions, power storage and site-specific power needs. The expansion of photovoltaic market has produced higher system integration and experienced system designers and installers. As a result, BOS cost reduced and this reduction are comparable to or even higher than module cost reductions.

5.2 PV Installation, Manufacturing, and Cost

Solar system is the fastest growing energy source in the world, powering homes, businesses and utility grids across nations. The solar photovoltaic (PV) industry has experienced 2012 to be an historic year. According to figures from the

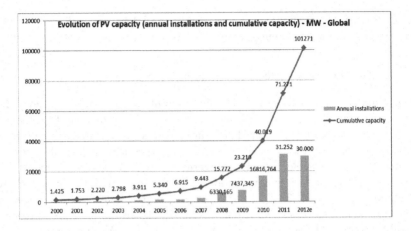

Fig. 5. Annual installations and cumulative PV capacity [28]

Table 4. Outlook for the solar sector (2011–2016) [29]

	2011	2012	2013	2014	2015	2016
Global installations (GW/yr)	28	34	34	43	52	54
Average Chinese module price ($/W)	$1.31	$0.74	$0.66	$0.73	$0.74	$0.66
Global revenue pool ($bn)	$103	$99	$96	$122	$138	$132
Manufacturing operating profit pool ($bn)	$0	−$9	−$7	−$3	$1	−$1
BOS and trading operating profit pool ($bn)	$14	$10	$11	$15	$16	$15
Global system operating profit pool ($bn)	$15	$0	$4	$11	$17	$14
Manufacturing operating profit margin (%)	1 %	−32 %	−31 %	−10 %	2 %	−2 %
Global operating profit margin (%)	14 %	0 %	4 %	9 %	12 %	11 %

EPIA [28], the cumulative global installed PV capacity passed the 100-gigawatt (GW) mark, achieving just over 101 GW in 2012. The solar PV industry has installed 30 GW capacity around the world and made it operational within 2012. In 2011, cumulative global installed PV capacity was around 70 GW. The exponential growth rate in installed capacity seen in recent years, global progression in PV installations outside Europe with a least 13 GW allowed the global market to reach the 30 GW mark again in 2012. Figure 5 shows the evolution of PV capacity globally, which indicate an exponential growth [28]. According to Photon consulting [29], installation volume is expanding rapidly across an extensive set of markets segments far from European countries, with bright prospects for growth in Brazil, Chile, China, India, Israel, Japan, South Africa, Thailand, Ukraine, U.K. and U.S. In 2010 more than 450 companies was active in PV manufacturing, within two years (by 2012) the figure is reduced to 154 which is even less than half. The reason is not being closer to the markets, most did not learn to adjust and adapt by listening to markets and getting closer to the customers. In reality, companies need tighter supply chains and more timely local market knowledge to adjust products, production, bundles, shipments and prices. It is expected that global PV installations will be 54 GW/year, module price reduction and increased revenue pool, manufacturing operating profit pool, BOS and trading operating profit pool, in 2016 [29]. The following Table 4 taken from reference [29] shows a comprehensive/forecast data of the solar sector; from installation, price revenue to BOS and profit etc., by the year 2016.

6 Conclusion

Today, Photovoltaic has more significant impact upon energy use, huge number of individuals making use of PV technology to power their homes and businesses, electric utility companies are also using it for large power grid stations. Photovoltaic costs have been gradually decreasing due to on-going advances in technology and rapid growing demand for photovoltaics system. Crystalline Silicon PV technology has highest efficiency but they are costly. Fabrication, installation and operational cost reduction is possible. We observed during the investigation of various technologies that we can expect small advances in the production efficiencies. However, the on-going research on new concepts for PV materials will certainly lead to greater efficiency and will make it less expensive in the coming years. The chances of getting to this goal are good due to wide variety of promising materials and the various concepts which have emerged [25]. Thin-film PV technologies requires only small amounts of material. It is advantageous for high-volume manufacturing and low material costs. Third generation PV technologies are new and not fully developed yet but expected to reduce the cost and enhance the performance of solar cells. Third generation technologies includes some multi-junction constructs and concepts based on the emerging fields of quantum technology, nanotechnology, optical meta materials and polymer semiconductor science.

References

1. Engineering the Solar Age: Suppliers for Photovoltaics, pp. 18–25, Report, Solarpraxis AG (2012–2013). http://www.suppliers-pv.com/fileadmin/user_upload/2012/pdf/esa12_GW-ES-Screen.pdf
2. Kippelen, B.: Organic photovoltaics. Opt. Photonics News **18**, 26–33 (2007)
3. PV Power Plants: Industry Guide, pp. 8–12 (2013). http://www.pv-power-plants.com/fileadmin/user_upload/pdf/PVPP2012_low_02.pdf
4. THE Solar CONSTANT. http://www.ips.gov.au/Category/Educational/The%20Sun%20and%20Solar%20Activity/General%20Info/Solar_Constant.pdf
5. Abdullah, M.O.: Applied Energy: An Introduction. CRC Press, New York (2012)
6. Photovoltaic Energy Factsheet. http://css.snre.umich.edu/css_doc/CSS07-08.pdf
7. El Chaar, L., Lamont, L.A., El Zein, N.: Review of photovoltaic technologies. Renew. Sustain. Energy Rev. **15**, 2165–2175 (2011)
8. Kothari, D., Subbarao, P.: Power Generation: Springer Handbook of Mechanical Engineering, pp. 1363–1419. Springer, Heidelberg (2009)

9. National Renewable Energy Laboratory (NREL): Silicon Materials and Devices R&D, 25 April 2012. http://www.daviddarling.info/encyclopedia/S/AE_solar_cell.html

10. Jha, A.R.: Chapter 5: Solar Cell Deploying Exotic Materials and Advanced Design Configurations for Optimum Performance: Solar Cell Technology and Applications, pp. 135–169. Auerbach Publications, Boca Raton (2009)

11. Handbook for Solar Photovoltaic (PV) Systems. http://www.bca.gov.sg/publications/others/handbook_for_solar_pv_systems.pdf

12. Electropaedia: Thin Film Silicon Solar Cells (2005). http://www.mpoweruk.com/solar_power.htm

13. Chen, C.J.: Semiconductor Solar Cell: Physics of Solar Cells, p. 179. Willey, Hoboken (2011). http://books.google.dk/books?id=dFKz6GwSVNEC&printsec=frontcover&source=gbs_ge_summary_r&cad=0&q&f=false

14. Bagnall, D.M., Boreland, M.: Photovoltaic technologies. Energy Policy 36, 4390–4396 (2008)

15. Photovoltaics Report. http://www.ise.fraunhofer.de/de/downloads/pdf-files/aktuelles/photovoltaics-report.pdf

16. Green, M.A.: Thin-film solar cells: review of materials, technologies and commercial status. J. Mater. Sci. Mater. Electron. 18(S1), 15–19 (2007)

17. Basol, B., Pinarbasi, M., Aksu, S., Wang, J., Matus, Y., Johnson, T., Han, Y., Narasimhan, M., Metin, B.: Electroplating based CIGS technology for roll-to-roll manufacturing. In: Twenty Third European PVSEC, pp. 2137–2141 (2008)

18. Eldada, L., Adurodija, F., Sang, B., Taylor, M., Lim, A., Taylor, J., Chang, Y., McWilliams, S., Oswald, R., Stanbery, B.: Development of hybrid copper indium gallium selenide photovoltaic devices by the FASST printing process. In: Proceedings of European Photovoltaic Solar Energy Conference, pp. 2142 (2008)

19. Powalla, M., Bonnet, D.: Thin-film solar cells based on the polycrystalline compound semiconductors CIS and CdTe. Adv. OptoElectron. 2007, 1–6 (2007). Article ID 97545

20. Doni, A., Dughiero, F., Lorenzoni, A.: A comparison between thin film and c-si PV technologies for MW size applications. In: 35th IEEE Photovoltaic Specialists Conference (PVSC), pp. 002380–002385 (2010)

21. First Solar: PV Technology Comparison. http://dev.firstsolar.com/~/media/Files/Products%20and%20Services%20-%20Product%20Documentation/Technology/PV%20Technology%20Comparison%20-%20English.ashx. Accessed 8 April 2013

22. Nazeeruddin, M.K., Baranoff, E., Grtzel, M.: Dye-sensitized solar cells: a brief overview. Solar Energy 85, 1172–1178 (2011)

23. Hagfeldt, A.: Brief overview of dye-sensitized solar cells. Ambio 41, 151–155 (2012)

24. Wei, D.: Dye sensitized solar cells. Int. J. Mol. Sci. 11, 1103–1113 (2010)

25. Goetzberger, A., Hebling, C., Schock, H.: Photovoltaic materials, history, status and outlook. Mater. Sci. Eng.: R. 40, 1–46 (2003)

26. Organic Solar Cell, 25 October 2012. http://murdockcapital.com/wordpress2/2012/07/23/organic-solar-cell/

27. Al Naser, Q.A.H., Hilou, H.W., Abdulkader, A.F.: The last development in III-V multi-junction solar cells. In: Computing, Communication, Control, and Management, CCCM, ISECS International Colloquium, pp. 373–378 (2009)

28. EPIA, European Photovoltaic Industry Association: Market Report 2012. http://www.epia.org/fileadmin/user_upload/Publications/Market_Report_2012.pdf

29. Photon Consulting: Solar Annual 2013: Build Your Empire. http://www.photonconsulting.com/files/reports/sa13.pdf

An Advanced Hyper-Efficient Design to Detect Random Peer-to-Peer Botnets

Isma Farah Siddiqui[1,2(✉)], Nawab Muhammad Faseeh[3],
Scott UK-Jin Lee[4], and Mukhtiar Ali Unar[5]

[1] Department of Software Engineering, Mehran UET, Jamshoro, Pakistan
[2] Software Engg Lab, Hanyang University, ERICA Campus,
Hanyang, South Korea
isma.farah@faculty.muet.edu.pk,
isma2012@hanyang.ac.kr
[3] Sungkyunkwan University, Seoul, South Korea
faseeh@skku.edu
[4] Department of Computer Science and Engineering, Hanyang University,
Hanyang, South Korea
scottlee@hanyang.ac.kr
[5] Department of Computer Systems Engineering, Mehran UET,
Jamshoro, Pakistan
mukhtiar.unar@faculty.muet.edu.pk

Abstract. Botnets have become one of the most solemn threats to Internet security. Botnets comprises over a network of infected nodes known as 'bot'. Bots are controlled by human operators (botmasters). Random nature of Peer-to-Peer botnets has influenced sinkhole researchers to compromise over occupation of hunted command and control in a complex manner and due to variable nature of action, they are often good deserters. In this paper, we present a design of an advanced hyper-efficient mechanism which has the ability to pursue Peer-to-Peer randomized botnets. It provides capacity to detain targeted sinkholes and identify arbitrary execution of contagion in infected nodes. In the end, method acquires the composition of different cubic formations for proper lookup of random natured Peer-to-Peer botnets.

Keywords: Botnets · Bot · Botmasters · Sinkhole

1 Introduction

Botnets are malicious programmed nodes, which are remotely controlled by botmasters. A botnet consists of bots and botmasters, postures a severe threat to internet security. The botmaster launch attacks such as Distributed Denial of Service (DDOS) and perform scam tasks such as phishing and spamming [1].

It is a matter of deep concern that the number of bot variants and the number of new bots are increasing every day. The huge propagation of botnets can be largely indorsed with the massive collection of computer nodes with 'always on' broadband connectivity that is tranquil to infect. The point of focus for a botmaster is to target home computers as well as the educational institutes computers because they are less

© Springer International Publishing Switzerland 2014
F.K. Shaikh et al. (Eds.): IMTIC 2013, CCIS 414, pp. 251–258, 2014.
DOI: 10.1007/978-3-319-10987-9_23

protected and have a huge storage with fast connectivity, and frequently direct connectivity with the backbone.

A command and control (C&C) system is a bridge through which bots connect to receive commands from botmaster. To this point, Internet Relay Chat (IRC) [1] protocol has been used by botnets to deploy C&C channels, so detecting patterns are customized to this protocol.

The botnets are programmed to achieve a target and are efficient enough to keep dispersing instructions, but they need to be familiar to get an interruption as the servers are recognized. In this way, it becomes rough for servers to distract all the information which becomes result of reducing the efficiency of botnets. In order to explain the scenario, it would be a disastrous for a botnet to shut down the C&C because it would lose all the effort done for the collection of bots and would result the termination of contact with botmaster. It is the reason for the propagation of peer-to-peer (P2P) botnets. P2P botnet does not hold any C&C server and the hierarchy of all nodes connected becomes complex in such a way that no any node recognize the C&C residing among one of them. The random natured P2P botnets have not only a decentralized C&C but it divide the central system in more than one location. In this paper, we present a design to identify such random P2P botnets.

The rest of the paper is drafted as follows. In Sect. 2, we briefly review the related work. In Sect. 3, we describe random P2P identification. In Sect. 4, we describe performance evaluation about the identification of random Peer-to-Peer botnets and discuss experimental results. Finally, in Sect. 5 we draw out conclusions and future work.

2 Related Work

Botnets have become a dynamics research area in recent years. An overview of bots and botnets was presented by Puri [2]. Botnets were monitored using honeynet by McCarty [3]. First built of P2P botnet named Slapper worm was analyzed by Arce and Levy [4]. The systematic dissection of botnets in details appeared in the past were given by Zhou and Xuxian [5]. Zeng et al. [6] presented a monitoring system to redirect DNS mapping of a C&C Server. Another researcher named Rafael [7] presented a passive detection of botnets by lookups of spam queries.

Botnets have an origin of using IRC for their C&C servers, most of the researchers detected and monitored network traffic to identify them. Abnormal IRC traffic detection modules were designed by Narang and Jagan [8]. P2P botnets have changed their straight intrusion in the shape of random attitude [9]. By random nature author describes the botnet attitude of changing C&C to random nodes so sinkholes could not be identified by security researchers as seen in Fig. 1.

3 Random P2P

To detect randomness in such an efficient system includes few components which are integrated with each other as follows:

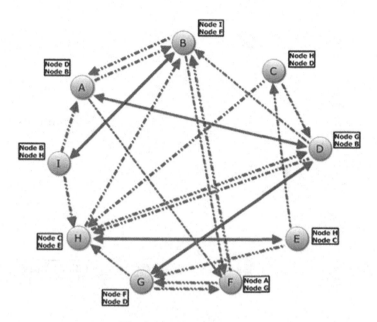

Fig. 1. Random P2P Botnet

3.1   Random P2P C&C Identification

Random P2P botnets apply botmaster-defined hierarchy to keep C&C among servant bots. Figure 2 illustrates the basic functionality of communicating infected client bots with medium layer servant bots. They are interlinked with each other in such a manner that acknowledgement mentioning infected bot and C&C can only be distinguished through detection between packet sampling among them.

Furthermore, paroxysm [10] is the only identification procedure through which information can be figured out over the network as illustrated from Fig. 2. Moreover, due to P2P decentralized nodes, all nodes are linked to networks and their subnets to attain the last node.

In order to identify malicious commands sent through a random C&C among bots, a paroxysm packet must be observed. It must have a sampling of destination with some defined attributes and randomization columns which are to be analysed for identification of temporary C&C node.

In the text below, D_a is used to identify nature of node paroxysm and D_s to recognize dispersed feature in the nodes. For ΔM time, t period samples are kept in considerations. Every node D network, links is structured in such a way that connectivity at each sample time forms a group $\{P_{d1}, P_{d2}, \ldots, P_{dq}\}$. W_{dr} is related with links of D node at the rate of R.

In a ΔM period, get the random average of the connections

$$P_s = \frac{1}{q}\sum\nolimits_{a=1}^{q} P_{sq}$$

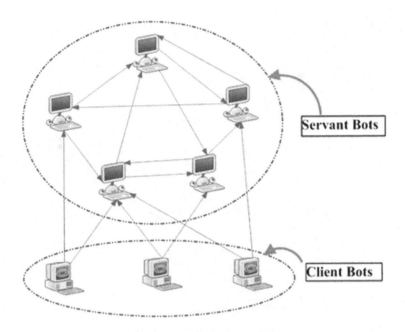

Fig. 2. Random P2P internal structure

At r, node D_{ar} is obtained with unit of paroxysm as:

$$D_{ar} = \frac{P_{dr}}{P_d}$$

Lets $D_{amax} = Max\ (D_{a1}, D_{a2}, \ldots, D_{am})$,
$D^x_{amax} = D_{amax} \times (1 - z\ \%)$, $D^y_{amin} = D_{amax} \times c\%$; [here z and c will remain fix.]
Furthermore, T_w is the number of sets to identify the criteria $\{D_{ai} \mid D_{ai} < D^x_{amin}\}$ and O_{Tw} has the collection of sets related to T_w. Furthermore, Q_z is the number of sets to identify the criteria $\{D_{ai} \mid D_{ai} < D^y_{amin}\}$ and O_{Qz} has the collection of sets related to Q_z.
D_a unit can be defined as:

$$D_a = \frac{O_{Qz}}{O_{Tw}}$$

$D_f = \frac{K_e}{K_u}$ is the dispersed node of D. T_w has a container which includes the set of nodes linked with it as K_u; T_w has a container which holds the set of subnets Q_z. As per the defined phrase, random P2P detection can be identified through Algorithm 1.

Alg. 1. P2P Detection of node

1. Calculate D_a and D_f of the node D;
2. If $D_a > D_{ca}$ and $D_f > D_{cf}$, wind up P2P node in the node D.

Samples of P2P nodes has delivered the paroxysm and dispersed values which are the properties related to D_{ca} and D_{cf}.

3.2 Random P2P Botnet Identification

Botnet which is of random P2P nature, bots have many similarities in action and reaction. The behaviour of such bots can include following properties [11]:

1. Scan Mode
2. DDoS Attack
3. Spam Sender
4. Binary Downloading
5. Exploits

Figure 4 illustrates different activities of random P2P botnet in a network. In Fig. 4 individual behaviour of botnets are identified with different nature of attacks like port scanners, spam senders with same SMTP destination locations, the behaviour of acquiring same files for a unethical activity, DDoS attack with lots of connections at the same time while engaging with exploits.

In order to extract bots attitude from defined method, given procedure can have some detections of bots. If we compare our method with other mechanisms, it is autonomous and does not relate with any given protocol.

In order to resolve different behaviours of botnets, let's assume set $D_p = \{D_1, D_2, D_i \ldots\}$ is the set of collection nodes in a P2P network. Assuming a sample of D_p as the collection of β_N. Let $N_{c\text{-}}$ as scanning behaviour, behaviour related to exploits is named as N_e and DDoS behaviour attack is related to N_o. In order to identify the individual action, evaluate the similarity of nodes in β_N.

As per the evaluation of the suspect attitude five groups $\left\{N'_c\ N'_s\ N'_d\ N'_e\ N_o\right\}$, we define their similarity as $\left\{T'_c T'_s T'_d\ T'_e T_o\right\}$ where $N_{\beta N}$ is the set of nodes into β_N.

$T_o = \dfrac{O_{\beta N}}{N_{\beta N}}$. $O_{\beta N}$ is set of nodes whose has the same DDoS parameters.

$T_e = \dfrac{E_{\beta N}}{N_{\beta N}}$. $E_{\beta N}$ is set of nodes whose has the same exploit parameters.

$T_s = \dfrac{S_{\beta N}}{N_{\beta N}}$. $S_{\beta N}$ is set of nodes whose has the same spam parameters.

$T_d = \dfrac{D_{\beta N}}{N_{\beta N}}$. $D_{\beta N}$ is set of nodes whose has the same downloading parameters.

$T_c = \dfrac{C_{\beta N}}{N_{\beta N}}$. $C_{\beta N}$ is set of nodes whose has the same scan parameters.

The similarity behaviour of β_N is $T = T_c + T_s + T_d + T_e + T_o$

As per the explained phrase, the random P2P Botnet detection algorithm is defined in Algorithm 2.

Alg. 2. P2P Botnet detection

1. Calculate the similarity of T of Ω_N
2. Determine set D_p as a Botnet if $T > M_N$.

Computation of M_N can be evaluated from the identified P2P botnets statistics.

---

4   Performance Evaluation

4.1   Random P2P Nodes Detection

To get results, we have taken into consideration three P2P protocol applications such as uTorrent, FrostWire and Transmission in a wired personal network to identify our required results based on specified criteria.

In order to get results, our simulation includes 100 nodes and the number related to P2P application user's nodes is 30. The mean time for the simulation is 3600 s, having x-axis as 1and y-axis as 10 illustrated in Fig. 3.

As shown in Fig. 3 common nodes are clearly separated from P2P nodes in the ratio of D_a & D_p. The threshold for this simulation holds the equity of: $C_{Da} = 10$, $C_{Dp} = 1$.

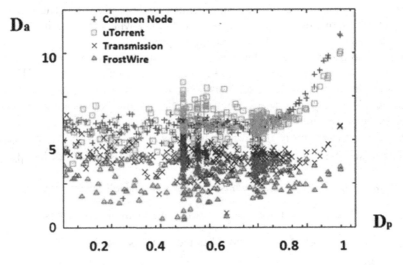

Fig. 3. Performance evaluation of random P2P Botnets

4.2   Random P2P Botnet Detection

Bots can perform their malicious activity many times in a single day. Zeus [12], Kelihos.B [13], ZeroAccess [14] and Sality [15] are the four types of botnets which are set for the simulation results. It can be clearly observed that our method identifies and differentiate the nodes of not having any botnets and the ones with the flavour of botnets through mentioned algorithm as declared in Table 1.

Table 1. Random P2P Botnet Detection result

Samples	T_c	T_s	T_d	T_e	T_o	T
No Bots	0	0	0.07	0	0	0.07
Zeus(silver)	0.1	0.8	0.4	0	0.9	2.2
Kelihos.B(Green)	0.9	0	0.9	0	0.8	2.6
ZeroAccess(Blue)	0.9	0.5	0.8	0.7	0.7	3.6
Sality(Gray)	0.3	0	0.3	0	0.5	1.1

The results of random P2P botnet detection algorithm are categorized and shown in Fig. 4 where we have mentioned four types of botnets in their prescribed categories.

After having results, main feature of Zeus is identified as sending spam, Kelihos.B and Sality depicts lots of scanning behaviour whereas ZeroAccess shows doing DDOS. By using detection algorithm, infected bots can be detected in a P2P network.

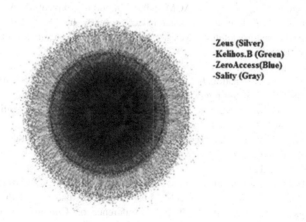

-Zeus (Silver)
-Kelihos.B (Green)
-ZeroAccess(Blue)
-Sality (Gray)

Fig. 4. Random P2P Botnet Detection

5   Conclusion and Future Work

A naïve user perform any activity on system related to IRC usage, lottery web sites, free advertisers and money web sites, anonymous conversations, encoded water mark pictures and free full version software. Such systems are easy resource to be contaminated to the network of botnets and enlist for the botnets into a ready position for unethical act.

In this paper, we have presented a mechanism for detecting random P2P botnets. It describes how unidentified C&C can be identified in a random P2P botnet network and the way it can be captured for extending to a sinkhole. The mechanism is based on an idea to shrink the strength of random P2P botnets.

In future work, we will focus on secure sinkholes and P2P botnets activities in captured sinkholes.

References

1. Grizzard, J.B., et al.: Peer-to-peer botnets: overview and case study. In: Proceedings of the First Conference on First Workshop on Hot Topics in Understanding Botnets (2007)
2. Puri, R.: Bots & botnet: an overview. SANS Institute 2003 (2003)
3. McCarty, B.: Botnets: big and bigger. IEEE Secur. Priv. 1(4), 87–90 (2003)
4. Arce, I., Levy, E.: An analysis of the slapper worm. IEEE Secur. Priv. Mag. 1, 82–87 (2003)
5. Zhou, Y., Xuxian J.: Dissecting android malware: characterization and evolution. In: IEEE Symposium on Security and Privacy (SP). IEEE (2012)
6. Zeng, J., Tang, W., Liu, C., Hu, J., Peng, L.: Efficient detect scheme of botnet command and control communication. In: Liu, C., Wang, L., Yang, A. (eds.) ICICA 2012, Part I. CCIS, vol. 307, pp. 576–581. Springer, Heidelberg (2012)
7. Rodríguez-Gómez, R.A., Maciá-Fernández, G., GarcíaTeodoro, P.: Survey and taxonomy of botnet research through lifecycle. ACM Comput. Surv. (CSUR) 45, 45 (2013)
8. Narang, P., Reddy, J.M., Hota, C.: Feature selection for detection of peer-to-peer botnet traffic. In: Proceedings of the 6th ACM India Computing Convention. ACM (2013)
9. Li, H., et al.: Modeling to understand P2P botnets. In: IEEE Second International Conference on Instrumentation, Measurement, Computer, Communication and Control (IMCCC) (2012)
10. Han, K.-S., Im, E.G.: A Survey on P2P Botnet Detection. In: Kim, K.J., Ahn, S.J. (eds.) Proceedings of the International Conference on IT Convergence and Security 2011. LNEE, vol. 120, pp. 589–593. Springer, Heidelberg (2012)
11. Xu, Z., et al.: Utilizing enemies' P2P strength against them. In: Proceedings of the 2012 ACM Conference on Computer and Communications Security (2012)
12. Lu, C., Brooks, R.R.: P2P hierarchical botnet traffic detection using hidden markov models. In: Proceedings of the 2012 Workshop on Learning from Authoritative Security Experiment Results. ACM (2012)
13. Greengard, S.: The war against botnets. Commun. ACM 55, 16–18 (2012)
14. Dave, V., Guha, S., Zhang, Y.: ViceROI: catching click-spam in search ad networks. In: Proceedings of the 2013 ACM SIGSAC Conference on Computer & Communications Security. ACM (2013)
15. Wichmann, A., Gerhards-Padilla, E.: Using infection markers as a vaccine against malware attacks. In: IEEE International Conference on Green Computing and Communications (GreenCom), pp. 737–742, 20–23 November 2012

Ontology Based Requirement Interdependency Representation and Visualization

Safeeullah Soomro[1], Abdul Hafeez[2]([✉]), Asadullah Shaikh[3,4],
and Syed Hyder Abbas Musavi[1]

[1] Faculty of Engineering Science and Technology,
Indus University, Karachi, Pakistan
ssoomro@indus.edu.pk, drhyderabbas@yahoo.com
[2] Hamdard University, Karachi, Pakistan
ahkhan@smiu.edu.pk
[3] College of Computer Science and Information Systems,
Najran University, Najran, Saudi Arabia
asshaikh@nu.edu.sa
[4] Department of Computer Science and Information Technology,
Institute of Business and Technology (IBT), Korangi Creek, Karachi 75190, Pakistan
ashaikh@ibt.edu.pk

Abstract. Requirement interdependency is being extensively studied with greater interest in software engineering research. However, existing tools and techniques have not properly characterized and visualized the requirement interdependency relationships between requirements. This research introduces ontology based representation of requirement interdependencies among requirements, and formal graphical notation for proper visualization of requirement interdependencies. There is evidence to point out that Ontology based approach is better technique for managing the requirement interdependency i.e., diagrammatic representation of requirement interdependency will improve the quality of software and will reduce the failure rates.

Keywords: Ontology requirements · UML ontology · Requirement traceability

1 Introduction

Software project should conclude on time, be within the specified budget and must fulfill the user requirements. All these aspects measure the quality of software. Unfortunately most of the software projects fail in at least one of these aspects. The primary factor of measuring the quality of software is fulfilling the user's requirements. Suppose that software is developed on time and within the budget but not fulfilling the user requirements then it is not considered to be quality software. Therefore, accomplishment of the user requirements is most important aspect of Quality in Software development.

© Springer International Publishing Switzerland 2014
F.K. Shaikh et al. (Eds.): IMTIC 2013, CCIS 414, pp. 259–270, 2014.
DOI: 10.1007/978-3-319-10987-9_24

Software requirement specification (SRS) is developed in the first phase of software development and it serves as an agreement between user and software development team. It specifies the features included in software. An important factor with SRS is that it continuously adopts change during the entire software development life cycle due to emerging changes in user's requirements. These changes affect the software development in dual perspective. Firstly Changes in requirements should be properly incorporated with release of software secondly changes can also affect the other requirements because software requirements have relationships with each other. Sometime software team overlooks these relationships among requirements due to their unclear visibility and improper representation [1]. Requirement traceability maintains complete track and trace of requirements during software development. Requirement traceability is considered more important in safety critical software [10]. Requirement interdependency being an integral part of requirement traceability is the study of understanding and managing relationships among requirements. Properly represented requirement interdependency can reduce the chances of software failure and the lack of the requirement interdependency information may lead to higher costs, wrong or unnecessary changes and wastage of time during its development. Therefore, well-managed requirement interdependency improves the quality of software.

This paper presents a formal approach in managing and visualizing requirement interdependency. Proposed methodology uses the ontology for the formal description of interdependency model and presents diagrammatic notation for representing requirement interdependency.

The remainder of the paper is structured as follows. In Sect. 2 the requirement interdependency types and current approaches of representation and visualization are explained. Ontology and web ontology language explained in Sect. 3. Section 4 presents the proposed methodology ontology based requirement interdependency management and diagrammatic notation for requirement interdependency that concludes with the results of the case study carried out thereon. Section 5 explains the tool support. In Sect. 6 related research is presented. Finally, conclusions are drawn in Sect. 7 along with future work.

2   Requirement Interdependency and Requirement Traceability

Requirement interdependency is a particular type of requirement traceability that focuses on change relationships among different requirements. Requirement traceability manages and specifies the relationship among different artifacts that are constructed during the software development. Gotel and Finkelstein [6] suggested the following common definition for the term requirements traceability: "Requirements traceability (RT) refers to the ability to describe and follow the life of a requirement in both a forwards and backwards direction (i.e., from its origins, through its development and specification, to its subsequent development and use, and through periods of ongoing refinement and iteration in any of these phases) [8]."

The core aspect of traceability is 'requirement to requirement traceability' that is also called requirement interdependency. It is used to discover the impact on other requirement when one or more requirements are changed.

2.1 Interdependency Types

Dahlsedt and Persoon [4] compile the different views expressed in the literature into an integrated model that is neutral as far as development of a new situation is concerned. They proposed nine interdependencies types within two categories vis-à-vis (i) Structural Interdependencies: Require, Explain, Similar To, Conflict With, and Influences (ii) Cost / Value Interdependencies: Increase/Decrease Cost, Increase/Decrease Value. We are defining the above interdependencies' types as under:

Require Interdependency describes the depending relationship among requirements. It illustrates one or many compulsory requirements for the accomplishment of other requirement. For example, calling a remote procedure requires network connection.

Explain Interdependency describes the composition relationship among requirements. It illustrates that a requirement is combination of many other requirements.
For example: A security requirement for data can be combination of authorization and authentication requirements.

Similar to interdependency describes the equivalency relationship among requirements. It illustrates that the requirement is equal to another requirement. For example, the information about students will be searched by name and the student information will be searched by roll number.

Conflict With interdependency describes the contradictory relationship among requirements. It illustrates that a requirement is inconsistent with other requirements. For example, all users can reset their account passwords and only administrator can change the password of users.

Influences interdependency illustrates that a requirement makes some effect on another requirement other than Require, Conflict, and Explain. For example, some legal requirements depend on industry and type of business for which software is developing.

Increases/Decreases cost interdependency type illustrates that a requirement can increase/decrease cost of another requirement. For example, A Copy of data should be stored on cloud platform. This will most likely increase the implementation cost of many other requirements such as security.

Increases/Decreases Value interdependency type illustrates that requirement increases/decreases the worth of another requirement. For example, online money transfer facility decreases the value of other payment mode like cheque, draft, etc.

Table 1. Traceability list [11].

Requirement	Depends-on
R1	R3,R4
R2	R5,R6
R3	R4,R5
R4	R2
R5	R6

Table 2. Interdependency types by [3,14].

Type	Meaning
R1 AND R2	R1 requires R2 and R2 requires R1
R1 REQUIRES R2	R1 requires R2, but not vice versa
R1 TEMPORAL R2	Either R1 has to be implemented before R2 or vice versa
R1 CVALUE R2	R1 affects the value of R2 for customer, either positive or negative
R1 ICOST R2	R1 affects the cost of implementing R2, either positive or negative
R1 OR R2	Only one from R1 or R2 needs to be implemented

2.2 Current Techniques of Requirement Interdependency Representation

Current practices are generally using traditional traceability techniques for representing requirement interdependency traceability. These are (1) Traceability List and (2) directed graph. Requirement traceability mainly focuses only one relationship called change. However, requirement interdependency has various relationships as discussed in Sect. 2.1 above.

Traceability list is a simple table of relationships describing dependencies among requirements as shown in Table 1. There might be several such lists, one for each type of relationship such as Require, Similar To, Conflict [11].

A directed graph (digraph) is also used for representing Requirement Interdependency. Carlshamre [3] visualized requirement interdependency through digraph for incremental software development. He also represents five interdependency relationships as shown in Table 2.

3 Ontologies

Ontology is the concept of metaphysics, and is used by philosopher from mid of sixteen century for categorization and representation of entities. Ontologies have various elements like classes, relations, individual, etc. for making clear the concept of entities. These are extensively used in knowledge Engineering, Artificial intelligence, ecommerce, natural language processing. Due to Ontology provides a great amount of expressiveness and facility of reasoning, it is widely

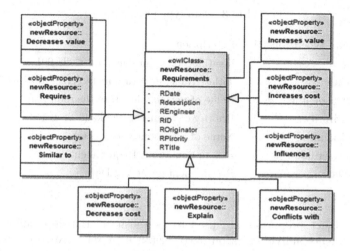

Fig. 1. Requirement interdependency ontology.

using in software engineering practices [7]. Web Ontology Language (WOL) is a declarative language for ontology development. It was developed in 2003 by W3C. It is designed to express a wide variety of knowledge as well as provide reasoning facilities to express the most important kinds of knowledge. It comes with three flavors: OWL Lite, OWL DL (description logic), and OWL Full. These three levels are in increasing order of expressivity.

4   Ontology of Requirement Interdependency and Diagrammatic Representation

In this section we are proposing requirement ontology and graphical notation for proper management and visualization of requirement interdependency. Here the requirement ontology is constructed for managing the various interdependency relationships among the requirements defined in Sect. 2.1. For managing requirement through ontology and generating requirement interdependency relationship diagram, we have built a tool that discussed the management, visualization of requirement independencies efficiently in Sect. 5 of this paper.

4.1   Requirement Ontology

The building block of present work is requirement ontology shown in Fig. 1. In this ontology a class is declared called Requirements. This class represents a concept similar to software requirements. Requirements class declared seven data types properties (RID, RTitle, RDescription, etc.) shown in Fig. 1 and complete details of these properties are listed in Table 3. Nine interdependency relationships those are explained in Sect. 2.1 are also declared in requirements class through object properties shown in Fig. 1.

Table 3. Data type properties.

S.No	Data type Properties	Description
1	RID	Identifier for requirements e.g. "U-001"
2	Rtitle	Title / Name of requirement e.g. "Add User" etc
3	ROriginator	Name of person who state the requirement
4	RPirority	Priority of requirement like (1 or 10)
5	REngineer	Name of requirement engineer
6	Rdescription	Description about Requirements
7	Rdate	Requirement gathering Date

These object properties are used to establish relationships among different requirements individual in ontology instance. A reflexive relationship (self relationship) is also specified on requirements class. For example one instance of requirements class associates with another instance of requirements class through object properties. Therefore, object properties establishing the interdependency relationship between different requirements. Finally, an external restriction is applied to specify that the object properties are 'established relationships' between only members of requirements class.

4.2   Requirement Interdependency Relationship Diagram (RIRD)

Requirement Interdependency is very important aspect of software development. Success factor of software is mostly dependent on proper management of requirement and their change relationships (interdependency). If software development team is not fully aware of requirement interdependency relationships then there is a risk that software could not fulfill the user need, exceed from estimated budget and schedule or even may be failed. Therefore, proper representation of requirement interdependency relationships for quality software development is very crucial. Earlier research shows that traceability list and diagraph have been used for representing the requirement interdependency. These methods are well suited for representing small number of interdependency relationships; however for large and complex interdependency relationships, these methods have some limitations. As an example, for the large amount of interdependency relationships, table and graph could be difficult to manage and understanding of interdependency will be difficult at a glance. Therefore, there is need of proper diagrammatic notation for representing the requirement interdependency. The RIRD is graphical representation for better representation and visualization of requirement interdependency relationships. In RIRD the requirement is represented by a rectangle and the title of requirement appears at middle of rectangle. Requirement interdependency relationships are represented by various symbols listed in Table 4 that are attached in the border of rectangle with in a circle called relationship circle. A unidirectional arrow shows the direction of interdependency relationships and optional label can be attached on arrow to show

Table 4. Symbols for requirement interdependency relationship.

S.No	Symbols	Interdependency Types
1	+	Requires
2	*	Explain
3	=	Similar to
4	X	Conflicts with
5	>	Influences
6	> .	Increases cost
7	< .	Decreases cost
8	>	Increases value
9	<	Decreases value

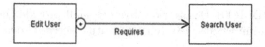

Fig. 2. RIRD for require interdependency relationship visualization.

interdependency type. For example a requirement "Edit User" Require another requirement "Search User" represent a RIRD as shown in Fig. 2.

Relationship circle will be attached to only those requirements that have interdependency relationship with other requirements. Also, the unidirectional arrow starts from that requirement as shown in Fig. 2.

When changes arise in requirements, RIRD diagram also shows its impact on other requirement through different requirement rectangles and arrow styles. A change requirement is shown with double border rectangle. The direct impact of change is shown by rectangle with thick border and thick arrow. Indirect impact of change is shown by dotted rectangle and dotted arrow.

Figure 3 is the complete illustration about requirement change impact. Here, requirement 3 is presented in double border rectangle that shows change in requirement 3. A thick arrow is moving from requirement 3 to requirement 4 indicates the direct impact change. Also requirement 4 is placed in thick rectangle. Dotted arrows are moving form requirement 4 to requirement 5 and requirement 5 to requirement 6 is showing the indirect requirement change impact.

4.3 Implementation

This section illustrates the proposed work with an example as a user management system (UMS). UMS is mostly part of large software. It provides security mechanism through user authorization and authentication.

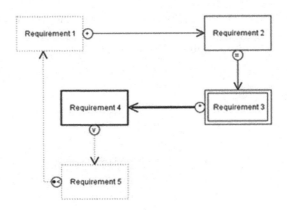

Fig. 3. RIRD of requirement change impact visualization.

1. Requirement ID: R001 Description: System shall provide the facility of edit user only by administrator like (change status, activate, deactivate etc.) and notification is sent to user
2. Requirement ID: R002 Description: Notification of 'status change' sent to user via email
3. Requirement ID: R003 Description: System shall provide the facility of search user
4. Requirement ID: R004 Description: System shall provide Search user option By ID and BY Name
5. Requirement ID: R005 Description: System shall provide the facility of Update user status
6. Requirement ID: R006 Description: Data cannot be accessed from outside the Local area Network due to security reason
7. Requirement ID: R007 Description: When the Users' status will be changed then the mobile message will also be sent to Users.
8. Requirement ID: R008 Description: User can be searched by User ID and Name from mobile

Requirement R001 has required interdependency relationship with R002 and R003 and the same with requirement R005. The value of requirement R002 is decreased by requirement R007. Requirement R003 is explained by requirement R004. Requirement R004's cost is increased by requirement R008. Requirement R008 and requirement R006 are conflicting. Figure 4 shows RFID of user management system.

Suppose User remove notification feature from the requirement R001. Figure 5 shows change impact in requirement 1 to other requirements. When the requirement R001 is changed, it will directly impact on requirement R002 and indirectly impact on requirement R007.

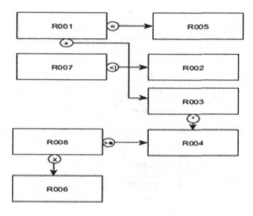

Fig. 4. RIRD of user management system.

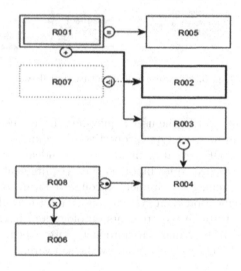

Fig. 5. RIRD after change of user management system.

5   Tool Support

This section will give the details about a tool that has been designed for managing requirement through ontology and generate requirement interdependency relationship diagram. Figure 6 is showing the structure of the mentioned tool. The software tool depicted in Fig. 6 has been built using java language with jena API for ontology processing. Jena provides management of OWL and RDFS ontology. It also provides rule based inference engine for reasoning on RDF and OWL. For diagram publishing, this software uses Graph visualization (Graphviz). Graphviz is an open source tool for creating the graph and is developed by AT&T labs for graph drawing that uses the script language DOT for specifying the graph.

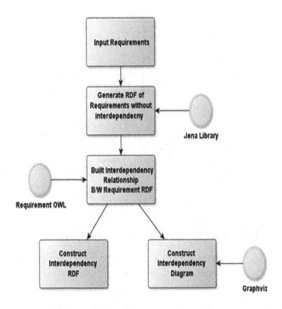

Fig. 6. Software tool structure and flow.

The proposed tool receives the user requirement from a user through a Form that captures the seven data type properties of requirement. The 'Requirements' are saved in RDF format without interdependency relationship among the requirement. After providing input as the "requirement", the user specifies the relationship among requirement through a form. When user finished the relationship specification then system creates interdependency relationship among requirements through requirements ontology and inserts them between previously generated RDF. Finally Requirement Interdependency Relationship diagram (RIRD) and RDF are generated by the software.

6   Related Research

In the early research of requirement traceability, Pohl [11] proposed 18 different types of dependency relationships between various types of trace objects used in software engineering. However, many dependency type presented in Phol [11] model cannot exist among requirements. Carlshamre and Regnell [2] proposed different types of interdependencies. In the extended work of [9] and [3], Carlshamre et al. [3] conducted an industrial survey on requirements interdependencies within release planning. He identified six different types of interdependencies, partially based on the types presented in [9], and relatively analyzed 20 high priority requirements within five different companies. Ramesh and Jarke [12] presented the reference models for requirements traceability. They did not focus on requirements interdependencies, but identified the 'requirements interdependencies' as a "traceability problem". The majority of the dependency types discussed by Ramesh and jarke [12] are related to requirements management and requirements evolution. Robinson et al. [13] reported on a field called requirements interaction management. This field focuses on managing relationships between requirements; those may interfere with each other's achievements. Robinson et al. [13] focused on conflicts between requirements, and recognize the problems with satisfying requirements at requirements definition time. He also gave explanation about different requirements interdependency types. Dahlstedt and Persson [4] in 2003 explained various types of interdependencies through literature and empirical study. He describes nine types of interdependencies exits between requirements. He also group requirement interdependency relationships into two main categories: structural and cost/value. Arda Goknil [5] introduced the way of representation and managing the requirement interdependency through OWL and semantic. He performed inferencing and consistency checking and proposed the mechanism to derived new relationships from existing ones and determined contradiction among requirement. He built a tool called Tool for Requirements Inferencing and Consistency checking (TRIC) that performs automatic inferencing and consistency checking. He also did impact analysis on requirement change with the help First order Logic (FOL). However he worked on only five interdependency relationships (Require, Refines, Partially Refines, Contain and Conflict) and did not focus on visualization and any diagrammatic approach for proper representation. Yuanyuan Zhang [15] worked on five interdependency types (And, Or, Precedence, value related and cost related). He is of the opinion that not much work has been carried out on entire five interdependency types collectively. He has taken Requirement Interdependency problem as a constraint satisfaction problem and has proposed three search based algorithms to tackle requirement interdependencies. He also investigated the impact of requirement interdependency relationship on the automated requirement selection process for release planning.

7   Conclusion and Future Work

Software Requirement Interdependency performs vital role in software development. Software success factor is entirely based on proper understanding of requirement interdependency. Therefore, proper representation of requirement interdependency plays a crucial role in software development. Current research in requirement interdependency mainly pays attention in identifying the interdependency relationship types but the representation and visualization is not being focused upon thoroughly. This research proposed ontology based representation of requirement interdependency relationships and diagrammatic notation called Requirement Interdependency Relationship Diagram (RIRD) for proper visualization of requirement interdependency. The RIRD is used to clarifying the requirement interdependencies aspect of software team, and when the requirement changes the RIRD diagram graphically shows its impact on other requirements. There are still some open issues like verification and validation of requirement interdependency relationship and ontology based impact analysis of different artifact of software engineering. We are working on developing an ontology based representation of interdependency of different artifacts in Object Oriented Software Engineering.

References

1. Ali, N., Gueneuc, Y., Antoniol, G.: Trustrace: mining software repositories to improve the accuracy of requirement traceability links. IEEE Trans. Softw. Eng. **39**(5), 725–741 (2013)
2. Carlshamre, P., Regnell, B.: Requirements lifecycle management and release planning in market-driven requirements engineering processes. In: Proceedings of the 11th International Workshop on Database and Expert Systems Applications, pp. 961–965. IEEE (2000)
3. Carlshamre, P., Sandahl, K., Lindvall, M., Regnell, B., Natt och Dag, J.: An industrial survey of requirements interdependencies in software product release planning. In: Proceedings of the Fifth IEEE International Symposium onRequirements Engineering, pp. 84–91. IEEE (2001)
4. Dahlstedt, Å.G., Persson, A.: Requirements interdependencies: state of the art and future challenges. In: Aurum, A., Wohlin, C. (eds.) Engineering and Managing Software Requirements, pp. 95–116. Springer, Heidelberg (2005)
5. Goknil, A., Kurtev, I., van den Berg, K., Veldhuis, J.-W.: Semantics of trace relations in requirements models for consistency checking and inferencing. Softw. Syst. Model. **10**(1), 31–54 (2011)
6. Gotel, O.C., Finkelstein, A.C.: An analysis of the requirements traceability problem. In: Proceedings of the First International Conference on Requirements Engineering, pp. 94–101. IEEE (1994)
7. He, H., Wang, Z., Dong, Q., Zhang, W., Zhu, W.: Ontology-based semantic verification for uml behavioral models. Int. J. Softw. Eng. Knowl. Eng. **23**(02), 117–145 (2013)
8. Hokkanen, M., et al.: Requirements traceability (2001)
9. Karlsson, J., Olsson, S., Ryan, K.: Improved practical support for large-scale requirements prioritising. Requir. Eng. **2**(1), 51–60 (1997)
10. Mc Caffery, F., Casey, V., Sivakumar, M., Coleman, G., Donnelly, P., Burton, J.: Medical device software traceability. In: Cleland-Huang, J., Gotel, O., Zisman, A. (eds.) Software and Systems Traceability, pp. 321–339. Springer, Heidelberg (2012)
11. Pohl, K.: Process-centered Requirements Engineering. Wiley, New York (1996)
12. Ramesh, B., Jarke, M.: Toward reference models for requirements traceability. IEEE Trans. Softw. Eng. **27**(1), 58–93 (2001)
13. Robinson, W.N., Pawlowski, S.D., Volkov, V.: Requirements interaction management. ACM Comput. Surv. (CSUR) **35**(2), 132–190 (2003)
14. Svensson, R.B., Gorschek, T., Regnell, B.: Quality requirements in practice: an interview study in requirements engineering for embedded systems. In: Glinz, M., Heymans, P. (eds.) REFSQ 2009 Amsterdam. LNCS, vol. 5512, pp. 218–232. Springer, Heidelberg (2009)
15. Zhang, Y., Harman, M., Lim, S.L.: Empirical evaluation of search based requirements interaction management. Inf. Softw. Technol. **55**(1), 126–152 (2013)

Turbo Multi-hop Relaying
for Co-operative Communications

Muhammad Suleman[1], Pir Shah Gul[2], and Amjadullah Khattak[1(✉)]

[1] University of Engineering and Technology Peshawar, Peshawar, Pakistan
sulemanktk@yahoo.com, amjad67@gmail.com
[2] University of Science and Technology Bannu, Bannu, Pakistan
shah_gul_khan@ciit.net.pk

Abstract. In wireless communication, several communication devices are limited by hardware complexity and their size; however, they can benefit from an increased spatial diversity due to the broadcast nature and cooperation of these devices with each other. Increased spatial diversity improves the coverage range of these devices and save the transmission power. Currently, amplify or decode and forward are two will known relaying techniques used for improving the spatial diversity: In this paper, the main contribution is the improvement in decode and forward by *using* turbo codes in all nodes of a particular cooperative communication system. In the proposed technique, we reduced the number of iteration at relay and accomplished the wanted bit error rate with lessen complexity. It results to fast and simple relaying techniques then that of other existing techniques. Secondly we used the turbo code with large interleaver which reduces the error floor as due to large interleaver the bit error rate reduces due to which iterations; delay and computing power at relay reduces. Simulations show that this S-*PDF* scheme outperforms both *AF* and *DF*.

Keywords: Partial decode and forward · Spatial diversity · Cooperation communication · Relaying techniques · Decoding iterations

1 Introduction

In cooperative wireless communication, relays assist mobile end nodes to achieve spatial diversity in single antenna environment. It helps to reduce path losses in fading transmission environment in a wireless channel. Cooperation can be achieved in a multiuser situation where mobile act as a relay and generate spatial diversity of ad hoc nature. However, in this research, our focus will be on relay networks rather the mobile networks. Relay and its protocols help the destination to get three folds benefit then that of single hop channel. Firstly; it achieved virtual MIMO which helps in providing spatial diversity against fading even with a single antenna. Secondly, it reduces the transmit power of transmitting terminal and finally the coverage range of system is increased [1]. Presently, there are three well known relaying techniques. First two basic techniques were presented and compared in [2, 3]. In AF, the relay only amplified the signal that it received from transmitter and process it to destination. It keeps soft information and requires less processing time and computational power. However, the

© Springer International Publishing Switzerland 2014
F.K. Shaikh et al. (Eds.): IMTIC 2013, CCIS 414, pp. 271–279, 2014.
DOI: 10.1007/978-3-319-10987-9_25

main problem of this relaying scheme is strengthening of noise which is quite nasty and reliability is very low. While the DF scheme destroys the soft information in the signal and require higher processing time and computational power but it suppresses the noise and reliability is quite high and regenerates efficient signals. The PDF scheme is a recent relaying technique with promising features; it would not through away soft information by making hard decision. It provides fast processing then DF and reduces the noise significantly and finally it avoids the hefty processing and it works in soft input/soft output fashion.

To assist the relaying process, recently, several protocols are proposed. In [4], they developed a protocol to use a spatial diversity accessible among the gathering of scattered terminal. The developed protocol performs averaging of fading at destination terminal with the help of relay. They achieved full diversity with a half symbol rate per channel use. In [5], they proposed a novel in which N partner and one cell site with partial delay coherent channel is used for cooperative transmission protocol. They achieved the efficient use of resources by not relaying on the orthogonal subspaces. The proposed protocol provides good result but it was complex and implementation was not done. In [6], partial DF protocol achieves full diversity and full symbol rate based on partial decoding at relays. The decoding and re-encoding are performed is soft input and soft output fashion in recently projected soft decode and forward protocol (SDF) [7] using the BCJR algorithm [8]. Recently in [5, 6, 10, 11] authors used soft modulation techniques to avoid bandwidth expansion. They modulated each soft bit directly to channel analog manner. They applied SDF in distributed turbo coding scheme (DTC) [9]. In spite of this research effort, it is derived that the relay node of DTC scheme does not employ iterative decoding due to which error can propagate to destination node.

In this paper we examine the ability of source, destination and relay that work in the same band and uses time division multiplexing (TDM) to separate the source and relay channel. Turbo codes [7] and iterative decoding BCJR [12] algorithm used as the basic decoders. With the help of soft cooperation protocol we examined the effect of number of decoding iterations performed at relay and SNR of channel. The iterative decoding increased the complexity of the relay node which is undesirable. So for that we proposed other relaying techniques which limit the number of decoding iterations called soft partial decode and forward (S-PDF) reduces the relay node complexity and transmits the soft information obtained using S-PDF.

The remainder of the paper is ordered as follows. Section 2 explains the proposed technique for relaying in cooperative communication environment. Section 3 explains experimental results and discussion on results. Finally, conclusions are drawn in Sect. 4.

2 S-PDF Scheme

Figure 1 shows the schematic of the cooperative scheme under consideration. All the channels used in the proposed scheme are additive AWGN channels. The time division multiplexing is followed for the cooperation of SN and RN. In first time slot the encoded information from SN is broadcast to relay and destination nodes encode. The relay node modifies the message in accordance to S-PDF protocol and forwards it to destination.

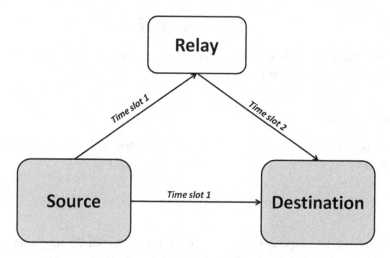

Fig. 1. Schematic of cooperative scheme under consideration

2.1   Source Node

As encoding the K-bit sequence is the initial process for that they used half rate turbo coder. Turbo codes are used as error correction codes described in [11, 17]. Turbo codes have parallel concatenated encoding structures with interleaver in between them and for their decoding we used iterative decoding algorithm BCJR. Turbo codes are the first practical codes closely approach the Shannon channel capacity [15] and provide the reliable communication in the presence of channel noise at a given code rate.

By using the π interleaver the bit sequence A is rearranges to another sequence B as shown in Fig. 2. To encode these un-coded sequence coded sequence C and D we use the parallel concatenation of unity recursive convolution encoders. Then these sequences are multiplexed to get N-bit sequence. By using BPSK this sequence is mapped to symbol Xs and transmitted to both relay and destination node using time slot 1 through antenna.

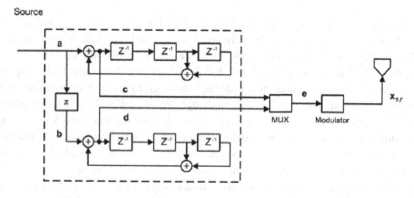

Fig. 2. Source node

$$x_{s,r} = x_{s,d} = (2e - 1)\sqrt{Es} \tag{1}$$

where Es is the energy radiated per symbol. The s *represent source,* r represent relay and d represent destination nodes.

2.2 Relay Node

The relay node received the signal $Y_{s,r}$ as $X_{s,r}$ is transmitted by the source node may be modeled as

$$y_{s,r} = \frac{|h_{s,r}|}{\sqrt{d_{s,r}^{\gamma}}} x_{s,r} + n_{s,r} \tag{2}$$

where γ the path loss exponent and $d_{s,r}$ is the distance between the supply and relay. The magnitude of the fading coefficient $|H_{s,r}|$ remains constant during the transmission. For AWGN channels fading coefficient is one while in quasi-static Raleigh fading channels has a complex value Gaussian distribution in which mean of both real and imaginary part is 0 and variance is ½. The noise vector $n_{s,r}$ also has complex-value Gaussian distribution in which the mean is 0 and variance is $\delta_{s,r}^2$. The spectral density of noise power is equal to $N_o = 2\delta_{s,r}^2$. The E_s/N_o represents the signal to noise ratio between source and relay nodes as shown in Fig. 3. Logarithmic likelihood ratios (LLRs) e_{γ}^{-a} is obtained by demodulating of received signals at relay by using BPSK. According to [14] for soft decision for corresponding bit e in the vector we use particular LLRs.

$$e_{\gamma}^{-a} = \ln\left(\frac{P\left(e = \frac{1}{Y_{s,r}}\right)}{P\left(e = \frac{0}{Y_{s,r}}\right)}\right) \tag{3}$$

At this node BPSK calculates LLRS according to below formula

$$e_{\gamma}^{-a} = \frac{2|H_-(s,r)|\sqrt{Es}\,(e = \frac{1}{Y_{s,r}})}{\delta_{s,r}^2\sqrt{d_-(s,r)^{\wedge}\gamma}} R[Ys, r] \tag{4}$$

The subscript a in the above equations show that LLRs are used as a priori for relay node. This priori information is demultiplexed to c_{γ}^{-a} and d_{γ}^{-a} which act as input for BCJR decoders as shown in Fig. 3. By alternate operation of these decoders provide iteratively the LLRs sequences a_{γ}^{-e} and b_{γ}^{-e} the subscript e shows that LLRs sequence used extrinsic information and there order is rearranged by using π *interleaver or* π^{-1} de interleaver in order to provide a_{γ}^{-a} and b_{γ}^{-a}. As shown in Fig. 3, the resultant a priori information helps the BCJR decoders operation for the next iteration. This help in providing even more reliable extrinsic information which gradually increases in iterative manner until the limit of complexity of RN node is reached or specific stopping criteria is met. LLRs sequence which used a posteriori information e_{γ}^{-p} is achieved by multiplexing and adding of decoders output with a priori LLRs sequences then relay node forward this resultant a posteriori information to DN in timeslot 2.

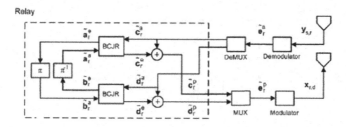

Fig. 3. Relay node

Soft modulation is employed in this node and is achieve by assuming that LLRs are Gaussian distribution [15] which is valid when we used AWGN channel. Model used to fit in below

$$e_\gamma^{-p} = \tfrac{1}{2}\delta\_(r,r)^{\wedge}2(2e-1) + n_{r,r} \tag{5}$$

Where $n_{r,r}$ is Gaussian distribution of real valued with the mean null and variance $\delta_{r,r}^2$. Soft binary phase shift keying symbol $x_{r,d}$ having average energy E_r are obtained using [5, 6, 10, 11].

$$x_{r,d} = \frac{2\sqrt{E_r}}{\delta_{r,r}\sqrt{\delta_{r,r}^2+4}} e_\gamma^{-p} \tag{6}$$

2.3   Destination Node

At destination, the soft modulated signal provided by RN is given below

$$y_{s,r} = \frac{|h_{s,r}|}{\sqrt{d_{s,r}{}^\gamma}} x_{s,r} + n_{s,r} \tag{7}$$

Yr, d shows that conventional BPSK signal is corrupted by AWGN. The signal energy per symbol is

$$\hat{E}_r = \frac{\delta_{r,r}^2 E_r}{\delta_{r,r}^2 + 4} \tag{8}$$

While noise appear to have variance

$$\delta_{r,d}^2 = \frac{4E_r}{(\,d\_(r,d)^{\wedge}\gamma\,(\delta_{r,r}^2+4)\,)} + \delta_{r,d}^2 \tag{9}$$

And signal offered by the source node are recovered in same manner according to

$$e_d^{-a} = \frac{2|H\_(s,d)|\sqrt{Es}}{\delta_{s,d}^2\sqrt{d\_(s,d)^{\wedge}\gamma}} R[Ys,d] + \frac{2|H\_(r,d)|\sqrt{Er}}{\delta_{r,d}^2\sqrt{d\_(r,d)^{\wedge}\gamma}} R[Yr,d] \tag{10}$$

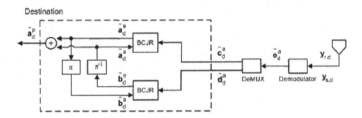

Fig. 4. Destination node

Finally the $e_d^{\tilde{\ }a}$ LLRs sequences are working as a priori sequence for Destination node. The turbo decoder used in the destination nodes is not limited by number of iterations it performs until convergence is achieved and the posterior LLRs sequence $a_d^{\tilde{\ }p}$ is obtained as shown in Fig. 4. For reconstruction of the original bit sequences we used hard modulation.

3   Results

In this study, we have conducted simulation for proposed S-PDF scheme to compare its performance with other corresponding scheme (PDF, AF, and DF). We proposed a particular setting for simulation where AWGN channel was used having a path loss exponent of $\Upsilon = 2$ and 1000-bit sequence is transmitted over it. Also, the space between transmitter and receiver has taken one where relay is placed between middle of them. Using the proposed scheme, the energy per symbol of $E_r = E_s$ is used for transmission of bit sequences from relay node to destination node. We also used pseudorandom interleaver π for interleaving the bit sequence which provides the better results. Figure 5 shows the effect of interleaver length on BER which is inversely proportional to each other which mean if interleaver length increases the BER decreases and SNR increases mean quality improved. Thus, we use the larger interleaver. Interleaver lengths of 10^4 bits sufficiently suppress tail effects.

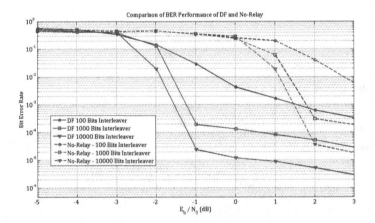

Fig. 5. BER and SNR comparison at different interleaver length

We use *EXIT* function for the erection of good iteratively-decoded turbo codes. The EXIT function and decoding trajectories predict 1 dB advantage of bit error performance. It shows that when SNR is increased the number of iteration is reduced as for $E_b/N_0 = -2$ dB we need 11 iterations and when this value is increased to 2 dB we need just two iterations to reach (1, 1) point mean to achieve low BER [18].

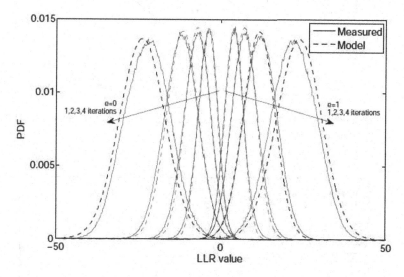

Fig. 6. Matching of Logarithmic Likelihood Ratios (LLRs) in the relay node a posteriori sequence $e_r^{\sim p}$, of the first 4 decoding iterations.

In Fig. 6, we explain the Logarithmic Likelihood Ratios (LLRs) in the relay node a posteriori sequence $e_r^{\sim p}$, of the first 4 decoding iterations. Also, Eq. 6 is used to measure the $\delta_{r,r}$ then these values are used to obtain the hypothetical LLR distributions which are implicit in Eq. 5. These obtained results are strongly matched with simulated results presented in Fig. 6 which reveal that our assumptions are valid.

In Fig. 7, the destination node *EXIT* function is presented at SNR of negative one dB for different number of decoding iterations in the relay node. This shows that the EXIT chart tunnel width depends on the decoding iteration performed at the relay node. If the number of iterations increased then the tunnel width increased.

Finally, we evaluated our proposed *S-PDF* scheme with respect to BER performance in Fig. 8. We took different E_b/N_0 values to evaluate them for different decoding iterations cases, i.e., 1, 2, 3, 4, 5, and 6 performed at *RN*. Figure 8 compare and characterize the proposed S-PDF scheme with other cooperative schemes. It shows that *PDF* is limited number of decoding iterations in the *RN* due to the use of hard modulation technique. Also, DF scheme uses a lot of iterations to achieve the convergence in the *RN* whereas AF scheme perform convergence without any iteration at *RN*. The proposed scheme uses the soft modulation of Eq. 7. For communication but hard modulation is adopted when early stopping criteria is met. Figure 8 also shows that if the iterations are limited to 1 then the proposed scheme offers nearly half dB gain over

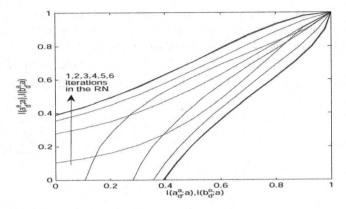

Fig. 7. Destination node *EXIT* function is presented at SNR of negative one dB for different number of decoding iterations in the relay node

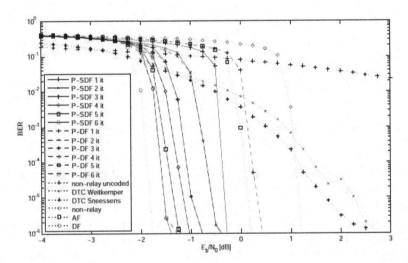

Fig. 8. BER VS SNR Comparison of over proposed scheme with other benchmarkers with different number of iterations

PDF scheme, however, the proposed scheme is same as *DF* if the iterations at *relay* node is not limited. In short, our proposed scheme provides significant gain over other Distributed Turbo Code schemes, owing to their elevated error floors.

4 Conclusions

In previous cooperation schemes, the distributive turbo coding was used only at destination node while convolution coding was used in *RN* and *SN*. In the proposed scheme, we used turbo codes on all the nodes to avoid the error floors. In this paper, we investigate the effect of pseudorandom π interleaver length used for encoding and found that Interleaver lengths of 10^4 bits sufficiently suppress tail effects.

Secondly we investigate the effect of number decoding iteration on the performance of relay from this we found that if we limit the decoding iteration at relay this will make the cooperation simple and fast but quality is degraded which is recovered by the turbo encoding at relay. We used the large number of iteration at destination node because there is no chance of error we need more confidence there. The improvement in partial decodes and forward signaling can be achieved by designing protocol and committed strategies in the cooperative communication techniques. The proposed scheme also tries to improve it by using distributed turbo coder, iterative decoding and soft and hard modulation both depend on situation and provide better results.

References

1. Pei, L., et al.: Cooperative wireless communications: a cross-layer approach. IEEE Wirel. Commun. **13**, 84–92 (2006)
2. Laneman, J.N., Wornell, G.W.: Distributed space-time-coded protocols for exploiting cooperative diversity in wireless networks. IEEE Trans. Inf. Theory **49**, 2415–2425 (2003)
3. Azarian, K., et al.: On the achievable diversity-multiplexing tradeoff in half-duplex cooperative channels. IEEE Trans. Inf. Theory **51**, 4152–4172 (2005)
4. Yang, S., Belfiore, J.-C.: Optimal space–time codes for the MIMO amplify-and-forward cooperative channel. IEEE Trans. Inf. Theory **53**, 647–663 (2007)
5. Sneesens, H., Vandendorpe, L.: Soft decode and forward improves cooperative communications. In: 2005 1st IEEE International Workshop on Computational Advances in Multi-Sensor Adaptive Processing, pp. 157–160 (2005)
6. Li, Y., et al.: Distributed turbo coding with soft information relaying in multihop relay networks. IEEE J. Sel. Areas Commun. **24**, 2040–2050 (2006)
7. Shannon, C.E.: A mathematical theory of communication. ACM SIGMOBILE Mobile Comput. Commun. Rev. **5**, 3–55 (2001)
8. Bahl, L., et al.: Optimal decoding of linear codes for minimizing symbol error rate (Corresp.). IEEE Trans. Inf. Theory **20**, 284–287 (1974)
9. Zhao, B., Valenti, M.C.: Distributed turbo coded diversity for relay channel. Electron. Lett. **39**, 786–787 (2003)
10. Weitkemper, P., et al.: Soft information relaying for wireless networks with error-prone source-relay link. In: 2008 7th International ITG Conference on Source and Channel Coding (SCC), pp. 1–6 (2008)
11. Qi, Y., et al.: Performance evaluation of soft decode-and-forward in fading relay channels. In: Vehicular Technology Conference, 2008. VTC Spring 2008, pp. 1286–1290. IEEE (2008)
12. Hagenauer, J.: The EXIT chart-introduction to extrinsic information transfer in iterative processing. In: Proceedings of the 12th European Signal Processing Conference (EUSIPCO), pp. 1541–1548 (2004)
13. ten Brink, S.: Convergence of iterative decoding. Electron. Lett. **35**, 806–808 (1999)
14. Berrou, C., et al.: Near Shannon limit error-correcting coding and decoding: turbo-codes. 1. In: IEEE International Conference on Communications, 1993. ICC 93. Geneva. Technical Program, Conference Record, pp. 1064–1070 (1993)
15. Burr, A.: Turbo-codes: the ultimate error control codes? Electron. Commun. Eng. J. **13**, 155–165 (2001)

NetFPGA Architecture Reconfiguration to Incorporate Support for IPv6 Addressing

Saad Zafar$^{(\boxtimes)}$ and Numair Zulfiqar

Department of Computer Engineering,
College of EME - National University of Science and Technology,
Rawalpindi, Pakistan
saadzafar31@ce.ceme.edu.pk

Abstract. NetFPGA has attracted interest in recent years as a high speed networking hardware platform. Despite rapid progress in this open-source project and growing adoption of IPv6 worldwide, the router support for this protocol is still not started. In this paper attempt is made to present an architecture based on 10 Gigabit NetFPGA environment which supports IPv6 protocol while still being backward-compatible with IPv4. Designed modules perform the pre-processing of headers, routing/ port-forwarding operations and packet encapsulation or generation. The architecture is described using Verilog HDL, translated and successfully synthesized for Xilinx Virtex-5 FPGA board. Results of this work provide the primitive layout of hardware for modern protocol support at very fast processing and forwarding rate of 10 Gbits per second. The new design will ensure that NetFPGA remains compliant with Layer 3 and ensure future-safety for the platform.

Keywords: Digital design · IPv6 · NetFPGA · Reconfigurable · Router

1 Introduction

Switches and routers are primitive network space components which are integral in Internet expansion. Switches allow inter-connect of devices within a local network, whereas routers help to join remote networks to create a Wide Area Network (WAN). Conventionally, universities teach the operation of these devices by implementing their respective tasks in software. The implementations carry out packet switching/forwarding by working in user-space sockets; and this is far removed from actual hardware-based implementations created by network vendors. NetFPGA is an open-source didactic hardare platform which provides cost-effective design of data networking hardware and this setup has been of particular focus in research on high-speed routing. The NetFPGA is a modular system which allows complex designs and easy expansion or integration of different elements [1].

Essentially, the NetFPGA v2.1 is composed of 1 Gigabit Ethernet interfaces, a user programmable Field Programmable Gate Array (FPGA) and banks of

© Springer International Publishing Switzerland 2014
F.K. Shaikh et al. (Eds.): IMTIC 2013, CCIS 414, pp. 280–290, 2014.
DOI: 10.1007/978-3-319-10987-9_26

SRAM and DRAMs [2]. There is also a separate Xilinx Spartan II FPGA that contains the controller logic for driving the PCI interface to the host computer. Over the last few years, there has been fast development on the NetFPGA platform by the open-source community. A packet generator and network traffic capture system has been implemented as discussed in [3]; also virtualized data planes for mapping networks on same physical topology have been completed [4]. This sharing of physical substrate greatly reduces the cost requirement of network infrastructure, and this hardware approach allows comparable isolation or packet-forwarding rates as compared to its software based virtualization techniques [5]. The architecture has even been ported for use in Data center networks which make use of specialized algorithms for packet forwarding [6,7]. A dedicated operating system for NetFPGA has also been introduced [8] to provide a united operating environment for the development and execution of hardware designs. This enables developers and users to easily access the NetFPGA through standard Unix binary utilities and filesystem access. The progress has not only been limited to router designing but has been successfully copied for implementing a high-speed switch [10] which allows easier network management and is built around the premise of security.

The next generation of these routers consists of a larger FPGA and greater memory but most importantly, it utilizes four 10G interfaces for greater performance. However, currently the NetFPGA designs only support IPv4 addressing scheme. With the global shift towards IPv6 network-layer addressing [11], the mentioned incompatibility poses a threat to the usefulness of NetFPGA routers in near future. An attempt was made at College of EME (NUST) in 2011–2012 to port the prevalent architecture to comply with IPv6 [12] however, the work could not progress beyond foundational algorithms. This paper attempts to build upon the initial start of our colleagues and address IPv6 support problem by proposing a reconfiguration of the current architecture while still being backward compatible with IPv4. The scope of this work is limited and restricted to high-level architecture design and modification just enough to provide support, and the interface controller will attempt to conform to the 10 Gigabit data rate.

2   Algorithm Overview

The algorithm as enunciated in [12] involves a packet which is received at the input port, then it is checked if the packet is from CPU. If true, it is forwarded otherwise the MAC address of the packet is checked to see whether the packet is destined for this network or not if yes accept the packet otherwise drop the packet. Then a check is performed to determine if it is IP packet or not. If not, then packet is forwarded to the host PC otherwise the version is checked. If it is IPv4 packet then it is directed to the underlying modules of IPv4, else it is directed to the corresponding IPv6 specific modules. If it is IPv4 packet then IP checksum field of the header is checked. If checksum is bad the packet is dropped otherwise we check the time TTL of the packet, if it is less than one it is dropped else the IP address is checked in the routing table and ARP tables to check whether it is available in the tables or not. If not, forward the packet to the host PC otherwise all the corresponding entities are updated, like decrementing TTL, generating new checksum, finding the next hop IP and MAC and send the packet to the appropriate port. In case the packet is IPv6, the next header field is checked whether there is a valid type of next header, if not the packet is forwarded to the host pc else the extension headers are checked. The next field to check is the flow label which checks whether the packet is of the same flow or not. If it is from different flow from the previous one it is sent to the host CPU otherwise the hop limit is checked if the hop limit is decremented to zero the packet is dropped otherwise the other information like set the destination, source address destination MAC address and decrement the hop limit. This sceheme is summarised in the flowchart of Fig. 1.

3   Architectural Details

3.1   High Level View

The modular design of NetFPGA router is shown in Fig. 2.

First of all the packet is received at one of the four input ports, a tag number is attached to the packet to show which port did the packet arrived. After that the packet is stored at the rx input queues. Then arbiter moves the packet from the rx queues to the FIFOs of the vertex-5, where the router is implemented.

3.2   Preprocessing modules

preprocess_control. In this module, the controller state machine is implemented and it asserts the appropriate signals for parsing the headers. It is always in communication with the op_lut_process sm block, giving and receiving signals from it. It is the first module parallel with fifo of which the packet passes. It directs the packet to its appropriate module according to the desired functionality. The working of this module is best explained by use of a state diagram, as given in Fig. 3.

oplut_header_parser. This module checks if the packet is arriving from the CPU or not. For instance, the packet may have arrived from any network for routing or it could be from the host PC. We treat these packets differently so its important that we know whether it has arrived from the host PC or network.

eth_parser. This module checks the 48-bit MAC address field of header of the packet and decides if the destination MAC address of the incoming packet is ours and whether the incoming packet is an ARP or IP packet. It has interfaces to the register block, preprocess block and process block. One of the signal is forwarded to eth_parser from both the preprocess and register block as show in Fig. 4.

The Ethernet parser checks to see if the destination port matches any of the native port MAC addresses. We need to make sure that this search is completed before end of the packet. This is shown in the state diagram of Fig. 5.

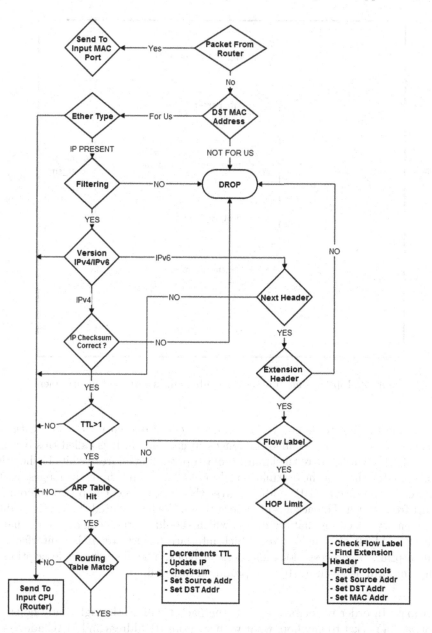

Fig. 1. Flowchart overview of the algorithm depicting router operation

3.3   Routing Modules

ip_lpm. Longest prefix match is algorithm used by routers in Internet Protocol (IP) networking to select an entry from a routing table, because each entry in a routing table may specify a network, one destination address may match more

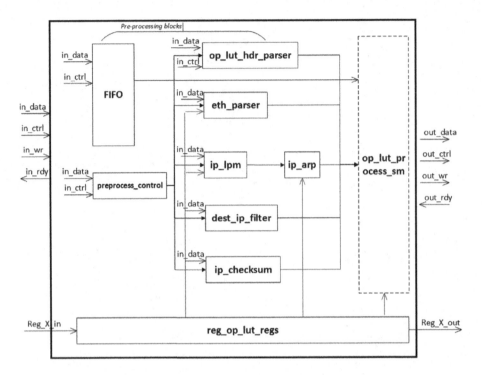

Fig. 2. Top level module showing submodules and their arrangement

than one routing table entry. The most specific table entry, the one with the highest subnet mask, is called the longest prefix match. It is called this because it is also the entry where the largest number of leading addresses bits in the table entry match those of the destination address. This module finds the longest prefix match of the incoming IP address, gives the ip of the next hop and the output port from which the packet will be forwarded. We have stored the routing tables in memory based on that we decide which should be the next hop and what is the IP address of that hop and which interface to forward. It has interfaces to the arp_lut, preprocess block and register block. The alogirthmic description in digram form as given in [10] is reproduced in Fig. 6.

ip_arp. In order to forward packet, the packet will go through many hops. To forward a packet to any hop, what we need is an IP address and MAC address of the next hop. IP address of next hop is found in previous module named ip_lpm. This module gives us the next hop MAC address which is required for packet delivery to the destination. We have an ARP cache stored in memory, which have MAC addresses of the hosts against their respective IP addresses. If we dont find a MAC address of the required user, then we make an ARP request message and we broadcast it. When the intended host receives this message he replies back with an ARP reply message by inserting his MAC in the source

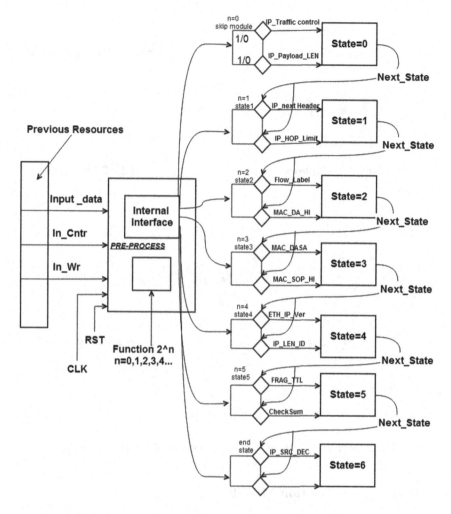

Fig. 3. State diagram illustrating the behavior of preprocess controller

MAC field. In this way, we get MAC address of a host. It has interfaces to the process block and the registers.

dest_ip_filter. This module finds the destination IP and sends the data packet to the appropriate router by using the next hop destination IP. This module matches the destination IP address to the addresses available in a list and indicates whether we find a match or not. We have routing tables stored in memory. If we dont find a match in the table against a particular IP address it means that destination is not reachable [12]. This module also checks the error/fault in the receiving packet data. The diagram showing the corresponding hardware implementation is given in Fig. 7 overleaf.

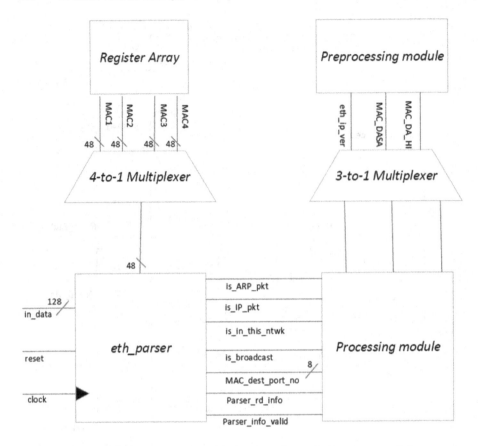

Fig. 4. Block arrangement showing interfaces of eth_parser module

3.4   Packet Encapsulation Modules

ip_checksum_ttl. This module checks the IP checksum over the IP header, and generates a new one assuming that the TTL field gets decremented and checks if the TTL is valid, and generate a new TTL. Checksum is checked by putting all zeros at the checksum field and then adding all the fields of header if it equals the checksum then the packet header have no error otherwise checksum is not correct in that case we drop the packet. Assuming that the checksum field is good, then we decrement the TTL field by one (time to live) which prevents packets from infinite loops. After decrementing the TTL field we calculate the new checksum and replace that in place of the checksum field.

ip_lut_process_sm. This module takes the information from the preprocess blocks, write a new module header for the output port, write the packet with the information from the pre_process block.

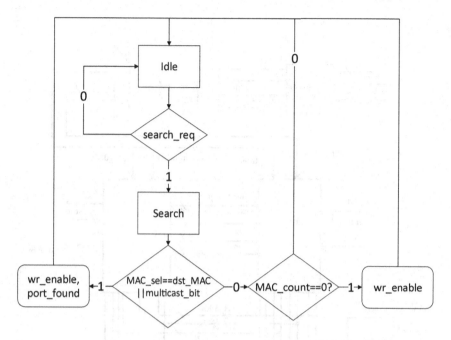

Fig. 5. ASM chart for eth_parser controller module

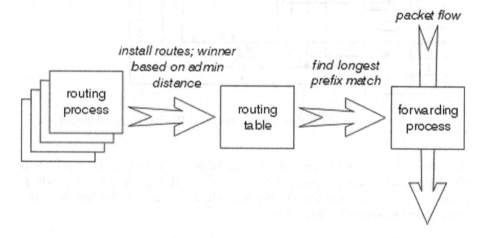

Fig. 6. Routing mechanism through longest prefix matching

Flow label module. Flow label is a 20-bit field used by a source for labeling a set of packets belonging to the same flow. The combination of source address and non-zero flow label identify a unique flow. Multiple flows may also exist from a source and destination as well as there may be traffic that are not associated with any flow i.e. flow label = 0. When a packet from a new flow is observed

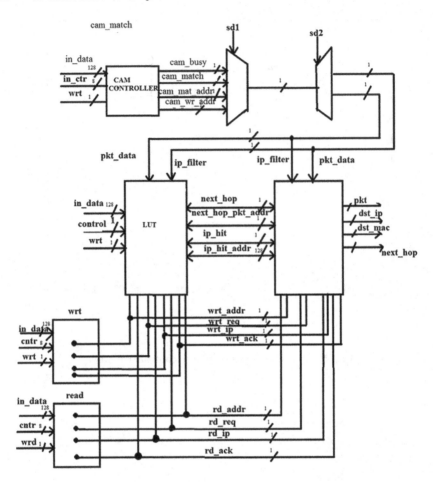

Fig. 7. Modualar block diagram of destination IP filter implementation

the information carried by the ipv6 header, routing header and the hop-by-hop extension headers are processed. The result is stored in a cache memory which is used to route all other packets belonging to the same flow having the same source address and same flow label.

4   Results

A self-checking and time agnostic test-bench was used for carrying out thorough functional verification of the modules. Intensive regression and simulation testing over a range of random values did not produce any unexpected results and every answer conformed to correct outputs. The Verilog description of the architecture was successfully synthesized for the Virtex-5 target device (xc5vlx110t-2ff1136). The utilization summary is given in Table 1.

Table 1. Virtex-5 utilization summary for data-plane components

Resource	Used	Available	Percent
Slice registers	83	69,120	1
Slice LUTs	140	69,120	1
Route-thrus	28		
Occupied slices	4000	300,000	1.3
LUT FF pairs	3000		
Bonded IOBs	15	640	2
BlockRAM/FIFO	12	148	8
BUFG/BUFGCTRLs	1	32	3

5   Conclusion

This paper presents an initial step for new generations of NetFPGA based reconfigurable hardware that can support IPv6 addressing scheme. The proposed architecture has been successfully translated and mapped to the Xilinx Virtex-5 board. The design is completely open-source and its Verilog description will be made available for future work. The research presents an important milestone in the shift of networking equipment which allow support for IPv6, and makes the design future proof. Like most 10G NetFPGA implementations, the performance gain compared to conventional network devices is profound and far ahead of software based implementations. Most importantly, this research can come useful in universities for teaching the architecture of routers capable of supporting newest network-layer protocol.

However, as the scope of the work was to present a simple and basic architecture just enough to support IPv6, there is room for some improvements. Firstly, the security routines are kept to a minimal in the present design and this may be compensated by incorporating a NAT module as discussed in [13]. Secondly, greater robustness can be achieved by utilizing Layer 4 checksums. Moreover, support for protocols like FTP can be included by mapping certain flow types to host-end processors. Even though the design has been simulated and verified, but a greater degree of confidence in functional performance can be obtained by using a Packet generator [3] to create 'artificial' traffic.

References

1. Lockwood, J.W., McKeown, N., Watson, G., Gibb, G., Hartke, P., Naous, J., Raghuraman, R., Luo, J.: NetFPGA - an open platform for gigabit-rate network switching and routing. In: MSE 2007, San Diego (2007)
2. Gibb, G., Lockwood, J.W., Naous, J., Hartke, P., McKeown, N.: NetFPGA - an open platform for teaching how to build gigabit-rate network switches and routers. IEEE Trans. Educ. **51**(3), 364–369 (2008)

3. Adam Covington, G., Gibb, G., Lockwood, J.W., McKeown, N.: A Packet generator on the NetFPGA platform. In: The 17th Annual IEEE Symposium on Field-Programmable Custom Computing Machines (FCCM), Napa, CA, 5–7 April 2009
4. Anwer, M., Feamster, N.: A fast, virtualized data plane for the NetFPGA. In: NetFPGA Developers Workshop, Stanford, CA, pp. 90–94 (2009)
5. Anwer, M.B., Feamster, N.: Building a fast, virtualized data plane with programmable hardware. In: SIGCOMM VISA, Barcelona, Spain, August 2009
6. Lu, G., Shi, Y., Guo, C., Zhang, Y.: CAFE: a configurable packet forwarding engine for data center networks. In: SIGCOMM PRESTO, Barcelona, Spain, August 2009
7. Guo, C., Lu, G., Li, D., Wu, H., Zhang, X., Shi, Y., Tian, C., Zhang, Y., Lu, S.: BCube: a high performance, server-centric network architecture for modular data centers. In: ACM SIGCOMM Barcelona, Spain, pp. 63–74, August 2009
8. Hamilton, B.K., So, H.K.-H.: BORPH: an operating system for the NetFPGA platform. In: 2nd North American NetFPGA Developers Workshop, Stanford, CA, 13 August 2010
9. Cisco: Route Selection in Cisco Routers, 2 Jan 2008. http://www.cisco.com/en/US/tech/tk365/technologies_tech_note09186a0080094823.shtml. Accessed 29 Aug 2013
10. Luo, J., Pettit, J., Casado, M., Lockwood, J., McKeown, N.: Prototyping fast, simple, secure switches for ethane. In: Hot Interconnects, Stanford, CA, August 2007
11. Google: IPv6 Adoption Statistic. http://www.google.com/ipv6/statistics.html. (Accessed: 24 Aug 2013)
12. Ali, I., Rabi, F., Dost, S., Salman, M., Implementation of IPV6 10G router. In: Bachelors thesis, College of EME (NUST), Pakistan, July 2012
13. Choudary, O., David, J.M.: NAT implementation for the NetFPGA platform. University of Cambridge

IBA: Intelligent Bug Algorithm – A Novel Strategy to Navigate Mobile Robots Autonomously

Muhammad Zohaib[1], Syed Mustafa Pasha[1], Nadeem Javaid[2], and Jamshed Iqbal[1(✉)]

[1] Department of Electrical Engineering,
COMSATS Institute of Information Technology (CIIT), Islamabad, Pakistan
zohaib.ciit@yahoo.com,
{mustafa.pasha,jamshed.iqbal}@comsats.edu.pk
[2] Center for Advanced Studies in Telecommunication (CAST),
COMSATS Institute of Information Technology (CIIT), Islamabad, Pakistan
nadeemjavaid@comsats.edu.pk

Abstract. This research proposes an intelligent obstacle avoidance algorithm to navigate an autonomous mobile robot. The presented Intelligent Bug Algorithm (IBA) over performs and reaches the goal in relatively less time as compared to existing Bug algorithms. The improved algorithm offers a goal oriented strategy by following smooth and short trajectory. This has been achieved by continuously considering the goal position during obstacle avoidance. The proposed algorithm is computationally inexpensive and is easy to tune. The paper also presents the performance comparison of IBA and reported Bug algorithms. Simulation results of the robot navigation in an environment with obstacles demonstrate efficacy and performance of the improved algorithm.

Keywords: Obstacle avoidance · Path planning · Robot navigation · Mobile robots

1 Introduction

The revolution in the field of Mechatronics has made it possible to see the 'fiction' robots in reality in various fields of life ranging from mobile robots [1], articulated arms [2–4]. Mobile robots permit human access to unreachable locations including accidental situations like fire, building collapse, earthquake and hazardous scenerios such as Nuclear Power Plant (NPP) [5], chemical industry, transmission lines etc. Deployment of a mobile robot in real world applications demands addressing several new issues regarding the robot interaction. The increasing development in robotics has brought up various challenges including obstacle avoidance, path planning, navigation, localization, autonomous control etc. Recent Japanese robotic competitions on field

This research has been funded by National Information and Communication Technology (ICT) R&D Fund under agreement no. NICTRRFD/NGIRI/2012-13/corsp/3 Sr. 5.

© Springer International Publishing Switzerland 2014
F.K. Shaikh et al. (Eds.): IMTIC 2013, CCIS 414, pp. 291–299, 2014.
DOI: 10.1007/978-3-319-10987-9_27

robotics has highlighted the need of multi-disciplinary research to accomplish challenging tasks [6].

Intelligence in the robot navigation to achieve autonomy is a challenging problem for researchers, as it is an important task to design the robot which can perform variety of tasks, such as surveillance, transportation, exploration or human locomotion [7, 8]. The existing robot navigation algorithms can be categorized into three main types on the basis of knowledge of environment: completely known, partially known and unknown environment. In a completely known environment, it is easy to tune a robot by simply creating a map and applying A* search algorithm [9] to generate a reference path. On the other hand, in a partially or completely unknown environment, an obstacle avoidance algorithm is required. Obstacle avoidance is the backbone of autonomous control in robot navigation especially in a fully unknown environment as it plays the key role in safe path planning. The algorithm for this purpose must be efficient enough, so that it can take a quick decision while encountering an obstacle without human intervention. Wide sample space of obstacle shapes that can be encountered in real world applications further necessitates the algorithm intelligence. In the field of mobile robotics, intelligent obstacle avoidance is the most important task, since every autonomous robot has to plan a safe path for its trajectory towards destination. This is achieved with an intelligent algorithm that uses knowledge of goal position and sensorial information of the surrounding environment.

With a focus on these primary features, the present research proposes an intelligent goal-oriented algorithm for autonomous navigation of mobile robots. The proposed algorithm does outperform the existing approaches and proves the convergence with relatively short, smooth and safe trajectory.

The paper is organized as follows. Section 2 describes the related work. Section 3 introduces the proposed algorithm. Section 4 depicts the simulation results. Finally Sect. 5 comments on conclusion.

2 Related Work

Several algorithms are used for path planning with obstacle avoidance to navigate mobile robots. The algorithm which plans a shortest and smoothest path with obstacle avoidance capability is considered as an ideal candidate for autonomous robots. Obstacle avoidance in some cases is difficult to cater since many algorithms suffer from problem of their local behavior.

Bug algorithms are fundamental and complete algorithms [10] with provable guarantees [11], since they let the robot to reach its destination if it lies in the given space. In case the destination is not reachable, the robot has ability of terminating the assigned task. Each algorithm in Bug family carries its own termination property [12]. Bug algorithms do not suffer from local minima problem. In these algorithms, the robot takes an action on the basis of current percepts of sensors without taking into account the previous path and actions. It is not a goal-oriented approach, as it does not consider goal's position and distance while avoiding an obstacle. It has two behaviors, *move to goal* and *obstacle avoidance*. In *obstacle avoidance* behavior, it avoids an obstacle by just following the edges. It then changes the behavior to *move to goal* after avoiding the obstacle i.e. it restarts moving toward goal without considering any other parameter. Bug algorithms are divided into three types that differ from one another on the basis of their behavior of obstacle avoidance i.e. decision taken when an obstacle is encountered.

2.1 Bug-1 Algorithm

Bug-1 is the earliest obstacle avoidance algorithm. It is easy to tune and does not suffer by local minima. However it takes the robot far away from the goal in some scenarios [10, 13]. In this algorithm, the robot after detecting an obstacle starts following the edge of obstacle until it reaches to the point from where the robot started following the edge. It simultaneously calculates the distance from current position to destination and finally stores the point having minimum distance. This point, after one complete cycle of the robot is considered as the leaving point. The robot restarts following the edge until it reaches to this calculated point. After avoiding obstacle, the robot computes new path from the leaving point (x_1, y_1) to destination (x_2, y_2) using straight line equation. The slope m and y-intercept c of this line are given by (1) and (2) respectively.

$$m = \tan^{-1}\left(\frac{y_2 - y_1}{x_2 - x_1}\right) \tag{1}$$

$$c = y_1 - m \times x_1 \tag{2}$$

The robot follows this line until it reaches the destination or another obstacle is encountered. One of the common drawbacks of Bug-1 algorithm is that when the robot is following the edge of obstacle 1, it may collide with a neighboring obstacle 2 in case when the later is in very close proximity to the first obstacle or the gap between them is less than the width of the robot.

2.2 Bug-2 Algorithm

Bug-2 algorithm is an improved version, which generates initial path from source to destination and stores slope of this path in its *move to goal* behavior. The behavior of the robot is changed to *obstacle avoidance* when an obstacle is encountered, where the robot starts following edge of the obstacle and continuously calculates slope of the line from its current position to the destination. When this slope becomes equal to the slope of initial path (from source to destination), the behavior of the robot is changed to *move to goal*. Therefore, the robot follows single non-repeated path throughout its trajectory. Bug-2 algorithm is more efficient than Bug-1 algorithm as it allows the robot to reach the destination in less time by following a short trajectory.

Both Bug1 and Bug2 algorithms demand minimum memory requirements. However, they do not have capability to make optimum use of sensors data for generation of shorter paths. An improved approach named as Dist-Bug algorithm addresses this problem [14].

2.3 Dist-Bug Algorithm

Dist-Bug algorithm is final improved version of Bug algorithm series. It traverses comparatively shorter distance by allowing the robot to reach its destination in less time. This algorithm employs different *obstacle avoidance* behavior. When the robot encounters an obstacle in its path, it starts following the edge of the obstacle simultaneously calculating and storing the distance from its current and next position to destination. The leaving point, where it switches the behavior from *obstacle avoidance* to *move to goal*, is selected based on the condition that the distance of destination from its next position is greater than the corresponding distance from its current position (i.e. $d_{next} > d_{current}$). The robot continues its obstacle avoidance behavior otherwise [15].

The objective of this research is to improve these algorithms by addressing their inherent problems and limitations. An algorithm having comparatively more intelligence and efficiency that can reach goal in comparatively less time by following smooth and short trajectory was the goal of this research. The proposed, Intelligent Bug Algorithm (IBA) attempts to achieve these objectives.

3 Proposed Algorithm: IBA

The detailed review of autonomous control strategies for mobile robot revealed that, in the category of Bug algorithms, Dist-Bug algorithm is most efficient as path cost is considered throughout the decision making process. However, it is not goal oriented and thus can take the robot far away from its goal position while avoiding obstacles. This is due to its decision of leaving point during edge detection in *obstacle avoidance* behavior since the goal information is not taken into account. This gives the clue to improve Dist-Bug algorithm by devising an approach to make it goal oriented and to take time to destination into consideration. Based on this, the proposed IBA offers an intelligent control to navigate the robot in maze environment. Decision of leaving point in *obstacle avoidance* behavior of the robot is based on the goal position as well as the path cost. This makes the robot goal oriented and improves the overall behavior of the robot, making it possible to achieve the goal in comparatively less duration of time by following a short and smooth trajectory. Bug algorithms are unidirectional as they are able to take decision in one direction only. In contrast, bidirectional mechanism is introduced in IBA using the sensor's configuration on the robot and their Field Of View (FOV). The improved characteristics of IBA make it efficient to prove its convergence with relatively smooth course.

The proposed IBA algorithm is also based on the two behaviors: *move to goal* and *obstacle avoidance*. Similar to Dist-Bug algorithm, the behaviors in IBA also depend on the present sensorial information of environment i.e. whether obstacles are sensed or not. Initially, in *move to goal* behavior, a reference path is generated from source to goal position and the robot is forced to follow it until an obstacle is encountered or destination is reached. The behavior of the robot is changed to *obstacle avoidance* when an obstacle is sensed and the robot is commanded to follow the edges of the obstacle until leaving point is reached. The leaving point, by taking the goal position into account, is selected on the basis of free path toward the destination. The robot monitors obstacles in the path towards destination while detecting edge in *obstacle avoidance* behavior. This condition, not introduced in Dist-Bug algorithm, offers goal orientation. The condition dictates that in IBA, the leaving point is not taken only on the basis of minimum distance to destination. The obstacle-free path towards goal is also considered. This ensures that the robot does not have to wait for the point having minimum distance to goal. The robot changes its behavior to *move to goal* in order to generate new reference path, in case an obstacles-free path is sensed (just like humans follow the straight path to avoid hurdles). The flowchart of IBA is shown in Fig. 1.

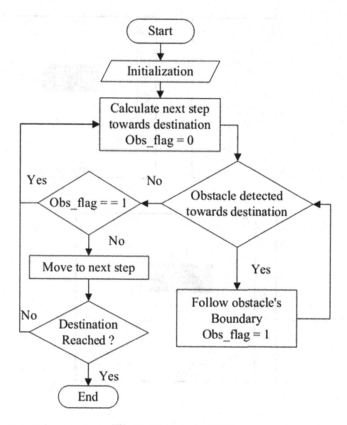

Fig. 1. Flowchart of IBA

4 Simulation Results

The effectiveness of the proposed algorithm (IBA) has been demonstrated using simulation results. The performance has been compared with other Bug algorithms reported in the literature. Consider an environment having a block shaped obstacle. Same environment is taken in all the cases to compare the performance of Bug variants and IBA. The designed simulation environment resulted in the robot trajectories corresponding to these algorithms. In case an obstacle is not sensed, the robot acts in a same manner in all the mentioned algorithms. Considering the scenario when no obstacle lies in the path (Fig. 2(a)), the robot generates a path from source to destination and starts following it until it reaches to destination. The next scenario involves placement of an obstacle in the robot's path. Figure 2(b) illustrates the behavior of the robot in Bug-1 algorithm as it avoids the obstacle by edge detection and finds the leaving point finally reaching to destination successfully. Figure 2(c) shows the robot trajectory in Bug-2 algorithm where the robot is following the initial reference path by comparing the slope at each step while avoiding the obstacle.

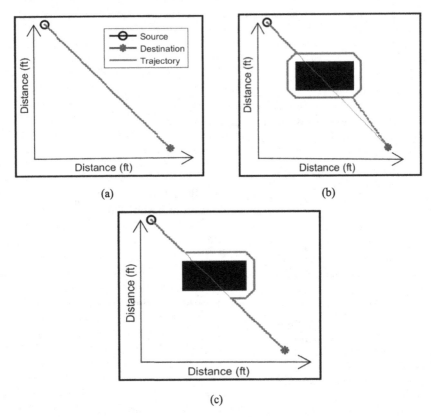

(a)   (b)

(c)

Fig. 2. Trajectories of Bug-1 and Bug-2 algorithms. (a) No obstacle (b) Bug-1 algorithm (c) Bug-2 algorithm

Figure 3(a) shows the performance of the robot in Dist-Bug algorithm, where the robot is following the edge of obstacle until it reaches to the leaving point having minimum distance to destination. Simulation result of the proposed IBA is shown in Fig. 3(b). The robot is following the edge until it finds a clear path towards the destination. Comparing the robot trajectories of Fig. 3(a) and (b) confirms that IBA improves the Dist-Bug algorithm since the path covered by the IBA is comparatively smaller and smoother.

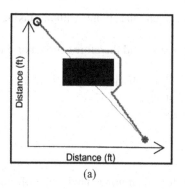 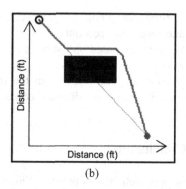

(a)   (b)

Fig. 3. Robot trajectories for performance comparison using (a) Dist-Bug algorithm (b) IBA

The distance-time graph of above mentioned algorithms giving the path cost is illustrated in Fig. 4. The minimum distance from source to destination is 172 ft, which is covered in 120 s when no obstacle lies in the path. This time increases by a factor dictated by algorithm efficiency in a path having obstacles. The most efficient variant of Bug algorithm i.e. Dist-Bug algorithm takes 179 s where as the proposed IBA takes 162 s to achieve the goal, which confirms the outstanding performance of IBA as compared to reported Bug algorithms.

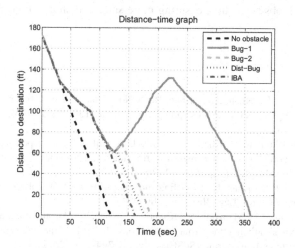

Fig. 4. Path cost v/s time for performance comparison

From above comparison, it can be seen that the IBA takes least time and has a smoother trajectory than other bug algorithms. However, there are certain limitations of IBA that existing Bug algorithms also exhibit. These limitations are listed below. Some of the limitations can be overcome by fusing IBA with the bubble band technique proposed by Khatib and Quinlan in [16].

- IBA/Bug algorithms consider the robot as a circular point without taking its dimensions into account.
- Decisions are based on the basis of current percepts and therefore sensor noise may result in a wrong decision.
- Collision may be possible in the presence of an obstacle adjacent to the robot especially while avoiding the edges of the obstacle.

5 Conclusion

A new approach IBA is presented in this paper for autonomous navigation of mobile robots. The proposed algorithm IBA follows short and smooth trajectory and achieves the goal in less time as compared to reported Bug algorithms. IBA is a goal-oriented approach. The improved characteristics of IBA make it efficient to prove its convergence with relatively short and smoother trajectory in contrast with Dist-Bug algorithm. A bi-directional mechanism is introduced in IBA which can be achieved by using the sensor's configuration on the robot and their FOV. IBA, though exhibiting better performance than any algorithm in Bug family, needs to be further improved in an environment having U and H shaped obstacles. An on-going work to propose a more robust algorithm, Intelligent Follow the Gap Method (IFGM) is intended for environments with symmetric as well as critical shaped obstacles by following the maximum gap among obstacles, thus ensuring more safer and shorter trajectory.

References

1. Iqbal, J., Nabi, R.U., Khan, A.A., Khan, H.: A Novel track-drive mobile robotic framework for conducting projects on robotics and control systems. Life Sci. J. 10(3), 130–137 (2013). ISSN: 1097-8135
2. Manzoor, S., Islam, R.U., Khalid, A., Samad, A., Iqbal, J.: An open-source multi-DOF articulated robotic educational platform for autonomous object manipulation. Robot. Comput. Integr. Manuf. 30(3), 351–362 (2014)
3. Iqbal, J., Islam, R.U., Khan, H.: Modeling and analysis of a 6 DOF robotic arm manipulator. Can. J. Electr. Electron. Eng. 3(6), 300–306 (2012)
4. Islam, R.U., Iqbal, J., Manzoor, S., Khalid, A., Khan, S.: An autonomous image-guided robotic system simulating industrial applications. In: IEEE International Conference on System of Systems Engineering (SoSE), Italy, pp. 344–349 (2012)
5. Iqbal, J., Tahir, A., Islam, R.U., Nabi, R.U.: Robotics for nuclear power plants — challenges and future perspectives. In: IEEE International Conference on Applied Robotics for the Power Industry (CARPI), Switzerland, pp. 151–156 (2012)
6. Nagatani, K., Kushleyev, A., Lee, D.D.: Sensor information processing in robot competitions and real world robotic challenges. Adv. Robot. 26(14), 1539–1554 (2012)
7. Zhu, Y., Zhang, T., Song, J., Li, X.: A new hybrid navigation algorithm for mobile robots in environments with incomplete knowledge. Knowl.-Based Syst. 27, 302–313 (2012)
8. Sgorbissa, A., Zaccaria, R.: Planning and obstacle avoidance in mobile robotics. Robot. Auton. Syst. 60(4), 628–638 (2012)

9. Nosrati, M., Karimi, R., Hasanvand, H.A.: Investigation of the *(Star) search algorithms: characteristics, Methods and Approaches. World Appl. Program. **2**(4), 251–256 (2012)
10. Sezer, V., Gokasan, M.: A novel obstacle avoidance algorithm: follow the gap method. Robot. Auton. Syst. **60**(9), 1123–1134 (2012)
11. Choset, H., Lynch, K.M., Hutchinson, S., Kantor, G.A., Burgard, W., Kavraki, L.E., Thrun, S.: Principles of Robot Motion: Theory, Algorithms and Implementations, vol. 1, pp. 17–38. MIT Press, Cambridge (2005)
12. James, N., Thomas, B.: Comparison of bug navigation algorithms. J. Intell. Robot. Syst. **50**, 73–84 (2007). (Springer Science)
13. Yufka, A., Parlaktuna, O.: Performance comparison of bug algorithms for mobile robots. In Proceedings of the 5th International Advanced Technologies Symposium, Karabuk, Turkey (2009)
14. Evgeni, M., Ehud, R.: CAUTIOUSBUG: a competitive algorithm for sensory-based robot navigation. In: Proceedings of IEEE/RSJ international Conference on Intelligent Robots and Systems (IROS), Japan, vol. 3, pp. 2757–2762 (2004)
15. Zohaib, M., Pasha, M., Raiz, R.A., Javaid, N., Ilahi, M., Khan, R.D.: Control strategies for mobile robot with obstacle avoidance. J. Basic Appl. Sci. Res. (JBASR) **3**(4), 1027–1036 (2013)
16. Quinlan, S., Khatib, O.: Elastic bands: connecting path planning and control. In: IEEE International Conference on Robotics and Automation (ICRA), pp. 802–807 (1993)

Author Index